Theatre Buildings

The Association of British Theatre Technicians produced its first guide to the design and planning of theatres in 1972. Revised in 1986, it became the standard reference work for anyone involved in building, refurbishing or creating a performance space. *Theatre Buildings: A design guide* is its successor.

Written and illustrated by a highly experienced team of international theatre designers and practitioners, it retains the practical approach of the original while extending the scope to take account of the development of new technologies, new forms of presentation, changing expectations and the economic and social pressures which require every part of the theatre to be as productive as possible.

The book takes the reader through the whole process of planning and designing a theatre. It looks in detail at each area of the building: front of house, auditorium, backstage and administrative offices. It gives specific guidance on sightlines, acoustics, stage engineering, lighting, sound and video, auditorium and stage formats. Aspects such as catering, conference and education use are also covered.

The information is supplemented by 28 case studies, selected to provide examples which range in size, style and format and to cover new buildings, renovations, conversions, temporary and found space. The studies include Den Norske, Oslo; the Guthrie Theatre, Minneapolis; the Liceu, Barcelona; Les Bouffes du Nord, Paris; The RSC's Courtyard Theatre in Stratford-upon-Avon; and the MTC Theatre in Melbourne. All have plans and sections drawn to 1:500 scale.

The book contains around 100 high-quality full-colour images as well as over 60 specially drawn charts and diagrams explaining formats, relationships and technical details.

First published 2010
by Routledge
2 Park Square, Milton Park, Abingdon,
Oxon, OX14 4RN

Simultaneously published in the
USA and Canada
by Routledge
270 Madison Avenue, New York, NY 10016

*Routledge is an imprint of the Taylor &
Francis Group, an informa business*

Typeset in Optima by
Gavin Ambrose
Printed and bound in India by
The Replika Press Pvt. Ltd., Sonepat, Haryana

British Library Cataloguing in Publication Data
A catalogue record for this book is available
from the British Library

*Library of Congress Cataloging-in-Publication
Data*
Theatre buildings: a design guide / Association
of British Theatre Technicians; editor, Judith
Strong.
p. cm.
Includes index.
1. Theatre architecture. 2. Theatres-Designs and
plans. I. Strong, Judith. II Association of British
Theatre Technicians.
NA6821.T447 2010
725'.822--dc22
2009040592

ISBN10: 0-415-54894-2 (hbk)
ISBN10: 0-203-85468-3 (ebk)

ISBN13: 978-0-415-54894-6(hbk)
ISBN13: 978-0-203-85468-6 (ebk)

Theatre Buildings
A design guide

Association of British Theatre Technicians
Edited by Judith Strong

Routledge
Taylor & Francis Group
LONDON AND NEW YORK

Contents

Foreword by
Sir Cameron Mackintosh

I unexpectedly became a theatre owner 20 years ago when I was invited to purchase an interest in two 1930s musical houses, the Prince Edward and the Prince of Wales. By 2002 a further five playhouses had been added to my portfolio, all designed by William Sprague and built 1900 – 1910. Now known as the Novello, Wyndham's, Noel Coward, Gielgud and Queen's, they have always been ideal for plays and medium-scale musicals. I discovered great pleasure in reinventing these remarkable historic buildings so that they would be glamorous, comfortable and practical. During this process my team collaborated with Westminster Planning Department, English Heritage, The Theatres Trust, and other specialist bodies. Their experiences have influenced this book which, I am sure, will prove an invaluable resource for anyone involved in renovating existing theatres or in building new ones.

I only agreed to take an interest in the first two theatres if a commitment was made to refurbish the Prince Edward, which had become faded and run down, a cold barn of a building that felt more like a cinema. With its auditorium seating 1,690, there was also a need to create a feeling of greater intimacy. We achieved this by introducing stepped loges at either side of the auditorium with glowing illuminated front panels decorated in warm shades of pink and red. Decorative plasterwork was added to the auditorium above the stalls; fretwork screens were installed down the side aisles of the stalls; and the anti-proscenium was dropped down.

As I acquired further theatres, we began planning a major refurbishment of them all. The work involved hours of planning, both on and off site, for me, my in-house team and my consultants Arts Team at RHWL. Although I hugely appreciate the benefits of digital design, nothing quite compensates for the reality of sitting in a theatre and physically assessing everything from sightlines to leg room to the visual impact of a decorative feature. I believe in being a very hands-on theatre owner.

My aim throughout has been to upgrade the theatre facilities to the standard expected by modern audiences and performers while being sensitive to the period style of each theatre, using and recreating original details wherever possible. The Prince of Wales Theatre gave us the greatest scope for realising a completely new vision as its original auditorium was in a terrible state and the cramped front of house was packed with unnecessary offices. We inserted a totally new auditorium into the building and ripped out the front of house to create spacious foyers and – what was previously completely missing – masses of public space and bars. My other theatres offered less scope for structural alteration; nevertheless, we improved access at the Novello, by breaking through walls and reusing old class-segregated staircases so that all the audience, whatever price they pay, can enjoy the same comfort and facilities. At Queen's, we remodelled the foyers and decorated and reseated the entire auditorium, even adding extra rows on all levels and installing two loges – a remarkable feat of organisation for my Theatre Division and our contractors, as we had to work around *Les Misérables'* eight performances a week.

There is no nook or cranny of my theatres that I don't know and love; each one has its intrinsic charms and eccentricities. I am proud that they are now in such a good state that they should last for at least another century, dramatically improving the experience of visitors to London's world-class theatres. They will be my legacy to West End theatre and my way of returning something to a profession that has given me so much fun and enjoyment.

Cameron Mackintosh
January 2010

Preface

The Association of British Theatre Technicians was formed in March 1961 by a group of enthusiasts, all professionally connected with the theatre, who believed that it was time to improve technical standards.

So began the introduction to *Theatre Planning* edited by Roderick Ham in 1972. This book builds upon that solid foundation which remains a prime work of reference in many architectural and theatre consultancy practices around the world. Like its predecessors, the book you are now reading represents the cumulative knowledge and experience of a large group of experts, all of whom have either worked in theatres or have been actively involved in the design, building and refurbishment of theatres for many years. Indeed, so great is this collective knowledge, it has often been harder to determine what to leave out as opposed to what to include. The section editors are an eclectic mix of the said architects and theatre consultants plus a theatre owner, a producer and theatre technicians, all of whom share a simple passion for 'supporting the actors in their craft'. They in turn have called upon some 50 experts in particular aspects of theatre working who have made contributions ranging from a few paragraphs to almost entire subsections.

Theatres are highly complex buildings that are visited and used by many people during the course of their lifetimes. We attend theatres to have our emotions shifted about and theatres need an element of emotional intelligence in order to ensure successful productions from both artistic and commercial points of view. Such is the complexity and the often arcane language employed in the design and running of a theatre, that no one book can be a simple work of reference. This book is in essence an aide-mémoire to those about to embark upon a theatre project, be they designers, clients, theatre users or students. This book will constantly remind you of the need of expert help, be it from planners, architects, theatre consultants, acousticians, structural engineers, theatre owners, producers, technicians or others required in order to ensure a welcoming home for an audience night after night.

This book is a prompt for those who know and an education for those who don't.

During the 20 or so years since the last edition of *Theatre Planning*, the technology of and legislation concerning theatres has much changed. Disabled access is an obvious example, as is the need for environmental sustainability, let alone the developments of, for example, automation of stage machinery and the projection of light. This is a book written in 2009 for publication in 2010 and some effort has been expended in not producing dated material. Look not in these pages for examples of modern equipment as such, but look instead for the space and the pathways of interconnectivity required both front and rear of house. Some of those principles have been with us since Elizabethan times.

The ABTT expresses its grateful thanks to the owners, managers and designers of the buildings featured in the Reference projects section of this book for supplying the information, photographs and drawings enabling us to produce these studies.

Mark White

Mark White
Chairman
Association of British Theatre Technicians

Section 1
Preliminary planning

Contents

1.1 Introduction

This section focuses on the preliminary planning for a new or refurbished theatre, covering the period prior to commencing design. This period is probably the least clearly defined in terms of actions, process and timescale but is crucial to the ultimate success of the theatre both as a completed building and as a continuing operation. Preliminary planning should culminate in a clear brief for the project, a chosen site, funding for the project, a business plan and the appointment of a design team. Once a brief is agreed and a design team appointed the project should then proceed through clearly defined stages of design and construction to the opening night.

Subsequent sections of this book explore the process of designing, detailing, constructing and equipping a successful theatre. The word theatre is used to embrace a range of performing arts spaces, including drama theatres, opera houses, dance spaces, recital rooms, educational theatres and concert halls.

Projects and communities all vary and the initial planning process can be radically different, even in an apparently similar set of circumstances. In some cases the process can run over many years, in others decisions are made quickly and funding obtained promptly to permit a project to proceed.

Two new opera houses, one in Copenhagen and the other in Oslo, both completed about the same time, demonstrate significant differences in their planning stage and process. The differences are used to illustrate issues discussed later in this section.

1.2 Two case studies – Copenhagen and Oslo

Copenhagen and Oslo, respectively the capitals of Denmark and Norway, have both built new opera houses. The Operaen in Copenhagen was a private project financed by the A.P. Møller and Chastine Mc-Kinney Møller Foundation that opened in January 2005. The Operaen in Oslo was a government-funded project that opened in April 2008.

Historically Denmark was the most successful of the Scandinavian countries, effectively ruling Norway for over 400 years until 1814. Norway was then ceded to Sweden and only became a sovereign nation in 1905. Denmark as the country of royalty and government developed significant cultural organisations and buildings. Det Kongelige Theater (The Royal Danish Theatre) building has been located at Kongens Nytorv in the heart of Copenhagen since 1748 when the theatre was established with royal patronage.

Norway was a relatively poor country and did not develop as sophisticated a cultural infrastructure. In the early twentieth century Norway was one of the poorest nations in Europe but with the exploitation of natural resources and industry it has become the third wealthiest country in the world (by Gross Domestic Product per capita).

At the end of the nineteenth century a new National Theatre was proposed for Oslo. This was initially conceived as a venue for drama and opera. This concept of dual use was opposed by playwright Henrik Ibsen who was concerned that such a theatre would be a compromise and that drama would be subsidiary to the opera. Consequently the Nationaltheatret opened in September 1899 exclusively as a drama theatre. It then took a further 109 years for an opera house to be built.

Opera in Norway remained undeveloped until the founding of Den Norske Opera and Ballet (the Norwegian National Opera and Ballet) in 1957 under the direction of the renowned Norwegian soprano Kirsten Flagstad. The opera was housed in an unsatisfactory theatre that had been converted from a cinema.

The recent successful attempt to build a new opera house in Oslo stretches back 20 years to the appointment of Bjørn Simensen as General Director of the opera and ballet company. He effectively became the project champion leading the initiative to generate public and political support for the new house. A brief was prepared in 1998 with active participation by Den Norske Opera and Ballet (DNO). Two sites were identified in Oslo – the favoured site of DNO was a lively animated area known as Vestbanen. The favoured site of politicians was on the fjord, the post-industrial, depressed area of Bjorvika in need of regeneration. In 1999 the Storting (Norwegian Parliament) approved construction of a new opera house in Bjorvika. An international, anonymous, architectural competition was held in 2000 and won by architects Snøhetta. Construction started in 2003 and the house opened in April 2008.

In Denmark, benefactor Mærsk Mc-Kinney Møller offered a gift to the nation in the form of an art gallery, but was persuaded of the greater need for an opera house to present the larger operas and major ballets that could not be accommodated in Det Kongelige Theater. The decision was announced in August 2000. Architect Henning Larsen was directly appointed and construction commenced in 2001 with the building opening for performances in 2005.

These two projects illustrate a number of issues that will be discussed and developed in this and subsequent sections.

Project champion

Both projects had significant project champions: in Copenhagen, Mærsk Mc-Kinney Møller, the benefactor who gave the project to Denmark; in Norway, Operasjef Bjørn Simensen gave leadership to the project. Most arts projects benefit from having a key individual who is dedicated to 'making it happen'.

Architect selection

In Copenhagen the project was privately funded, allowing the architect to be selected and directly appointed by the donor. The Oslo opera house was a government initiative and an international architectural competition was held to select the architects. The competition took over a year to complete but generated massive publicity for the project both nationally and internationally.

Brief (disagreement)

In 1890 Oslo almost built a theatre to house opera and drama. Such a theatre would probably not have been successful as the needs of the two performing arts are significantly different. There was a dispute about the roles of the new Nationaltheatret, with the views of playwright Henrik Ibsen dominating, and the brief eventually favoured drama over opera.

Users' roles
For speed, the users (opera and ballet companies) in Copenhagen were kept at arm's length from the project with the majority of design decisions being made by the donor Mærsk Mc-Kinney Møller, advised by his consultants. By contrast in Oslo the user client, Den Norske Opera and Ballet, were at the heart of planning the building.

Site
In Oslo the choice of site was entirely political – the new opera house was to be located in an area requiring significant urban renewal. In Copenhagen the site on Dokøen Island was originally used by the military and needed redevelopment; the opera house is on a city axis which passes through the Royal Palace.

Time
Initial discussions about a new opera house in Oslo took place over 100 years ago. As a government initiative, financed by the Ministry of Culture and executed by Statsbygg (the state building agency or public works department), the project was subject to government requirements for consultation, open and transparent processes, etc. These are important but add time to the project. Oslo took over ten years to plan, design and build. Copenhagen, an entirely private initiative, took just under four years from brief to handover.

Procurement
As a private initiative the Copenhagen Opera was not constrained by any government procurement requirements. Although Norway is not a member of the European Union (EU) it participates in the EU's single market and any state-funded project is subject to both EU and Norwegian government procurement policies.

The two projects are for very similar buildings – new opera houses – yet illustrate very different approaches to the planning and design of a performing arts building. Both show the importance of a project champion. Oslo had significant participation in design by the eventual users while Copenhagen took a different route. One selected an architect by direct appointment; the other through a major competition. Oslo was a government project and being subject to government regulations took significantly longer to design and build than Copenhagen.

Both projects are illustrated in the Reference projects at the end of this book (pp. 206 and 254 respectively).

1.3 The project – phases and time

As demonstrated, every new theatre building follows a different timetable. Politics, availability of funding, organisation and so on, will all have an effect on the timing. What follows is a broad outline of the phases between inception and opening night. More detailed guidance on design and construction phases and timetables is available in publications from architect institutions and other agencies. The entire project can be divided into three stages, as shown in Figure 1.3.1.

It is often suggested that each of these steps takes about two years – giving a $1/3$, $1/3$, $1/3$ model. In reality it is almost impossible to predict how long the preliminary planning stage will take. A more realistic generalisation is that preliminary planning takes at least two years and, while design may be completed in 18 to 24 months, construction will often take 18 to 36 months.

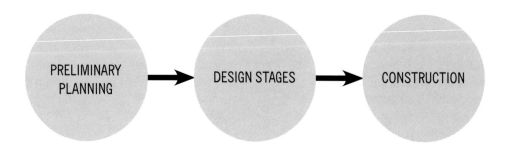

1.3.1

1.3.1 Gantt chart illustrating a typical design and construction process

The design stages of a project have different names in different countries. The British refer to stages of work (B, C, D, etc.) as defined by the Royal Institute of British Architects. In other countries the stages are named according to the work involved. However, they generally follow the same sequence:

Concepts

The creation of initial concepts by the architect. This may involve the development of a number of options or alternate designs for discussion with the client and stakeholders. These options may be tested and evaluated before a preferred concept emerges. The concept design illustrates a broad direction for the building, its positioning on the site and the general placement of the major elements.

Schematics

This stage involves the development of the design with more detail on the planning of the rooms in the building and will include sections and elevations. The overall parameters of the building will be fixed and preliminary input will be received from consultants and engineers.

Design development

The plans for the building will be developed to a greater level of detail. All external materials will be selected and coloured architectural drawings and 3D visualisations will illustrate how the building will look within the context of the existing environment. The design of the auditorium and stage will be developed by the architect in conjunction with the specialist theatre consultants. The interior plans of the building will also be developed.

Engineers will develop the design under the leadership of the architect to ensure that the correct area is allowed for the structure and building services.

In most towns and cities an application for planning consent would be submitted during or at the completion of this phase.

Tender documents

Once the design development drawings and documents have been accepted by the client, stakeholders and funding bodies, a detailed set of documents will be prepared to enable tenders to be obtained for the construction works. The quality and clarity of the tender documentation is integral to the reliability of the tendered construction costs and ultimately to the successful outcome of the project.

During this stage the entire design team will be preparing a coordinated set of drawings, schedules and specifications. Regular design reviews will be undertaken to coordinate the interface between individual parts of the design and to ensure the proposals meet the project goals as well as all relevant statutory regulations.

It is not unusual for a project to have problems with affordability at this or earlier stages and cost-cutting or value-engineering exercises may be undertaken to ensure the design meets the project budget. Such exercises are generally more productive and less disruptive the earlier they are done.

At the end of this phase a set of documents – drawings, schedules and specifications – will be prepared and coordinated in sufficient detail to enable contractors to submit tenders to execute the works.

Tender

The traditional route to appoint a contractor is through an open tender in which potential contractors submit prices against a full set of tender documents. This is still a good route giving considerable price certainty. Other procurement routes are increasingly used including two-stage tendering, construction management, guaranteed maximum price contracts, partnering arrangements, etc. The eventual outcome is to appoint contractors to build the new theatre.

Construction

Construction of a new theatre typically takes 24 to 36 months depending on its complexity. There is usually a sequence of site establishment, excavation, foundations, substructure, superstructure, cladding, interior walls and floors, mechanical systems, fit out, specialist equipment installations, etc. This normally leads to a commissioning stage in which the building and its systems are examined and tested by the relevant consultants and engineers to ensure that deficiencies and problems are resolved before the new building is officially handed over to the client. Ideally, there is a familiarisation period between handover and opening night.

Opening night

Throughout the design and construction period the management and leadership of the project will have been developing an artistic plan, an organisation structure, business plans, and staffing to ensure a successful opening and continuing operation.

Post-contract

There is a one- or two-year period after the project is completed in which defects are resolved and while the final accounts and payments for the building are made.

1.4 Preliminary planning – the process

While the preliminary thinking and planning process can follow many tracks, there are three steps which have to be undertaken in sequence as each is dependent on the previous work having been carried out. They are:

Step 1 – Project inception
The emergence of an initial vision for a new building, initial discussions, building of support and establishment of an informal organisation or lobby group. Deciding what the goals of the project are, what is required and why. The key question at the end of this stage is 'Is it a good idea?'

Step 2 – Project development and studies
Further development and testing of the viability of the project. The organisation becomes more formalised. Funding is sought for a more detailed appraisal to be made of the project, testing its viability and achievability. Several studies may be initiated. The key question at the end of this stage is 'Do we have a viable project?'

Step 3 – Brief writing and design team selection
The brief is the single most important document in the life of the project. It defines what the architect and other professional advisers are to design and so needs careful preparation and consideration. The selection of an architect and design team is also crucial to the success of the project. The client group also needs to grow into an effective organisation able to manage a significant design and construction project. The key question at the end of this stage is 'Do we have the funding, site, organisation, team and business plan to undertake a capital project and achieve a successful outcome?'

1.5 Step 1 – Project inception

There are many different ways in which a project for a new theatre can be initiated. An existing drama or dance company could have outgrown its existing space and need a new home to nurture its future. A local authority could decide that the development or image of their town needs a new theatre or cultural building. A group of concerned citizens might feel that the performing arts in their community need development and that this can best be achieved with a new theatre. A commercial company could decide to build a new theatre as a commercial profit-making venture. A government agency may want to place a new theatre at the heart of an urban renewal or regeneration project.

There are also different ways in which the project can start but each one requires a small number of people to share a vision for a new building. These people may be artists, community leaders, politicians, educators or business people and any one of them may become the project champion. In the early stages of a project the client organisation is often small and informally organised.

What is the vision for the new theatre? What are its goals? What benefits will it bring to the community, its arts groups and audiences? Projects without a clearly defined vision rarely succeed. Sometimes the vision and goals will be clear-cut. For example, an educational institution requires a new performance space to support its programmes; or an orchestra needs a new concert hall to replace its current acoustically inadequate space. More generally, the reasons for building a new theatre are complex with several differing (and occasionally conflicting) requirements having to be met. These may include:

Artistic need An existing arts organisation needs a new or refurbished building in which to continue its artistic growth and development.

Civic goals A town or city has developed and the political and community leadership determine a need for a new theatre, opera house or concert hall to enhance the quality of life and to support and encourage the growth of community.

Educational A school, college or university may need a theatre to support its arts education programmes. Or a community may determine that its young people should have greater opportunities and involvement in the performing arts.

Status Some performing arts buildings are planned and constructed because a government ministry or other agency sees a need for such a building to enhance the status and reputation of that country or city.

Regeneration Theatres can be very successful at drawing people, life and animation to an area. Many communities use theatre buildings as an integral part of their urban renewal and regeneration strategies.

A useful test or question to be asked of the proponents of a scheme is 'If we meet five years after the project has opened how will we judge its success?' Some of this assessment could be quantitative – size of audiences, number of performances being presented, breadth of educational programmes being offered, etc. Other goals and achievements may be less tangible – has the perception of the community been positively changed by the new theatre? Is business attracted to the city? Has the artistic quality of what is being presented improved?

Art forms and performance genres

There are many forms and types of theatre; they vary considerably in size and function. An opera house, for example, has a radically different form and size from an intimate drama theatre. The advocates for the project must therefore decide what is to be built and, specifically, what the new building will accommodate.

The table below (Figure 1.5.1) gives an incomplete listing of performing arts genres, but it serves to illustrate the considerable variations in the type of activity that may be presented. For example, in music, a performance could run the gamut from a solo performer to a full symphony orchestra complete with choir and organ. Similarly, the scale and complexity of the performance can vary significantly within other art forms.

Different types of performance are typically housed in particular types of theatre; for example, opera and classical ballet are traditionally housed in an opera house; symphonic and classical music in a concert hall and drama in a drama theatre or playhouse.

In a major city or large metropolitan area a number of different types and forms of theatre will generally be found. These auditoria and theatres are used to accommodate specific activities. In smaller communities or cities the activities may need to be concentrated into fewer theatres able to accommodate a wider range of activities.

Drama
Greek, medieval, Elizabethan, Jacobean
Asian, American,
Chinese, European
Tragedy, comedy, farce
Puppetry, mime, physical theatre,
multimedia

Entertainment
Singers
Stand-up comedy
Magic
Poetry
Spectaculars
Variety
Circus and circus arts
New media
Revue
Headliners
Skating

Dance
Ballet
Contemporary dance
Folk and ethnic dance
Mime
Ceremonial dance
Social dance
Street and modern dance

Opera
Chamber opera
Grand opera
Operetta
Contemporary
Pop opera
Chinese opera
Musical theatre
Rock opera

All forms
Traditional, contemporary, exploratory,
interactive, improvisational

Music
Symphony concert
Symphony concert with chorus
Symphony concert with organ
Chamber orchestra
Baroque orchestra
Recital
World Music
Jazz
Headliners
Folkloric
Sacred
Blues
Electronic
Pop
Brass bands
Country
Fusion

1.5.1

Producing and receiving theatres

Before discussing a typology of theatres it is important to distinguish between two broad categories: producing and receiving theatres. A producing theatre is one which originates its own productions. This will involve choosing or commissioning scripts, hiring actors, rehearsing, designing and building sets, and all the other activities associated with the mounting of new productions. To do this the theatre will need a larger artistic and administrative team and space for rehearsals and the making of sets, props and costumes (although these activities may take place off-site). A receiving theatre (sometimes called a touring theatre or roadhouse in the USA) is one which predominantly presents touring shows or events that have originated elsewhere. This type of building will need to be geared to efficient and rapid changeovers between productions, where one show will often load-out and the next show load-in within a 12- to 24-hour period. It will generally have a smaller administrative team and no, or minimal, production facilities.

There are many variations on the producing/receiving model and these have different needs. To give three simple examples:

Theatres which produce and receive
Many producing theatres cannot afford to rely solely on their own productions. They will therefore produce their own shows for part of the year and take in touring productions for the remainder.

Long-run receiving theatres
Typically found in major cities such as London and New York, where shows will run for as long as they are commercially successful, for months or even several years. These theatres often have quite simple technical facilities with the technical equipment being brought in specifically for each production.

Repertory and repertoire
Theatres can also operate on a repertory or repertoire basis. Repertory (sometimes called stagione in opera or stock in the USA) implies a theatre that produces a play, opera or dance piece for a brief but intensive run of performances. Repertoire is more common in opera houses where an opera and ballet company share a theatre when there are a series of productions running on alternate evenings. This is often done to minimise vocal stress on singers' voices by not requiring them to perform the same role on consecutive nights. An opera house or theatre operating this way requires considerable space to store multiple sets and stage facilities to make set and production changes easy.

Theatre typologies

The auditoria and stage requirements for the different types and forms of theatre are more extensively discussed in Section 4. They are introduced in this section as the form is relevant to the brief for a new theatre. The types of theatre most commonly encountered include:

Opera house
An opera house typically provides a home for an opera and ballet company. While there are considerable variations, opera houses usually seat audiences of between 1,800 and 2,200. Opera houses frequently have a horseshoe form of auditorium confronting a large well-equipped stage with a large orchestra pit for musicians.

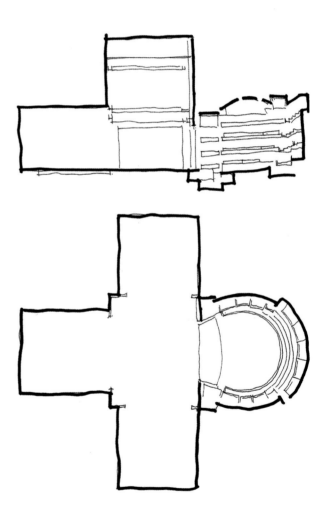

1.5.2 Typical opera house form

Concert hall

This provides a home for classical music including symphonic concerts, chamber music and recitals. Almost all concert halls also accommodate a wider range of amplified and contemporary music. Concert halls typically seat audiences of between 1,500 and 2,000. There are two broad approaches to concert hall design as illustrated in Figures 1.5.3 and 1.5.4: the shoebox form and the vineyard form.

Recital rooms

These are used for the performance of smaller-scale classical music typically to audiences of 200 to 600.

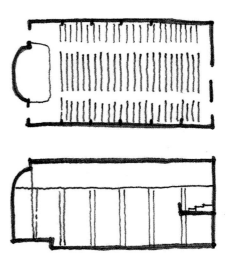

1.5.5 Typical recital room form

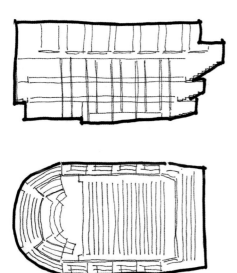

1.5.3 Typical shoebox form concert hall

Dance theatres

These are less common than other forms of theatre. With generous stages and sightlines focused on the stage floor, they vary considerably in size from say 600 to 1,400 seats.

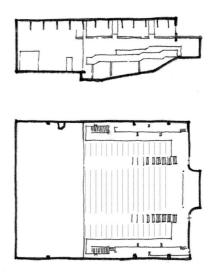

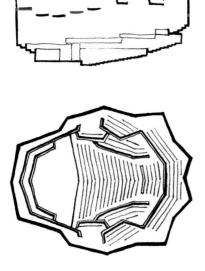

1.5.4 Typical vineyard form concert hall

1.5.6 Example of a dance theatre format

Drama theatres

Theatres for drama probably show the widest variation in form and seating capacity. Drama theatres can range from 100 up to around 1,200 seats. Above this capacity it is difficult for actors to communicate effectively with their audience. The staging of drama can also be in many different formats. The stylised diagram in Figure 1.5.7 illustrates six different formats – (clockwise from top left) arena or in-the-round, thrust, end stage, promenade, traverse and an alternate traverse.

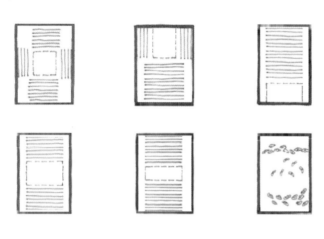

1.5.7 Six different drama theatre formats

Musical theatres

London's West End and Broadway in New York have many theatres used specifically to house large-scale musicals. Many cities have built new theatres to house these larger-scale attractions. Theatres for musical theatre typically seat an audience of between 1,500 and 2,000.

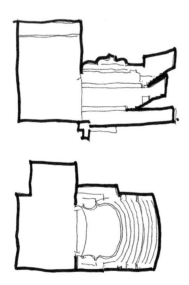

1.5.8 Typical musical theatre form

Entertainment venues

There are some theatres planned and built specifically for more popular entertainment – pop music, circus shows, etc. These venues fall into three broad seating capacities:

1 Smaller-scale venues seating from 1,500 up to 6,000
2 Mid-scale arenas seating 6,000 to 12,000
3 Larger-scale venues seating 12,000 plus.

These latter two categories are beyond the scope of this book.

Others

There are inevitably some venues that defy categorisation. The Royal Albert Hall in London is a heavily used historic venue that accommodates everything from the BBC Promenade Concerts through popular music, sports events and annual visits by Cirque du Soleil.

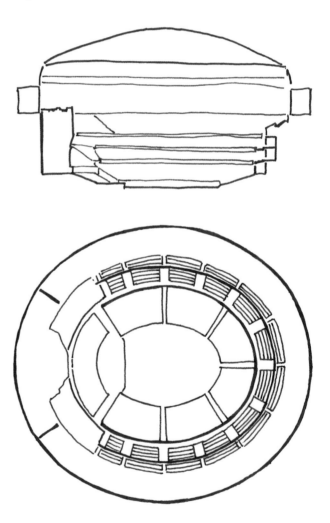

1.5.9 Royal Albert Hall, London, UK

Flexible theatres

There have been many attempts at creating multi-purpose theatres. These have generally failed to meet expectations as the architectural, theatrical and acoustic needs of different types of performance cannot be successfully resolved in a single 'multi-purpose' room. However, there have been successful experiments in flexible and multi-form rooms.

Flexible rooms are ones in which technology is deployed to allow the room to be successfully used for a number of activities. For example, it is not unusual for a larger-scale theatre to be able to accommodate opera, musicals and ballet/dance. It would need devices to vary the acoustics of the room, to vary the proscenium width and height, and to create differing sizes of orchestra pit (see Section 4).

Recent years have seen the development of 'multi-form' theatres in which the fundamental architecture and form of the room is changed to enable one auditorium to successfully house many different types of event. The multi-form theatre is a good solution for a town or city that needs one auditorium to house a number of types of performance. However, one auditorium still cannot house everything. One of the earliest multi-form theatres was the Derngate in Northampton in the UK. The concept was further developed in the Cerritos Center for the Performing Arts in California. Cerritos is a city of only 56,000 people but as part of Los Angeles county has 11 million people in a one-hour isochrone (travel time). The theatre can be configured as a shoebox concert hall, as a drama theatre, as a theatre for musicals and dance, and as a flat floor room (Reference project: p. 202).

Renovation, restoration, refurbishment or reconstruction

Often a group or community will decide to renovate or restore an old building in preference to building anew. Sometimes an existing structure will be found that can be converted into a theatre or performance space. Section 9 discusses renovation and restoration in more detail.

It is not the role of this book to provide a history of theatre buildings going back to Greek amphitheatres; there are many excellent books on that subject. It is, however, appropriate at this point to consider five types of building that may still be encountered:

Architecturally outstanding theatres

Some towns and cities may be lucky and have an unused or underused theatre of significant architectural merit. Examples would include the Theatre Royal in Bury St Edmunds (Reference project: p. 266) or the Georgian Theatre in Richmond, Yorkshire. The historic Zhengyici Theatre in Beijing, believed to be the oldest Chinese theatre in the world (1688), would also fall into this category. The faithful renovation of such a theatre will generally provide an excellent venue and attraction for the community.

Old theatres

The nineteenth century saw many theatres constructed, often by commercial managements. A significant number were destroyed by fire in a period of gas and candle lighting. Those that remain are often attractive and can serve a useful role in their community.

Movie palaces/super-cinemas

Many towns and cities have large cinemas dating from the 1920s and 1930s. Some have been tripled or otherwise adapted. While originally built as cinemas, often with a small stage, some can be effectively converted to house performances.

Failed or outdated theatres

During the 1950s and 1960s many poor or simply bad theatres were constructed. Often these buildings no longer serve the needs of their communities or are simply dated and obsolete. In some cases they can be upgraded to provide a successful new facility. For example, the St Lawrence Centre in Toronto was recreated to create a 'new' drama theatre. The Mahaffey Theater in St Petersburg, Florida was radically transformed to give it a new life (Reference project: p. 248).

Conversion

Many different types of building and structure have been converted to performing arts use – warehouses, sports halls, swimming pools, Masonic temples, etc.

Client and user

On occasions the client and user will be the same organisation. For example, if a college wants to build a new theatre for its academic programmes then the college will be both client and user. This has the advantages of easing decision making and ensuring that the resulting project is designed to fulfil the requirements of the eventual user exactly.

Frequently however the legal client for the project will be a different organisation. For example, a local authority/municipality may decide to build a new theatre as a home for the local theatre or dance company. The division of responsibility can bring advantages but also challenges, and communication between the relevant bodies needs to be extremely good to ensure the project is successful.

Typical client bodies include:

Arts group
An arts organisation (drama, dance or other company) becomes both the user client and the legal client for the construction project.

Local authority or government department
A local authority or government department through its architects or public works department could be the legal client for the project.

Private trust or benefactor
In some situations a new non-profit, charitable organisation may be established to become the client for the design, construction and delivery of the project.

Commercial organisation
Some theatres are built by private enterprises.

Educational organisation
Some theatres are constructed by schools, colleges or universities.

Support

A key role of the founding group of advocates for the new theatre is to generate support for the project. Such support can be political support, community support, support from the artistic community, media support, etc. Of equal importance is generating support that can be turned into funding for the project. In the short term there is a need for modest seed money. As the project develops and moves into the more detailed planning stages then more significant funding will be required to undertake studies, engage staff and advisers, etc.

In planning a new theatre it is easy to overlook the needs of the audiences and the wider public. There will be many articulate arts organisations and lobby groups who want to participate and have some role in the development of the theatre or in its future life once it is completed. There will also be pressures and inputs from politicians and funding bodies over the planning of a new arts building. However, a theatre is being built primarily for the audiences of the future.

On a number of occasions during the planning of a new theatre the client or group leading the project will need to decide whether to go ahead with the project. At the conclusion of the initial 'project inception' stage the group will need to confidently address the question 'Is it a good idea?'

1.6 Step 2 – Project development and studies

After a period of deliberation, examination and review, the client group may then decide to proceed with the project. At this point a more structured and professional client body is needed and more significant funding will be required. The challenge in Step 2 is to develop a strong case for the project sufficient to generate the support and further funding needed to bring it to fruition.

Feasibility study

During this stage one or more studies may be undertaken to assess the viability and achievability of the project. Some clients commission a comprehensive feasibility study to address all the key issues; for example, market analysis, needs assessment, business planning, site analysis, capital cost estimating, funding plan, etc. Alternatively, studies or explorations can be separately commissioned to cover each specific area. Their scope and contents are discussed in the following list:

Needs assessment
An objective, clear-sighted assessment is required of the needs of the arts groups in a community. Do they need a new venue? Do they have the potential to use a new venue successfully? How will they grow and develop into the new venue?

Market analysis
Is there an audience for a new theatre? There is little reason to build a new theatre or refurbish an old one if there is not a significant audience to support the completed project. The market for a new venue can be assessed in a number of ways – through desk research, quantitative analysis, focus groups, benchmarking against existing venues, original market research, etc. All of these methods are valid routes to build a picture of likely future attendance.

Programme planning
Based on the needs assessment and market analysis, a programme plan should be prepared for the venue. This would be a typical year's plan listing the events, the source of the events, number of performances, etc. The programme plan is a key document as it conveys to all involved in the project the types of programmes and levels of activity anticipated in the new or refurbished theatre. The programme plan needs to be prepared for a single year and, in outline at least, for an initial three- to five-year period to show the projected growth in activity in the new building.

Business plan
There are two parts to creating a successful new theatre building – its construction and its operation. A great building must have similarly creative management, operating and financial strategies. The business plan will be developed from the needs assessment and market analysis and use the programme plan as the basis for many of the projections and assumptions about the operation and finances. The business plan should include:
- Governance – advice on the governance and management of the building and its activities
- Artistic programming
- Role of resident companies
- Management structure proposed
- Staffing requirements
- Marketing structure
- Financial planning including realistic estimates of all incomes and expenditures
- Projections of operating support required for the project and sources of such support.

Site analysis
The location of a new performing arts building is clearly critical to its success. In many cases, where an existing building is being remodelled or enlarged, the location is already determined, but in the case of a new building it will be necessary to ensure that a suitable site has been secured before commencing the design process.

Technical issues related to a preferred site need to be identified, criteria established, and the potential site critically evaluated to ensure it fulfils the stated needs.

Where there is more than one site to choose from, it is common to carry out an options appraisal, using a rational methodology and scoring system, to help ensure the best possible site is chosen.

Site requirements are discussed at the beginning of Section 2.

Capital costs

The capital costs of refurbishing an existing building or of creating a new building need to be realistically assessed. These capital costs will be estimated and recalculated many times during the development of the project. The estimation of costs requires skilled input from both a cost consultant or quantity surveyor and the theatre consultant. It is outside the scope of this book to describe the costing process in detail but the following paragraphs outline some of the processes involved.

Before looking at cost estimating at the different stages in the process, it is useful to introduce some terms:

Net area

The net area of the building is the net usable area within all the individual rooms in the building. The net area excludes any circulation – corridors, stairs, elevators, etc. It also excludes any mechanical spaces, ducts, voids and wall thicknesses.

Gross area

This is the gross built area of the building including circulation, plant rooms, etc. In the early stages of planning the gross area is calculated by applying a grossing factor or multiplier to the net area. Compared with other more conventional buildings, theatres are inherently inefficient in their use of space due to the generous circulation spaces required as well as escape routes and mechanical systems. It is not unusual for the net area to be multiplied by 1.55 to 1.65 in order to calculate the gross area.

Construction cost

This is the total cost of building the new or refurbished theatre including all specialist equipment, fit-out, finishes, etc.

Specialist theatre equipment cost

The construction costs include the costs of all the specialist theatre equipment such as:
- Production lighting systems
- Stage equipment – flying systems, elevators, etc.
- Sound, communications and audio-visual systems (AV)
- Movable acoustic devices
- Seats and movable seating systems.

Budgets for the specialist theatre equipment are normally developed by the theatre consultant and will typically amount to around 10 per cent to 18 per cent of the total construction cost.

Den Norske Opera - Nytt Operahus Romprogram - Oppsummering - Summary	Version 3 - 2 December 1998					22-Jun-09 DNO - romprogram.xls	
Sone Zone	Rom Room	Rom Room	10-Nov-98 Net kvm	01-Dec-98 Net kvm	% of Total	Area Change	% Change	Kommentarer Comments
1. 0. 00 Publikumsarealer	Public areas		4,339	3,614	19%	725	16.7%	
2. 0. 00 Store sal	Large auditorium and stages		4,464	4,524	19%	-60	-1.3%	
3. 0. 00 Stottefunksj. Forest. Store sal	Performance support - large theatre		672	672	3%	0	0.0%	
4. 0. 00 Studioscene	Small auditorium and stage		898	898	4%	0	0.0%	
5. 0. 00 Stottefunksj. Forest. Lille sal	Performance support - small theatre		183	183	1%	0	0.0%	
6. 0. 00 Areal - utovere	Performers areas		2,131	1,924	9%	207	9.7%	
7. 0. 00 Provelokaler	Rehearsal		3,522	3,322	15%	200	5.7%	
8. 0. 00 Verksteder	Workshops		4,951	4,714	21%	237	4.8%	
9. 0. 00 Kontorlokaler	Management		2,166	2,347	9%	-181	-8.4%	
	Total net building area		23,326	22,198	100%	1,128	4.8%	
	Grossing to include							
	HVAC rooms							
	Mechanical and electrical rooms							
	Corridors							
	Vertical circulation - lifts & stairs							
	Ducts							
	Inaccessible spaces							
	Wall thickness							
	Allow 55% of net building area		12,829	12,209	kvm			
	Gross building area		36,156	34,407	kvm			

Notes
1   HVAC = heating ventilating and air conditioning.
2   Level 0 is assumed to be stage level, therefore +1 is one level above stage, -1 is one level below stage.
3   Dimensions - height, width and depth are only given for theatrically critical spaces, they are clear dimensions.
4   Some room areas are shown as 0kvm - this room is therefore not being provided at this time.

1.6.1 Specimen summary page from a Schedule of Areas chart for a large theatre building

Soft costs

Any project will incur a series of costs outside of the actual construction costs. These are often referred to as the soft costs and will include:

- Fees for architect, consultants and engineers
- Client costs – project office and staffing
- Site acquisition
- Permits and licences
- Fundraising costs
- Business planning
- Taxes (including VAT where relevant)
- Architect selection costs
- Loose furniture and equipment
- IT and box office systems
- Removal costs/temporary accommodation
- Site investigations and surveys
- Administration, staff recruitment and training
- Opening costs.

Typically the soft costs can be some 20 per cent plus of the overall project costs.

Contingencies

Every project should include reasonable contingencies to cover unknown or unexpected events. It is common for a percentage to be allowed for contingencies and for that percentage to vary and be reduced as the project proceeds. At an early stage when there are considerable unknowns a contingency of 25 per cent or even 30 per cent may be allowed. As the project is more clearly defined, with a firm brief and concept and schematic drawings, the contingency can be reduced. Some projects allow separate contingencies for the design and construction periods. The design contingency is available to cover changes or fluctuations that occur during the design stages. The construction contingency, as its name implies, is to cover unforeseen situations and circumstances that may arise during the construction period.

Inflation

Every project is subject to the effects of inflation on design fees, construction costs, etc. This can be a significant factor in the overall project cost.

Project cost

The overall cost of the project including all the costs – construction, equipment, soft costs and contingencies.

At the inception of the project there is generally a vague brief or ambition for the project. Some idea of capital costs will be required. This will be based on comparable projects and the experience of the advisers. There are hundreds of new office buildings, housing, schools, etc. completed each year which provide a good database of comparative costs. By contrast there are few new or refurbished theatres completed around the world. Each project is often unique and significantly different from others. There is therefore a lack of reliable cost information on comparable projects.

International comparisons are even more difficult given differences in construction costs and exchange rates. However it is possible to benchmark costs even at this stage as long as the factors that generate cost differentials, such as location, quality, acoustic performance, flexibility and accommodation mix, are recognised in the benchmarking analysis. Costs based on overall area are always more reliable than costs based on seat count.

As the project concept is developed and an initial and then a firm brief are prepared, a clearer cost plan can be drawn up. This will usually be based on a schedule of areas for the building giving a total area for the building in square metres. Applying a rate per square metre for the project will give a more accurate indication of the construction cost as it has been found that there is a degree of consistency between the costs per unit area for similar building types. This can be refined by breaking the building down according to the types of space to be provided – auditoria, rehearsal rooms, stage areas, administration, storage, circulation, etc. Such an approach also allows comparative assessments for alternative proposals. With any of these proposals one needs to be mindful of costs that are not specifically area related (such as the specialist stage equipment) and ensure that the allowances made reflect the technical vision.

When the design team starts work, then drawings of the building will be developed. These can be used by the cost consultant to calculate more accurate cost estimates. The theatre consultant will produce lists and budgets for the specialist theatre equipment.

As the design process proceeds, more detailed estimates of the costs will be prepared. The costs will be analysed by element and quantity (e.g. excavation – number of cubic metres to be excavated; structural frame – quantity of steel or concrete required).

Almost every theatre building project experiences cost overruns or budget difficulties. The costs need to be constantly checked and reconciled against the budget. Almost inevitably there will be a need to reduce or rationalise costs. This is done by the client and design team through a process of cost cutting or 'value engineering'.

Prior to tender, a detailed cost plan and bill of quantities are usually prepared. This sets a benchmark against which tenders from contractors can be assessed and compared.

Tenders received for the construction work are carefully assessed and compared by the design and client teams. They are assessed not only on the basis of the price submitted but also for the qualitative aspects of the proposals – contractor expertise, experience, team, resources, etc.

The careful assessment and measurement of the costs and expenditure needs to continue throughout the construction stage. The cost consultant's final task on a project is to prepare and agree the 'final account' for the building.

Funding plan

Once the anticipated 'hard' and 'soft' costs for the project are known then a funding plan is required showing how the capital costs will be met and the sources of project funding whether government or private. The plan needs to look at timing as well as total amounts. The amount needed on a month-by-month basis will fluctuate, peaking early in the construction period.

All of the above studies may not necessarily be required. Equally, funding bodies or the dictates of a particular situation may require other studies to be carried out. For example, in the case of urban renewal or regeneration projects more detailed studies may be required to demonstrate the role the theatre can play in the overall development. Some projects have an economic impact assessment prepared, others detailed studies of the educational programmes they are to offer. Where historic buildings are involved a Conservation Plan may be required (see Section 9).

The key question at the end of this stage is 'Do we have a viable project?'

1.7 Step 3 – Brief writing and design team selection

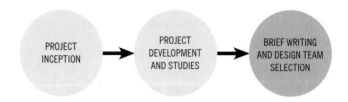

The brief is probably the single most important document for the project. The brief contains significant factual information about the proposed building but must also convey the rationale behind the building, the client's goals and aspirations. The brief is the document on which the architect and design team will base their plans and designs for the building, its systems and equipment. It needs to find a balance in providing sufficient information to the design team to ensure they fully understand the requirements but not be so prescriptive that it inhibits the creativity of the design team.

A typical brief for a new or refurbished theatre will include:

- The vision
- Goals and aims for the project
- Rationale for the building
- Background and context
- Project organisation
- Site – plans, description, opportunities and constraints
- Description of the type of building required – to give guidance to the architect and design team
- Description of the building functions by area or zone – auditorium, stage, public areas, backstage area, etc.
- Room schedule – a listing of all the rooms in the building with their net areas and other key parameters
- Acoustic brief
- Etc.

Scope of information required

The following list summarises the range of information required for each part of the building. The subsequent sections of this book provide more detailed analyses.

Auditorium
Form, seating capacity, flexibility, design guidance, acoustics, accessibility, sightlines (see Section 4).

Stage
Size, capabilities, flexibility, technologies, orchestra pit, concert platform (see Section 5).

Public areas
Foyers, box office, cloakrooms, catering, retail, visual art spaces, informal performance spaces (see Section 3).

Backstage areas
Rehearsal space, dressing rooms, band room, green room and related provision (see Section 7).

Production spaces
Get-in, scene dock, workshops, wardrobe, etc. (see Section 7).

Exterior
Appearance, accessibility, servicing, parking, etc. (see Section 2).

Ancillary accommodation
Office space, education and community areas, conference facilities and storage (see Section 8).

The design team

The timing and process for selecting an architect and design team will vary from project to project. In some cases, the client will need architectural advice early in the process (for example, to test the feasibility of a potential site, or the scope for adding to or adapting an existing building). In other situations, the client may feel confident to develop the initial brief before making the decision as to which architect/design team is best suited to undertake the work. The theatre consultant may be appointed to advise on this process, often before the appointment of the architect.

Composition of the team

The exact make-up of the design team will vary depending on the nature, scale and complexity of the project. A typical core team will include:
- Architect
- Theatre consultant
- Engineers – structural, mechanical and electrical
- Acoustic consultant
- Cost consultant or quantity surveyor
- Project manager.

Depending on the needs of the particular project, the team could be extended to include any of the following specialist consultants:
- Landscape architect or designer
- Fire and safety consultant
- Traffic consultant
- Planning consultant
- IT consultant
- Security consultant
- Accessibility adviser
- Sustainability consultant
- Conservation expert
- Management consultant
- Architectural lighting consultant
- Catering consultant.

The client can choose to select a full design team working under the responsibility and control of the architect (see Figure 1.7.1). This has the advantage of making one person or firm, the architect, responsible for the work of all the other consultants. (Note: the cost consultant is nearly always a separate commission as they need to be independent and responsible direct to the client.)

While this is a valid route, it can lead to difficulties and many clients choose to separately select and contract with key members of the team. Typically the client will separately select the architect, theatre consultant, cost consultant and project manager. Such a structure is illustrated in Figure 1.7.2.

Many teams include a professional project manager. This person or group can join the project at different times. Many project managers have direct, practical experience of construction and can be valuable in ensuring the construction process stays on time and on budget. A smaller number of project managers have experience and knowledge that is valuable to the client and the design team during the planning and design stages. Few project managers have direct experience of the planning, design and construction of theatres.

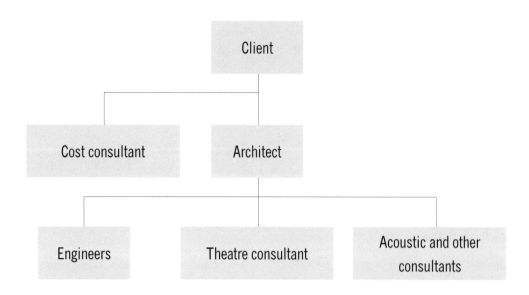

1.7.1 Organisational diagram: architect-led team

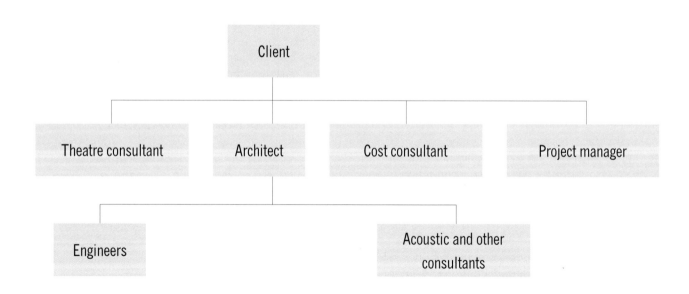

1.7.2 Organisational diagram: separate appointments

Where a project manager is appointed, they should be an integral part of the team without taking away from the architect's leadership of the design process.

Selecting the architect/design team

There are several methods of selecting architects and consultants including recommendation, design competition, competitive interview and research and analysis. While private sector clients are free to choose whichever selection route they prefer, most theatre projects will be subject to government or other funding body rules and regulations. A government or city project will be obliged to follow government procurement rules. Similarly, any project in receipt of significant government funding will also probably be required to follow government procurement policies.

Projects within European Union countries in receipt of significant government funding (or funding which originates from publicly funded organisations) will generally be required to fulfil the EU procurement regulations. The EU rules require an open, fair, competitive selection process (but do not specify that this has to be by architectural design competition). The interview system can be used provided certain conditions are met.

The selection can be considered in two ways:
1   A selection process to find the correct architect for a project.
2   A selection process to find the most appropriate design for the project.

Where the client wants to choose on the basis of a design, some form of competition should be considered. Where architects from more than one country are invited to submit designs, a competition can be run using the regulations of the UIA (International Union of Architects). The EU also has rules governing 'Design Competitions'.

Within the UK, the competition system is a very flexible one ranging from an 'Open Project Competition' which any qualified architect can enter and where anonymity is maintained throughout the whole process, to a competition in which a number of selected architects are invited to prepare designs and present them to the client. Procedures such as discussion forums, interviews, site visits, public exhibitions and formal presentations can form part of the selection process.

Open design competition

This route would see a public advertisement of the architectural competition that invites appropriately experienced architects or teams to enter the competition. A clearly written brief, along with the rules of the competition and a specification of the amount and detail of information to be submitted is issued to those invited to enter. The competition documentation should also set out the selection criteria. Architects are then given an appropriate period (typically around three months) in which to prepare their submissions.

This type of competition is a major undertaking in terms of time, cost and the effort required from the promoting organisation and so tends to be used only for schemes which have a particular significance. The Oslo Opera House competition, for example, attracted 238 entries from around the world. All were put on public display (anonymously, in a disused aircraft hangar at the old Fornebau airport in Oslo). The public and press were invited to view and comment on the schemes and this formed part of the selection process.

Two-stage competition

A two-stage competition is sometimes held to overcome some of the difficulties of handling the number of entries which an open single-stage competition might attract and to reduce the amount of unpaid work undertaken by the architectural profession.

The first stage of such a process can include:
• Submission of credentials. Each of the teams are requested to submit their credentials, experience, team, etc. and/or
• Submission of ideas and concepts in response to an outline brief. It is common to limit the amount of information that architects are allowed to submit (to say ten A3 pages).

Following the first stage, a fair and objective evaluation of the submissions is made against selection criteria set out in the invitation or outline brief. Several architects may be invited for interview, following which the jury will select a shortlist of three to five architects to enter the second stage of the competition. It is increasingly common for architects to be paid a modest fee towards the cost of preparing their entry for the second stage of the competition.

A more detailed brief is issued at the beginning of the second stage. Judging will be by an acknowledged jury with input from professional advisers.

Competitive interview

A competitive interview can fulfil EU procurement regulations and the requirements of government funding bodies within the UK. In response to an advertisement and/or invitations, expressions of interest credentials are sought from appropriately experienced architects. The documents received are then fairly evaluated and ranked against agreed criteria. The shortlisted architects are invited to attend an interview and to make a presentation demonstrating their experience and ability to undertake the project. They may also be asked to outline their approach but are not normally required to prepare site-specific designs. An interview is valuable in helping the client assess the possible working relationship with the architect.

Other

There is considerable flexibility in selection processes. The government of Singapore used an interesting approach in selecting an architect for the Esplanade (their national performing arts centre). An open first stage led to a shortlist of four practices. All four were invited to Singapore for one week. During that week they could visit the site, meet the potential users for the building, meet and hold workshops with the client, the theatre and acoustic consultants. At the end of the week each team was invited to make a presentation on their responses to the brief, the site and the opportunities presented. They were specifically requested not to present a design for the building. This was a thorough process that allowed client, users and consultants to fully assess the architects and their capabilities.

1.8 Conclusion

At the completion of the preliminary planning stage the client should have:

- A clear vision for the project
- A detailed brief for the building
- A site, selected against appropriate criteria
- A detailed view of the capital costs and source of funding for the project
- A robust programming, business and financial plan for the operation of the building
- An architect and specialist consultants, selected and appointed.

The key question at the end of this stage is 'Do we have the funding, organisation, site, team and business plan to undertake a capital project and achieve a successful outcome?'

SECTION EDITOR

David Staples	Chairman, Theatre Projects Consultants

CONTRIBUTORS

Gary Faulkner	Gardiner and Theobold (cost management)

Section 2
Broad principles

Contents

2.1 Introduction

This section explores some of the basic design principles that need to be considered in the early stages of planning a new theatre. It aims to answer questions about the location of the building and how the various elements of the brief can be organised within the design of the theatre building. Key factors which influence the planning of the building such as access for people with disabilities, fire safety, acoustics, and the integration of mechanical and electrical services, and environmental sustainability are discussed in this section, insofar as they relate to the building as a whole. More specific information is given in the relevant later sections.

2.2   Location

The theatre within the local economy

A city or town centre location is usually preferred to an out-of-town location. A visit to the theatre is often only part of a 'night out' and proximity to other facilities, such as shops, bars and restaurants, is therefore helpful both to the theatre and to the night-time economy of the district as a whole. A theatre, by definition, should attract large numbers of people. This will generate 'footfall' which will in turn benefit other businesses and bring greater activity to an area. The creation of new arts projects is often seen as a means to kick-start the regeneration of a particular area as a 'cultural quarter'. While there are many situations where this approach has succeeded, some caution is required. First and foremost, the new arts building must fulfil a genuine need and be well managed to ensure it provides a programme which will attract an audience. Even when successful, regeneration is a process which often takes many years to come to fruition. Conversely, there are many examples of small theatres starting up in old buildings in less salubrious low-rent districts, which have succeeded in attracting audiences through their sheer dynamism, the quality of their work and the alternative experience they offer audiences, particularly younger people.

Ultimately, it is the quality of the programming of a venue that attracts audiences. Good design, however, can stimulate creativity and enhance the audience's experience of an enjoyable evening out.

Travel plan

It has been estimated that the energy consumed by an audience travelling to a theatre is almost as great as the total energy used by the building itself. For this reason, the quality, quantity and proximity of public transport is an important consideration when selecting a site. Generally, car travel should be discouraged, although for theatres with large rural catchment areas or where there is limited late night public transport, there may be little alternative. In such cases, sufficient car parking facilities will need to be made available and the overall number of spaces within reasonable walking distance of the theatre will need to be assessed. In some cases, theatre patrons may be able to make use of public car parks in town centres as these are often under-used in the evening. Where theatregoers are forced to park in residential streets it will inevitably generate conflict with the needs of residents and this should be avoided. Drop-off points for taxis and parking for people with disabilities must also be considered.

Deliveries

The ability to deliver scenery, equipment and other supplies is an essential requirement. For larger theatres, this may involve the use of several large articulated vehicles, which need space to manoeuvre and park off-street at the delivery doors. Achieving this, particularly in an urban environment, can be challenging. Loading and off-loading will often take place at night and needs to be organised in a way that it will not cause disturbance to nearby residents.

Further information about loading requirements is set out in Section 7.

Visibility

Theatres, particularly larger ones, are major public buildings and need to be located in a prominent position within the town or city and to be easily recognisable. This may be achieved through location, the architecture of the building itself, and clear signage. Every theatre needs signage both to say what it is and to advertise the current and forthcoming productions. This needs to be recognised as a design requirement at an early stage. If no provision is made it is likely to result in unplanned additions by the users at a later stage that could well detract from the appearance of the building.

Views into the building from the street are also important in promoting a venue and encouraging the public to enter. Older theatres often have small doors and windows, with little opportunity for people to see in. If this is the case, it will be important to ensure that the building is highlighted with good external lighting and signage and made as welcoming as possible.

With new buildings or new additions, a more transparent entrance and foyer area that allows the activity within the building to be seen from outside, particularly at night, will help to animate the theatre and make it appear more accessible for new audiences. The Edinburgh Festival Theatre illustrates this approach (Reference project: p. 224).

Acoustic environment

Consideration of the acoustic environment is important when selecting a site for a new theatre as it can have a significant impact on the cost of the building. The ability to create a quiet environment within an auditorium is essential and this is made much more difficult if the building is located close to external noise sources such as railway lines, airports or major roads. While there are construction techniques available to exclude high external noise levels, they are generally expensive and can be avoided if a quieter site is chosen, although this may conflict with the need for a city centre location.

Noise break-out from the theatre is also an important consideration, particularly for venues that may wish to present shows with loud amplified music. Close proximity to housing may provoke complaints from residents, which can lead to restriction of the operating hours of the theatre by the local environmental health authority or, in extreme cases, to enforced closure. It is possible to solve these problems through the use of heavy construction and of separated structures to prevent air-borne and structure-borne noise from leaving the building, but this can prove expensive.

The involvement of an acoustic consultant to advise on these matters at an early stage of the project is recommended.

Audience catchment area

When planning a new theatre an assessment needs to be made of where its audience will come from. This information will be needed in order to produce a coherent travel plan (see above) as well as informing the overall business model. The catchment area will vary considerably for different types of theatre and for different locations. For example, a small community-based theatre will draw its audience from a relatively local area, whereas a larger theatre will need to attract audiences from a wider area.

Travel time to the theatre is usually used to gauge the size of the catchment area. This means that a theatre in a provincial town will need to attract its audience from a larger geographical area than a theatre located in a major city centre. A specialist marketing consultant can be appointed to analyse the likely catchment area and predict attendance for a particular theatre and location. Where the building is for an existing organisation their marketing database can also provide valuable information about where regular supporters live and what their attendance patterns are.

Additional income streams

Most theatres rely heavily on generating additional income from activities other than the sale of tickets.

This includes bar and merchandise sales, catering and hiring out facilities for conferences, rehearsals, corporate entertainment, meetings and other events. The commercial success of these activities will rely on attracting a market for them and this will be dependent on various factors, including the quality and style of services offered and the availability of other similar facilities in the vicinity. Theatres often struggle to get their catering offer right and it may be advisable to engage a specialist catering consultant to help advise on this aspect.

The provision of these additional facilities needs to be carefully considered as part of the business plan and included in the design brief to ensure adequate space is provided. Further information is given in Sections 3 and 8.

2.3   Components of a theatre

There are three main areas of activity which go to make up a typical theatre building. Their scale and character will vary enormously for different types and sizes of theatre but the basic characteristics and relationships are similar. Understanding how they work is an essential first step in the early planning of any theatre. The main components are:

- Auditorium and stage
- Front of house
- Backstage.

Auditorium and stage

The auditorium is the heart of a theatre building, where the primary activity of experiencing and presenting performances takes place. The auditorium can range from a simple studio space with fewer than 100 seats to a multi-level room with several thousand seats and a large mechanised stage house. In both cases, audience seating is arranged to view the stage and the stage is a platform from which the actors perform to the audience. The relationship between the two is the crucial factor that determines the success of the space. A live performance is an interactive event where the chemistry between audience and performer is central to the experience and rarely the same twice. It is essential that the design of the auditorium facilitates this process. How that can be achieved is discussed in Section 4.

The auditorium must be planned with the optimum arrangement of seating to enable the audience to see and hear the performance. This may be in a fixed format or may be flexible, allowing seating and staging to be rearranged to create different actor/audience relationships.

The stage may be a simple platform (or just a designated area) within the same space as the audience (Reference project: The Young Vic, London, p. 278) or a stage with a flytower, where the acting area is within a separate compartment, which is viewed from the auditorium through a proscenium opening (Reference project: The Lowry, Salford Quays, p. 244). Whatever the size of the theatre, the performance is supported by a considerable array of technology in the form of lighting, scenery handling equipment and sound systems, all of which need to be integrated with the architecture of the auditorium. Advice on these installations is normally provided by a specialist theatre consultant who, in consultation with the end-users, will advise the architect on what is required and the space provision needed to accommodate them. Further information is given in Sections 5 and 6.

Above all, the auditorium is the heart of the building, where the audience and performers meet to participate in a live performance. The other elements of the building, the front of house and backstage, are designed to serve the needs of these two separate groups and to deliver them to the performance space in the best possible frame of mind.

Auditorium acoustics

It is important to understand at the briefing stage that the acoustic requirements of a particular auditorium will have a significant effect on its volume and form. Put at its simplest, there is a direct relationship between the volume of a room and its reverberation time. This means that a concert hall for un-amplified (e.g. classical) music will require a much higher volume per seat than a drama theatre, which needs a good acoustic for speech and mainly amplified music. An opera house will require a volume that lies somewhere between the two. These issues are examined in more detail in Section 4, but it is worth noting here that establishing the approximate volume (e.g. height) of an auditorium, relative to its use, is critical at the initial planning stage, as it will have a significant impact on the overall massing of the building and on its cost.

Front of house

The front of house encompasses all of the foyer facilities, which provide for the needs of the audience and will often also be open throughout the day. Unlike most other building types, the main users of a theatre building will all arrive shortly before the performance starts and will move en masse during the intervals and at the close of the show. This phenomenon requires the building to be planned to accommodate large numbers of people moving through a sequence of activities as they progress to and from the auditorium.

Many of the audience may be visiting the theatre for the first time and it is essential that the building is clearly laid out and legible, with the facilities arranged in such a way that movement through the foyers is not impeded, particularly when those who arrive at the last minute want to take the 'fast track' to their seats. It is surprising how many theatres are arranged so that people queuing at the box office and bar counters impede the flow of others or where those moving from the bars to the auditorium meet others, going straight to their seats, coming in the opposite direction. In larger theatres it is helpful to disperse the bars and toilets around the building, near to the different seating areas in order to avoid contra-flows and the congestion this creates.

A theatre foyer will require clear way-finding signage to enable the audience to find their seats and the other facilities around the building, but a well-planned front of house will be much easier to navigate without the need for excessive signage. No amount of signage will mitigate the problems created by poor planning.

A more detailed analysis of front of house requirements is given in Section 3.

Backstage

The backstage areas of a theatre must meet the needs of both the performers (rehearsal, dressing, preparation and relaxation) and of the production and technical staff responsible for the delivery and preparation of sets, costumes and technical equipment. These are activities that will generally need to take place away from public view if the mystique of the performance on the stage is to be preserved. Access routes to the stage from delivery doors, technical areas and dressing rooms should not, therefore, pass through any areas of the building occupied by the public.

Dressing rooms

Accommodation is required for performers to dress, make-up and prepare for the performance. The scale of these facilities will vary enormously depending on the size and type of theatre and may range from a single dressing room to accommodation for up to 200 performers. Dressing rooms must be provided with adequate toilets and showers. They will require additional support facilities nearby, such as a wardrobe, for the maintenance of costumes, and a green room, where actors and other staff can relax, eat or wait, away from their dressing rooms or offices. Dressing facilities should generally be as close to the stage as possible but with sufficient separation to prevent noise from reaching the stage.

Stage get-in

Ease and speed of delivery of large items of scenery and equipment to and from the stage is essential, particularly in touring or repertoire theatres where shows change frequently. For this reason it is highly desirable for the delivery doors, or 'get-in', to be at the same level as the stage. Where this is not possible, it will be necessary to provide a large elevator to move scenery and equipment from delivery level to stage level. This is expensive, adds considerably to the time and labour required to double handle large items, and poses the risk of performances being cancelled if the lift breaks down. In large multi-level venues, double handling is sometimes avoided by using large lifts designed to move the entire scenery trailer to stage level.

Technical areas

There will need to be sufficient scene dock space between the get-in and the stage for the off-loading, handling and storage of sets and equipment. The scale of this will depend on the size and type of theatre and on whether more than one show needs to be stored within the building at a time. Significant amounts of storage are also required for stock items that are used regularly, such as access equipment, rostra, seats, lights, drapes and musical instruments. Producing theatres may also require workshops for the manufacture of sets, props and costumes and for the maintenance of equipment, although the cost of providing these facilities on a city centre site means that, increasingly, they are located off-site or the work is outsourced to specialist contractors with their own facilities.

Stage door

Larger theatres will usually require a stage door, providing a separate entrance for actors and staff and acting as a reception and security point for the whole backstage area with space for visitors to wait and for deliveries to be received. Some smaller theatres may choose to dispense with the expense of providing and staffing this facility and actors and staff will then have to access backstage areas via the front of house.

More detailed information on these backstage areas is given in Section 7.

Administration

A theatre will require office space for the staff who work in the building. The size of this will be determined by the staff structure of the organisation concerned and it is important to gain an understanding of this structure at the briefing stage. It is often desirable to group all the offices together in one location, but in some cases, such as front of house management, technical or catering staff, the offices may need to be located close to their respective areas of responsibility. The ideal location for the offices is mid-way between the backstage and front of house zones so that easy access to both areas is possible. More detailed information is given in Section 8.

Other activities

A theatre may require a range of accommodation in addition to the main foyers, backstage and performance areas. These can include restaurants, private hospitality rooms, education facilities and art galleries in the front of house zone; and studios, rehearsal rooms and meeting rooms backstage. Large rooms, such as studios and rehearsal rooms, are often used for occasional performances and other public events and should therefore be positioned where they can be reached from both the foyers and the backstage areas. These facilities can all provide additional income streams for the theatre, and so need to be considered when the business plan is being prepared and provision made in the design brief.

Theatres for schools and communities

Most of the elements of a theatre building outlined above will be found in large or medium-scale theatres designed for professional use. There are, however, an increasing number of smaller theatres being built for use by schools and communities which, while they contain the same essential elements in microcosm, are quite different in scale. They pose a number of specific issues that are worth considering here.

Drama and performing arts courses are often part of the curriculum in secondary schools and colleges and their theatre spaces are therefore used for both teaching and performance. In addition, schools and communities will often expect to be able to use a theatre for many other activities, including music, assemblies, lectures, meetings and even examinations and sports. Most schools, however, now need purpose-designed theatre spaces, with good technical installations.

Multi-purpose halls, of the type commonly provided in the past, are unlikely to meet current expectations. Multi-use spaces are problematic, not only in terms of the different physical needs of different activities but also in terms of scheduling and the labour involved in frequent changes of format. It is often better, therefore, to consider several spaces, each dedicated to a specific use, rather than one single space that will do nothing particularly well. School theatres are likely to take the form either of a flexible studio or of a more conventional theatre space with a fixed stage and seating.

Studio spaces need a flat semi-sprung floor (not concrete), a ceiling height of at least 5m, a technical grid over the whole space for suspension of lighting and technical equipment, a perimeter curtain track to create a black box when required, and a flexible seating system, capable of providing several different layouts. Daylight is valuable for many activities, such as teaching and rehearsal, and will reduce energy use, but all windows must be provided with effective blackout for performances. There needs to be sufficient storage to accommodate seating and equipment when it is not in use. Typical seating capacities will be in the range of 80–150.

More conventional theatre spaces will have the stage in a fixed position, allowing for better technical installations in that area. Provision of a flytower is unusual but the stage will be provided with suspension equipment in the form of curtain tracks and flying bars, operated by hand-lines or winches. Seating may be fixed or movable, the latter often employing a retractable seating tier which can be withdrawn to provide a large area of flat floor for teaching or other non-theatrical uses. This may sometimes be combined with seating galleries at the rear and sides. Typical seating capacities will be in the range of 250-350 seats. The temptation to build over-large auditoria for big occasions such as speech days and concerts should be resisted, as the space will work less well for theatre.

The ability of students to participate in technical theatre activities, such as lighting, sound and set building, is important and it is therefore necessary to give careful thought as to how this can be achieved safely, particularly in relation to access to lighting at high level. Lighting walkways or grids, with appropriate fall arrest systems, should therefore be considered.

A school theatre will often be part of a larger complex of buildings, which may be used to provide foyer and changing facilities. However, educational facilities are increasingly used by the wider community, providing valuable income for the school. A well-equipped theatre may well be in demand for amateur and professional productions, both in connection with local arts festivals and as part of a regular cultural programme. It is therefore important to consider whether the theatre can function independently at times when the rest of the school is closed. This will require provision of adequate dedicated foyer space and toilets to meet current standards, sufficient backstage facilities to accommodate a small visiting company, and independent means of escape.

2.3.1 and 2.3.2 Parabola Arts Centre, The Cheltenham Ladies' College (2009: Tim Foster Architects)

School arts centre, created by building a new 300-seat theatre linked to an existing historic house, which provides foyers, dressing rooms and teaching spaces.

Photograph: Tim Foster

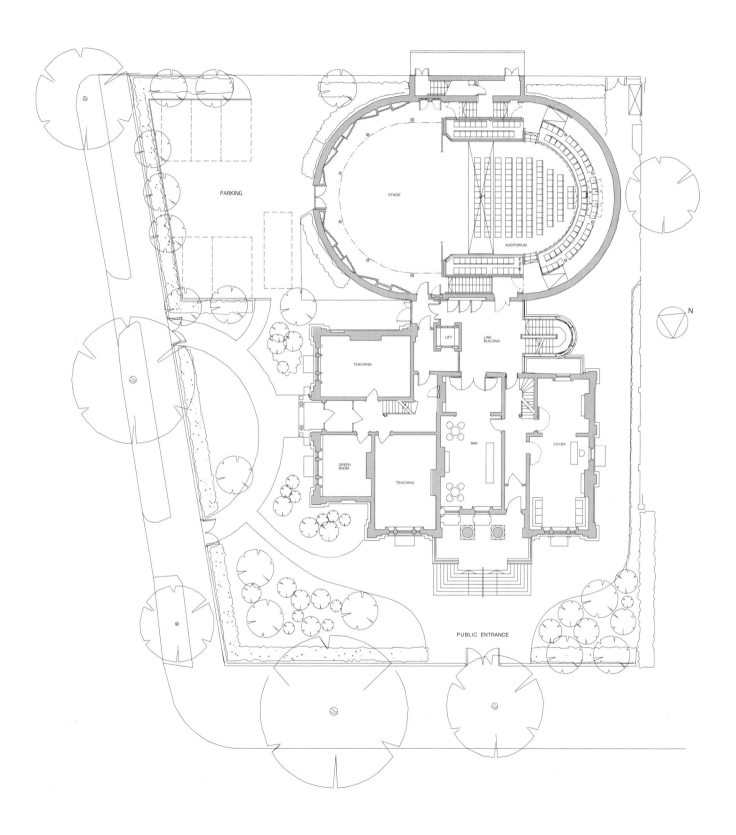

PARKING

STAGE

AUDITORIUM

N

LIFT

LINK
BUILDING

TEACHING

GREEN
ROOM

TEACHING

BAR

FOYER

PUBLIC ENTRANCE

2.4 Planning the building

While much of the logic of how the various components of a theatre should be organised has already been outlined above, it is worth examining the key adjacencies of the various areas in a little more detail.

A theatre consists of several very different elements that must be organised into a coherent architectural whole. It is a public building at the front, a semi-industrial production facility at the back, with an auditorium and stage at its centre, usually an acoustically sealed space, often of considerable volume.

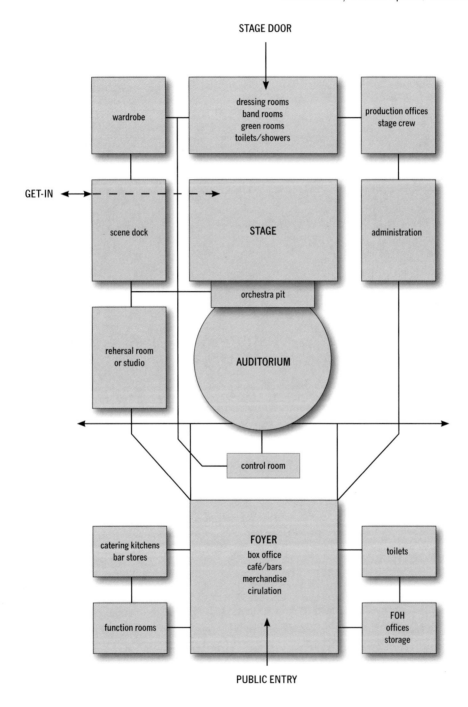

2.4.1 This typical organisational diagram shows the relationships of the key functional elements which make up a theatre

A traditional theatre building, built within a city block, such as in London's West End, has a relatively clear organisational diagram. It is approached by the public from a main street at the front where the treatment of the façade is suitably imposing to indicate its significance as a public building. The backstage faces a less important street at the rear and is less imposing, while the auditorium and stage, with its considerable height, sits at the centre of the block where its size is least apparent from street level. Side streets may also provide for escape routes from the auditorium.

A theatre on an island site, however, poses a more complex design problem as it must present itself as a coherent piece of architecture from all sides.

In this case it is often more difficult to handle the backstage elements, which take on greater visual significance. This can sometimes be resolved by wrapping the foyers and backstage areas, like a doughnut, around the larger volumes of the auditoria and stages at the centre of the plan but such a solution can lead to the foyers and backstage areas becoming larger than the brief demands or becoming too narrow to function well. It may also be necessary, particularly on a tight urban site, to arrange the elements vertically so that the foyers are located at ground level with the auditorium and stage above them (Reference project: RADA, London, p. 262). This approach does, however, create the problem of stage deliveries having to be made via a lift and the audience having more extended routes to their seats.

Acoustic separation

Acoustic separation between spaces is an important consideration in the early planning of the building. If noise-generating areas can be kept away from quiet areas it will avoid the need to employ expensive acoustic isolation techniques. For example:

- If there is to be more than one auditorium they should be separated from each other in both plan and section, with no shared walls or floors, to prevent noise crossover.
- Rehearsal rooms and workshop areas should be well separated from stages and from each other.
- Auditoria and stages should be provided with acoustic lobbies at all entry points to prevent noise from foyers, bars and backstage areas from entering the performance spaces.
- Plant rooms should be located well away from performance spaces and other quiet areas, to prevent plant noise and vibration from transferring to them.

If a building is to be used to its full potential it is essential that all areas can be used simultaneously without causing acoustic disturbance. An acoustic consultant should be involved in the early stages of design to advise on appropriate separation techniques.

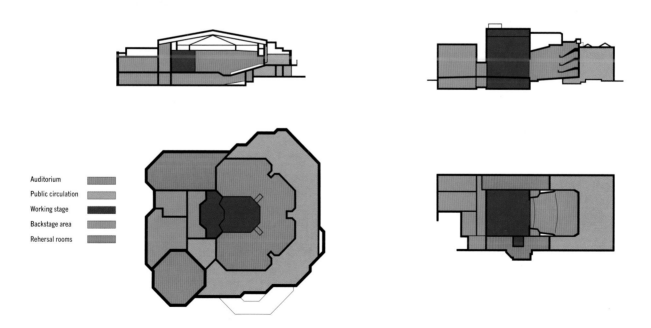

Auditorium
Public circulation
Working stage
Backstage area
Rehersal rooms

2.4.2 and 2.4.3 Typical planning of two theatres; island site (left) and city block (right)

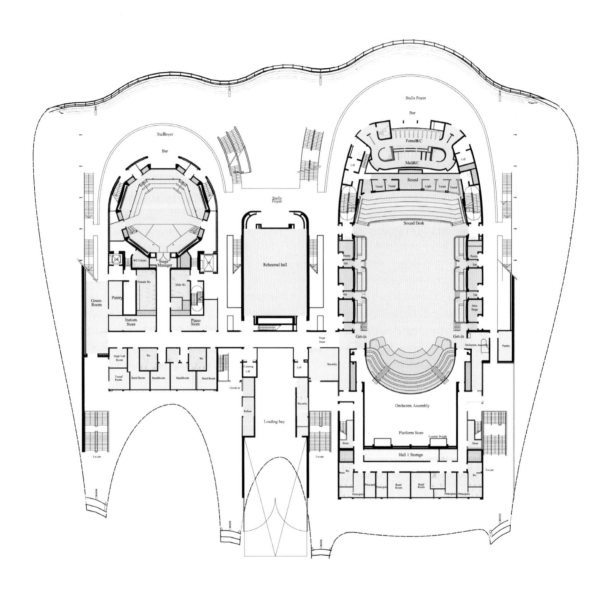

2.4.4 Plan of The Sage Music Centre, Gateshead, UK
(2004: Foster and Partners)
Two auditoria and a rehersal hall are arranged side by side, with acoustic seperation
between them, all under a single curving roof.

2.5 Mechanical and electrical services

Theatres are one of the most highly serviced building types, incorporating as they do a very diverse range of facilities from public foyers, bars and restaurants in the front of house, stage lighting and technology in the auditoria and stages, and semi-industrial activities backstage. In a new building, the cost of the services installations will typically be approximately one-third of the total construction cost and in a conversion or fit-out may well be more. It is therefore crucial to have a clear understanding of the services requirements and to have a strategy for their integration into the design at an early stage. A specialist mechanical and electrical services consultant will need to be employed who will ideally have previous experience of the building type. It is not within the scope of this book to provide detailed advice in this area but rather to give general guidance on the key issues and installations that need to be considered at the design stage. The following are key issues relating to the building services, which the designer should be aware of.

Ventilation

Ventilation systems in auditoria and other performance spaces must be extremely quiet with background noise levels of around NR20 and sometimes lower in a concert hall. They must also be capable of maintaining comfortable conditions despite the considerable heat generated by a closely packed audience and stage lighting and equipment. The design of low noise ventilation systems necessitates delivering air at low velocities, resulting in large duct sizes and significant amounts of acoustic attenuation. Adequate space for duct routes needs to be established early in the design process. It is generally accepted that displacement ventilation systems – where the supply air is delivered through vents in the floor, close to the audience, and rises through natural convection as it heats up – are the most effective and energy efficient. To achieve this necessitates the formation of plenum voids under the seats.

Where this cannot be achieved, air may have to be introduced from overhead and forced down to reach the audience, which tends to be noisier and less efficient. Where climatic conditions allow, there have also been significant developments in recent years in the use of natural ventilation systems for theatres. These, however, require large areas of air inlets and outlets with significant quantities of acoustic attenuation to prevent noise from entering or leaving the building through

the vents. This will only be possible if sufficient space has been allowed at the design stage. The provision of mechanical cooling in auditoria is increasingly normal, although it may be avoided through careful design of the building fabric to utilise night-time cooling and to prevent external heat and cold from entering the building. (See Subsection 2.8 'Sustainability' later in this section.)

In public areas there are likely to be kitchens and other catering areas with significant amounts of heat-generating equipment that will require ventilation and cooling. In backstage areas, theatre control rooms and rooms containing electrical equipment will also require ventilation and cooling. Workshops and wig rooms may need specialist extraction systems, to remove heat and toxic fumes.

Architectural lighting

Public areas will require high-quality architectural lighting with appropriate controls to allow different moods to be created at different times of day and evening and for different uses. Externally, lighting and illuminated signage will be important to highlight the public nature of the building. In auditoria, lighting plays an important role in setting the mood for the performance and must be highly controllable to cater for other uses, such as conferences. There will also usually be a separate working light system for use during cleaning, maintenance and technical fit-ups. The control of auditorium lighting must also be integrated with the production lighting systems. In backstage areas there must be lighting appropriate to the various tasks being undertaken, for example, the application of make-up in dressing rooms.

Maintenance access to change lamps, particularly in high spaces such as auditoria, is an important design consideration.

Emergency lighting

There will need to be an emergency lighting system throughout the building, including illuminated exit signs. Lighting levels in auditoria are particularly critical during the performance where it is necessary to strike a balance between safe levels of illumination for those who may need to find their way out and the demand for 'blackouts' on the stage for scene changes and special effects.

Production lighting

Production lighting, for the lighting of the performance, is in a state of constant evolution and is becoming increasingly sophisticated with the development of new light sources, controls and mechanisation. While this is dealt with in detail in Section 6, there are some key issues which affect the architecture of the building. In particular these relate to the provision of front of house lighting positions in the auditorium. These will normally be proposed by the theatre consultant and are likely to be required at high level in the ceiling, at lower levels on balcony fronts and side walls, and possibly in the form of forward suspension points in the ceiling, for hanging temporary lighting trusses in front of the stage. All of these require careful integration if they are not to disfigure the architecture of the auditorium and are particularly difficult to introduce sensitively into existing historic interiors. The electrical services to these positions are also extensive and require careful planning if unsightly surface mounted containment is to be avoided. Safe access to these positions, to hang and focus lanterns, is also a requirement, which may involve the provision of walkways, ladder rails and fall arrest systems.

Stage technology

In larger theatres, there will be considerable stage engineering installations to accommodate, including items such as flying systems, wagons, bridges and elevators. These are becoming increasingly mechanised and sufficient space provision needs to be made for them at the design stage. They will also demand significant electrical loads, which must be provided for.

Sound and communications

This encompasses all of the equipment used to provide both live amplified and recorded sound for a performance; public address systems in the front of house and backstage areas; and video links and communications between staff and performers. This will require the provision of a comprehensive wiring infrastructure throughout the building, which needs to be capable of serving all likely requirements. In the auditorium, it will be necessary to integrate positions for loudspeakers and a range of positions for live sound mixing desks, located where operators can see and hear well. This often necessitates the removal of seats to create appropriate positions for different performance types and equipment. Integrating these positions into an auditorium so that they do not compromise the sightlines and escape routes from adjacent seating requires careful consideration.

Data

Like most modern buildings, theatres now rely heavily on data wiring to allow a wide range of equipment around the building to be controlled and to communicate with other systems. This includes office computer networks, wireless systems, video links, box office computer systems, display screens, point of sale equipment (tills), production lighting and sound control systems, stage equipment installations, and control systems for mechanical and electrical services. The quantity of data wiring is therefore very significant and requires careful design and integration.

Plant rooms

The size and location of plant rooms to house mechanical and electrical plant and specialist theatre equipment are significant in such a highly serviced building type and need to be established early in the design process. The location of plant away from noise-sensitive areas such as auditoria is particularly important.

2.6 Access for people with disabilities

Attitudes to the provision of access for disabled people to buildings and the activities they house have changed dramatically in recent years and this has had a fundamental effect on the way buildings are designed. This section seeks to highlight some of the issues to be considered in the design of theatres. More detailed design guidance can be found in specialist publications and in the building codes. On a major project, it is often desirable to employ an independent access consultant to provide specialist advice.

Legislation

In most developed countries there is now anti-discrimination legislation in place, making it a legal requirement to provide access to buildings for people with many different types of disability. Key design principles are also now enshrined in most building codes. Access can be interpreted as not only covering the physical design of buildings but also the means by which an organisation communicates with its customers and staff, such as print, telephone and the Internet. The legislation remains open to some interpretation and its full application continues to evolve as a result of experience, case law and the rising expectations of those whom it affects. In the UK, the Disability Discrimination Act 1995 (the DDA) distinguishes between the duties of service providers, education providers and employers. Service providers are those who operate a building which is open to the public or who provide goods and services. The basic duty is to provide reasonable access to such goods and services.

In the employment context the duty is not related to the physicality of the building but in terms of reducing barriers to full participation in the workplace so there is more scope to make ad hoc adjustments.

The UK legislation applies to existing buildings as well as new ones and aims for a standard of reasonable accommodation. This means that in some existing, and in particular historic, buildings there can be a lesser standard of access than in a new building where there are fewer constraints.

Design principles

In terms of physical provision, the broad principle is that people with disabilities should be able to access and enjoy a public building in the same way as any other member of the public, in a seamless and integrated manner, without having to use special routes or facilities (toilet accommodation being an obvious exception to this principle). The most demanding requirement is to provide for wheelchair users but the needs of ambulant disabled people and those with visual and hearing impairment must also be considered.

Wheelchair users and people with walking disabilities should be able to enter the building by the same route as able-bodied people and enjoy easy access to all services. This will affect the detailed design of various elements, such as counters, toilets and seating in the auditorium.

Visually impaired people

Provision for visually impaired people should include:
- Good colour contrast in choice of materials, particularly relating to floors, walls, doors, steps, ramps and signage.
- Clear signage of sufficient size. Braille and raised signage is also sometimes provided but only a small proportion of visually impaired people are able to read Braille.
- Audio description of selected performances.
- Large print programmes and publicity material.
- An accessible telephone booking and information service.

Audio description will require the provision of a separate soundproof describer's booth at the rear of the auditorium, with a good view of the stage.

People with hearing disabilities

Provision for people with hearing disabilities should include:
- Sound enhancement systems in the auditorium and at service counters.
- Signed interpreted performances.
- An accessible website and booking page.

Wheelchair users

The particular design considerations relating to wheelchair users in the various areas of a theatre building are discussed below:

Auditorium
The DDA requires there to be sufficient wheelchair places in an auditorium. This is generally considered to be 1 per cent of the total seating capacity or six, whichever is the greater. These spaces are often provided in the form of seats which can be removed to provide wheelchair spaces, when required, or used by the general public when not required. The plan area of a wheelchair is such that up to four seats may have to be removed to provide one wheelchair space. Some fixed seats (companion seating) should also be provided adjacent to wheelchair positions and some locations should allow for two adjacent wheelchairs.

Some design standards suggest wheelchair users should have a choice as to where they are located in the auditorium in order to select from a range of prices and because different disabilities can require different viewing angles to the stage (e.g. if looking up or down is difficult). In North America, wheelchair positions must be provided at all levels of a multi-level auditorium, although in Europe this is not common practice. Wheelchairs, particularly larger motorised models, place the occupant at a higher level than those sitting in a normal chair. Placing wheelchairs in the centre of a block of seats can, therefore, cause sightline problems for those sitting behind them and adjustment of floor levels may be necessary to overcome this.

Foyers

Wheelchair users should be able to enjoy all the facilities of the foyers. In multi-level buildings this will normally require the provision of lifts to upper floors. Bar and box office counters will need to have lowered areas for the service of those in wheelchairs, although box offices are increasingly being designed with lowered counters for all customers.

Main entrance doors should be fitted with automatic opening devices. Accessible toilets should be provided adjacent to main toilet blocks and preferably at every level of the building and with a choice of transfer side.

Backstage

Performers who are wheelchair users need to be provided with accessible dressing, toilet and shower accommodation, preferably at the same level as the stage. Where this is not possible, lifts will need to be provided. Wheelchair users must be able to gain access to the stage, orchestra pit and communal facilities such as green rooms. Directors and technicians who are wheelchair users must be able to gain access to the stage, auditorium and technical control rooms. Some

theatres provide for wheelchair users to have access to technical galleries and lighting walkways but there is considerable debate as to whether these are safe areas for them to work in.

Emergency evacuation

In designing buildings for wheelchair users particular attention must be paid to their safe evacuation in the event of an emergency. More detailed information is given later in subsection 2.7 under the heading of 'Fire safety'.

Consultation

Consultation with disabled user groups is highly recommended at strategic stages in the design process. These groups, which exist in most areas, are made up of people with disabilities who offer advice on their needs. They can often provide valuable insights, both at the design stage and post-completion.

2.7 Fire safety

Historically, when theatres were lit by candles and gaslight, utilised timber construction and scenery and had inadequate means of escape, they represented a very serious fire risk. In the nineteenth century, in particular, there were many major fires in theatres, resulting in serious loss of life. Much of the legislation we have today, relating to materials, compartmentation and means of escape, has evolved over time to mitigate those risks. This section seeks to provide general guidance on the principles of fire safety in theatres, though local regulations will apply. A list of legislation and guidance which applies in the UK is provided at the end of this section.

2.6.1 Example of a wheelchair position within an auditorium, Royal Opera House, London, UK
Photograph: Mark White

2.6.2 Box Office at Norwich Theatre Royal, UK
Desk height box office counter, suitable for all, with built in leaflet racks and seats.
Photograph: James Morris

Design approaches

Essentially, there are two basic approaches to fire safety design, although similar principles will apply in both cases. These are:

- Code-based design – which satisfies the standards laid down in local building codes. This will be appropriate for many conventional buildings.
- Fire-engineering design – which develops a project-specific fire safety strategy that may offer more flexible solutions for complex buildings.

Code-based design

Building codes prescribe the key functions that must be satisfied in a building. In fire safety terms, most codes will require that a building must:

- be designed with a suitable means of early warning of fire;
- be provided with internal escape routes which lead the occupants to safety outside the building;
- contain internal surface linings which resist the spread of flames over the surfaces relevant to the location of the surfaces and the risks presented;
- be designed so that in the event of fire its stability will be maintained for a reasonable time;
- to inhibit fire spread, be sub-divided with fire-resisting construction and fitted with automatic fire suppression systems appropriate to the size and use of the building;
- have external walls and roofs which adequately resist the spread of fire from one building to another;
- be designed and constructed to provide reasonable facilities to assist the fire fighters in protection of life.

By adopting the regulations contained in the building codes a scheme should be approved by the relevant approving authorities. This represents a code-based approach to achieving a safe building.

Fire engineering

A fire-engineering solution takes a more holistic approach, which develops a design from first principles and creates a framework for the design, construction and management of a building and which more accurately reflects the bespoke nature of that building. This alternative approach may be the only practical way to achieve a satisfactory standard of fire safety in some large and complex buildings. The solution, which will normally be developed by a specialist fire-engineering consultant, will be a building-specific strategy to provide a flexible and unique design.

Fire engineering is the application of engineering techniques to define a total package of fire safety measures, which may include enhanced passive fire protection, active fire suppression, fire and smoke ventilation and automatic fire detection and alarms. Some advantages of a fire-engineering approach may be:

- Increased travel distances
- Reduction in widths of escape routes
- Reduction in the number of exits from a building or more appropriately located exits
- Reduction in the standards of applied fire protection
- Large compartment sizes facilitating open, multi-storey and interconnected spaces
- Creation of more flexible theatre space including removal of the traditional fire safety curtain.

Fire risk assessments

In some countries, including the UK, legislation has been introduced which shifts the emphasis of responsibility for fire safety to those who manage a building and requires that a fire risk assessment is undertaken by the management. This represents a major shift of responsibility to designers and operators of buildings and in a complex building makes it more likely that a specialist fire safety consultant will need to be employed to prepare the assessment and ensure that the terms of the law are being met.

The fire risk assessment is a dynamic process, which must be constantly reviewed and must consider the building's needs in terms of fire safety. Under previous legislation, reviews of fire safety were somewhat static and would typically be carried out annually to ensure that provisions were appropriate. Under the new legislation, a review of the fire safety arrangements must be undertaken whenever there is a change in the risk of fire; for example, where there is a change in the way the building is used, a new risk is introduced, a fire safety system stops working, or the building is spatially replanned. Under this system, the management of a building has much greater responsibility to ensure that both the building itself, and the procedures which are in place for its management, remain safe. The local fire and rescue authority will usually have the power to inspect a premises to check that its operators are complying with their duties.

Entertainment licensing

In most regions, there will be legislation governing the operation of buildings used for public entertainment that aims to ensure that the building is appropriately designed and managed. This will cover not only fire safety but may also include other matters, such as operating hours, noise control and the sale of alcohol. The relevant local authority will have its own policies. These are likely to include a requirement that the local fire and rescue service is consulted on fire safety matters, although responsibility for safe management will ultimately remain with the operators.

Means of escape

In case of an emergency, occupants must be able to escape quickly and easily to a place of safety. A building should be arranged and managed so that a safe and orderly evacuation will not be impeded. The solution developed must take a holistic view of the requirements for fire safety in terms of the design, management and operation of the building.

Total simultaneous evacuation of an entire building is not normally the philosophy adopted in theatre design, as this not only places a high burden on the management of an evacuation but also increases the number and width of escape routes required. Therefore the means of escape and means of warning of fire and fire protection measures should be configured to support the evacuation of only those parts of the building that are directly affected by a fire.

The minimum requirements for the number and location of escape routes are flexible and should be tailored to the requirements for the building's use profiles. A key principle is to assume that any designated escape route may be affected by fire. Therefore, in any part of the building, where a floor or room requires two or more escape routes, one of those routes will be discounted. This principle ensures that the number, location and dimensions of escape routes are adequate for the number of people who may need to use them.

To support the means of escape design, it will be necessary to divide the building into a number of fire evacuation zones, separated from each other by fire rated walls along lines dividing the main functions of the building. This approach enables an area at risk to be evacuated upon activation of the fire warning system, while adjacent spaces remain occupied. This is particularly beneficial for auditorium spaces, where evacuation for a remote fire incident may not be required.

Fire detection and warning systems

In order to be able to manage an emergency, the management must be aware that the emergency has occurred and must be able to communicate instructions to the staff effectively. Automatic fire detection and warning systems and staff communication systems are therefore essential tools in the event of a fire. It has been proven that a directive warning and evacuation system (i.e. a staff and public address announcement) is the most effective way to encourage people to leave a building. This is particularly important when fire could be part of a performance, as the audience will not be aware when the performance changes to a real fire risk. The design of the fire detection and warning system needs careful consideration to ensure that adequate and appropriate fire detection is provided at all times. Evacuation will normally be under management direction and carried out in a controlled and orderly manner. In order for this to happen there must be effective emergency planning and training of staff.

Disabled persons

Access for disabled persons will normally be provided throughout a building and it is therefore essential that appropriate means of escape are provided for these occupants and that they have a choice of escape route. The requirements to achieve this are focused around the needs of wheelchair users, as they are considered to require the greatest assistance. The provisions within a building will be a combination of:

- passive structural provisions (e.g. refuge areas, lifts, ramps);
- active protection systems (e.g. fire warning installations which include visual and sensory devices in addition to audible signals);
- assistance or direction (e.g. building operational management procedures and actions).

It should be noted that it is normally the management's fire safety team who are responsible for the safe evacuation of disabled persons and not the fire and rescue services. It is the responsibility of the management to define an evacuation policy and emergency plan, to be implemented in the case of a fire.

When designing a building, it is important that the design team and client discuss and agree the approach to the evacuation of disabled persons. For an auditorium, the maximum number of wheelchair spaces is defined, therefore the size and location of refuges and the expected management assistance can also be defined. For other areas, such as restaurants and bars, it may be more difficult to pre-define the maximum number of wheelchairs likely to be present.

Legislation in the UK

In the UK there are three key pieces of legislation to be met in order to ensure that a building is suitably safe for all its occupants in the case of a fire:

1   *The Building Regulations*
    Relating to building works for new, extended, refurbished or remodelled premises.
2   *The Regulatory Reform (Fire Safety) Order, 2005*
    Relating to the ongoing control in any building.
3   *The Licensing Act, 2003*
    A single integrated scheme for licensing premises used for the supply of alcohol, regulated entertainment and provision of late night refreshment.

To support this legislation there are a number of Approved Documents and Codes of Practice, which give guidance on how to meet these regulations. These include:

- *The Building Regulations Approved Document B (Fire Safety)*
  The fire safety design document used for the majority of common building designs.
- *The Technical Standards for Places of Entertainment, 2008*
  Published by the ABTT and the District Surveyors Association (sometimes known as the Yellow Book), which provides specific guidance on fire safety matters in theatres.
- *British Standard 9999, 2008*
  Gives recommendations and guidance on the design, management and use of buildings to achieve acceptable levels of fire safety. It promotes a more flexible approach to fire safety design through the use of structured risk-based design and includes specific advice relating to theatres.

2.8 Sustainability

Theatres consume prodigious amounts of energy and much greater efforts are now being made to create more sustainable theatres, which respond to modern environmental, social and economic requirements. Sustainable buildings are designed from a holistic standpoint and require a collaborative effort between designers, occupants, building owners, community, government and suppliers.

The following six objectives should be addressed from the beginning of the design process, through the means suggested below:

Operational carbon neutrality

A building is operationally carbon neutral when the annual carbon emissions are matched by an equal amount of carbon reductions.

- Match operational energy consumption with renewable sources
- Maximise the efficiency of the energy-using systems
- Produce greatest reduction in carbon while minimising impact to resource systems, economic security or human health.

Self-sufficiency in Water Use

Reduce the use of water through lower use, rainwater collection and recycling.

- Develop conservation and recycling techniques which treat water as a precious resource
- Effectively discriminate between 'grey water' and 'black water'
- Combine water-saving technology with education for building occupants.

Use of Sustainable Materials

Building materials should be selected to be local, recycled, recyclable or renewable.

- Discover and promote the use of less inherently wasteful materials
- Increase the proportion of recovered materials used in new construction
- Consider the waste associated with the entire life cycle of the building from the extraction of materials to their final disposal
- Build compact buildings
- Reuse existing buildings whenever possible.

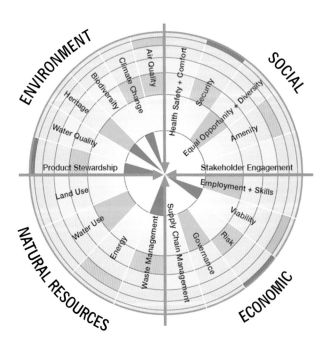

2.8.1 Arup's SPeAR® tool measures sustainability performance (SPeAR stands for Sustainable Project Appraisal Routine)

Ability to Cope with Future Climate Change

Buildings last a long time and need to be designed to adapt to anticipated changes in the weather.

- Design buildings to produce lower carbon emissions
- Update existing buildings with energy-efficient measures and technology
- Equip new buildings with the ability to cope with higher temperatures, rising sea levels and changing soil conditions.

Make a Positive Contribution to the Community and Built Environment

Buildings and their users, particularly theatres, interact with and shape their communities. They can be designed to achieve positive social, economic and environmental effects through outreach, education, access and programming.

- Identify community engagement process and options
- Discuss how the building fits within the overall built environment
- Identify links to public transport.

Sustainability in Operation

Ensure that buildings can be operated easily and efficiently throughout their life. This will help provide both a low carbon footprint and a better environment for the occupants.

- Educate occupants on how to operate building systems and ensure building management systems are appropriate
- Propose how to minimise and recycle waste
- Identify maintenance and replacement requirements
- Implement a sustainability management system.

Key considerations

A well-designed theatre should not only be environmentally sustainable but will, as a result, show significant financial savings over its life cycle. Whole life costs should therefore be considered in relation to initial capital costs. Some key issues to consider in the design of the building will include the use of:

- High levels of thermal insulation
- Materials which provide thermal storage
- Materials with low embodied energy
- Natural ventilation
- Renewable energy sources
- Low-energy lighting
- Control systems which reduce energy use
- Good orientation and avoidance of solar gain
- Avoidance of unnecessary space and equipment.

SECTION EDITOR

Tim Foster	Senior Partner, Foster Wilson Architects (formerly Tim Foster Architects)

CONTRIBUTORS

Lisa Foster	Access
Paul Gillieron	Acoustics
Stuart Martin	Fire safety
Arup	Sustainability

Section 3
Front of house

Contents

3.1 Introduction

Today's theatre audiences are not only able to compare one theatre with another but also able to compare the modern theatregoing experience with a wider range of contemporary leisure activities. Theatres need to compete with these in terms of comfort and service as well as artistic, educational and entertainment programming.

The front of house (FOH) design can make a positive contribution to the enjoyment of a visit to the theatre. The foyers are not there purely to process an audience from the collection of their tickets, via the toilets, to their seats, while selling them refreshments on the way. They provide an opportunity to animate both the building and street-scene: they are the showcase for the organisation – a place to see and be seen.

The foyers now normally account for around a quarter of the built area and can be larger than the auditorium in area. They are no longer just a pre-performance and interval space, the capital investment is too great. In fact, these spaces are perhaps the hardest working part of a theatre. Their design needs to:
- attract people in and encourage them to find out more;
- promote additional income generation;
- provide space for additional activities such as conferencing, exhibitions, education and community events.

A most important but probably unquantifiable contribution is that of improving public perception of the arts and, above all, helping to build audiences.

For the purpose of this section, FOH is defined as the space occupied by the public and its support facilities, excluding the auditorium. It comprises:

Public areas
- Arrival and drop-off
- External display
- Entrance doors and draught lobby
- Foyers and open-plan circulation paths and stairs
- Reception and information counter
- Box office and ticket collection
- Kiosk sales – confectionery and programmes
- Show merchandising
- Cloakroom
- Toilets
- Bars
- Catering and food service
- Hospitality suites (conference breakout spaces)
- Education suite
- Informal performance areas
- Exhibition area.

Support areas
- Duty manager's office and security office
- FOH equipment store
- First aid room
- Attendants' changing rooms and briefing office
- Telephone, internet and mail bookings office
- Box office manager's and cash offices
- Merchandising, programme, ice cream and confectionery stores
- Local and central bar stores, chilled cellar, spirits and empties stores
- Kitchens, cold and dry stores
- Local and central cleaners' stores
- Refuse store, compacting and recycling space.

3.2 Basic principles

Accessibility

All public areas must be accessible – not just physically but also conceptually. Front of house design must be inviting for those with disabilities and inclusive to those who would not normally attend cultural events with:
- Level approach negating the need for separate entrances or complicated ramps and handrails
- Wide automatic doors avoiding queues or obstructions – physical and psychological

- Clear points of entry and unintimidating views of the activities within.

Further information on access is given in Section 2. Specific requirements (such as the height of the box office counter) are detailed at the relevant points later in this section.

Legibility and ease of circulation

The circulation needs to be simply laid out, creating a point of arrival where all the facilities are set:
- Ticket office
- Cloakroom
- Sales points (confectionery and programmes)
- Stairs and lifts
- Toilets
- Bars, cafés, restaurants and shops
- Entrances into the auditorium
– and clearly identifying the auditorium as the eventual destination.

The facilities need to be designed and sited to avoid creating bottlenecks or generating long queues or cross routes which could impede easy circulation.

Loose fit

Foyers and the facilities available within them need to be adaptable to meet different tastes and changes of use. Audiences vary with different types of performance. The behaviour and expectations of an audience for comedy gigs, for example, are different from that for drama and different again for opera.

Most theatre foyers need to be able to accommodate a range of activities including special events related to the theatre's programme as well as generating income from sales and catering and from hosting outside activities such as conferences and meetings.

A distinction needs to be made between 'foyers' that are essentially auditorium-related and usually contain the theatre bars and areas for those attending a performance and 'concourses' found in larger developments with free access to the general public, encouraging 'cultural tourism' and having education facilities, cafés, restaurants, shops, public toilets and other arts facilities opening from them. Examples of the latter include Wales Millennium Centre, Cardiff; The Lowry (Reference project: p. 244); and the Milton Keynes Theatre complex (Reference project: p. 252).

3.3 The journey through front of house

The theatrical experience commences upon arrival at the theatre. Routes from car parks and pedestrian walkways to the main entrance need to create the sense of arrival while taking account of safety and security requirements.

In larger cities it is helpful to have taxi ranks located at or near the theatre entrance. Off-road drop-off for taxis and for less ambulant visitors is the ideal solution. Many theatres are reliant on group bookings and effective set-down and pickup points for coach parties must also be considered.

Theatres in busy streets can cause overcrowding on pavements and danger with passing traffic. This needs to be avoided by providing forecourts or entrance foyers that allow audiences to enter quickly into the building. After a show the reverse happens, with exits discharging a large number of people rapidly onto the street.

At the entrance, protection from inclement weather is welcome. Popular shows can create queues for tickets and managing these queues needs to be planned for if nuisance to neighbouring properties is to be avoided.

A clear sign displaying the name of the theatre helps patrons locate the building from a distance or a side street. For theatres with long runs it may be the name of the show that is significant.

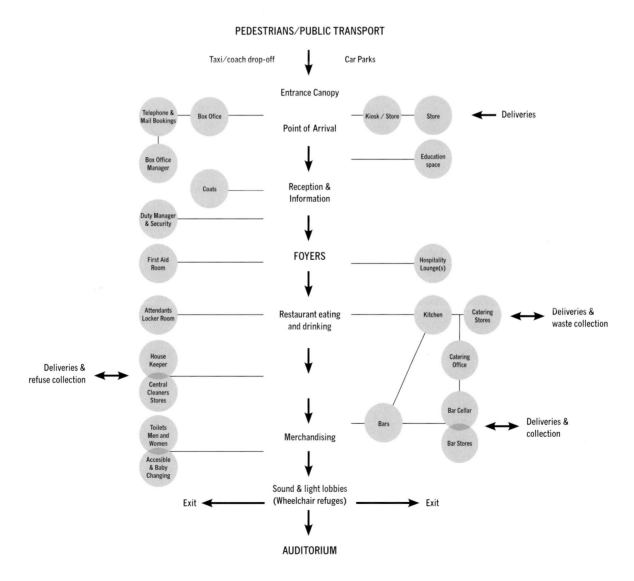

3.3.1 Diagram showing spatial relationships

3.3.2 Exterior of the Prince Edward theatre
The lighting of the Prince Edward theatre emphasises a sense of welcome and anticipation of the performance to come. A well-lit entrance with a canopy guides patrons to the main public entrance – it should be arranged to give a significantly enhanced light level to the pavement or forecourt area. Accent lighting to billboards along the façade and beneath the entrance canopy is of equal importance to emphasise the advertising of current and future productions.
Photograph: RHWL. John Walsom

The style, quality and dominance of 'show signs' is the province of the theatre owners, producers and their advertising agents. This can take many forms but should be considered at the briefing and design stage as a large number of poster panels, external banners and flags, etc. can detract from the appearance of the building. Alternatively a large LED (light-emitting diode) screen, linked to the box office media display, is a highly effective and flexible method.

All visitors should enter through the same main entrance enjoying all the facilities regardless of where they are sitting within the auditorium. A good management will aim to ensure that they are greeted and welcomed. From this moment the theatregoers may need to collect their tickets, leave their coats, wait for friends, buy a drink or get something to eat, and buy a

programme. These needs have to be met with minimum effort and without queues. The customers may also need toilet facilities before heading into the auditorium for the start of the performance.

During the interval, bars, toilet facilities and a change of space are the basic needs of an audience before they return to their seats for the second or even third act. If a range of different types of area can be provided – a place to stand to look around, a quiet intimate corner to sit and chat, or an open space to drink with a party of friends – so much the better.

At the end of the evening some of the audience may want to stay and talk to friends and perhaps again use the bars and toilet facilities before collecting their coats, etc. and heading home.

These activities represent around 30 per cent of the audience's time in the theatre and everything needs to run efficiently if the whole visit is to be a pleasant experience.

3.4 Foyer design and layout

Space requirements

The foyer is essentially the open-plan circulation area which leads to the auditorium, where the audience assembles before a performance and during intervals. All the public support facilities open onto the foyer. The ability to understand the overall layout of a space makes a big difference to perceptions of the venue while complex multi-level layouts can confuse or intimidate new visitors.

Consideration needs to be given to the movement of people around the foyers:
- Drawing visitors into the building avoiding logjams in the entrance lobby
- Avoiding paths crossing
- Queues obstructing circulation routes
- Adequate space on landings and in front of lifts and counters
- Ensuring passage widths and stair widths are sufficient.

3.4.1 Bridgewater Hall foyer

The Bridgewater Hall, Manchester, UK, with its clean, modern lines avoids the foyer clutter which can detract from the arrival experience. The purpose-designed and carefully positioned poster panels and leaflet racks are located close to the box office away from the main arrival point.
Photograph: Dennis Gilbert

The size of the FOH accommodation is normally determined by the seating capacity of the auditorium. Foyers, i.e. the circulation area excluding stairs and counters, range in the provision of space from 0.6m^2 per person to 1.2m^2 per person; although smaller foyers may exist in historic theatres and larger ones for grand civic statements.

Regardless of the format of the auditorium, foyer space should aim to be distributed to match the population in the various sections of the auditorium and to consolidate the audience in physically and visually connected spaces, maintaining a bond among members of the audience.

Additional uses

To contribute to the social and economic sustainability of a venue, all parts of the foyer need to be adaptable for alternative purposes which may include:-
- Specialist bars (champagne bar, bottle bar or confectionery point)
- Educational activities (breakout spaces, meeting rooms and hospitality rooms)
- Festival events or activities which may require a small stage, PA mixer position, lighting and power
- Sponsor recognition
- Merchandising opportunities

- Large-scale catering use with hot cupboards, tabled areas and plate clearing
- Business centre
- Conference registration
- VIP reception areas
- Links to other local facilities.

Also depending on the proposed business model for the theatre thought needs to be given to the inclusion and location of:
- Studio space
- Meeting rooms
- Reception rooms
- Public bars
- Café
- Restaurant.

These spaces need to look open and available when in use but not detract from the visitors' theatre experience when they are closed.

Secondary spending is an important part of a venue's income. Sales points need to be provided for:
- Bar sales and catering
- Programmes, ice creams and confectionery
- Show merchandising – i.e. branded T-shirts, masks, CDs and play texts, etc.

Environmental design

The foyer is a transition zone between the street and the events on stage. It should provide an environmental gradient between the outside noise and bustle and the controlled environment within the auditorium. While daylight is desirable, foyers should avoid stark contrasts of light (such as direct sunlight or glare) and excessive differences in temperature with the auditorium.

Acoustic design

The acoustic design of a foyer should be tailored to the uses to which the foyer will be put. As well as hosting the theatre audience before, during and after performances, the space may be used for impromptu presentations, small-scale musical performances, receptions and possibly parties.

A traditional foyer with a plush carpet and high ceiling with lots of ornamentation on the walls will sound radically different to a contemporary one with hard floors, lots of plain glazing and a plasterboard ceiling. The latter will have less absorption and so will be louder, noisier and less appropriate for informal uses.

It is always desirable to include a significant quantity of sound absorption. This will assist in controlling noise levels and will provide an environment suitable for a range of activities and informal events. Carpeting the main circulation area is desirable to control noise from footsteps and from the movement of chairs and tables.

There is a drive for energy minimisation in theatres and where possible natural ventilation should be considered for the foyer. In some instances external noise levels might render the simple opening window solution impracticable. However, attenuated inlets and discharges are possible and should be considered. Conversely, noise emanating from the foyer through opening façades could disturb people in nearby buildings. Mixed-mode solutions should be considered with, perhaps, daytime ventilation being provided through a natural system, while peak hours (pre-show and during the interval/s) are mechanically ventilated.

Lighting design

Lighting plays an important part in setting mood and atmosphere and needs to help make the FOH areas feel warm, welcoming and also dramatic.

Foyer lighting can aid navigation, helping to draw audience members to the box office, bars and the auditorium entrance doors. Lighting can be coordinated with way-finding to highlight the position of key signs.

It is important that some means of adjusting the light levels and general mood of the FOH lighting is incorporated. This could take the form of a programmable scene-setting control system that can dim or switch individual circuits and store pre-programmed lighting scenes. Centralised control systems of this type are also important in the reduction of energy usage. Scenes can be programmed in for daytime usage where the light levels can be attenuated and some lighting circuits switched off completely, while the use of daylight-linking can be of assistance to further reduce energy usage.

Finishes

Building finishes should be carefully selected and detailed to create the right impression, to avoid safety hazards, and for their durability and ease of cleaning and maintenance. Floor surfaces need to be selected for slip resistance, especially at entrances and potentially wet areas, and junctions between floor finishes must avoid trip hazards. Balustrades must prevent drinks glasses and other objects from falling below.

Furniture

Thought needs to be given to the range of people who are likely to use the venue, with the effective use of ramps, lifts, handrails and seating being factored in to the foyer design. Some older audience members will need to be dropped off or picked up from the building entrance and wait for companions to join or collect them. While younger audiences may be happy to stand during the interval, older people may expect to be able to sit down, so bars and foyers need to be furnished accordingly. Seating can be problematic. If it is fixed it can make the foyer inflexible but movable seats (especially where they have extended rear legs) can become trip hazards and seats can be moved into dangerous positions.

People who come with young children may welcome seating or tables so that children can enjoy their visit and refreshments without spilling their drinks. Space for parking children's prams and buggies could also be needed in community-based theatres.

Waste bins are required in the theatre foyers for wrappers and cartons purchased from confectionery or bar kiosks and there is an increasing expectation from customers that waste will be recycled. How these items are specified or designed needs to be thought through. (Housekeeping will almost certainly line any bin provided with a plastic sack which can make for an unsightly arrangement.)

Literature racks and poster sites are prized items as far as the marketing department is concerned. Good information display needs to be designed to ensure that audiences can be made aware of future productions without the foyers being cluttered with assorted display units.

3.5 Facilities within the foyer

Reception and information point

The venue may choose to have a foyer reception and information point available to customers throughout the day. This information point could be staffed or could provide an electronic concierge facility so that customers can learn more about the building and performances.

3.5.1 Open Box Office, Royal & Derngate Theatres, Northampton, UK
The open plan box office and information counter is the focus of activity within the foyer.
Photograph: James Corbett, courtesy of Royal & Derngate Theatres

3.5.2 Enclosed Box Office, Broadway Theatre, Barking, UK
Photograph: Mark White

Box office

Box office services are often outsourced and increasingly serviced by websites including 'print your own ticket' systems but on arrival some customers will still need to either purchase their ticket in person or collect pre-booked tickets.

The box office is normally located in the entrance foyer and may be open at times when the rest of the theatre is closed. It is useful for the entrance foyer to be configured to prevent access to the remainder of the theatre at such times. The style of the box office should reflect the ethos of the venue. Box offices vary from small enclosed kiosks separated from the customer by glass security screens, to open-plan counters.

To ease communication, it is best for the box office counter not to have glass separating the customer from the cashier as glass restricts sound and information exchange. Eye-level contact with the customer is preferable for staff. Customers who are purchasing tickets also like to see where they are to sit; therefore seating plans need to be displayed or computer screens used that can be turned to face the customer.

Little cash is actually held in the box office. Most customers who are purchasing tickets will use debit or credit cards so positioning for easy use of chip and pin machines needs to be considered. Cash needs to be quickly transferred to a secure location.

If an open style of box office is adopted, care must be taken to ensure that the staff are secure, that it is arranged so that customers are not able to get behind staff, and that it is sited in a position which is free from draughts and has local environmental controls.

Ticket collection immediately prior to the performance can be handled from the box office or from a separate counter. Alternatively tickets can be printed on demand, an arrangement which may be augmented by automated ticket collection machines. Press tickets or a special 'on the night deal' may also need additional counter space.

Induction loops at the box office counter will help those with hearing difficulties. Wheelchair users will also expect to get up close to the counter at a comfortable level for both parties to conduct the transaction. This applies to all sales positions.

- A separate box office counter may be available for advance booking with customers choosing to book in person for future performances.
- Displays around the box office may include poster panels and leaflet racks.
- Video screens/TV monitors are becoming a popular and more flexible method for promoting forthcoming events.
- Despite mobile phones a public telephone should be available.
- A wall-mounted, fixed IP address screen allows customers to browse future events from the venue's own website.

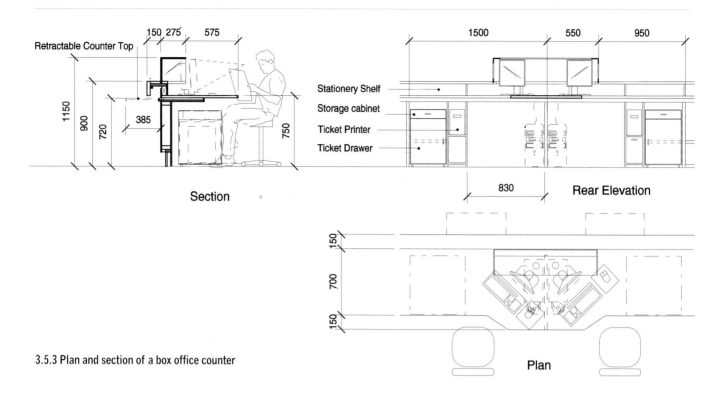

3.5.3 Plan and section of a box office counter

Box office manager's and cash office, telephone, internet and mail bookings office

These support spaces are best located behind the box office. The office needs to accommodate the mail and telephone sales team, the manager's office, a safe (for cash from ticket sales), box office server, ticket stock and post room. As cash handling is carried out in this area, consideration needs to be given to the security of doors, windows and alarm systems.

If possible the rear office and manager's office should be located adjoining the counter with visual connection enabling supervision and deployment of staff at busy times, either at the counter or on the telephones. With the growth of telephone sales the space required can be extensive and may have to be located elsewhere – within the administration department or even off-site.

Cloakrooms

The need for and capacity of cloakrooms is much debated. Continental theatres often have one coat peg per seat while in the UK experience is that only 25–35 per cent of the audience leave their coats; although a gala event or exceptionally bad weather will affect this. A guide is to allow 0.1m² per coat for storage. A cloakroom service is more important when auditoria use displacement air delivery systems as coats stuffed under the seats can reduce the flow of fresh cool air.

Cloak systems may be provided on a complementary basis or charged but the speed of service is a key feature particularly on exit. The choices are a manned cloakroom or a self-service system or a combination of the two.

An effective system depends upon a fast service and good space for circulation. A manned service requires a long counter over which staff can collect and return coats using a numbering system that is easy to follow with easily accessible shelving for briefcases, wet umbrellas, hats and shopping bags. A self-service system needs more space to circulate while the audience negotiates the locking system.

The cloakroom needs to be easy to secure once the 'house is in'. If left unattended some licensing authorities require the cloakroom to be a separate fire compartment.

3.5.4 Cloaks counter at the Barbican Arts Centre, London, UK
Designed by Allford Hall Monaghan Morris Architects /Studio Myerscough/
Cartlidge Levene

Kiosk and confectionery store

For many, the confectionery kiosk is an essential part
of the visit. Usually located in the entrance foyer it
needs a very prominent position but without causing
queues where they might obstruct.

The kiosk is one of those elements that needs to
be highly adaptable. Confectionery may be very popular
for one type of show but the kiosk may be far better
branded as a champagne bar or a coffee bar for another
type of show. The display system needs to be flexible
and adaptable, able to stock and display a variety of
merchandise.

The merchandise store needs to be secure and
properly ventilated, located immediately behind the
kiosk. It should be spacious and equally adaptable
with space for a freezer and/or fridge, even water and
drainage.

Programme sales points

Programmes and brochures are an integral part of front
of house revenue streams; the selling of them needs to
be from a location that is highly visible, does not block
circulation and is conveniently close to the central
distribution point.

Show merchandising

A further retail opportunity is 'show' and related
merchandising. Venues with resident companies may
operate their own shop while in receiving houses the
production managements may operate a merchandising
service themselves or franchise the service out.
Whichever system is followed, theatre operators earn
a percentage of the sales and will be keen to maximise
the opportunity. This will result in highly visibly
locations outside the auditorium doors being occupied.
Show merchandising can be an eyesore if not well
presented or thoughtfully positioned. Failure to design
in potential spaces results in trestle tables and flightcases being located in awkward or even potentially
hazardous positions.

Facilities should include:
- Display space that does not inhibit way-
finding, circulation or escape routes.
- Each sales point will need electricity
supplies for lighting and data-cabling for tills
and credit card authorisations.
- Storage will be required (unless the
franchisee brings in merchandise on each
occasion) and displays will be set up prior to
each show.

3.6 Bars and catering

Options

Food and drink are increasingly seen as significant
components of a theatre visit and their provision needs
to be considered early in the planning stage. Bar sales
are usually far more profitable than food sales and can
make a significant contribution to overall income.
While a theatre may forgo food service it is unlikely
to forgo 'wet sales'.

The theatre may choose to run the bar and catering
services in-house or contract them out, though
contracted-out bar services rarely make the same level
of financial contribution to the theatre as directly run
operations. In some cases, the contractor will have a
very clear view about the design and layout. Care needs
to be taken that this does not conflict with the overall
design and ethos of the theatre and its foyer space.

Theatre catering can be more risky and there
is a wider range of options to be considered, from
pre-theatre and interval bar snacks to a stand-alone
restaurant, open to the general public. The choice of
what is to be provided will impact on the design and

3.6.1 Bar at Northern Stage, Newcastle, UK
Photograph: Anthony Coleman

layout of the foyer area, the additional facilities required and the amount of space needed.

Bars and 'wet sales'

The location and scale of bars is a matter of choice. To maximise sales, audiences need to be confident that they will be served quickly enough to enjoy their drinks. Theatres (unlike pubs and bars) have very high peak/short duration demand in the half an hour pre-show and during the interval. It is therefore usual to keep product choice narrow.

Design considerations

The detail design of the bar front counter and back bar and local storage will vary or need to be adaptable to work with the type of venue and genre regularly staged. Opera and ballet audiences will provide higher sales of wines and spirits while comedy gigs or rock concerts will have higher beer sales; children's shows will sell mostly soft drinks; while matinees will see more tea and coffee sales.

Thought needs to be given to:
- The ergonomics of the staff task in reaching and walking within the bar area.
- The correct counter height is important for those working behind the bar and for wheelchair users. If lowered sections are incorporated, these should not be relegated to one end where they risk being ignored by staff or used to serve just coffee or to clear dirty glasses.
- Electronic Point of Sale (EPOS) systems are popular with customers and increasingly theatres are taking credit cards for bar sales.

Coffee service is a regular demand. This is a high-profit service which can be delivered from a bar or from a specific service point. There is no consensus on the best arrangement for this other than that coffee will need to be served hot and speedily so individual serving systems will be unsuitable for an interval use.

Location

The size and location of bars depends on the audience numbers seated at each level of the auditorium. Bars need to be easily accessible and designed to aid quick and efficient service so that people can buy a drink and then withdraw to a less crowded space. If these expectations are not met, members of the audience will

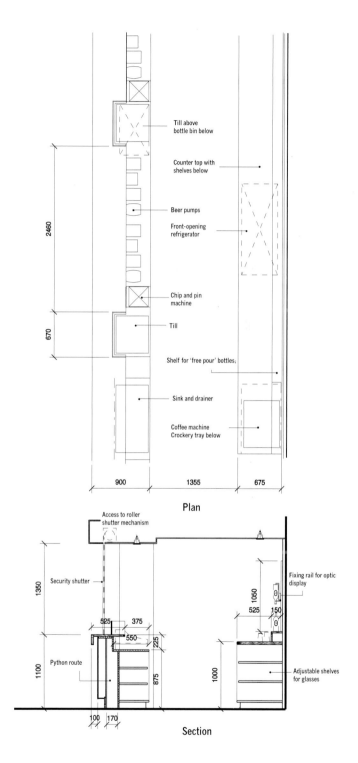

3.6.2 Plan and section of a typical bar

remain in the auditorium and valuable sales will be lost. Long straight bars with multiple cash tills produce quicker service while segmented bars with specific serving positions encourage the customers to queue in front of each section.

The design of bars needs to take account of cultural differences. In some countries alcohol consumption is not encouraged or not permitted. Those that can sell alcohol may need facilities that are discreetly located or within enclosed lounges.

Bars in the foyer should be located away from walls adjoining the auditorium, as should their associated pot-cleaning machines, dishwashers, compressors and fridges. If space planning results in these adjacencies, additional independent walls need to be provided and all noisy and vibrating equipment efficiently isolated from the auditorium structure.

To reduce delays, audiences are frequently encouraged to pre-order their interval drinks. This requires shelving where drinks can be laid out away from the bar and out of busy circulation paths. Drinks shelves need to be sufficiently long to allow drinks to be found and removed for consumption in comfort.

The bars should be divided into 1.5m–1.8m modules to suit a typical servery workstation; this is predicated by the width of equipment, i.e. bottle fridges, a range of spirits, soft drink dispensers, beer pumps, clean glasses and a till. Each workstation, with one well-trained and experienced member of staff, is able to serve drinks to an audience of 100 people during a normal interval.

Some interpretation is necessary as, in practice, some people will not buy anything and some areas will sell more than others (i.e. the more expensive seats). For example, a theatre with 500 people sitting in the stalls, 250 in the circle and 250 in the gallery would expect to have three bars, one related to each level.

Based on the seating capacity of each:
- The stalls would have 5 serving positions say 7.5 to 9.0m long
- The grand circle 3 serving positions 4.5 to 5.4m long
- The gallery 2 serving positions 3.0 to 3.6m long.

Local and central bar stores, chilled cellar, spirits and empties stores

Each bar should have a local bar store for spare stock, a white wine fridge, possibly a coffee maker, and a wash-hand basin.

Central storage, easily accessible from all parts of front of house, will be needed for:
- Secure wine and spirit store
- Chilled cellar, where beer and soft drinks are stored
- Empties/recycling store.

Finishes in these areas and along delivery routes need to be very durable and capable of being washed down.

Where draught beer and mixers are on offer, the location of the cellar is of importance. Kegs, gas cylinders and pumps will be kept in the cellar and connected to the individual bars by a python. (A python is a cluster of small plastic supply pipes with intertwined cooling pipes usually supplied and installed by the contracted brewery.) It requires a 225mm diameter conduit, with accessible large swept bends, linking the cellar and each sales point. The route should be thought about from an early stage and be as short and as direct as possible in order to minimise the pipe run to reduce wastage.

Food service options

Theatres need to decide why they want to serve food and should be conscious of the fact that catering is not the core function of the organisation. Theatres may well find it difficult to compete with surrounding restaurants, particularly if they are only offering a pre-show (single-sitting) service.

A catering consultant, if appointed at an early stage, will be able to advise on the market opportunities and the type of food service required. Later, the consultant can advise on the layout and equipping of the catering provision.

There may be a variety of reasons for including a food service:
- To generate additional income.
- Insufficient quality catering nearby.
- The theatre wants to be open for food during the day to attract non-theatregoers into the building.
- The theatre wants to offer catering for functions, and wants to be able to deliver this in-house.
- A local caterer wants to be associated with the theatre.

Some venues choose to offer a food service pre- and post-show. Sometimes these services will be a stand-alone public offer and sometimes they will be specifically for theatre customers. If this service is provided the client will need to be clear about the service proposition. Options are:

- table service (usually plated service from the kitchen or occasionally silver service);
- assisted service (usually a buffet or counter service);
- food court (a series of autonomous counters where customers may either order or eat);
- kiosk (an outstation used to provide service for peak demand).

Many theatres find that customers want a quick meal before the show, as they may not have had time to go home from work, eat and travel to the theatre. They will want to eat quickly and consideration needs to be given to the best way of achieving this.

Location

The location of the restaurant/eating area needs careful consideration. If it is intended just for theatregoers and integrated into the main foyer, it needs to be in an area which is not disrupted by the movement of an incoming audience or by the draughts that may be produced by constantly opening doors pre-show.

If the facility is intended to deliver catering for both theatre and non-theatre customers, it will need to be in a location where, for example, a schools matinee audience will not cause disruption. Conversely, if open to the general public during performances it must not inhibit access to the bars or allow noise and smells to intrude upon the auditorium.

Anyone considering food service for a non-theatre audience must be aware that a successful café/restaurant needs to be available at regular times and consistently each day it is scheduled to be open. It is not practicable to run a café/restaurant which is intended to be open for non-theatregoers during the day, but has to frequently close for theatre operational reasons.

Kitchens, cold and dry stores

If the venue offers a catering service then appropriately sized provision is essential. Not being the core business the catering 'back of house' accommodation is usually considered secondary and so can suffer from being undersized. Space of similar area to the eating area is required to accommodate:

- Kitchen, preparation and cooking
- Servery
- Wash up
- Dry stores
- Cold stores
- Crockery and cutlery store
- Linen store
- Wine store
- Administration
- Staff changing with separate toilets and a 'chef's shower'
- Goods delivery
- Waste disposal.

When locating kitchens and serveries hygiene regulations may require separate service routes for food and food waste.

3.7 Provision for other activities

Informal performance spaces

Informal performances either during the day and before or after the show will enliven the foyers. They need:

- A focal point at which to perform
- A raised platform for suitable sightlines
- Space for spectators to assemble or sit around
- Possibly acoustic treatment to surrounding surfaces
- Infrastructure for temporary sound and lighting rigs
- Adjacent storage (say for a piano).

3.7.1 Bridgewater Hall, Manchester, UK
Photograph: Dennis Gilbert

Sponsors' lounges, hospitality rooms and conference breakout space

Sponsors, VIPs and patrons are a necessary part of every theatre's life and the provision of well-appointed reception rooms or at least one sponsors' lounge is essential. Depending on the capacity and policy of the theatre, the type of hospitality will vary. The majority of events may only be entertaining 5-10 guests at a time or there could be two or three groups on the same evening. On other occasions, say a first night or a last night, larger parties may be held with 50 or more guests. Again flexibility is essential, for example, one large space that can be divided into two or three smaller rooms.

Sponsors expect recognition. They will bring display boards, banners or images to project onto screens or display on monitors.

Sponsors and hospitality areas will need:
- Ready access to kitchens or a food preparation space
- A suitable clearing area for dirty plates and glasses
- Lounge furniture
- Separate bar facilities
- Easy access from the front of house
- Accessibility even when the auditorium is not open to the public
- Quick direct access to the 'house keep' seats for VIP visits.

Hospitality rooms will be used in different formats – lecture, party or dining layouts, etc, so it is essential to have adequate furniture storage immediately adjacent.

If the theatre offers conferencing or banqueting facilities, room capacity will be determined by seating layouts and table sizes. To be successful in a competitive market these rooms need to be able to accommodate state of the art audio-visual presentations.

(See also Section 8 – Additional space.)

Education and outreach facilities

When education facilities are provided they should, wherever possible, be in addition to the hospitality suites. Education spaces should be adjacent to or part of the foyers. An interactive zone can be a major contributor to the liveliness of the public areas. It should include:
- Special educational exhibition area
- 'Dirty room' for children's workshops involving paint, water and dirty materials, etc.
- A defined quiet storytelling area for around 30 children sitting on cushions
- Somewhere for school groups to eat a packed lunch.

(See also Section 8 – Additional spaces.)

Exhibition space

Theatre foyers may be used to stage exhibitions associated with the show or its sponsors, or in the case of conferences - a trade show.

Exhibitions will:

- Need sufficient floor to ceiling height
- Impose high floor loadings
- Need variable lighting
- Need power supplies.

Exhibitions must be positioned so as not to cause obstructions to escape routes.

'Get-in' and 'get-out' of exhibitions may be more convenient if carried out through the front doors in which case sufficient clear openings should be integrated into the design of the front entrance. For example, in a large 'concourse'-style theatre, a car or similar-sized object may need to be got into the building.

The foyers may also provide a gallery for a more cultural programme; such as displaying paintings, photographs, sculpture or work for sale by local craftspeople. They will need additional requirements:

- An integrated hanging and display system should be considered in the overall design
- Suitable lighting and environmental conditions
- Additional security measures
- Location that enables fit-ups and dismantling not to interfere with other activities
- High-level and floor-level power supplies, even water and drainage
- IT and data outlets, a lot of modern exhibitions use projectors, film and video, digital art, etc.

The exhibition space will also need adequate storage for display systems as well as for exhibitions awaiting display or collection, after being dismantled.

3.7.2 Knitwits – Underground at the Royal & Derngate, Northampton, UK
Photograph: Alex Soulsby, courtesy of Royal & Derngate Theatres

3.7.3 Exhibition of Gary Hume's work in the foyer of the new Sadler's Wells Theatre, London, UK
Photograph: Gary Hume

3.7.4 Copenhagen Opera House
Large lamps of semi-permeable glass facets, designed by Icelandic artist Olafur Eliasson, illumine the central foyer and create a beacon from across the water.
Photograph: Lars Schmidt, courtesy of Copenhagen Opera House

Public art installations

Where projects are supported by public funding, there could be a requirement that work by artists and craftspeople be incorporated into the overall design. To be properly integrated, installations should be planned from an early stage. Clients may choose to select artists themselves, or with their architect, or use an art commissioning consultant to organise the process.

The foyers present an ideal opportunity. There is considerable scope for artists to be involved with design and fabrication of building elements such as:

- Floor finishes
- Balustrades and handrails
- Doors and door furniture
- Bars and counters
- Lighting
- Carpets and drapes
- Furniture.

There are examples where artists have successfully integrated donor names into commissioned work – for example, an etched glazed screen, a tiled area, decorative brickwork and even a chandelier.

3.8 Routes and signage

Auditorium entrance doors and lobbies

Entrances into the auditorium are a very important architectural element within the design of the foyers. Every member of the audience has to pass through these doors. Movement between the foyer and auditorium is an opportunity to build anticipation for the audience entering the auditorium and to reflect on the performance when leaving.

The aim should be to enable people to find the correct door without confusion. Each entrance has to be controlled by a member of staff to check tickets so it is good practice to avoid unnecessary doorways.

Doors should be wide enough for people to get into the auditorium without queuing but manageable for checking tickets, with space nearby for selling programmes and, if drinks are allowed in the auditorium, space for changing from glass to plastic containers. It should also be noted that with the advent of 'PYO' tickets stewards increasingly use bar code readers to check tickets. This activity, along with regular ticket checking, means that lighting levels near entrance doors need to be heightened so that customers and staff can read tickets easily.

Between the foyer and the auditorium there need to be lobbies. These lobbies are required to provide fire separation, reduce sound transference and avoid light spill into the auditorium. They need to be planned so that one set of doors closes before the next set opens. To aid circulation, doors should be on hold-open devices (as permitted by the licensing authority) and swing inwards for entry and outwards when leaving. Double swing doors will need careful specification to meet fire and acoustic requirements.

Latecomers

If the theatre holds a tight policy on the admission of latecomers to the auditorium, thought should be given to accommodating them with either a box at the rear of the auditorium, accessible without interrupting others' enjoyment of the performance, or good audio and visual relay to a position in the foyer. If late entry is permitted then latecomers' video monitors should be located near their entrance doors for quick entry at the appropriate point in the performance. At other times the same monitors can be used for promotional and advertising purposes. Viewing ports may also be necessary in the auditorium doors to enable attendants to usher latecomers quickly to their seats at a suitable moment in the performance.

Escape routes

It is as important to plan escape routes from the foyer as it is from the auditorium. The practical way of achieving this is to position escape routes from the lobbies between the foyer and the auditorium. If this approach is followed, the maximum capacity of the public spaces needs to be considered. While on most occasions the auditorium seating capacity will be the required escape capacity, licensing authorities may argue that if the foyers are used for additional events (e.g. restaurant, bar, ancillary performance or relaying productions to a wider audience via video screens) then the escape capacity needs to be increased.

On the upper floors, within fire protected zones, refuges – safe spaces for people in wheelchairs awaiting rescue – will be required with one refuge space for each wheelchair position in the adjoining part of the auditorium. (See Section 2 for more detailed information on fire safety.)

3.8.1 The doors into the Crucible Theatre in Sheffield, UK, are easily located by their large over panels, colour coded with bold directional arrows, matching graphics and tickets.
Photograph: John Danet, courtesy of RIBA Library Photographs Collection

Way-finding and signs

Clear, well-thought-out signposting is an issue for most public buildings. Signposting is all too often an afterthought and does not take account of where people actually look. This can lead to a raft of ad-hoc signage being added later. The more legible the building the less need there will be for a proliferation of signs.

For those with sight impairments, signs, changes of level and obstructions need to be identified. Braille or raised lettering, colour contrasting and tactile surfaces, and the avoidance of glare all need careful consideration.

Signs need to be well thought out from the point of view of the theatregoer and be consistent in terminology and graphic style. A hierarchy of signs needs to be developed to suit the journey around the building. The more complex the auditorium seating layout is and the more entrance doors there are, the more complex the signs are likely to become. The following information needs to be conveyed:

- Auditorium (if not obvious or where there is more than one auditorium)
- Seating level (e.g. stalls, circle or gallery)
- Door or aisle (e.g. auditorium left or right)
- Seating row
- Seat number.

The information given on signs within the foyers needs to correspond exactly with that printed on the tickets. To ensure consistency, consideration also needs to be given to integrating all the ancillary signs such as:

- Statutory signs
- Bar tariffs
- Disclaimers and warnings regarding the performance including explicit scenes, strobe lighting or cast changes, etc.

A proliferation of other items could appear in the foyer (such as clocks, posters, donor recognition, plaques, etc.). Slide projection or video screens may help control some of this but generally provision is best made in advance, thought through at the design and briefing stage.

Lifts

In normal circumstances it will not be possible to have sufficient lifts for all the audience to use at the beginning or at the end of the performance but adequate provision should be made for those who may need them such as the elderly, infirm or families with young children. Lifts

should be carefully positioned so that they can be easily located.

- Lift and escalator installations need to run as silently as possible, isolated from the auditorium structure.
- Have floor numbers in Braille and/or in raised numerals.
- Lift cars need to be large enough for wheelchairs to turn around.
- Have 'talking' level indicators which should be coordinated with the nomenclature used for parts of the auditorium.
- Lift cars should have easy-to-maintain walls and floors.
- Lift cars should be provided with hooks and protective wall coverings.

There should be more than one lift available in the event of servicing or breakdowns.

3.9 Toilets

Toilets have a marked impact on customer perceptions. Given the peaks of demand pre-show and at the interval, toilets need to be easy to maintain and service. For women, theatre toilets have long been synonymous with queuing. This is not only undesirable for the female sector of the audience but also for the management which loses bar and related sales when people are standing in queues rather than socialising with their companions. The ratio of male to female toilets needs to reflect audience composition and some toilets may need to have the facility to be switched to women's use for certain performance types.

Where a building type or form of entertainment is subject to license, the minimum scale of provision and the location and arrangement of the toilets has to be agreed with the licensing authority. In the UK the design of sanitary facilities in assembly buildings should be in accordance with clause 6.8 and table 7 of BS 6465-1:2006 or the similar table 23 in section G1 of the Technical Standards for Places of Entertainment.

If the toilet provision is to achieve a reasonable level of user satisfaction, its design needs to consider key features from the customer perspective:

- Counters that can be kept clean and dry.
- Materials that enable floors, wall and tiled services to be easy to clean.
- Ample ventilation to avoid odours.
- Easy-to-maintain lights, hand-dryers and other electrical fittings.

3.9.1 Barbican Centre in London, UK, notoriously difficult to navigate, has completely new way-finding signs
Designed by Allford Hall Monaghan Morris Architects/Studio Myerscough/Cartlidge Levene

- Cubical doors that swing open and do not appear to be locked when unoccupied.
- Cubicles that are sufficiently wide to accommodate sanitary dispensers.
- Easy-to-maintain taps and waste systems with flushing systems.
- Well-positioned mirrors, complementary lighting and dry handbag shelves.
- At least one full-length mirror.
- Movement-sensitive taps.
- Basins with wastes and overflows that cannot be maliciously blocked.
- Easy-to-see and use towel dispensers and waste bins.
- Choice of paper towels and hand-dryers. (Hand-dryers create less rubbish but are noisy and cause queues.)
- Toilet paper holders that contain a spare roll and cannot be tampered with.
- Local storage for toilet paper, soap and towels.
- Avoid views of urinals from adjacent areas.

Toilets should be located away from walls adjoining the auditorium or special measures taken to ensure that cisterns and hand-dryers do not cause intrusive noise.

Toilets for disabled people should be provided in accordance with BS 6465-1:2006 Clause 8. In addition to fulfilling these requirements, accessible toilets should:

- Be close to where the wheelchair users are seated and in sufficient number.
- Have a travel distance not exceeding 40m.
- Be unisex cubicles enabling carers to assist if necessary.
- Where more than one disabled person's lavatory is provided, offer a left or right or centrally positioned WC pan.
- And also wider cubicles with outward-opening doors and grab rails should be provided in all male and female toilets to aid the less ambulant.

Baby-changing facilities should not be sited within the disabled persons' toilets. They should either have their own space or be in the principal female and male toilets which must be large enough to accommodate the changing table in use with circulation space around it.

3.10 Support areas

The following areas are not usually open to the public and access needs to be controlled.

Duty manager's and security office

This is the hub of the FOH activity, as important as the stage door is to backstage. It usually has to accommodate two or three staff and a multitude of activities, including pre-performance briefings and the cashing-up of programme, ice cream and other sales money, requiring a safe that is separate from the one used for box-office takings.

The duty manager needs to maintain contact with other departments in the theatre throughout the evening. Radios are the usual means of communication between staff but if a large amount of steel is used in construction signals can be weak and thought needs to be given to how communications are maintained during show time. Most theatres still use a bell system to alert customers to the start of a performance and this is often accompanied by foyer announcements from the duty manager or from the stage manager. Dimming the foyer lights provides a visual signal to deaf people.

The proliferation of CCTV has extended to the exterior of theatres and sometimes includes the foyers. The CCTV monitoring may be carried out off- or on-site. If the plan is to have a security presence on-site then a control room or CCTV space may be needed.

Traditionally the stage door is the focus of security and fire control but fire panels are a vital part of emergency equipment and need to be readily accessible to the duty manager and possibly the Fire Brigade. Small area zoning is appreciated by theatre staff who have to check areas and establish exit routes in an emergency.

At various times of operation different sections of the building may be active or inactive. To help manage energy consumption and minimise waste and disturbance, zoning parts of the building's lighting and public address system should be incorporated.

First aid room

A first aid room should be provided in larger venues, with a bed, a supplies cupboard and a screened space to store a wheelchair and stretcher/carrying chair. A washbasin, with drinking water, will be required and ideally an en-suite WC. The room needs to be close to the point where ambulances arrive and positioned so that a full-length stretcher can be manoeuvred out.

Staff briefing and changing rooms

Where staff are expected to wear a uniform they should be provided with changing facilities and locker space. Many of these staff will be part-time or job sharing, requiring more lockers. These areas should be close to a suitable briefing area for attendants. They should be equipped with notice boards and full-length mirrors, next to doors leading to public areas, and have vending machines for drinks or snacks.

FOH equipment store

Storage is a real issue for theatres. The items that need a home in the front of house area are:
- Door locks, once removed from emergency exits, available for easy inspection
- Key safe
- Radio recharge point
- Infrared headsets (usually dispensed from the cloakroom)
- Tables and chairs not in use
- Sponsors' materials
- Conference print
- Meeting equipment including flipchart or electronic equivalent, projectors, screens and audio equipment
- VIP equipment; visitors' book, umbrellas, red carpet
- Photocopier for rotas, etc.
- Cash bags for programme sellers
- Programme boxes for current show.

Merchandising, programme, ice cream and confectionery deliveries

Unless decided otherwise, all these goods should be delivered via the stage door where they can be checked and kept secure. The eventual storage of these goods should be located close to FOH, where the items will be sold. Print notices of future events, programmes, promotional leaflets and posters will be delivered in bulk and require a significant amount of storage space.

Ice cream store

The sale of ice cream requires freezer space, sales trays and cash bags. The number of freezers will depend upon the size of the theatre and the frequency of delivery. Sales will vary between shows: not surprisingly ice

cream sales during the Christmas pantomime season frequently exceed alcohol sales. Freezers should be:
- Centrally located in a well-ventilated dedicated space
- With a suitable reliable power supply that is hard to switch off by error
- Located near to the attendants' changing rooms.

When demand requires, additional freezers can be loaned from suppliers but these will need space and a power supply.

Housekeeping and cleaners' stores

Maintaining good front of house cleaning standards requires adequate storage for vacuum cleaners, mops, buckets, brushes, dustpans, back-pack vacuums, buffing machines and items restricted by the control of substances hazardous to health (COSHH). As well as a central store there should also be cleaners' cupboards on each floor, both front of house and backstage. Cleaning staff will also need locker rooms. The housekeeper may need space for administration, duty rotas, ordering, etc. The cleaners' room should:
- Contain a sink or bucket sink, where buckets of water will be used during cleaning, and space for the storage of cleaning appliances and materials.
- Be ventilated to allow for drying of equipment.

Refuse store, compacting and recycling space

These facilities should be located close to the stage door where the collection can be monitored and controlled. This space needs to be operated separately from stage waste, which will be bulky and produced mainly during 'fit-ups'. Rubbish coming from the foyers, bars and auditorium needs to be sorted between waste, paper, plastic and glass. Where breweries do recycle bottles, space is needed for crates. To reduce volume and frequency of collection, compactors should be considered. Refuse stores need power and water supplies and drainage to wash down the area.

3.11 Future technology

Theatres are built with long lifespans and technology that is unforeseen when the building is being planned will inevitably arrive. This is true of theatre FOH services as much as any other business. Wireless (e.g. Wi-Fi) coverage of the foyers, conduit width and optical cabling are already must-have services for new buildings, and Bluetooth routers and other informational systems need to be considered when trying to future-proof the facilities.

SECTION EDITOR
Barry Pritchard — Arts Team, RHWL Architects

CONTRIBUTORS
John Botteley — Theatre Director
Colin Chester — Ambassador Theatre Group (ATG)
Stewart King — RHWL Arts Team
Ian Knowles — Arup Acoustics
Jim Morse — Lighting Design Associates
Howard Raynor — World Class Service Ltd
Ian Smith — King Shaw Associates
Roger Spence — National Concert Hall, Dublin
Nadia Stern — Rambert Dance Company
Alan McKenzie — RHWL Arts Team

Section 4
Auditorium design

Contents

4.1 Introduction

The auditorium is the most important part of any theatre. The design of this space holds the key to the scale, form and layout of the whole building. As the engine room that drives the theatre machine – it has to be right.

This section explores the factors that need to be considered. It looks at the crucial relationship between performers and audience and how this is interpreted to serve different styles of production and different art forms. It also looks at the practical issues of getting the audience to their seats, ensuring that they can see and hear what is being presented, and that they are both comfortable and safe.

As modern performance practice has evolved so has theatre design. A wider range of formats has emerged, each suited to different art forms and differing presentational styles. In many ways a review of auditorium design during the course of the latter half of the twentieth century can be seen as a quest to break free from the restrictions imposed by the proscenium

format – the division between the world of the actor and that of the audience. This led to exploration of shared 'open space' and a preoccupation with the degree to which the audience encircled the stage.

At the same time, changes in society encouraged theatre designers to create more egalitarian and democratic layouts. These developments were also allied to ideas such as 'the point of command' (the focal point of interaction between a performer and the audience) and the creation of spaces that could deal simultaneously with epic and intimate theatre.

Technological advances also have an influence, offering directors opportunities for experimentation and theatre designers scope to extend the uses to which a single space can be put.

4.2 Factors influencing size and scale

Seating capacity

Seats generate income but deciding on the optimum number of seats is not a case of the more the better. With modern technology it is possible to create a space which can accommodate tens of thousands of people but such a space will only be effective for large-scale, electronically enhanced productions. At the other end of the scale, theatres are still being commissioned for fewer than 100 people though these may require some form of subsidy; through public funding, donations, 'add-on' activities, or by being part of a larger complex.

A range of factors influence the number of seats that should be provided and that can be accommodated within different types of theatre.

Visual and aural limits

Traditionally, the size and layout of the auditorium was determined by the distance people can see and hear what is being presented to them. For the spoken voice, the usual accepted maximum distance is for the audience to be within 20m of the setting line of the proscenium stage or the front of an open stage. This distance is also determined by the need to see the actors' expressions.

Contemporary standards of safety, comfort and access have reduced the number of seats which can be accommodated within these visual and aural limits and a working norm now sets the maximum at around 1,000 seats for drama.

For musicals and opera, where the sound of the voice carries further, the maximum distance for communication can be up to 30m. In opera, as in epic theatre, sets are often more striking and the costumes and gestures are enlarged. This helps performers communicate with the audience over a longer distance, thus enabling greater numbers to be accommodated without losing their sense of engagement with the action. For example, The Coliseum in London, home to English National Opera, has a seating capacity of 2,358 over four levels.

With the advent of amplified sound, much larger audience capacities can be contemplated (with arena-style venues seating 20,000 or more) but aesthetic factors come into play when considering whether amplification is appropriate for any particular art form.

Space for music and the sung word

Sung words carry further than spoken words, enabling a singer to fill a much larger volume of space. Musical instruments carry further than the voice by sustaining the sound for longer.

Spaces which are designed to house music need a certain amount of interior volume and carefully specified contours. Different styles of music, however, require different volumes. For concert halls, the primary emphasis is on the quality of the sound while in an opera house a balance needs to be struck between designing for clarity in the spoken word and for the fullness of the musical sound.

Intimacy, immediacy and audience cohesion

Theatrical intimacy, immediacy and audience cohesion are the essential tenets of good auditorium design. For the audience, the experience of live theatre involves a sense of participating in the 'event', of shared responses and of being part of a homogeneous group. From the actors' point of view, a good space achieves the feeling of being embraced by the audience.

Theatrical intimacy is about enclosure and envelopment. One way it can be achieved is by increasing the angle of the rake of the audience relative to the stage. Some directors find that a 'wall of people' in a steeply raked auditorium gives a perception of closeness as well as a clear view of the stage. Alternatively 'painting' the walls with people in a series of shallow balconies can help achieve the desired effect, a technique demonstrated by the boxes in the traditional opera house and galleries in courtyard-style theatres. A degree of 'closeness' in which each gesture and nuance of the actors' expression is clearly seen by every member of the audience requires a smaller auditorium and a format that wraps the audience around the production or even intermingles the action with the audience.

Some productions are bound to be more successful than others and blocks of empty seats can destroy the quality of the theatre experience. This can be counteracted, in part, by a design which allows the audience to be concentrated in the parts of the auditorium where the interaction with the actor or production is greatest.

4.3 Auditorium formats

The proscenium theatre format emerged in Italian opera houses in the seventeenth century and then dominated auditoria design for over two hundred years, reaching its heyday in the latter part of the nineteenth and early twentieth centuries. Since then, various different formats have evolved, gradually eroding the proscenium division of space and exploring ideas of the single room theatre.

This subsection describes the different auditoria formats, indicating aspects of their historical development, typical use, opportunities and limitations. It creates a narrative which starts with the proscenium theatre as the predominant form and works out from this, gradually eroding the proscenium opening itself and exploring the idea of the open space theatre. The narrative follows a course of gradually increasing the degree of audience encirclement and the preoccupation with theatrical intimacy. In the course of the narrative aspects of auditoria design, or performance type, are articulated as separate headings. This is not to categorise them as particular formats, but to include them as part of the quest for greater theatrical intimacy.

Proscenium theatre

In the proscenium theatre model the stagehouse and the audience chamber are separate but interlinked volumes. The scenery and action are contained on the stage and the audience views the performance through the proscenium opening. Directors and designers often refer to this opening as the 'fourth wall' of the stage while in the more ebullient theatres of the latter part of the nineteenth century, the proscenium surround was treated as an enlarged and elaborate picture frame. Above the stage is the stagehouse or flytower where scenic elements can be suspended or flown.

In this format, the audience has to be placed substantially end-on within the auditorium to maximise their view through the proscenium opening onto the stage beyond. Over time sightline imperatives have evolved and the audience chamber in a proscenium theatre has adapted to take on many different configurations. Different performance types require differing widths of proscenia and various widths-to-height relationships for the opening. These are detailed in Section 5.

While performance practice and audience tastes ebb and flow, the proscenium format retains a key advantage which ensures its continued relevance: it remains the primary format for the presentation of large-scale and elaborate scenic effects.

Modern proscenium theatre designs may tend to play down the proscenium opening, blurring the boundary between two spaces in order to reduce the sense of separation. In smaller venues, the full flytower may be replaced by simple suspension and the proscenium itself can be a temporary construction of panels, pelmets and drapes.

See Reference projects:
- The Opera House Oslo, Norway: p. 254
- Jerwood Vanburgh Theatre, RADA: London, UK: p. 262
- Hackney Empire, London, UK: p. 236.

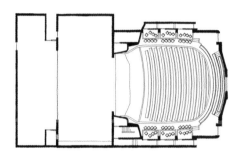

4.3.1 Proscenium format: Wexford Opera House

Forestage and apron stage

A forestage, or apron stage, is not a defined auditorium format. It is more accurately described as an adaptation or an aspect of a proscenium theatre design.

In the proscenium theatre there is a limit to which scenic elements can be brought downstage towards the audience. This is normally about 1m back from the rear face of the proscenium wall and is known as the setting line. The zone between the setting line and the edge of the stage riser is termed the forestage. When this extends well out into the auditorium it is known as an apron stage. In contemporary performance practice an apron stage can help break down the perceptual barrier of the proscenium and bring actor and audience closer together.

The forestage can be seen as a subtle erosion of the restrictions of the proscenium and a first step towards end stage and the more open staging formats. In terms of performance style, a deep forestage within a proscenium format can allow directors and designers to combine epic scenic effects with intimate scenes played well forward. The facility to do this is an essential part of modern proscenium theatre.

End stage

The end stage can be seen as an abstraction of the proscenium theatre model. The audience is oriented end-on directly in front of the stage. There is no encirclement.

As the audience form a single body, in opposition to the stage, it is harder for an actor to make an aside, or be conspiratorial with just a part of the audience. The format can be criticised for placing the audience in a passive relationship with the performance but an upside of the layout is that it is easier for an actor to address the audience as a group and hold their full attention – as they are unified and less fragmented.

A characteristic of this format is that all four corners of the acting area can be visible which means that it is well suited to contemporary dance and some forms of physical theatre – particularly those that combine multimedia projection with live action.

End stage spaces may, or may not, have a stage riser. Spaces without a riser tend to be single tier and fairly steeply raked. Spaces with a stage riser may have more than one tier, with a shallower rake at the lower level. Rows can be parallel to the stage edge or softened by being set out on a radius while still contained within parallel walls. The stage end of the space may have a flytower or more modest suspension above the acting area.

Within the end stage environment actors and audience effectively share the same physical space. So while there are some similarities between the end stage and the proscenium, in this respect they are fundamentally different.

Examples:
• Netherlands Dance Theatre, The Hague, the Netherlands.
• Stage 1, Northern Stage, Newcastle upon Tyne, UK.

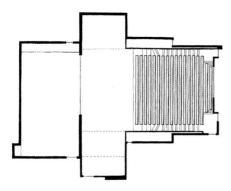

4.3.2 End stage format: Northern Stage, Newcastle upon Tyne, UK

Corner stage – 90° arc

Setting the stage in a corner of the room creates, broadly speaking, a 90° arc arrangement. Philosophically, and geometrically, it is set somewhere between an end stage and an amphitheatre. While there is an enhanced degree of encirclement with the audience embracing the front edge of the stage, the performance itself takes place primarily against the stage walls or some form of scenic backdrop.

When supported by a flytower and appropriately planned upstage wing space, this arrangement retains a high degree of scenic potential. However, staging and set design are limited by the extreme side seats and their lateral sightlines.

In some respects, the performance technique is not radically different from that of the proscenium or end stage. However, performers can come forward into the audience zone and the overall staging composition can be more clearly three-dimensional. The most successful examples of the format tend to be fairly modest in scale – up to around 600 seats.

The form can be developed with or without an upper tier.

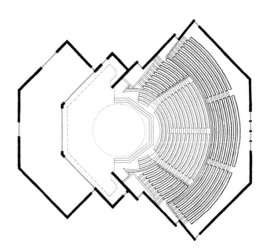

4.3.3 Corner stage format: the Olivier auditorium at the National Theatre, London

Larger capacities, such as the Olivier at the National Theatre in London with its 1,150-seating capacity, tend to suffer from a number of common problems. As the fan arrangement is extended outward from the stage, row lengths increase and the space becomes wider. Although an individual seat may not be physically distant from the stage, there can be a loss of aural inclusivity. It can also prove difficult to establish a strong focus on stage, although the use of side boxes or raised tiers can address this shortcoming. The inherent scale of larger auditoria is perhaps more suited to epic theatre than to more intimate styles of production.

Examples:
- The Olivier, National Theatre, London, UK
- Arc, Stockton-on-Tees, UK.

The wide fan

Extending the encirclement of the stage by the audience to around 135° brings to the fore the idea of the actor's 'point of command'. This theory was strongly espoused by Sir Peter Hall and John Bury during the development of the Barbican Theatre in London in the late 1970s. It works on the principle that there should be a position, approximately 2.5m back from the leading edge of the stage, from which an actor can command the attention of the entire audience, without the need to turn the head. In practice this was perceived to be an arc of 135°.

As with the 90° arc arrangement, increasing the width of the seating plan and pushing the stage forward can increase the sense of visual immediacy but does so at the potential expense of visual and aural intimacy. The width of the audience seating and stage can be daunting and achieving a balance between an epic scene and a more intimate moment can be problematic.

In practical terms, while the point of command theory demonstrably works, the degree of wrap-around means that at any given time some actors are facing away from large sections of the audience. Allied to this, the extreme side sightlines limit the amount of stage setting that can be viewed by the audience as a whole.

Examples:
- Barbican Theatre, Barbican Arts Centre, London, UK
- Bayreuth Opera, Germany.

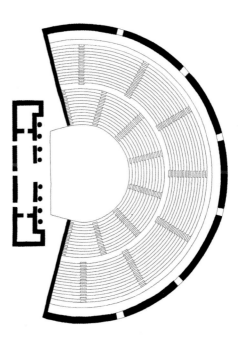

4.3.5 Amphitheatre format

Amphitheatres

The Greek amphitheatre wrapped its audience around a central stage, with the degree of encirclement extended to 220°. These spaces were carved into the landscape and open to the sky.

While Roman arenas fully encircled a central stage, their amphitheatres were semi-circular in form, giving 180° encirclement. Here, while the seating block was geometrically focused on the semi-circular 'orchestra', the action took place on the 'proscenium', a linear strip running across the back of the circle. A multi-storey architectural stone façade created a permanent back-drop.

The format is still in common use for external performance spaces – with 'amphitheatre' used as a generic term for an outdoor venue.

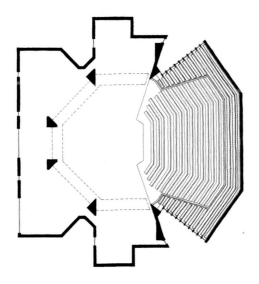

4.3.4 **Wide fan format: the Barbican Theatre, London**

Thrust stages

The next step in pursuit of theatrical intimacy is the thrust stage where the audience is positioned around three sides. For a pure thrust stage they are equally distributed, with the group on one side providing a backdrop to the action for those seated opposite. Large scenic elements are limited to the back wall.

Performers enter from the rear of the stage or through the body of the audience. The audience sees the performance from a range of differing perspectives. Performance style is three-dimensional to ensure that no 'side' misses the action. The 270° envelopment around the stage edge ensures that a high degree of immediacy can be achieved for audiences of up to 1,000 seats.

The format is often associated with single, fairly steeply raked spaces. Larger capacities have shallower rakes. There are also two-level auditoria, such as the Donmar Warehouse in London.

The resurgence of interest in this format can largely be attributed to theatre director Tyrone Guthrie (working with his designer Tanya Moiseiwitsch). His ground-breaking theatre in Minneapolis inspired a generation of theatre practitioners and theatre builders.

See References projects:
- The Crucible Theatre, Sheffield, UK: p. 216
- The Donmar Warehouse, London, UK p. 220
- Guthrie Theater, Minneapolis, USA: p. 232.

In-the-round

As the name implies, this format places the performance in the centre of the room with the audience encircling the action. The 360° wrapping of the audience around the stage is also occasionally referred to as an island stage (particularly when there is a stage riser), arena or centre stage format. There is no scenic backdrop and sets and props have to be fairly minimal to ensure the actors remain in view from any angle. Performers enter through the body of the audience, often sharing entry routes.

Historical precedent for the format can be found in spaces designed for activities not reliant on scenic backdrops such as circus. To a degree a lineage can also be traced in the informal and impromptu use of galleried spaces such as the yard of a medieval inn.

At the smaller scale, in spaces such as the Orange Tree Theatre in Richmond, Surrey, the format can be astonishingly intense and demanding for both actors and audience. (The theatre seats 172 people.) Spaces can be single-rake or multi-level and volumes can vary considerably with the single-rake format tending to lead to a fairly large volume.

The Stephen Joseph Theatre in Scarborough is a good model of a single steeply raked arrangement. The Royal Exchange Theatre in Manchester is a successful multi-level space, surprisingly compact for the format and providing a strong sense of focus.

Examples:
- Stephen Joseph Theatre, Scarborough, North Yorkshire, UK (see p. 194)
- The Royal Exchange Theatre, Manchester, UK (see Reference project p. 264)
- The Orange Tree Theatre, Richmond-upon-Thames, Surrey, UK.

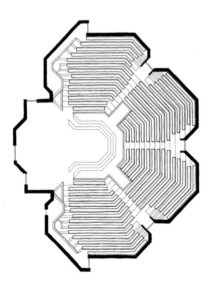

4.3.6 Thrust stage format: The Crucible Theatre, Sheffield

4.3.7 In-the-round format: the Royal Exchange Theatre, Manchester

As well as exploring different degrees of encirclement, theatre directors and designers looked to earlier forms for examples of formats which encouraged interaction and intimacy.

Courtyard theatre

The theatre model of the English Renaissance, the format that held the work of Shakespeare and his contemporaries, was compact, multi-levelled and open to the sky. The discovery of the Rose Theatre in London's Bankside has greatly increased the knowledge and understanding of these buildings.

The stage was thrust well out into the auditorium, with the two or three levels of shallow audience galleries providing a high degree of encirclement often in a broadly circular form. The stalls audience stood. The architectural form of the space extended behind the stage to provide a permanent setting. Audiences in such spaces were much closer to the action than in classical theatre forms and there would have been a strong sense of audience participation and involvement with the live event. Visitors to the reconstruction of Shakespeare's Globe in London can gain a genuine sense of how exhilarating these original venues must have been.

The 'courtyard theatre' is a modern term. The form derives from the English eighteenth-century playhouse. While such space can be viewed as a rectangular version of the European opera house model, the format also has strong parallels with the Elizabethan stage. The space was multi-level and, as the modern name implies, rectangular in form. The action of the play took place on what we would now describe as an extended forestage. Behind this was the scenic zone with suspension and stage machinery. Unlike the Elizabethan model, the stage was directly flanked by the parallel side galleries and boxes. Side doors also gave actors access directly onto the acting area.

Performance spaces such as the Cottesloe at the National Theatre and the Tricycle Theatre in Kilburn, both in London, helped to re-establish interest in the courtyard format. The creation of the Swan Theatre in Stratford-upon-Avon in the 1980s was a deceptively refined meditation on the Elizabethan model and thrust stage.

These two models have now begun to converge in the development of the modern courtyard theatre. An important part of this process has been the creation of the temporary venue for the Royal Shakespeare Company – a full-scale working prototype for the new permanent space. In both the RSC spaces, the thrust stage is surrounded by a gently raked stalls and a

multi-level gallery structure on three sides and supported by a stagehouse for scenic backdrops and enhanced staging depth. The central stage is supported by extensive technology above and below. The furthest seat is only 15m from the edge of the stage, creating remarkable immediacy in a space accommodating 1,000 people. While tailored to meet the particular needs of the RSC, the spaces combine theatrical intimacy, the ability to stage epic and intimate moments, and a high degree of adaptability and aesthetic neutrality, making them exemplars in the pursuit of the actor and audience sharing the one room.

See Reference projects:
- The Theatre Courtyard, RSC, Stratford-upon-Avon, Warwickshire, UK: p. 212
- The Cottesloe , National Theatre, London, UK: p. 210.

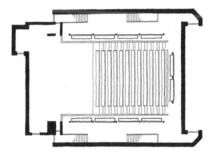

4.3.8 Courtyard format: the Cottesloe at the National Theatre, London

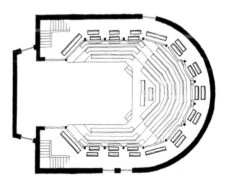

4.3.9 The Swan, Royal Shakespeare Company, Stratford-upon-Avon, UK

Other formats draw inspiration from earlier theatricals, where a performance might take the form of a street procession or where a wagon forms a simple stage in an inn yard or market square.

Traverse

The traverse format places the stage as a linear performance platform down the centre of the room with the audience arranged in equal blocks on either side. The audience watches the performance with other members of the audience as the backdrop. Scenic potential is minimal with larger elements restricted to either end of the space.

Although permanent traverse stage auditoria are rare, built examples do exist, the National Theatre in Mannheim being an example. The format is more generally associated with small- to medium-scale adaptable venues, with the staging arrangement one of a range of potential formats.

Example:
*   National Theatre, Mannheim, Germany.

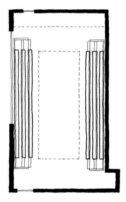

4.3.10 Traverse format

Promenade

As with the apron stage, promenade is not technically a permanent theatre format. In a promenade performance the choreography of the standing audience forms an inherent part of the work itself. The relationship between actor and audience is continually changing as the audience follows the performance around the space – the complete opposite of an audience sitting passively in its seats.

This style of production experienced a major revival in the 1970s with ground-breaking productions such as *The Mysteries* at the then unused Lyceum Theatre in London and *The Ship*, a site-specific piece, at the McGovern shipyard in Glasgow. The interest in experiential theatre productions, such as *De La Guarda* and *Fuerzabruta*, have more recently engaged a new younger audience.

Adaptable space

Adaptable spaces are not a defined performance configuration. They are primarily flat-floored spaces that can accommodate a wide range of performance configurations. Like courtyard auditoria they often have a default setting, which is their primary mode of operation. At a larger scale such spaces change between clearly defined formats – concert to proscenium, for example. At a smaller scale they are essentially studio venues (up to around 300 seats) capable of achieving a wide range of ad-hoc loose-fit layouts.

An adaptable studio is often a second space within a performing arts complex, enabling a more experimental programme to be mounted to complement the primary venue. The format is also often used within the educational environment, where the variability and potential for experimentation are important.

See Reference projects:
*   Cerritos Center, California, USA: p. 202
*   Milton Keynes Theatre, UK: p. 252
*   Studio space at Copenhagen Opera House, Denmark: p. 206.

Found space

The idea of found space needs to be touched upon as a concluding part of this overall sequence. Once again this is not a prescribed seating configuration or auditorium format though the term will often surface in conversation on 'types' of performance venue. Found space refers to a production taking place in space not designed for the purpose. This is often a redundant building but any space can be used from railway arches to churches.

Found spaces are often temporary, to host a particular performance or season of work. Once 'found' some spaces can go on to become formalised performance venues. They can also be re-found, or rediscovered, theatre spaces such as Peter Brook's BAM (the Brooklyn Academy of Music which reclaimed the Majestic Theater) in New York.

The appeal of such spaces is in part the ephemeral nature of their existence as theatres. They also allow a unique creative dialogue for the director and designer as they work with and respond to the quality and character of a particular building.

As a performance aesthetic and practice, the found space movement has grown in influence and has had a profound impact on the design of many new experimental spaces, both in terms of physical and philosophical adaptability and also ideas of aesthetic neutrality.

See Reference projects:
- The Roundhouse, London, UK: p. 258
- Théâtre des Bouffes du Nord - Paris, France: p. 198
- King's Cross Almeida, London, UK: p. 238.

4.4 Positioning and seating the audience

The experience

The sense of participating in a shared experience is one of the key factors in live theatre, where audience reaction impacts on the performance and there is a two-way transference of energy. From an actor's point of view the audience is a community of people so it is important that the audience is cohesive and does not appear overly segregated or dispersed. In larger auditoria side boxes, or galleries, can assist the performer in providing a direct link out and upward to seating tiers. From an audience perspective such devices can help lead the eye down to the scale of the stage. Side seating also serves to unite levels of audience who may otherwise not be aware of one another, critically enhancing the sense of audience cohesion.

Sectional considerations

The primary objective in the design of an auditorium is to bring as many people as close as possible to the performance area. This has to be done within optimum viewing and aural limitations. An understanding of historical precedent can be invaluable in knowing how best to arrange an audience.

As outlined in the previous discussion on formats (in subsection 4.3), one way of increasing the numbers of people with proximity to the stage is to increase the degree of envelopment. An alternative strategy is to add levels or tiers enabling a greater number of seats to be accommodated without increasing the distance between the stage and those seated furthest away. Actors also respond well to the sense of envelopment offered.

The various levels have had a profusion of names over time: at or below stage level the audience is referred to as the stalls, orchestra stalls, parterre or pit; one level above the stage they can be referred to as the circle, dress circle, royal circle or grand tier; the audience located two levels above from the stage can be referred to as upper circle, balcony, gallery or 'gods' and the shallow side rows as slips. These terms have served to convey the level of luxury and prestige – and the extent of social segregation. They may now be simply referred to as 'levels'.

The complexity involved in designing multi-level spaces comes in balancing sightline requirements to achieve good standards throughout the auditorium. The theoretical angle of rake in the stalls needs to be reduced to ensure that upper tiers are not pushed up too high or their rakes too steep. The rake of an upper tier is determined by visibility of stage front and by regulations. The impact on upward sightlines from rear rows also needs to be considered. A qualitative balance needs to be sought as tiers set too close together can create the effect known as a letter box – where the stage is viewed through a narrow slot between two seating levels.

In this respect several shallower tiers can be more effective than one or two deeper ones – a model characteristic of the traditional European opera house, where a series of tiers, in line with one another, wrap around a gently raked parterre. These tiers were generally subdivided into separate boxes (in part reflecting the way the buildings were funded), with divisions radiating from the centre of the stage. Generally such boxes allowed for two rows of seats. The small group of audience, particularly those in the sides, could improve oblique views by leaning forward onto the balcony rail – without disrupting the view for others. With the removal of the box division an extra row or two could be added. However, restricted ceiling heights limit the degree of elevation of these rows.

The sale of individual boxes and loges, combined with structural limitations, had a significant effect on the development of the opera house form. Commercial imperatives also had a profound influence on the configuration of the nineteenth- and early twentieth-century theatre. In order to fit in as many paying customers as possible, tiers facing the stage became deeper. Structural developments (such as the cantilever) enabled upper tiers to be stepped back in order to maximise sightlines. Side boxes and slips remained as the oblique angles restricted the depth of any overhang.

Auditorum design was also influenced by the emergence of dedicated spaces for cinema. Oblique side views of the screen were unacceptable. Auditoria became a stalls and circle only – often almost separate spaces within a single volume. When such ideas were transposed into live performance spaces, many lacked the fundamental sense of atmosphere and audience cohesion.

In contemporary auditoria the section is still largely determined by sightlines. However, the depth of overhang is heavily informed by acoustic parameters. Spaces reliant on a natural acoustic require shallower overhangs. A good rule of thumb is to limit the depth of the overhang to the vertical clear height between the tiers themselves. In spaces supported by amplified sound the overhang can be deeper. (Auditorium acoustics are discussed in subsection 4.6.)

Seating layout

The following commentary is in part based on the ABTT Technical Standards for Places of Entertainment and British Standard BS 9999 – Code of practice for fire safety in the design, management and use of buildings – Annex D. The latter replaced the earlier BS 5588 in 2009. While non-UK authorities will adopt their own regulations, BS 5588 has done much to harmonise requirements. BS 9999 and the ABTT Technical Standards provide a robust basis upon which to plan international projects. However, in acknowledgement that different regions will have their own particular standards, good practice guidance is set out alongside the minimum requirements.

Useful dimensional data

- The minimum back-to-back dimension between rows of seats with backs is 760mm. A good practice minimum is between 850mm–900mm.
- The minimum width of seats with arms is 500mm centre of arm to centre of arm. A good practice minimum is between 525mm–550mm.
- The minimum width of seats without arms (individual seats or benches) is 450mm. A good practice minimum is 500mm.
- The unobstructed vertical space between rows (seatway or clearway) should be a minimum of 300mm. However, see detailed table in Figure 4.4.1.
- Distance from seat to gangway is now more normally associated with number of seats in a row (i.e. assuming typical seat width in the order of 500mm–550mm). See Figure 4.4.1, as number of seats in row dictates seatway.

- Row lengths exceeding 28 seats – this is sometimes referred to as 'continental' seating.
- The minimum unobstructed aisle width is 1100mm. (Note, as with escape staircase the handrails can project into this minimum zone.)

Number of seats in a row		
Seatway width mm	Maximum number of seats in a row	
	Gangway on one side	Gangway on two sides
300 to 324	7	14
325 to 349	8	16
350 to 374	9	18
375 to 399	10	20
400 to 424	11	22
425 to 449	12	24
450 to 474	12	26
475 to 499	12	28
500 or more	12	Limited by travel distance to place of safety

4.4.1 Table D.1 from British Standard BS 9999:2008. This illustrates the clear seatway required for the number of seats in a row

Seating and seatways

The replacement of seating, to improve audience comfort, is often a high priority in the refurbishment of existing theatres.

Achieving the right balance between comfort, safety and commercial imperatives requires careful consideration in both new build and refurbishment projects. Seating should ensure the audience's comfort, while keeping them alert. The spacing of seats is key to enjoyment of the visit but must not be so generous that the cohesion of the audience is threatened. Large seats, popular in cinemas, are not appropriate because in theatre it is important to relate to fellow audience members as well as to the actors on stage. One way of doing this is to be aware of other people's presence by sharing an armrest or sitting close on a bench, or seeing them in the peripheral vision.

There are significant cultural and regional sensitivities. Each country has its preferred seat width relating to the anthropometric data of its population. Today, some historic theatres are reconfigured so that, in a given floor area, they seat about half the capacity of the original theatre when built. This is not just because people have grown, but more that they require a certain level of personal space, and safety, compared to the crowds who attended variety and music halls a century ago.

Seat module

Auditorium seating falls into three broad categories: benches (with and without backs), fixed seats and tip-up seats. Each of these can be with or without arms.

The requirements outlined above define the minimum. It is not uncommon to find 500mm module tip-up seats with arms in the commercial theatres. However, subtle distinctions exist between what audiences will accept in a historic theatre and what is expected in a new cultural facility. As noted, a good practice module for preliminary planning is a 550mm seat with a row depth of 900mm.

It is important to establish the seat module early in the design process, taking account of the need to balance individual comfort with the imperatives of keeping the audience compact to retain theatrical intimacy.

Seatway

The seatway is the unobstructed distance between two rows of seats, with the seat in its closed position if a tip-up type. The table on p. 74 outlines how the width of the required seatway rises as the number of seats in the row increases. The clear seatway is primarily focused on means of escape but is equally important in terms of access. The longer the row the more people will have to pass one another within the row and the wider the seatway the easier this is. A seatway of 500mm clear, normally associated with continental seating, allows audience members to pass by without needing seated members to rise.

Seat design has evolved rapidly. Greater comfort can now be achieved in more compact seats, with flatter (less heavily profiled) backs. This can radically alter the dimension when closed, enhancing the seatway and sense of leg room. Such seats are particularly useful when reseating existing tiers.

Extended row length

The term continental seating is used in the UK for longer seating rows (28 seats plus). In the longer rows, the seatway is set at 500mm, with the limiting factor for the number of seats defined by the travel distance to a place of safety. Consideration also needs to be given to the width of side aisles due to the greater concentration of people using each aisle.

Longer rows have pros and cons. None of the best viewing positions are lost by having a central aisle and, for the actor, the audience is undivided. As row depths need to be wider, audiences have increased leg room. While seats are gained where there would have been aisles, some are lost due to wider row spacing. Continental seating is therefore not necessarily a method for achieving more seats. However, hybrid solutions mixing longer rows at the front of the stalls with traditional seating arrangements behind can be very helpful in creating a strong sense of focus.

Means of escape

Individual regions will have their own regulatory requirements. UK guidance on the distance from a seat to a place of safety for means of escape is set out in BS 9999. A maximum travel distance of 15m in one direction is permissible, with 32m as a limit when escape is possible in two directions (of which only 15m can be in any one direction).

A minimum of two escape routes is required for an audience or tier of up to 600, and three routes minimum for above this figure. The escape route needs to lead either directly to a final exit or via a protected route/ space. Escapes should be equally distributed around the edge of the room, ensuring that audience members can turn their backs on a fire.

The width of escape routes is dictated by the numbers of people exiting and as outlined in documents such as BS 9999. The clear width is measured at its minimum point – which is often a door set, not the corridor. Within the auditorium, circulation should be designed to ensure the smooth flow of people, particularly if radial and traverse aisles intersect. Aisles should remain a constant width, with seat edges in line; however, they may get wider in the direction of escape so long as they do not narrow upon leaving the space. (See also subsection 2.7 – Fire safety.)

Balcony/tier front design

The height of the balcony front guarding in front of fixed seating should be a minimum of 790mm from the floor of the first row. This can be reduced to 750mm if the top profile has a minimum width of 230mm.

The detailed design of the balcony front needs to take account of a number of factors. The top element is often referred to as a 'rester rail'. This is a misnomer, as the last thing the rail should be used for is resting on or placing items such as programmes or drinks. Canting the top profile back towards the seat discourages this activity and reduces likelihood of items falling onto the audience below. The higher, narrower guarding, say a 50mm diameter rail, pulled as close to the seated audience member as the seatway will allow, can negate the need to lean forward. Additional toe space should also be allowed for in the front row.

A full guard rail must be provided at the end of a stepped gangway, for the full width of the gangway. This must be 1100mm high. Consideration needs to be given to the impact of such rails on lateral sightlines.

4.5 Sightlines

Context

Aiming to give members of an audience a good view of the performance is an obvious starting point in the design of an auditorium. That said, sightline imperatives have evolved over time so it is therefore important to understand what is meant by 'good' sightlines as part of the overall qualitative experience.

Throughout the seventeenth, eighteenth and nineteenth centuries attending a theatrical performance was, for many, as much about being seen, as seeing. The side boxes of the proscenium theatres of the period offered a relatively inferior view of the stage. However, they enabled ample opportunity for public display. To some degree, the restricted view was offset by the proximity to performers delivering major speeches and arias downstage – in a time before amplification.

The development of sophisticated cantilevered structures in the late nineteenth century brought new opportunities to auditorium design. Column-free tiers reduced restricted lateral sightlines. Creating spaces for ever larger audiences, specialist theatre architects of the day responded by pushing sightline design to the limits. Auditorium tiers sometimes stacked four high, developed by highly complex three-dimensional geometries.

With the advent of the modern movement in architecture and design in the early twentieth century, technological advancement was mirrored with rapidly changing social conditions. Auditorium design broke away from the highly segregated and hierarchical forms of earlier centuries. In attempting to democratise the auditorium, sightlines became a key tool.

The viewing criteria up to the early part of the twentieth century were dictated by the sightlines required to see a performer standing on the stage. Auditoria were generally designed for a single use. A contemporary auditorium, by comparison, may host an opera one night, drama the next and dance the following evening. Audiences' expectations for viewing opera are less demanding than say dance, where it is important to see a dancer's feet on the setting line on the stage floor – and all four corners of the stage space. In some auditoria variations in format may radically shift the focus, while the resurgence in circus and experiential performance has increased the importance of the upward sightline.

The sightline criteria need to be established by the auditorium designer, defining how much of the stage floor, back and sides of the acting area must be seen. From this starting point it is possible to develop the geometrical volume within which the required number of seats can be contained. The seating rakes, disposition of audience members and integration of tiers or balconies are all determined by acceptable visual limits and the lateral and vertical parameters for viewing the performance. The ultimate form of an auditorium is therefore a blend of anthropomorphic limitations, structural possibilities and performance imperatives.

The methodology set out below is a guide through the basic geometrical sightline criteria. It should provide a robust basis upon which to establish an initial design. 3D modelling and interactive modelling of sightlines can then explore more complex sightline issues and be invaluable in helping to explain and guide client bodies through the development of the viewing criteria.

Establishing the stalls rake

To develop the vertical, downward sightline a number of key points need to be established.

P: point of sight
This is the lowest point to be clearly visible on the stage or acting area. Its position can vary considerably both vertically and horizontally. The stage can be a flat floor, a riser can vary from 300mm to 1100mm, Point P can be located on the leading edge or on the setting line (approx 1.0m back from the proscenium). Point P can also be set at the level of the stage – or to an agreed elevation above this.

Point P may also have to take account of a variable stage edge – forestage. If there is an orchestra pit Point P may be deemed to be the head of the conductor.

For dance, audiences need to see the performers' feet. Point P is therefore set at the stage floor – and normally on the setting line. Added to the restrictions on lateral sightlines this factor contributes to giving dance the most onerous sightline criteria. For drama, P can be raised up to around +300mm from the stage datum, but this needs to be evaluated in the context of the scale of the space and size of the stage riser.

For classical music performance it is not uncommon to raise Point P to 450mm above the platform (the musician's knee), as partially masking other musicians is not normally such an issue. Again, the height of the platform also has a bearing on setting this level.

The higher Point P is set, the more gentle the incline of the seating rake can be.

It is critical that the criteria for determining the position of Point P are clearly defined by the auditorium designer and clearly understood by the user.

HD: horizontal distance
This is horizontal linear distance between the eye positions of the audience members in consecutive rows. The dimension normally equates to the row dimensions.

O: offset
While HD is determined by the back-to-back dimensions of the individual rows, it does not normally coincide with the tread or risers. In reality the degree of offset from the riser is determined by the design of the seat, how upright it is and the amount it oversails the structural riser. For early planning, 100mm offset allows for an assumption of the ultimate eye position in relation to the riser.

When a seat is selected, the detail ergonomics should be refined – particularly in regard to tier front geometries.

EH: average eye height
A theoretical working height of 1120mm is normally assumed. The final eye position ultimately depends on the seat design.

TH: top of head
Distance taken from the centre line of eye to the top of the head – normally 100mm for the basis of the sightline calculation. Enhanced allowances can be made up to 125mm. However, it is normally argued that an angled, between-heads view combined with 100mm provides a good basis.

D: distance front row eye position to Point P
The closer this distance the steeper the resulting rake will be.

Using the above guidance, working from Point P back through the auditorium establishes the theoretical rake of the stalls seating. This gives a parabolic curve to the seating profile, getting steeper as the distance from Point P increases. Each member of the audience achieves a similar viewing condition.

While licensing authorities do allow parabolic floor profiles with an incremental increase in the risers in stepped aisles (as the increase is generally imperceptible) larger rakes are often reduced to a series of angled sections.

For theatrical formats and dance use, the theoretical rake as described above can lead to a fairly steep profile. While acceptable in smaller scale and single-level spaces this can be problematic in larger venues, with bigger capacities, and where upper tiers of seating are introduced.

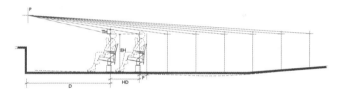

4.5.1 Vertical sightline with high-level viewing point (P)

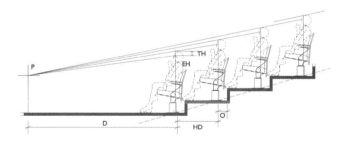

4.5.2 Vertical sightline with low-level viewing point (P)

The view between heads

To reduce the degree of rake in the stalls seating, an assumption can be made that point P is seen between heads. Sightlines on this basis can be developed graphically or with an assumption of distance between the eyeline and the top of the head reduced to 65mm.

When working with between-heads sightline criteria, it should be on a basis that the seating is set in a staggered/offset arrangement. This is normally established on the auditorium centre line. As the rows extend to the side, particularly in curved auditoria, seats invariably come into line again; however audiences to the side of the auditorium are more likely to be looking diagonally towards the stage.

Refining the sightline in this manner illustrates the balancing of requirements necessary in the development of larger auditoria. Here visual and aural imperatives have to be considered alongside the degree of elevation of the audience in relation to the stage (from the actor's point of view) and average height and volume. Reduction in the height of the rake at lower levels leaves more room to accommodate upper balconies.

4.5.3 Sketch showing the view of the stage between heads

Performers' perspective

In small auditoria, particularly where a limited number of rows encircle or embrace the stage, a steeper rake can be helpful in offering both a sense of enclosure and good sightlines. This should be balanced with the subjective view that it is preferable for a performer to have half the audience below their standing eyeline.

Upper tiers

The criteria for upper seating levels are fundamentally the same as in the stalls - with seated members needing to see the full three-dimensional performance. Allied to the vertical downward sightline is the upper sightline, which, for example, allows the rear row of the stalls to have an uninterrupted view of the top of the proscenium.

P2: point of sight
As with position P, Point P2 is the lowest and nearest point that a balcony audience member needs to be able to see. This can be the same as the position for the stalls audience – on the leading edge of the stage or the setting line. It can also be different to the stalls, hence the suffix, and be out into the auditorium for a forestage extension, or a view of the conductor in a pit, or within the stalls seating enabling upper levels to be aware of other audience members (contributing to a sense of audience cohesion).

DP: depth of the stage
This is the working depth of the stage or normal acting area.

HP: clear visible height
This is the clear height to be visible at the back wall of the stage or back of the performance area. This requirement can vary – for example, in opera to see Tosca on the battlements, for music spaces to see a raised area of choir, or for dance to see a lift at the back of the stage. This height is a subjective one and needs to be developed with the client.

PH: proscenium height
This is the height of the proscenium opening or the upper defined limit in an open stage space. Note: the panel above the proscenium may be used to provide surtitles.

When working within the constraints of a historic space, visibility of the proscenium head can be reviewed as part of a qualitative assessment of sightlines. Upper sightlines are normally dictated by the position of the overhang –and vice versa.

BF: balcony front height
For the sake of calculation 790mm should be assumed, but take cognisance of any requirements for raised 1100mm rails at aisle intersections.

D: Distance to front row
Distance from Point P2 to the front row.

Sightlines across lateral gangways
Lateral gangways can be problematic for sightlines. Generally ensure vertical rake continues uninterrupted, despite the wider width of the gangway aisle.

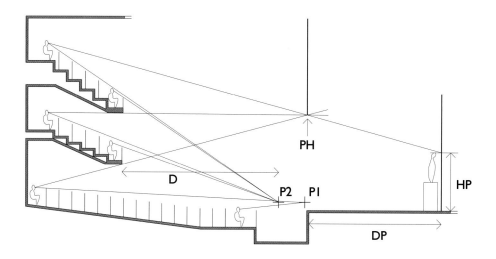

4.5.4 Vertical sightline diagram

Horizontal sightlines

Restrictions on horizontal sightlines only need to be considered in proscenium theatres, end stage spaces, and platforms for classical music. Given a particular performance area, defined by a proscenium opening, sightline requirements limit the width of the seating block. The view of the proscenium opening cannot be too oblique or members of the audience will lose too much of the stage from view.

When considering horizontal or lateral sightlines, consideration should be given to reduced proscenium widths, particularly associated with the compact scale of touring productions. Audiences, in unrestricted view seats, should be able to see at least two-thirds of the back wall of the acting area, unless the space is primarily for dance where all four corners of the performance area need to be clearly visible.

Side seats

Side seats can be problematic in the early stages of a design – with the term 'restricted view' ringing alarm bells for many. While the seats may offer an oblique view of the action (depending upon the format) it should always be remembered that they offer proximity to the performance, enhance theatrical intimacy, contribute to a sense of cohesion and animate the side walls. The amount of side seats needs to be balanced as part of the overall provision. Simple 3D modelling can be very helpful in communicating the viewing restrictions of these positions.

4.6 Acoustic considerations

Auditorium form and volume

The task of the acoustician is to ensure that the construction, geometry and finish of an auditorium is such that every member of the audience hears the performance clearly without colouration and that performers can hear each other well to enable them to play as an ensemble. Many factors contribute. Close to the stage, the listener hears mostly direct sound, which dominates the weaker late reflections from the room surfaces. Further from the stage, listeners hear a combination of direct sound and reflected sound arriving as a series of discrete reflections, spaced in time. The reflected sound should arrive in an ordered way, maintaining the realism of the direct sound, reinforcing it and not containing strong long-delayed reflections or echoes, which affect its quality.

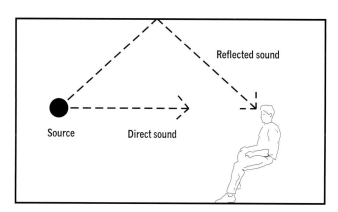

4.6.1

The volume of any room has a direct relationship to its reverberation time and it is therefore important to establish the correct volume for a particular performance type, or range of types, at an early stage. For example, see Figure 4.6.2.

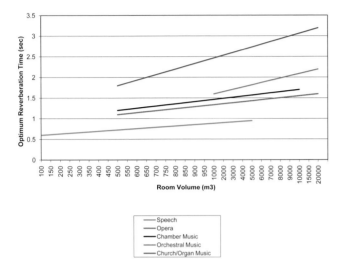

4.6.2 Chart showing volumes and reverberation times

Speech

For speech, the auditorium volume can be fairly low, around 5m³/per person. The early to late energy ratio should be high – late energy arriving beyond 100m at a high level affects intelligibility. Reverberation times should be appropriate to the use, around one second at mid-frequencies. In theatres, seating should be as close as possible to the stage, favouring a fan-shaped seating plan and multiple balconies. Good sightlines generally make for good acoustics as what the eye can see the ear can also hear. Theatres for unamplified speech work well up to around 1,000 seats but beyond this the skills of the acoustician are taxed.

Music

For music, the early to late energy ratio must be lower. Clarity is less significant and reverberance and envelopment are more important. To provide this, the reverberation time should be close to 2.0 seconds, with a rise in the bass. This means a volume of around 10m³/person or more. The shoebox form, often a double cube, was used in many eighteenth-century concert halls and is still favoured by many acousticians. It guarantees high ratios of lateral energy, so important to instrument

localisation and the listening experience. Audience size is optimum up to around 1,800 seats, after which acoustic excellence becomes more difficult to achieve. Overhead reflectors with variable height can be used to provide early reflections to the audience and to improve communications between musicians.

Other auditorium forms have been and are successfully used, most significantly the vineyard layout, used by Hans Scharoun at the Berlin Philarmonie, completed in 1963. Here, the end stage format is subverted, with the orchestra placed in the centre and the audience in terraces with connecting walls to enhance lateral reflections. This provides a different experience acoustically and spatially and was probably informed by developments in the design of open stage theatres. In a music room the sound should be enveloping, unlike a speech acoustic, which is directional, to ensure high intelligibility.

Orchestral balance is important within and between orchestral sections and sufficient diffusion or scattering should be applied to room surfaces to control the middle- and high-frequency response of the hall. Conditions on stage should ensure good communications between musicians and the conductor.

Developments in acoustic design

Until the middle of the last century, auditorium design evolved through experimentation and imitation. There were some spectacular failures. After this, acoustic scale models were built with sound absorption and sound sources scaled to around 1:20. As a result acoustic prediction and guarantees of excellence began to improve. Physical scale-modelling is still used today but more recently, with the advent of low-cost processing, computers have been used to predict performance using acoustic-modelling software. This is an extremely powerful and accurate tool, but its success depends on acousticians having an understanding of the acoustic parameters that they know will ensure excellence. After decades of research, listening and consultation with conductors, these parameters are now generally well understood.

Multi-purpose spaces

Many spaces can be used, with some success, for a range of purposes requiring different acoustic conditions. However, these tend to be smaller spaces, with a chamber music or opera acoustic, where staging and curtains can be used to reduce the reverberation time for speech. Above 200 seats or so, significant measures have to be taken to ensure a good acoustic for speech or music and each measure takes something away from an ideal acoustic for one or the other, as conflicts of geometry will always limit their effectiveness. In some communities, however, economics have dictated the demand for multi-purpose spaces, particularly those suitable for both amplified and unamplified music, and many such auditoria have been built.

Variable acoustics

To vary an acoustic, the room volume and/or the amount of absorption must be varied. A range of measures have been used, which include:

- Concert halls with large reverberation chambers to increase reverberation times beyond 3 seconds
- Concert halls with acoustic panels and curtains to vary reverberation time
- Concert halls with movable ceilings.

The full range of variability between a theatre and concert hall acoustic is, however, often difficult to achieve.

Improving existing rooms

This is a large and growing area of endeavour for acousticians. Projects include refurbishment of eighteenth- and nineteenth-century theatres and the remodelling of existing school halls, town halls and former industrial buildings. The need for change is often a result of the need to renew mechanical and electrical services or a desire to cater for a wider range of performance types. Increases in urban noise levels also mean that building envelopes need to be upgraded to exclude external noise. If the volume of the space is right, then much can be done to improve existing acoustics. Rooms are measured acoustically, compared with the achievable changes and aspirations of the user, and then modified accordingly. There have been many successes.

Electronic architecture

Acousticians must create spaces for performers and audiences which are fit for their purpose, whether it is for public speaking, drama, musical or lyric theatre,

or spaces for music. It was realised early on that spaces that worked well for speech, with volumes of around 3m³ to 6m³ per person, were not good for musical performance. Speech needs a 'dry' acoustic, that is, one which is not reverberant, allowing each speech syllable to be heard separately.

Amplified music works well in theatres – the performance acoustic can be artificially set up within the sound system and imposed on the space. Orchestral music performed in such spaces however feels lifeless. There is poor communication between performers and between musicians and audience, since direct sound predominates.

Other parameters are now known to be important and relate to the way, and from which direction, reflected sound arrives at the listener. Since the 1950s, when manipulation of sound on a large scale using electronics became possible, acousticians have considered imposing acoustic conditions on theatres and halls to give more flexibility to their use and to correct acoustic faults. Experiments were carried out in Europe and in America. In the 1950s, the Royal Festival Hall in London was fitted with an early analogue 'Assisted Resonance' system to increase reverberance.

As systems became more sophisticated, other acoustic features were added, such as early and late reflection sequences and lateral energy. Systems have evolved from electromechanical to analogue to digital. The latest systems are extremely stable and are preset from a small control panel with about five settings. These systems, described as 'Electronic Architecture' or EA systems, work extremely well, altering the reverberation time and reflection sequence of a space to simulate a range of geometries and acoustic environments. They create strong lateral reflections, which are important in giving a sense of envelopment. Each system consists of an array of high-quality microphones connected to a large processor. This processor adds early and late delays, reverberation and lateral information, distributed by a number of small wall- and ceiling-mounted loudspeakers. They can be set over a range of values to suit different types of music.

In use, one is not aware of the system working, although the room acoustic is clearly altered. Properly tuned, the system will merge imperceptibly with the natural acoustic of a theatre. The installation of EA systems can extend the range of use considerably and give excellent listening conditions in all seats for chamber and orchestral concerts and all types of acoustic music performance.

4.7 Lighting and sound in the auditorium

Section 6 gives a detailed explanation of the requirements of the production lighting, sound and video equipment, how they are controlled and where they need to be positioned.

It is essential that the auditorium designer understands these requirements as they will have a significant impact on the design and detailing of the auditorium and must be considered at an early stage in the planning process. If appropriate, workable positions for rigging lighting and sound equipment are not considered within a design, theatre technicians will have to make their own adaptations. These can be unsightly.

Integration of technical equipment can be relatively straight forward in an open stage, or studio – where the technology is part of the aesthetic. The problems become slightly more complex within an aesthetic design that aims to conceal part of, or all, the production equipment. The summary below focuses on the proscenium format.

Equipment

Lighting requirements within the auditorium include boom boxes and slots, both of which are side lighting positions. The advance bar/ bridge, lighting bridges, tension wire grids, slips or side bridges, and follow spot platforms are all high-level lighting positions. Low-level front lighting is also often required and supported by circle fronts lighting bars, or bars located discretely under tiers. Rigging requirements for sound within the auditorium may include proscenium side booms, a central speaker cluster set above the proscenium and delay 'under balcony' speakers.

Control points

The control room (or rooms) for lighting and sound is ideally situated on the centre line and at the back of the auditorium. It should be an acoustically separate volume. The connecting window should be openable and non-reflective. The sightline should give clear visibility of the stage with the downward sightline taking account of seeing over the audience members seated immediately in front – and ideally not be interrupted by someone standing in the rear row. The upper sightline should give a clear view of the top of the proscenium. The success of this space for mixing live sound will depend on the particular auditorium design and programme. It is often necessary to provide an additional sound mixing position within the auditorium, particularly for touring shows. Some theatres integrate such positions as permanent installations. Access routes for heavy equipment and mobile kit need to be thought through to avoid damage to seating.

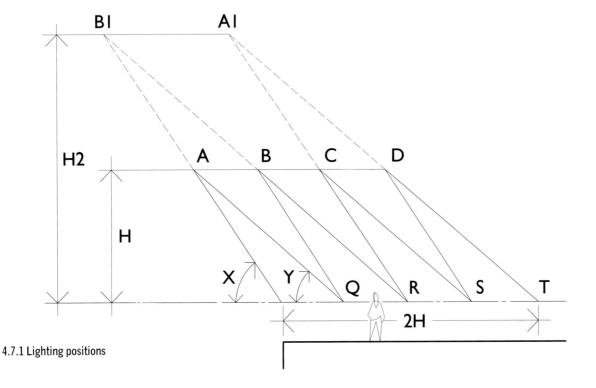

4.7.1 Lighting positions

Lighting bridges in a proscenium space

Stage lighting must provide the ability to light any part of the stage from a wide range of angles. Some positions are fundamental, outlined below, but there will be other production-specific requirements. As some stage lighting is required to the front of the stage, this is by necessity with the auditorium space.

Lighting the actor's face at around 45° above the horizontal is essential to avoid unflattering shadows, while a lower angle may cause unwanted shadows on the set. Spotlights are rarely directed straight at the actor and are more normally crossed. This means that setting positions out on a cross-section requires an angle in the order of 55° to achieve 45° when crossed.

The diagram sets out the basic geometry of required lighting positions. A luminaire at A will light the actor's face at 55° on the edge of the stage and 45°–50° when crossing. As the actor moves away from the edge of the stage, this angle will decrease. At Q it will only be 40° and 35° when crossing which is the absolute minimum. It is therefore necessary to have another luminaire at position B – which covers the area between Q and R.

This diagram illustrates the imperative of end-on performances. In the proscenium format positions A and B correspond to front of house lighting bridges – with C and D the numbers 1 and 2 spotbars. The diagram also indicates the impact of the elevation of the luminaires. Positions A1 and B1 give the same coverage as four positions set lower.

Lighting bridges require thoughtful integration into the ceiling design of an auditorium. While the basic diagram indicates a linear position, installation can be curved in form or treated as sculptural objects within their own right, as part of the room aesthetic – exemplified by the installation at the Glyndebourne Opera House in Sussex (Reference project: p. 228).

4.8 Ventilation and air handling

Introduction

In the United Kingdom, during the theatre-building boom of the Victorian and Edwardian eras, auditoria relied upon natural ventilation systems. Air was generally drawn in at low level and exhausted through the roof of the auditorium. Such systems were fairly erratic in operation. Centrally located seats received little air, while audience members at the sides were affected by draughts.

The introduction of regulatory requirements for fresh air supply made reliance on natural ventilation systems more complicated. By this time, mechanical systems had been developed which were easier to design, substantiate and more reliable.

The increased interest in sustainability, alongside refinements in how natural ventilation systems work, has led to this viewpoint being questioned. While considerable design challenges are set by the need to balance the large amounts of air needed with the attendant acoustic issues arising from the large openings required in the external building fabric, it is now perfectly feasible to ventilate a small auditorium by natural means in a temperate climate and in a quiet location. Venues such as the Auden Theatre in Holt, Norfolk, UK, and the Contact Theatre in Manchester, UK demonstrate the viability of the natural approach.

Larger projects in urban areas, on congested and noisy sites, or in more demanding climatic conditions, still remain reliant on mechanical ventilation. However, when these systems are designed to work with natural air movement patterns and are combined with heat recovery, they can become far more environmentally efficient and cost-effective to operate.

Theatre ventilation via wind towers

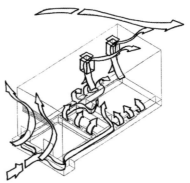

Natural ventilation schematic

4.8.1 Diagram: Auden ventilation strategy

Auden Theatre in Norfolk, UK. The natural ventilation strategy draws cool air into the building at low level, as the air is warmed it rises within the auditorium volume and is exhausted at high level through wind towers, assisted by the prevailing winds.

Internal design criteria

Statutory regulations set high targets for air changes within the auditorium - with a fresh air input normally 8 litres per second per person. Acoustic criteria mean these large volumes of air need to be delivered at low velocity. This necessitates that supply and extract ducts have large cross-sectional areas. Threading these elements through an existing building, or planning into a new one, can be complex.

In temperate climates, deciding between a full air conditioning system or a more simple heating and ventilation strategy can be marginal. In more extreme climates full air conditioning is a necessity.

Acceptable comfort conditions for audiences are those that maintain suitable levels of temperature, humidity and air velocity, avoiding the extremes of stuffiness (stagnation) and draughts (too much air movement).

Acceptable internal air temperatures depend on local climatic conditions. People living in warmer climates are able to accept higher internal temperatures. In the UK, an internal design temperature of 22°C, with a relative humidity (RH) of 50 per cent, would be regarded as normal while in tropical climates audiences might find 35°C and 80 per cent RH acceptable. Similar variations apply in cooler climates and during winter periods.

Natural ventilation

The inherent logic of a natural ventilation strategy is that it makes use of natural forces. Rising warm air has the potential to draw in cooler air from outside a building by what is termed the stack effect. While external wind pressures can override this internal effect, there are simple mechanisms for adjusting and compensating.

There is an undeniable logic in allowing air to move in the manner natural laws dictate, rather than expending energy to make it move in contrary directions. Such strategies reduce the reliance on heavy mechanical plant, assist in energy conservation and reduce associated running costs.

Whether or not natural ventilation strategies are fully adopted there is an acknowledgement that working with natural forces, nudging and gently assisting as required, is the sensible way forward. The design of the building fabric can also assist. Heavy structures can attenuate heat gain and be used for night-time cooling.

Air conditioning and mechanical ventilation

Air conditioning as a terminology is often misused to describe simple mechanical ventilation systems and comfort cooling. In full air conditioning the air is conditioned, i.e. filtered to remove particles and odours while its moisture content and temperature are also adjusted. Such a system needs to be able to work in variable conditions of humidity and temperature. This can necessitate cooling air via refrigeration to lower humidity in warm sticky summers and then having to reheat it before reintroducing it into an auditorium. Conversely, low humidity in winter months may require air to be treated with humidifiers.

In hot weather, and warmer climates, it is the relative humidity that contributes significantly to audience discomfort. The body can tolerate higher temperatures and feel comfortable if its natural cooling mechanics are allowed to work but warm moist air does not allow perspiration to evaporate and so regulate comfort. In winter months and cooler climates, if warmed air is too dry discomfort can come in the form of sore throats and eyes. The method of tackling humidity (without recourse to removing all the moisture) is to increase the flow of air over the body – the cooling effect associated with sitting in a draught. This is the basis of auditoria mechanical ventilation systems.

Air distribution

In temperate conditions, heating is generally only required for warming up the auditorium prior to audience arrival. The imperative during a performance is the supply of clean cool air.

There are two primary models for air distribution. The first introduces cool air at high level which mixes with the room air to give, on average, a comfortable condition throughout the space. Extraction is generally at low level and located to promote good circulation throughout the space. The second provides the cooled air at low level, adjacent to the audience members. This cooled air is then drawn upward as it warms and is extracted at high level.

High-level supply

The cooled air is supplied through high-level diffusers. The air is supplied cooler than required by the audience as it absorbs heat from high-level lighting equipment and the rising heat generated by the audience itself. Air is exhausted, or returned, at low level under seating tiers

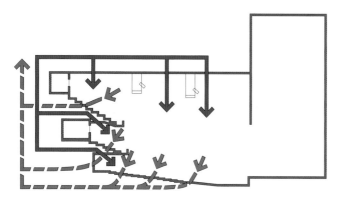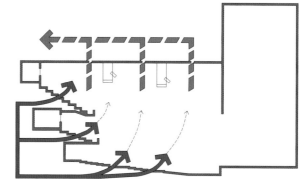

4.8.2 Diagrammatic illustrations of auditorium with high- (left) and low- (right) level supply strategies

or seats. High-level supply can be from the ceiling alone or combined with delivery at the back of seating tiers in multi-level spaces.

Auditoria are large-volume spaces with high ceilings. Warm air rises, through the stack effect, creating stratification. Supplying air at high level means that the higher temperatures are adjacent to the point of delivery and the effect on the incoming air needs to be considered as it can increase the demands placed on mechanical plant.

In top-down systems, balancing air velocity with low noise levels can result in insufficient air distribution into parts of the auditorium. Therefore the return air system needs to draw the air downward to avoid uneven distribution. This is rarely effective. Jet-type diffusers, located at high level, can assist where a longer throw is required. Such systems give an increased sense of freshness as the air is being moved faster but the increased supply velocity has the inherent danger of raising noise levels.

A number of theatres, particularly those in London's West End, have mechanical ventilation with cooling introduced into buildings built around 1900 or earlier. In general these were the best that could be achieved at the time they were installed. A number of the buildings have both the supply and the extract at high level, usually via the central domed ceiling above the chandelier. Such systems can suffer from short-circuiting and 'dead spots' where the air distribution is not effective.

Low-level supply

This is now a preferred air distribution method. With this system, known as 'displacement', the air is supplied to low level, at around 20°C under the seats, in the riser or seat base. The air supplied at low velocity and at a temperature of only 2°C below the design temperature picks up heat from the audience so that a comfortable

temperature is achieved in the seating zone. Cooled air is thus supplied directly where it is required – adjacent to the audience. Air velocities need to be low to achieve comfort with no draughts, reducing supply air noise problems. Exhaust or return air is then extracted at high level. Such a ventilation system works with the natural stack effect of warm air rising.

Both basic delivery methods require extensive ductwork outside the auditorium volume to move air around the building. Low-level supply is usually localised to seating and best achieved by a plenum chamber. Integration of the plenum in stalls and tiers has spatial and cost implications.

Pre-cooling and pre-heating

The use of a pre-cooling strategy can assist in reducing plant size. As auditoria are not in constant use, there is an opportunity to pre-cool the body of air within the space prior to audience arrival. The air is cooled several degrees below the design temperature. The air temperature then gradually rises as the audience arrives and the performance takes place. Pre-cooling time is normally about an hour, although some theatres have facilities to provide larger amounts of cooler air during intervals to restart the process.

Pre-heating works in a similar way in the winter months. The auditorium is pre-warmed before the audience arrives. The heat given off by the audience, lighting and equipment then offsets the fabric and ventilation heat loss, allowing the mechanical plant to minimise requirements by only heating the fresh air.

Air distribution to the stage

Air distribution on stage is notoriously difficult, particularly in proscenium theatres, where the large volume of the flytower is often exposed to the external elements. Also it has to assume that scenery may be stacked against any available wall space.

Heating on stage is generally provided at low level by recessed wall-mounted radiators or convectors. Radiant panel heaters may also be considered. These could be located at high level in the wings and under the fly galleries. The use of air distribution systems for heating or cooling is problematic as scenery is a variable and unknown quantity – often lightweight and easily disturbed by relatively gentle air movement.

The stage floor plays a crucial role in performance. Supply grills or ducting is therefore not practicable on stage. Equally when there is a flytower, low-level extract is unlikely to be able to compete with the considerable stack effect occurring in the flytower. Provision for return air should be made. This is best achieved at high level, under the loading gallery, tying up with exhaust air taken from the top of the flytower, together with any exhaust air from auditorium lighting bridges.

In winter conditions, and cooler climates, provision should be made to adequately heat the stage volume to avoid a column of cold air collecting in the flytower and flooding over the stalls audience as an icy blast when the curtain is raised. Allied to this is the need to prevent the stage curtain from billowing out due to the stack effect in the flytower. This is caused by the temperature differential between the stage and auditorium and good air flow and temperature distribution can greatly assist in balancing this.

Other areas

There are a range of spaces coupled to the auditorium which require consideration within the ventilation strategy. The pit is open but a tightly packed orchestra in a closely confined area needs a fresh air supply. This should be a separate system.

Control rooms may be open (during technical rehearsals or in a performance) or closed off during a performance. They should be provided with an independent supply and extract system to avoid any cross-talk issues within the auditorium volume. Removal of heat build-up in other technical spaces, dimmer rooms, etc. also needs be considered.

Noise Levels

The target NR (Noise Rating) for theatre use should be NR 20, unless specifically required to be lower by the acoustic consultant. NR 25 can sometimes be acceptable with NR 30 as an absolute maximum.

Achieving an NR 20 level is onerous. It means that noise levels generated by mechanical plant cannot exceed NR 15, when the noise from adjacent areas or the external environment is taken into account. This can have a critical bearing on the basic planning of a building. It necessitates locating plant away from the auditorium or within an independent structure and the installation of large attenuators in the ductwork systems.

4.9 Orchestra pit

Pit size and modes of use

An orchestra pit for a large opera house may need to accommodate up to 120 musicians. Pits in larger historic theatres may accommodate in the order of 60–70 players, while other auditoria, for example, those designed for musical theatre or contemporary dance, may accommodate no more than 10–12 people. As general guidance, an allowance of $1.1m^2$ should be made for musicians in open space; $1.5m^2$ for those under the overhang; $5.0m^2$ for a piano; and around $6.0m^2$ for the timpani.

To avoid extending the divide between stage and audience the pit can be partly under the stage. This is not normally an acoustic disadvantage, as it helps to balance the orchestral sound with that of the vocalists on the stage above. However, consideration needs to be given to the acoustic environment for the musicians and 'control of noise at work' regulations.

In an opera house the pit is a fixed feature. In other theatres, designed perhaps mainly for drama use, a permanent pit will act as a barrier that can damage the actor-to-audience relationship so there needs to be some adaptability in the pit zone. The area forward of the fixed stage edge defines the adaptable area. In most such pits there are three key modes of operation:

1 Orchestra pit
2 Extended stalls
3 Forestage extension.

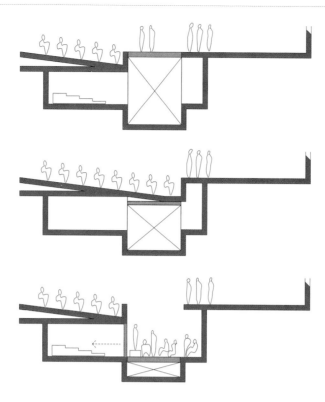

4.9.1 Diagram illustrating the primary orchestra elevator positions

Pit operation

How this adaptability is achieved depends on the frequency of changeover from one configuration to another and on available funding. The change can be effected manually with panels installed over a demountable framework. This involves labour and time. Alternatively mechanical systems in the form of a pit lift, or lifts, can be used. Even in fairly modest projects the initial investment in this piece of stage engineering can have a huge benefit in the flexibility and long-term sustainability of a venue. A pit elevator can also be useful in moving large and heavy items, such as pianos, between stage and basement/orchestra pit levels.

A single lift can be installed to create the three basic configurations noted. In larger pits, split lifts offer refinements in the size of pit or forestage and the degree of extra seating in an extended stalls area.

When the pit is in position a handrail, or pit rail, is required in front of the audience. This will need to retain the appropriate seatway and leg room. It also needs to conform to the regulatory requirements in terms of loading and height. The rail needs to be demountable, usually achieved by dropping uprights into sockets along the pit edge.

Methods of pit lift operation include spiral lifts, screw jacks and hydraulic cylinders. Where deep construction is not feasible, a scissor lift mechanism is an alternative, although these are generally regarded as less rigid and more sensitive in operation. Side guides are generally needed. Any guide or elements which intrude into the pit itself need to be detailed so as to not impinge on functionality of the pit.

Detailed design

As with any area of adaptability, the geometrical configuration is only one aspect of the design. The front edge of the stage, the pit walls and orchestra pit rail zone all need to be carefully thought through for each of the key positions. Electrical points, microphone outlets and traps need to be considered. Details need to be robust and durable, particularly on the audience side, where there may be interfaces with finer finishes.

Safety

The pit operation diagrams indicate the potential health and safety issues related to the operation of these large mechanical units. The requirement for safe edges, enclosing blinds, warning bells and dual-operating controls is all part of the theatre equipment consultant's area of expertise.

Where fire separation between auditorium and stage is required the pit is deemed to be a part of the auditorium. Continuity of fire separation means that the rear wall of the pit and the overhang need to be fire resistant. Any opening between the stage and auditorium, outside of the proscenium with its safety curtain, needs to have protected lobby entrances with self-closing doors. This includes the pit access below stage level.

Smaller pit types

While the traditional pit described above is the primary form, some smaller studio spaces have a pit that is more akin to a shallow recess in the floor zone. Usually designed to accommodate small numbers, the pit recess needs to be low enough for seated musicians not to interfere with the view of the acting area. Such pits are often accessed from the stage or audience side, and form part of an adaptable pit/forestage zone.

4.10 Adaptability, flexibility and variable formats

As performance typologies evolved, auditoria became dedicated to single functions: opera house, musical theatre, concert hall, drama theatre, etc., but it has become less common in more recent times to find spaces that are designed exclusively for a single purpose. Adaptability, to a lesser or greater extent, is often inherent in the brief for a new performing arts venue, as the costs associated with creating these highly serviced and technically sophisticated facilities necessitate that they host a wider range of performances. Even in larger arts complexes with complementary auditoria supporting different performance types and scales of event, each auditorium is likely to have its set of adaptable features. Adaptability can range from modest flexibility in one particular area to wholesale reconfiguration of the space. The usual areas where some form of adaptability is introduced are:

- Orchestra pit and forestage zone
- Variable audience capacity
- Adjustable proscenium width and height
- Adjustable acoustics
- Format change and variable formats.

Orchestra pit and forestage

The orchestra pit and forestage is perhaps the most common area of adaptability in auditoria, and one of the most straightforward to achieve. It is associated with proscenium and end stage formats.

Variable audience capacity

Aesthetic or management reasons may require the scale of a space to be reduced for particular productions. At its simplest, this can involve closing off an upper tier, or part of a tier, through the use of drapes, screens or lighting. More complex solutions can require the movement of large-scale architectural elements, such as the mobile ceiling in the Milton Keynes Theatre (Reference project: p. 252), fully closing off the upper tier. Any variable capacity arrangement needs to be planned in advance, particularly with regard to entrance points.

Adjustable proscenium

To accommodate smaller scale productions some variability in the proscenium width and height may be required. These can be integral installations or production-specific – and are normally located behind the house curtains. Tormentors and teasers or a show portal can also be used as a way of varying the proscenium opening. In developing an adjustable proscenium it is important to consider the lateral sightline constraints of the smallest format.

Adjustable acoustics

This kind of adaptability is required in spaces that change between music and drama use. For the performance of symphonic music in a natural acoustic setting the volume requirement for the space is in the order of 10m³ per seat. This requirement drops for musical theatre, amplified music spaces and drama. Changes between music and drama also impact on the degree of diffusion, reflection and absorption required, as well as changes in ambience.

Such adaptability is relatively easy to achieve at the smaller scale of around 300 seats. The deployment of wool serge drapes can be highly effective in reducing reverberation time and changing the aesthetic tone of the interior. At large scale (again illustrated at the Milton Keynes Theatre) the mobile ceiling element can radically adjust the physical volume of the space to suit classical music, lyric theatre or drama. Sadler's Wells Theatre (London, UK) adjusts its reverberation time through the use of concealed absorbent banners.

In spaces designed for drama or where the volume cannot be readily adapted to create the acoustic space required for music assisted resonance systems can be integrated to create a longer reverberation time. (See subsection 4.6.)

Format change and variable formats

A subtle distiction exists between spaces that convert from one format to another – a format change – and spaces that are designed to facilitate multiple performance formats. Variability of format is more readily achieved in smaller scale spaces. A more limited and prescribed format changeover is normally associated with larger venues where, for example, it could involve a transition from lyric theatre mode to classical music presentation.

Hierarchy

The key to creating a successful adaptable auditorium is to develop a clear hierarchy of use for the space. This hierarchy needs to articulate the qualitative and quantitative imperatives. This is probably best illustrated with a simple example:

An auditorium is to be built to host classical music concerts and popular entertainment. There are to be 12 classical concerts per year, with the remainder of the programme featuring events such as popular music and comedy.

On a *qualitative agenda* the demands of classical music performance, in a natural acoustic environment, is the most demanding use and would set the design agenda for the space. This would define the overall volume and geometry. This volume would then be adapted to host the other, more regular events. The compromise here is building more physical volume than is generally required.

On a *quantitative assessment* the space is designed around what it hosts most often. With this agenda the auditorium would have a fundamentally lower physical volume, dictated by what is necessary to support the most frequent use. Classical music would be then presented in a less satisfactory environment (as it is only an occasional use) – or an assisted resonance system could be used to enhance the room's acoustic response.

Each scenario presents a valid approach. A balance has to be struck between the qualitative and quantitative agendas. A commissioning body may decide, for example, that the cachet of a premier classical music facility is worth the cost and the compromise required in hosting the more regular uses. Weighing up such criteria is complex and requires detailed exploration by the consultant team in close collaboration with the client body and the business case adviser.

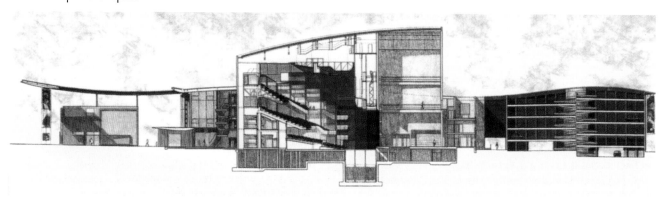

4.10.1 Milton Keynes Theatre, UK
Drawing of the theatre complex showing the interrelationship of the foyer and auditoria. Courtesy of Andrzej Blonski Architects

Key components of the adaptable auditorium

While many components (such as large mobile ceiling units) are highly bespoke, there are a number of 'standard component' types that help to make up the adaptable venue.

Retractable seating unit

This is a block of retractable raked seating, where each row folds back in on itself to create a compact linear unit when stored. The units can be manually or electronically operated and turnaround time can be a matter of minutes. They are ideal in spaces where flat-floor usage is required for alternative functions or as the basis of other formats.

Rostra

These are demountable components comprising frames, legs and floors units used to create raked seating or stages. Manufactured in steel or lightweight aluminium they are fairly labour-intensive and used where a fast turnaround is less critical and changes are infrequent.

Seating wagons

An alternative way of changing from a raked/stepped stalls to a flat floor is the use of seating wagons. These are raked or stepped floor units, complete with seating, made mobile by the use of castors or air castor technology. Wagons allow large seating blocks to be moved out of the auditorium, as a low-rise alternative to the retractable unit described above. When not deployed within the auditorium they are usually moved on the forestage elevator and stored below the front of stalls.

Mobile towers

These multi-level units can contain seating and are moved on floor tracks or air castor technology. These essentially architectural components are particularly useful in radically remodelling the end stage zone of a space transforming from concert to lyric theatre use.

Floor lifts

These are very similar in operation to the orchestra pit lifts described in subsection 4.9 above. They can be as simple as a complete stalls floor plate on screw jacks, lowered to facilitate a standing area for pop and rock events. Alternatively, they can be a modular panel section in the form of scissor lifts to create a variety of profiles within the floor zone. One of the most notable installations of this arrangement is Schaubuhne Theatre in Berlin.

4.10.2 Small scale retractable seating unit in operation: Winterflood Theatre, City of London School, UK
Photograph: Philip Vile

Tension wire grid

A tension wire grid (TWG) is a fine, open mesh working level, which allows production lighting to be rigged and focused with ease of access. The performance is then lit through the grid itself. Such grids come into their own when used to match the flexibility at stage and auditorium floor level and where safety, for example, in spaces for young people, is a priority. A tension wire grid is illustrated in Figure 5.6.1.

Large acoustic door sets

These allow the capability for interlinked spaces to be used either as two smaller venues, combined to make one larger one, or connected to allow epic scenic opportunities (where a studio is linked to a main stage area).

Banners, blinds, drapes and reversible panels

Changing the format or configuration often requires changes in the acoustic response of the room. Acoustic banners, blinds and drapes can be deployed at high level or on wall surfaces. Revisable panels are also very effective in changing the acoustic response and aesthetic character of a room.

Specific elements

In addition to the basic components described above, there are many specialist interpretations from mobile lighting gantries to individual row lifts which can stow away their own seating to create a flat floor. In practice an adaptable auditorium will contain a combination of the different components to suit the particular needs. It is worth noting that any substantial repositioning of the performance area has an impact on the technical rigging.

Aesthetic adaptability and ambience

Consideration should also be given to aesthetic adaptability. If the format change is from a thrust stage to an in-the-round scenario, then the adjustment in ambience is not too demanding. Where the change is from classical music venue to drama, the aesthetic implications are more demanding. Concerts take place in an illuminated room, drama in a darker and more subdued setting. Spaces that play host to both activities need to establish an aesthetic treatment that supports both.

A guiding rule should be to ensure that a space looks convincing and fully intended in each of its formats. This is perhaps exemplified by the main theatre at the Cerritos Center for the Performing Arts

in California, USA (Reference project: p. 202) and its predecessor the Derngate in Northampton, UK. Here the structural adaptability of the venue informs the overall architectural treatment of the space. The theatre is completely flexible, capable of being transformed into five possible configurations: arena, concert, lyric, drama and banquet (flat floor).

The theatre at Milton Keynes tackles the aesthetic problem in a different manner, creating a very precise close-fitting interior design for each of its modes of operation. An alternative strategy is the 'loose-fit' approach (both physically and aesthetically) taken by Northern Stage, in Newcastle, UK, where the industrial aesthetic of a dark timber box allows a variety of ad-hoc performance configurations.

4.10.3 Northern Stage
A strong sense of materials is used to achieve a neutral aesthetic at Northern Stage in Newcastle, UK.
Photograph: Philip Vile

4.11 Materials and finishes

Atmosphere

The primary concern of this section has been to explore the key physical, geometrical and technical parameters that underpin auditoria design. However, successful spaces are always a blend of both these practical imperatives and aesthetic factors.

Individual responses to auditoria can be highly subjective. Asking a director, designer or theatre practitioner to consider their preferred performance spaces can be a sobering experience for an auditorium designer. Often such lists will have a bias towards historic theatres and found spaces – such as those associated with Peter Brook. While new auditoria will also feature, the exercise does perhaps indicate the importance of ambience – and how difficult it can be to achieve.

Getting the balance right between the competing technical requirements and the more poetic aesthetic considerations can lift a space beyond the simple mechanics of engineering and architecture. These are the spaces that inspire and delight both practitioners and audiences; the ones that have that elusive and often indefinable quality – theatrical soul.

Themes and approaches

The architecture of the auditorium is critical in setting the scene and preparing the audience for the performance. The degree to which it remains apparent during the performance depends upon the type of space and the nature of the particular production.

Whatever the format of an auditorium, the materials, texture, colour and lighting are fundamental in defining its character. Different auditoria formats and types of performance require different architectural responses. An experimental studio, for example, has a very different aesthetic agenda from a large modern lyric theatre.

The open stage space requires neutrality. The performance takes place within a space shared with the audience and an overly dominant architectural treatment could conflict with the work on stage. Here architects and auditorium designers should resist the temptation to play set designer – these are spaces that should allow directors and designers the freedom to create their own worlds.

Over the past 20 years the starkness of the 'black box' aesthetic has gradually been eroded. A new approach, exemplified by venues such as the Donmar Warehouse and the Young Vic (Reference projects: pp. 220 and 278 respectively), exploits the tactile and sensory quality of the elements of their construction

4.11.1 Brooklyn Majestic
Peter Brook's re-found theatre space, the Brooklyn Majestic, demonstrates the aesthetic freedom temporary spaces can offer.
Photograph: Durston Saylor from the book 'Theatre Builders' by James Steel, published by Academy

4.11.2 The main auditorium of Wexford Opera
House, Ireland
Photograph: Courtesy of Keith Williams Architects

o define a studied neutrality. The architectural features of these spaces are both present and neutral, without the need for black paint.

This design approach has strong parallels with the Found Space movement. Found spaces allow directors and designers a unique freedom and the creative opportunity to work with the individual character and atmosphere of a particular building. While found spaces can be used many times over, some host only a single production. There is an appeal to both practitioners and audiences of the fleeting nature of their existence – see it while you can. Allied to this is the often unprecious, sometimes dilapidated, nature of the spaces themselves, which allows a subtle balance between the performance and the space. The character of the space informs the work, but its underlying neutrality does not dominate.

A similar design sensitivity can also be found in more traditional proscenium spaces such as the new opera houses in Wexford, Ireland and Norway's Den Norske (Reference projects: pp. 272 and 254 respectively), both of which have auditoria where the elements of construction are clearly on show. Both spaces combine a restricted palette of materials with crafted geometries – blending a sense of austere neutrality with opulence. These unfussy, but appropriately civic, spaces provide a highly sympathetic setting for the contemporary performances they house.

Learning from the past

The sheer exuberance of the late nineteenth- and early twentieth-century theatres interiors contributed hugely to generating a sense of excitement and anticipation.

Many were hedonistic palaces of entertainment, taking liberties with the established architectural mores of the day. Though tastes and performance styles have moved on, there is much to be learnt from the sheer verve and glamour of these buildings.

The Grand Canal Theatre in Dublin and the Lowry in Salford, a modern lyric theatre, illustrate the importance of the architectural elements in creating a sense of excitement and anticipation while the Egg, in Bath, combines a bold sense of colour and choice of material to 'mirror' the neighbouring historic theatre in ways which engage its young, contemporary, audience (Reference projects: pp. 244 and 222 respectively).

Collaborative process

Whenever possible, designers should work closely with a theatre company or an organisation's creative team on the design of an auditorium. Like a production, a successful auditorium is the result of the creativity and collaboration of a cast of many players.

SECTION EDITOR
Julian Middleton   Director of Arts Team, RHWL
                          Architects

CONTRIBUTORS
John Eames   Services engineer
Paul Gillieron   Acoustics
Anne Minors   Performance consultant

Section 5
The stage and stage machinery

Contents

5.1 Introduction

The two technical sections that follow are collaborations between theatre consultants, practising designers and technicians. The contributors have been selected for their particular expertise representing many years of practical experience and in-depth knowledge.

Proscenium houses are considered first, but open stage theatres that feature thrust or in-the-round stages are also discussed in some detail. Subsections 5.2 and 5.3 provide an overview of the subject, while subsequent subsections describe the equipment in detail.

Technological advance

Computer power has dramatically increased since the ABTT first published *Theatre Planning* in 1972, while the amount of space required to house it has diminished – the computer power that once filled a room can now be carried in the pocket.

If cars had improved at the same rate as personal computers since 1972, then a typical family car in 2009 would travel 43,000 times faster than a Formula One racing car and would travel 200 times around the world on one litre of petrol (Professor Chris Bishop, Royal Institute Lecture 2008). This degree of technological advance has been reflected in the quantum leap of theatre technologies over the same period.

Programmable control desks for stage engineering; stage lighting and AV; digital audio; motorised remote controlled luminaries; powered flying systems that can be plotted off-line in 3D: these have all led to changes in the way get-ins, production design and rehearsals, as well as performances, are now scheduled and conducted.

Technology and people

It is heartening that despite such advancement, technical theatre remains a very personal craft, as exhibited throughout this section. People are still more important than technology; and though theatres are essentially factories that create performances, they are factories with a particular atmosphere of creativity, collaboration, interaction and (mostly!) joy.

It is a common misconception that theatre technicians love 'toys'. Many theatre technicians would be happy to work with outmoded technology, if their building is a pleasure to work in and a source of pride and inspiration to its resident company. The right space in which to do technical theatre work is more immediately important than filling a space with the latest technology.

Section format

Each subsection in this section and the next follows a common format – a provocation from a theatre practitioner and a response from the section author.

Key spatial design issues are addressed along with safety and sustainability issues and each author has chanced a look into the future. The detail of this 2010 technical section will inevitably become outdated – but the principles of good design, safe operation and joy will remain valid.

...and finally

It should go without saying that the following subsections are no substitute for proper professional advice.

A set of guidelines followed do not alone a good theatre make.

5.2 Sets and scenery

The task for the design – whether it is to reach out into the audience, to suggest other worlds or barely to contain momentous events – is to inspire an audience which wants to be transported, debated with or enchanted.

Kate Burnett,
Society of British Theatre Designers

The role of the stage designer is to create a space in which a theatrical performance can take place. The stage setting is more than decoration or illustration; it is an integral part of a production. It presents a visual stimulus to the imagination as well as emphasising the mood of the play.

This subsection considers the facilities that set designers might hope to find in a theatre and what they might wish to avoid, as well as introducing some of the elements that are brought into play when working on the design.

Through discussion with the director, the designer will develop proposals, making sketches and rough models before producing working drawings and visual references to communicate the design to the workshops. The design may develop further through the rehearsal period and even while on stage.

Designing for a producing theatre

In many theatres the format of the stage and its relationship with the auditorium is predetermined. The building itself may only be modified within narrow limits so sets have to be tailored to fit onto whatever stage exists.

When designing for a new producing theatre, where the scenery will be designed specifically for that stage, there is greater scope for the architect to determine an unusual theatrical space in collaboration with the theatre user. For example, particular formats such as the thrust stages at the RSC in Stratford-upon-Avon and the Crucible Theatre in Sheffield, or the in-the-round space

5.2.1 Bunny Christie's model for After Miss Julie at the Donmar Warehouse, London, UK
Photograph: Peter Ruthven Hall

at the Manchester Royal Exchange Theatre, establish unique physical parameters for the designer (Reference projects: pp. 212, 216 and 214 respectively).

Theatres such as these do not readily accommodate touring product.

Touring scenery to receiving houses

Where a production is to be shown in a series of different venues, the designer might determine the spatial parameters by overlaying the footprint of each stage and the extreme sightlines onto a single composite drawing. This may result in a lowest-common denominator approach to the set, or perhaps, as with large-scale opera productions, the need to tour 'large' and 'small' versions of the same set.

Standardisation of touring houses – stage depth, width, height and space in the wings; position of suspension points; lighting positions and sightlines – would help immensely. Although this is not readily achievable in the UK given the wide range of theatre stock still in use, those planning new receiving venues need to be aware of the implications of straying too far from the norm. Later subsections, particularly 'Setting out the stage house' (5.3), provide useful minimum design criteria and benchmarks for different types and scales of venue.

How might a set designer respond to a proscenium house?

The proscenium frames the human figure and places it in proportion to the scenic elements and to the frame itself. Whether two- or three-dimensional, these elements operate within the convention of a picture frame and create perspectives in which a foreground, mid-ground and background can be understood.

The provocative element is the line between stage and audience. Music Hall and Vaudeville traditions use it to tease and strut; architectural and domestic sets use it as the edge between different worlds. The frame – ornate or simple, historic or contemporary – presents the performance to the audience. So, choice over the shape, dimensions and style of the proscenium offers welcome opportunities for the set designer. However, such flexibility is not often available.

Behind the proscenium, scenery and technical equipment is supported by a variety of mechanisms. Stage machinery can also create illusions and special effects in its own right. It may either be part of the permanent installation or installed specifically for a production. Later subsections discuss the methods for setting or changing scenery in greater detail.

How might a designer respond to an open stage?

Flats and cloths cannot be used in the same way on the projecting portions of a thrust stage, nor upon a stage set in-the-round across which spectators need to have a virtually unobstructed view.

In such open-stage settings any scenery must be kept low or 'transparent'. Design elements may be restricted to a floor surface, furniture and props, costumes and lighting, perhaps with a 'picture' wall on one side only. Overhead suspensions are still required but their operation will need to adapt readily to the designer's response to the sightlines of that particular space.

On an open stage, devices such as lifts and turntables, revolves or even the double-height drum-revolve such as in the National Theatre's Olivier Theatre in London, enable scene changes to be made and enhance the sculptural quality of the design by offering a changeable point of view from the otherwise fixed viewpoint of a theatre seat.

Introduction to the scenic materials and effects that a designer might employ

Drapery

Drapery is a significant part of any stage setting, from the lavish red plush front or 'house' curtain which conceals the scenery behind it, to the more austere 'black box' within. This latter neutral setting is created from side masking panels ('legs'), headers ('borders') and a backing ('tabs' or 'full blacks'). As fabric can be stretched, hung, seamed, folded and draped or painted to look three-dimensional, theatrical drapery may take on a sculptural quality.

Cloths

The flying system which is installed may need to suit a range of different cloths including:

- The painted front-cloth or 'show drop' which might introduce a pantomime or vaudeville act and hide a scene-change taking place behind it.
- The backcloth which may depict the sky or a distant view, or be left plain (as a 'cyclorama') to take lighting or projection.
- A cut cloth – or series of them – typically representing trees or architecture can add perspective and depth.
- A gauze or 'scrim' offers a device for distancing the action or scenery or enables one picture (painted on it) to dissolve into another behind it simply by a change of lighting; striking effects can be achieved in this way.
- Black velvet/serge is used to imply infinite depth or may be pricked with numerous fibre optic endings to represent a night-time sky (a 'star-cloth').

Painted cloths still predominate in traditional ballet and pantomime design because they take up least floor area and can be changed simply. They are also widely used in many other forms of performance. Cloths are light and can easily be folded or rolled when being stored and transported.

The stage surface

Floors may be treated with a painted heavy duty canvas, a vinyl or sprung wooden flooring suitable for dancers, or a raised and sculpted surface. A raked stage is commonly used when a chorus or crowd need to see the conductor as much as to be visible to the full audience. A raised 'show floor', often required

for musicals, may be a box of tricks accommodating travelators, traps, tracks and concealed lighting.

Two-dimensional scenery

Behind a proscenium, three-dimensional effects can be represented by cleverly painted cloths or rigid panels, referred to as 'flats'. The lightest flats are made from canvas stretched over a timber frame much like a fine artist's canvas but at heights of up to 8.0m. Equally, skin plywood or a heavier construction, perhaps on a steel or aluminium frame, might be adopted. Relief applications such as timber or plastic mouldings can add architraves, bricks, foliage or texture, which help suggest 3D qualities.

Three-dimensional scenery

Sculptural scenery provides interest from all aspects, especially when lit. It tends to become heavier in construction as it contributes to a representation of a more substantial or robust setting. Elements include rostra, ramps or 'raked' stage decks, stairs, balconies, rocks, columns, trees, etc.

Stage properties – or 'props' – are equally significant 3D objects which support the stage action and narrative. They might range from small hand-held items to furniture or rock formations, inanimate vehicles or practical machines. On an open stage, the costumes also assume a significant role in establishing locale as much as individual character.

Multi-dimensional scenery

Projected scenery can change, dissolve or even disappear. Technical developments now enable optical devices or projectors to track in line with moving scenic surfaces or for LED panels to operate in motion, thereby opening up all sorts of opportunities for the designer.

The use and production of still images, moving images, multiple images and lighting effects are discussed further in Section 6.

The requirements relating to making, handling and storing scenery are set out in Section 7.

Theatre type	Seating	Proscenium width (m)	Proscenium height (m)	Grid height (m)	Main stage depth (m)	Wing width (m)	Height under galleries (m)
Opera/dance	1,200- 2,000	12–18	8–10	24–30	15–20	8–10	8–12
Large touring	1,200-2,000	12–15	7–9	22–28	14–18	6–10	7–9
Medium touring	900-1,200	10–14	6–8	18–22	12–15	5–8	6–8
Drama and small touring	400-1,000	8–12	5–7	14–20	10–14	5–8	5–7

5.3.1

5.3   Setting out the stage house

Plenty of space and height, with walls at right angles to each other and free of all obstructions above and on and beneath the stage level.

Actor, producer and director Basil Dean.

As long as you are sure of what 'plenty' means, the above is still a very good summary!

This subsection covers the planning of a proscenium stage with flytower and the variations in the layout which are needed for different types of use and size of auditorium.

Figure 5.3.2 shows the normal components of the flytower, with side galleries and an overall grid for high-level access and temporary rigging.

5.3.2 Section through stage with single purchase counterweights

Stage level – how wide are the wings?

Intrinsically, a proscenium stage needs to accommodate scenery. The stage arrangement must make the setting up and changing of scenery and lighting as easy and as flexible as possible. Scenery may be moved during a performance, or to make way for a new production. Movement can be horizontal into the wings on either side or into a rear stage. It can also be vertical up into the flytower or vertical down into a stage basement.

The easiest places to move scenery into are the wings so these areas are important. The wing spaces also need to accommodate prop tables (for the setting and running of props during a performance) and quick change areas (a temporary booth constructed often on a show-by-show basis to facilitate a performer changing a costume with some degree of privacy when there is insufficient time to return to the dressing room). For certain productions the wings will also provide clear space to the side of the stage for dancers and other performers to run off the stage at speed and decelerate out of sight without colliding with a wall or piece of equipment.

As well as issues of cost and available site area, the amount of wing space is influenced by the choice of flying system. An understanding of flying methods is therefore needed before the stage plan can be decided.

Flying systems

Detailed information on flying system equipment is set out in subsection 5.4. What follows here is a brief summary indicating how the choice of system impacts on the size and layout of the wing space.

With traditional rope sets or winches operated by hand from a gallery well above stage level the scenery load is directly suspended and there is no obstruction to the extent of the wings. With counterweight flying which has largely replaced ropes and hand winches, the load on a flying bar is counterbalanced by weights in a cradle running in guides on the side wall.

Counterweight sets can be either single purchase or double purchase. It is usual only to install counterweight cradles on one side of the stage. A full installation forms an unbroken row of equipment. If single purchase sets are installed, their cradle travel comes down to stage level and limits the wing space to the flytower width. With double purchase the cradle travel is in the upper half of the flytower so does not necessarily limit the wing which can then be as wide as necessary. There are, however, disadvantages to this system (see subsection 5.4).

For the past 70 years the flying system of choice has been single purchase counterweights, which is why so many stages have an asymmetric plan with one wing much deeper than the other. The narrow wing results from a balance being struck between wing space and tower width. A very wide flytower is uneconomic and moves the operating position for the flying system a long way offstage. This restricts the flyman's view and limits other gallery uses such as sidelighting.

With the ever-increasing availability and affordability of powered flying systems the wheel has come full circle. Like the original rope sets, motors for flying at high level on galleries or the grid do not obstruct the wings. Without the intrusion of counterweights there is freedom to set flytower and wing widths to the ideal dimensions and cost is the only limiting factor.

5.3.3 The wall frame of a single purchase counterweight installation
Photograph: Peter Angier

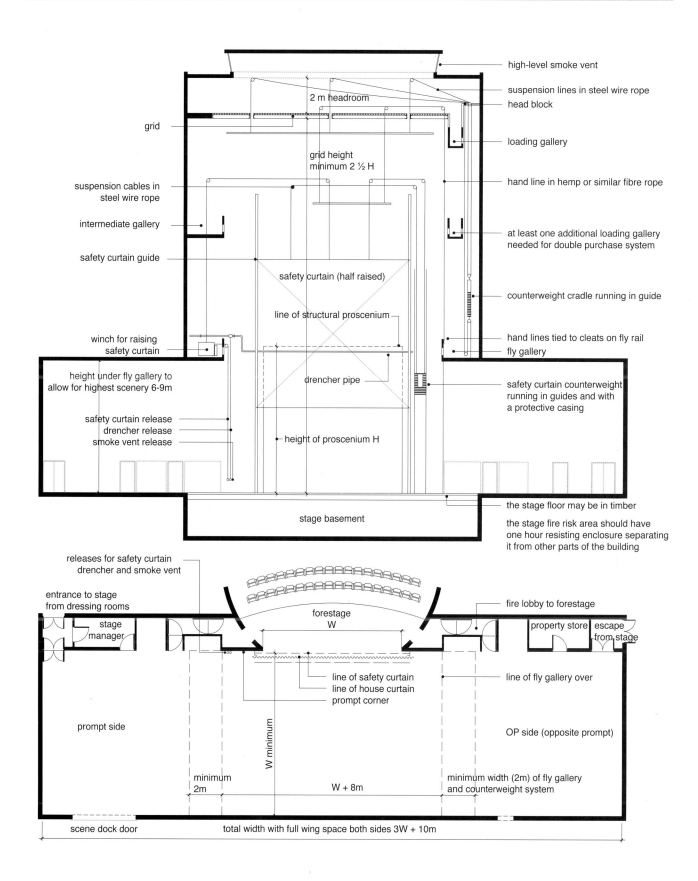

high-level smoke vent

suspension lines in steel wire rope

head block

2 m headroom

grid

loading gallery

grid height minimum 2 ½ H

hand line in hemp or similar fibre rope

suspension cables in steel wire rope

intermediate gallery

at least one additional loading gallery needed for double purchase system

safety curtain guide

safety curtain (half raised)

counterweight cradle running in guide

line of structural proscenium

winch for raising safety curtain

hand lines tied to cleats on fly rail

fly gallery

height under fly gallery to allow for highest scenery 6-9m

drencher pipe

safety curtain counterweight running in guides and with a protective casing

safety curtain release
drencher release
smoke vent release

height of proscenium H

stage basement

the stage floor may be in timber

the stage fire risk area should have one hour resisting enclosure separating it from other parts of the building

releases for safety curtain drencher and smoke vent

entrance to stage from dressing rooms

fire lobby to forestage

stage manager

forestage W

property store

escape from stage

line of safety curtain
line of house curtain
prompt corner

line of fly gallery over

prompt side

W minimum

OP side (opposite prompt)

minimum 2m

W + 8m

minimum width (2m) of fly gallery and counterweight system

scene dock door

total width with full wing space both sides 3W + 10m

5.3.4 Diagram showing the layout of a stage equipped with a double purchase flying system

The proscenium and rear stage

Figure 5.3.4 relates wing width to proscenium opening. This is a good guide but regardless of proscenium width the wing space from proscenium opening to a single purchase wall frame should not be less than 4m.

The proscenium structural opening is the reference for setting out the wings, galleries and stage depth. The dimensions of the opening are closely linked to the size and general design of the auditorium. The width needs to give adequate sightlines for the audience to the full playing area while avoiding acute sightlines into the wings. The height must also be adequate for the view from upper seating tiers. Too large a proscenium results in a need for wider wings, higher grid, and big events to fill the opening. Too small and the contact between player and audience is cramped or lost. The table (Figure 5.3.1)gives some typical dimensions as a guide.

It is common to install a vertically moving safety curtain which can close the proscenium opening when released. Its historic purpose was to protect the audience from a stage fire. While it is not mandatory nationally in the UK (although it may still be locally and elsewhere) it still has a useful role in keeping the auditorium clean and warm during stage operations, providing a temporary stacking wall and masking a noisy interval change. For all these reasons safety curtains remain common. There are various curtain types but the simplest should be the target, which is a flat, rigid, counterweighted, one-piece unit made of steel.

It should be noted that including a safety curtain is likely to have other implications for fire breaks above and below the proscenium. (More information on fire safety is given in Section 2.)

Conventionally the proscenium opening can be reduced in width and height on the upstage side with variable black masking, sometimes called a 'tormentor'. It is desirable if this masking can be easily adjusted and quickly moved completely out of the way for those shows where it is not needed.

In larger theatres a permanent adjustable proscenium system may be provided. Small platforms, offstage of the black masking forming proscenium wall perches, have a number of production uses. These should be detailed so as not to intrude into the working stage area and designed to move in tandem with any large adjustable proscenium system.

A rear stage (without full flying height) is useful for storage and as an extension of the acting area (perhaps with a perspective set), but sightlines may limit its performance use. The opening width into the rear stage should not be less than the structural proscenium dimension and the clear height should not be less than the clearance under the lowest stage galleries. Extra height should be allowed over the rear stage to install hoists used for performance, assembly and storage.

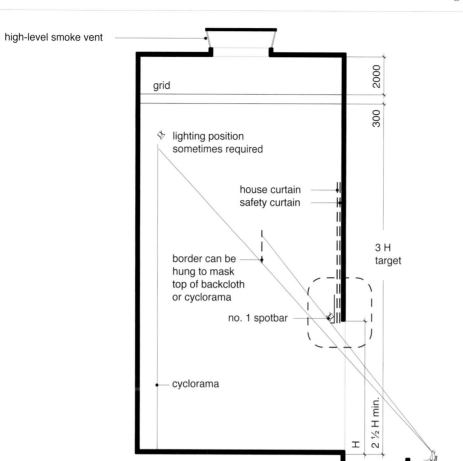

high-level smoke vent

grid

2000

300

⬦ lighting position
sometimes required

house curtain

safety curtain

3 H
target

border can be
hung to mask
top of backcloth
or cyclorama

no. 1 spotbar

cyclorama

H

2 ½ H min.

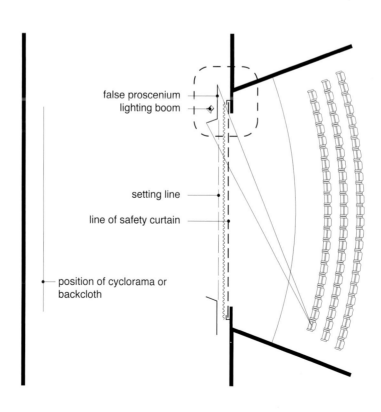

false proscenium

lighting boom

setting line

line of safety curtain

position of cyclorama or
backcloth

5.3.5 Plan and section showing
front row sightlines

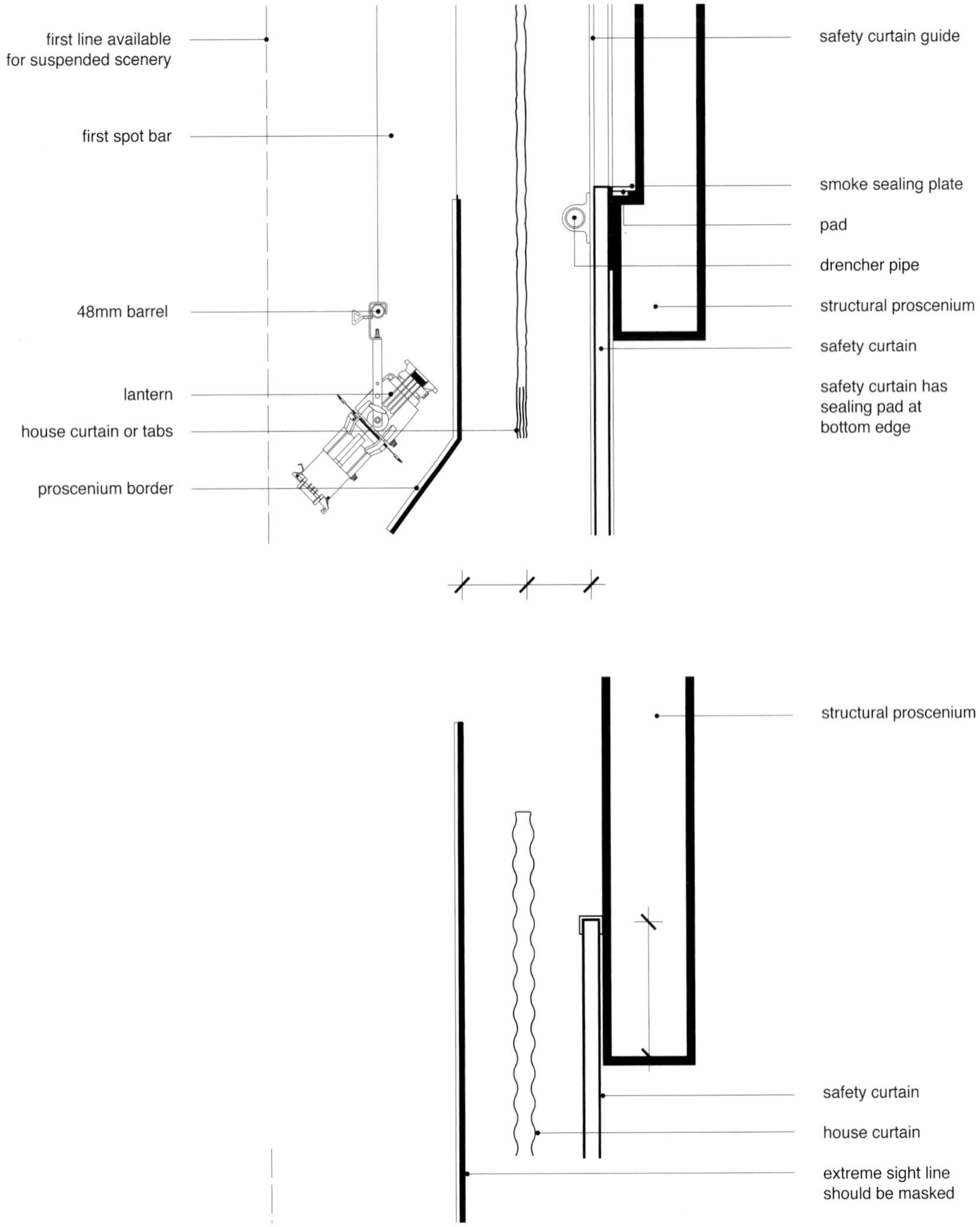

first line available
for suspended scenery

first spot bar

48mm barrel

lantern

house curtain or tabs

proscenium border

safety curtain guide

smoke sealing plate

pad

drencher pipe

structural proscenium

safety curtain

safety curtain has
sealing pad at
bottom edge

structural proscenium

safety curtain

house curtain

extreme sight line
should be masked

5.3.6 Typical plan and section of a proscenium arch

5.3.7 The grid
Photograph: Peter Angier

The flytower grid

The grid is the maintenance and access deck for the stage suspension systems. It may also carry equipment loads.

Care needs to be taken over the height of the grid as there is no substitute for grid height when it is needed and no remedy if it is lacking. While 2.5 times the structural proscenium height should be taken as a minimum, extra height is a production bonus and three times the structural proscenium height should be the target. This additional height may also be necessary where an unusual stage/auditorium relationship creates awkward upward views into the flytower. It should be noted when checking sightlines into the stage that the end seats of front rows are usually the worst case.

Powered flying and control systems can now provide the sensitivity for in-show movement which was previously only possible with single purchase counterweights. Flying motors can easily be accommodated at grid level. They should be located at the sides to leave the central area clear for temporary rigging. Additional area at grid level, upstage of the stage back wall line, is useful for housing spotline hoists, again leaving the central area of the grid clear for safe and easy access.

All permanent suspension lines over the grid should be mounted at high level above head height, leaving the grid surface clear of pulleys. The grid structure should be sufficiently open to allow a chain hoist hook to pass through. It is desirable to form a suitably guarded opening section in the grid which can be used to hoist heavy production items to grid level. This may also be useful for powered flying hoist maintenance access if there is no lift to grid level for heavy loads – though such a lift should be incorporated into the design where funds permit.

The flytower galleries

Side galleries within the flytower have a number of uses apart from being the best operating position for the flying system (whether manual or powered). These include side lighting, 'breasting' and 'brailing' of fly bars (that is, the securing of flying bars in a lateral position up or down stage of their natural position), various special effects and (with counterweight systems) loading weights.

5.3.8 The fly gallery
Photograph: Peter Angier

Conventionally the majority of stage lighting gallery outlets for spotbar connection are concentrated on the side away from the flying system. This leaves the flying operating area as free from trailing cables and sockets as possible. With powered flying, where the controls are likely to be small and portable, this separation is slightly less important but still valuable.

High-level galleries for loading counterweights are only required on the counterweight side. Normally one is needed for single purchase systems and two or three for double purchase because of the longer cradles.

All other galleries should be in pairs, one on each side of the stage, with their onstage edges set back from the proscenium opening and lining up vertically.

The onstage edges should be symmetrically spaced about the proscenium centre line. The dimension from the proscenium structural opening to the onstage edge of galleries is important. It should be large enough to accommodate up/downstage flying bars beyond the cross-stage suspensions but not so large that all gallery activity is remote from the stage central area.

The lowest level of galleries is usually the best position for operating the flying system. With counterweights which are operated from the offstage side, the gallery should be relatively narrow to allow the operator a view down to the stage floor. A crossover, connecting galleries at this level, is highly desirable but should not take up valuable flying space. It is best placed behind the back wall of the stage and can often make use of a dressing room corridor.

Good vertical circulation for the flytower should be planned from the beginning, with at least one dedicated stair rising from stage to grid. Such stairs should be located outside the working rectangle of the flytower plan. Cat ladders should not be used for primary access and should be avoided where possible. A grid lift for personnel and small hoists will save much time and labour. The lift should have the principal gallery levels as intermediate stops.

The stage floor and substage

The stage floor should be level, without steps or ramps. Vertical movement of scenery below the floor on a large scale involves mechanisation using lifts. This sort of installation is often combined with horizontal movement of scenery on wagons. Wagons usually run into the wing and rear stage areas. Such extensive machinery generally only earns its keep in opera houses working in repertoire. In other types of theatre where it has been installed, it rarely remains in use. Mechanised methods for scene changing tend to impose a certain rigidity on methods of constructing and of operating scenery.

A more useful general purpose stage floor is supported on demountable modules over a stage basement. This allows the formation of traps or extended open areas to suit a particular production. The module size can be based on plywood sheet dimensions for ease of replacement. The modular area should be symmetrical to the proscenium centre line, equal to the proscenium opening as a minimum, and extend as far downstage as possible. The central module should straddle the centre line.

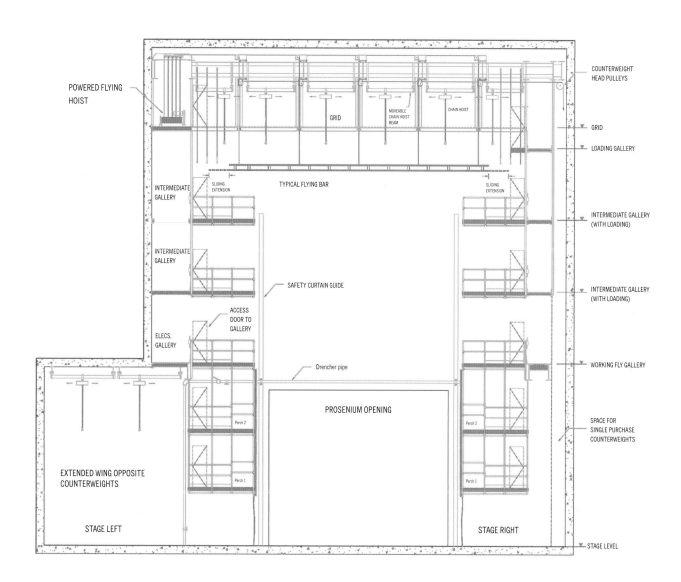

5.3.9 Section through the stage house
Diagram: Peter Angier

The clear basement depth should not be less than 2.5m. Although likely to be expensive, for a resident company a double-height basement extending down for 5m or more will be useful. If this is further divided into two levels by a demountable floor it will significantly extend the range of production uses.

Demountable stage floors are most used in producing theatres where the designer can exploit the in-house facilities. In these buildings the area of removable floor should be a square, with sides the same dimension as the structural proscenium. Touring theatres make the least use of the floor because touring circuits rarely have a common floor module facility throughout the network. In these theatres a small area of demountable floor of about 18m²–20m² in a central and downstage position is usually adequate.

5.4   Overstage machinery

The installation of power flying machinery at the Grand Theatre in Leeds has been very successful; making change-overs, builds, and strikes safer and faster whilst providing much higher levels of control and repeatability in performance.

Ric Green, Technical Director, Opera North

Any equipment which suspends or moves loads overhead has to be extremely safe and must be designed, fabricated, installed and tested to the highest standard. Codes and regulations in most countries control what can be done and must be complied with. In addition to ensuring that the equipment is fit for purpose, it is vital that everyone using overhead equipment is thoroughly trained and that a comprehensive training regime continues for all new operators and for those involved in repairs and maintenance.

The operator of any moving overhead equipment must be able to see the loads that he or she is controlling, whether these are moved by hand or by machine.

Manual flying

A large number of theatres are fitted with a form of manual flying, although many are moving towards powered systems as these become more economic and health and safety considerations become more important. The most basic form of suspension is to use ropes, which although historically referred to as 'hemp', should be Grade 1 Manilla or a quality polyester rope.

Hemp

Direct haul theatre suspensions either have a single rope carrying a small piece of decoration, like a chandelier, or a number of ropes, normally three or four, attached to an (aluminium) pipe to which the scenery is tied. The operator raises and lowers this scenery from a gallery at the side of the flytower. The ropes pass over pulleys on the grid and are tied off to cleats or pins fitted to a substantial rail on the onstage side of this gallery, which must be wide enough to accommodate the many operators required for this form of flying and for all the loose rope when the scenery is raised.

5.4.1 A hemp fly gallery
Photograph: Richard Brett

Single purchase counterweights

Single purchase counterweights are the most common form of scenery suspension. Wire ropes from each fly bar pass over drop and head pulleys before being attached to a counterweight cradle. The cradle is a steel frame which carries cast iron, lead or steel weights to balance the weight of the scenery. A hauling rope is attached to the counterweight cradle and reeved over pulleys at both top and bottom of its travel. It passes vertically through a rope lock device on the operating, or 'fly' gallery. This rope makes the work of moving the scenery relatively easy, although considerable effort is required to load and unload the counterweights.

5.4.2 The rope lock of a flying system
Photograph: Richard Brett

The counterweight cradle is guided on one wall of the flytower. The cradles pass behind the galleries on the 'working' side of the flytower where a space, usually about 800mm wide, needs to be available to accommodate the wall frame, counterweights and hauling ropes.

It is not good policy, either operationally or from an engineering viewpoint, to put counterweights on a rear wall or to distribute them on both sides of the stage. (See subsection 5.3 – Setting out the stage house.)

Double purchase counterweights

The vertical movement of the cradles can be halved by doubling the weight in the cradle and double purchasing the wire ropes so that they pass over a pulley on the top of the counterweight cradle and are fixed to the head steels. This permits doorways, openings and side stage access through the lower part of this wall and increases the available wing space.

The disadvantage is that twice as many weights have to be loaded and unloaded, and the reaction forces on the head steels are increased. The hauling rope is also double purchased but the cradles of double purchase sets can be very long (over 4m on occasion) and the effort involved in accelerating and stopping a double purchase set is increased by 50 per cent over that for a single purchase set, which adds

strain to the operator's body.

Such a system should only be contemplated after considering other options, including a powered system.

Powered flying

With the development of relatively economic AC inverter drives and control systems, powered systems for moving scenery have become practicable. These take two basic forms:

- Powered assistance (counterweight cradles operated by an electrical motor)
- Direct lift (the suspension wire ropes are wound directly onto a drum rotated by an electrical motor).

These systems must be designed to exacting standards by professionals, as the inherent risks cannot be understood without training in these disciplines. A number of proprietary systems are available but these must be capable of complying with current safety standards, such as being designed to an appropriate safety integrity level under EN 61508.

5.4.3 The winch motor room
Photograph: Richard Brett

Powered assistance to counterweight systems
Powered assistance is only a solution where a suitable counterweight installation already exists: elsewhere it is more economic to install a direct haul system. This can be either electrical or hydraulic, and can raise or lower the scenery by moving the counterweight. Wire ropes attached to the counterweight wind on a suitable hoist which can be mounted in the basement, on the grid or on a gallery – wherever sufficient space can be found.

It is also possible to drive the hauling line with a motor at fly gallery level, though this system is less commonly used.

Direct lift hoists

Direct haul systems can use wire ropes or steel bands, and these hoists can employ either grooved or pile-winding drums. Where hoists need to be synchronised (as in most modern installations) pile-winding drums should not be used, as the winding diameter of two hoists at varying heights will be different and they will therefore be unable to lift at sufficiently identical speeds to maintain a level lift.

Most direct lift systems use a hoist with a grooved winding drum. This can have a single or multiple wire ropes on it and can be made in many sizes with a range of performances. Typical units operate with loads up to 1,000kg at maximum speeds of up to 2m/sec. These hoists have a self-weight of between 50 per cent and 75 cent of the load they are rated to lift.

Modern hoists are relatively quiet but should be enclosed or mounted outside the flytower in acoustically critical situations, such as in a drama theatre. Typically a winch room should be between 3m to 5m deep, and run the full depth of the stage. Often winch rooms will be located on both sides of the stage to achieve the close centres required, and to better distribute the structural forces across the building fabric. Occasionally a winch room may be situated above the grid, with a footprint in plan comparable to the grid, in a separate acoustic enclosure (for example, in the Copenhagen Opera House, Reference project: p. 206).

Where quiet operation is not a particular requirement (where the hoist is being used for suspension rather than live flying), line shaft winches can be a lower-cost alternative.

Space near the hoists will be necessary for the variable speed drives as this allows cross-plugging in the event of a drive failure.

Control systems

Modern flying control systems control a number of 'axes', each of which is the movement of one piece of equipment. As well as handling overstage hoists, the system can control stage elevators, stage wagons or revolving stages. Thus they are referred to as 'stage control systems' and will generally consist of a control centre, incorporating a server, and some control panels.

The hoists are connected to the control centre by Ethernet or similar protocols. Advanced systems enable the operation of the installation to be monitored and any errors diagnosed remotely by the manufacturer over an Internet connection. The control centre should be located outside the stage area but reasonably adjacent to the main control panel positions.

Emergency stop facilities will be required by regulations relating to rotating machinery. The emergency stop should be one system that stops all moving equipment: hoists, elevators, wagons or dividing shutters.

Safety curtains, dividing shutters

Where a sound-reducing shutter is required to separate a side stage, rear stage, or scene dock from the stage, this may move vertically rather like a safety curtain that seals the opening between stage and auditorium in a proscenium theatre. Safety curtains are sometimes required to provide sound separation in addition to fire protection, in a similar way to most dividing shutters. To achieve these functions, sound-reducing shutters are heavy, up to 130kg/m^2 and, being counterweighted, require suitable structural support.

Chain hoists

Chain hoists are relatively slow and noisy but reliable and are used for static rigging. The grid must be strong enough to take the load of the hoist plus its payload. An alternative is to hang these chain hoists overhead on fixed or rolling beams.

Advance bars and other special rigging

Overstage rigging can extend into the auditorium when scenery, lighting or action is required above the audience. This will need load-tested attachment points on the roof structure, a facility required increasingly as touring shows with three-dimensional flying become more popular. Some coordinated openings in the auditorium ceiling are also necessary to accommodate chandeliers and lighting and sound equipment, or performers who might 'fly' through the ceiling or appear from above.

Operating life expectancy

The life of the mechanical equipment can be expected to be 40 years with that of the drive equipment between 15 and 20, but the components in the control system may only be available for 7–10 years.

Therefore it is essential to buy stage rigging and machinery installations with professional advice.

5.5   Understage machinery

Understage machinery is not a new idea. According to historian Allardyce Nicoll, even Greco-Roman theatre utilised machines and scenery a lot more freely than one might think. Writing in the second century AD, Pollux listed some 19 theatrical devices including the 'Anapiesmata' which apparently raised the spirits mechanically from the depths.

Theatre technicians have been building machines to raise the spirits ever since.

The stage structure

The stage has to be strong so that scenery and lights do not wobble when a vigorous dance routine or fight scene is staged. It may be required to support heavy scaffold structures, with several raised levels, stairs, ladders and walkways. It will also be subject to rolling loads from heavy moving scenery, grand pianos, cherry pickers, forklift trucks, tow trucks and other vehicles. It must be capable of adapting to varied production requirements and this means that most of it should be removable. (NB: It is much easier to loosen some bolts and dismantle a steel structure than it is to demolish reinforced concrete.)

The understage structure must also provide stable support for actors, dancers, musicians, scenery, props, mechanical effects and technical equipment. It might also at times allow any of these things to appear or disappear through the floor into the void below. Wherever possible a cavernous space with generous headroom, sometimes several storeys deep, should be provided below the stage.

Historically many stage floors were raked to improve the sightlines, an effect enhanced by the perspective of scenes painted on flat scenery. The current preference is to build theatres with flat stage floors to reduce hazard in operation and provide dancers with their preferred surface. A raked floor can always be added on top when needed. Other special types of flooring may be built on top of the normal stage floor temporarily – a sprung floor for dance, for example, or a raised show floor with tracks for scenic effects.

Various useful technical features may be built into a stage floor including projection screen boxes; dip traps (for hiding cables); float troughs (for downstage lighting instruments); and carpet cuts (for fast removal of stage coverings). Many stages are constructed with removable timber floor modules which make it simple to open up large holes in the floor wherever needed (Figure 5.6.3).

Understage machinery

Understage machinery might be used to facilitate rapid scene changing and produce spectacular effects in front of an audience or to aid manual handling when changing over from one show to another. It may also be used to help reconfigure the auditorium for different types of event. These are important distinctions. Apparently similar items of equipment may have very different noise or speed requirements, depending on how they are to be used.

Machinery may either be built in as a part of the infrastructure of the theatre building or it may be temporarily installed for a specific show or a season of shows. Big budget musical productions employ much machinery that is often custom designed along with the scenery. In some cases this may require major structural alterations or in extreme cases an entirely new theatre to be built around a specific show (e.g. recent Cirque du Soleil productions).

At the other end of the scale, a repertory theatre that is producing its own shows may build up a collection of portable items of machinery or a kit of mechanical parts that can be adapted and reused for different roles in many shows.

Some examples of the different types of understage machinery that are commonly installed in theatres are described in the following paragraphs.

Traps
The simplest type of understage machine is the hinged or sliding trap door that may be opened to enable an actor to make an entrance from below or to exit down stairs into the understage area.

For rapid appearances, popular in pantomime, a fast trap device is installed below. This is a counterweighted rising platform that lifts a performer up to stage level and fills in the opening in the floor using a 'sloat' lid. Used in reverse, it enables a genie to disappear behind a puff of pyrotechnic smoke.

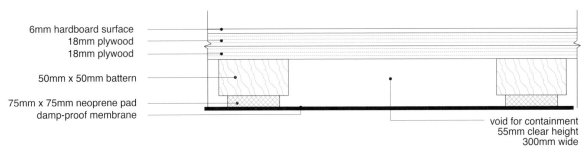

6mm hardboard surface
18mm plywood
18mm plywood

50mm x 50mm battern

75mm x 75mm neoprene pad
damp-proof membrane

void for containment
55mm clear height
300mm wide

Semi-sprung floor construction. Total depth approx 110mm

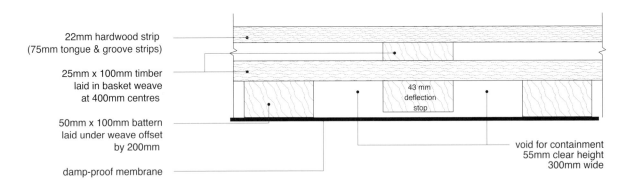

22mm hardwood strip
(75mm tongue & groove strips)

25mm x 100mm timber
laid in basket weave
at 400mm centres

50mm x 100mm battern
laid under weave offset
by 200mm

damp-proof membrane

43 mm
deflection
stop

void for containment
55mm clear height
300mm wide

Fully-sprung dancefloor construction. Total depth approx 125mm

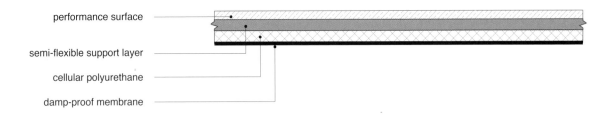

performance surface

semi-flexible support layer

cellular polyurethane

damp-proof membrane

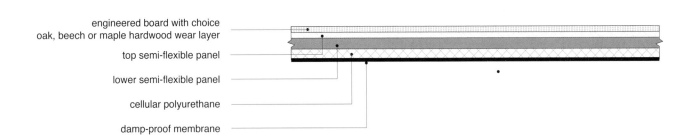

engineered board with choice
oak, beech or maple hardwood wear layer

top semi-flexible panel

lower semi-flexible panel

cellular polyurethane

damp-proof membrane

Vinyl performance surface proprietary fully-sprung floor. Total depth approx 45mm

5.5.1 Stage floor build-up diagram
Diagram: Charcoalblue

Stage lifts

Stage lifts are used to raise and lower both larger items of scenery and groups of actors. Lifts are particularly good for growing forests of trees, for sinking ships and for elevating heavenly choirs. They vary enormously in size and style, but may cover the entire stage area and travel deep down into the basement. More powerful lifts are capable of shifting tens of tons of scenery and some will rise several metres above stage level to create instant raised acting platforms, often in modular form.

Lifts may have a double-deck construction. The lower deck services the main stage floor which can be equipped with trap doors and may support supplementary lifting equipment. The top level of a lift can be made to tilt to create a raking stage floor at whatever slope may be required. Lifts within lifts are not uncommon.

To protect people on stage from falling into the hole left by a lift, various automatic rising barriers or folding safety nets may be incorporated into the system and doors below stage need to be interlocked. Shear edges must have protective devices to reduce the risk of injury and even of amputation. Generally though, safe operation depends on careful management, risk assessment and lots of rehearsal.

Revolves

Another popular scene-changing machine is the revolve. This can be a simple circular platform either built on top of, or recessed into, the stage floor. Two or more scenes can be built on a revolve and rotated into view as the show proceeds, often in full view of the audience. They are particularly good for chases or for switching from an exterior to an interior scene.

Revolves, like lifts, may be built with a second floor below, allowing entrances to be made while rotating. Larger revolves might incorporate smaller revolves or lifts within. Drum revolves are even more complex and incorporate large elevators in a tall rotating structure that facilitates spiralling scene changes.

Wagons

Scene changes can take place at stage level by rolling scenery on and off the stage from the side or rear. This may be done by building wheels into individual scenic elements or by constructing the scenery and props on top of big flat, wheeled platforms or wagons. The largest wagons may fill the stage and be capable of carrying an entire three-dimensional standing set in one piece. Wagons might incorporate a built-in revolve or may have trap doors that align with traps in the stage or lift floor.

In some installations, wagons are designed to precisely match the size and shape of stage lifts and the lifts are used either to transport the wagons, loaded with scenery, to another level in the theatre or to sink the wagon into the stage floor. Adjacent compensating lifts can provide a sunken pathway so the wagons traverse with their top surface flush with the surrounding floor, thus avoiding awkward steps and enabling fluid scene changes to be made.

Traditionally wagons are guided by tracks in the floor and are hauled by motorised systems mounted under the floor. More recently automated vehicle technology has been employed to guide and position wagons remotely so they can wander freely around the stage area.

Special purpose lifts

Aside from stage lifts, various other special lifts that aid efficient operation and smooth presentation may be required, particularly if the theatre is to host musical events or classical concerts. These can, for example, include piano lifts, organ console lifts, microphone stand lifts and orchestra riser lifts.

Building for future use

For a theatre building to be sustainable it should be planned to support the unpredictable demands of show business and to anticipate future development, even if no machinery is to be installed initially. Allowances for suitable anticipated structural, electrical and mechanical loadings, as well as sensible acoustic protection, are essential elements of such pre-planning.

5.6 Stage machinery for the open stage

Theatres with open stages may wish to make provision for flying and suspension of three-dimensional settings.

Roderick Ham 1972

The growth in popularity of the open stage in the UK over the past 30 years has certainly caused a re-evaluation of Roderick Ham's 1972 gentle suggestion. Space and provision for suitable stage machinery should be considered an imperative for the open stage in the twenty-first century.

Although the basic engineering concepts are the same for both the 'conventional' proscenium format and open stage, the particular constraints of the open stage format require innovative thinking when designing the stage machinery. The open stage in all its forms sets challenges for the stage machinery to solve:

- Scenery tends to be 'three-dimensional' rather than linear.
- Delivery of scenery and performers to the stage area occurs in full view of the audience.
- It is necessary to ensure that any machinery in view does not undermine the magic of the image; for example, the audience around an open stage is more likely to have a sightline to below stage when a trap is opened or elevator descends.
- Noise. Systems tend to be much closer to the audience; actors waiting to enter and technicians operating the equipment will also be in close proximity.
- Suspension methods. Ropes are much closer to the audience and thereby more attention must be paid to visible size, colour and reflectivity. Some suspension carriers are perhaps unsuited to open stage use – for example, steel bands.
- Flying height and masking. Stored scenery may be very visible to the audience and this can undermine the element of surprise in scene changes.
- Safety issues. Flying over the audience and the creation of voids near to the audience may require consideration of barrier systems or other precautions.

Setting out the overstage areas

Sufficient clear height above the stage is desirable to hide scenery beyond audience sightlines. This space may also be used to install temporary bridges and access platforms to enable performers to be hooked up, suspended and made ready to fly in on cue.

In some cases, where roof heights are restricted, it may be necessary to consider having no grid at all and suspending directly from the ceiling to achieve the maximum possible flying height. While this approach may improve flying capability, careful consideration must be paid to access methods used for rigging and maintenance. Preferably a permanent means of access should be provided, for example, mobile gantries and drawbridges, rather than relying on access equipment.

For overstage rigging, a traditional grating-type grid with high 'transparency' is desirable. As described below, the grid becomes the 'blank canvas' onto which the particular suspension layout to suit the production design is sketched. This may be achieved by diverting suspensions from high-level structure using travelling beam systems and such like or, by using the grid surface itself with appropriate diversion components, to route suspension ropes to the necessary drop point.

A grating grid with cell size of nominally 50mm x 100mm (in order to achieve good porosity for chain hoist and winch hooks and suspension terminations) and floor load capacity of the order of $5kN/m^2$ provides a 'systematic' surface to which standard diversion components may be mounted.

5.6.1 A tension wire grid (RADA)
Photograph: Byron Avery

5.6.2 Egg Crate Grid at the Young Vic
Photograph: Charcoalblue – Jack Tilbury

Tension wire grids (TWGs) may also be considered but these are not particularly easy to work on if intensive rigging work has to take place. A TWG surface is typically made of narrow gauge steel wire and therefore not easy to fix pulleys or equipment to.

Egg-crate grids may also be considered. These are ideal for lighting positions and may be used to provide access at high level for rigging purposes. However, while bridges provide ideal access to lighting positions the stage engineering elements generally have to be rigged in the void areas with all the resulting 'working at height' concerns.

Overstage machinery

Although there will be some requirement for regularly set-out 'linear' flying as in a conventional proscenium stage house (for example, masking borders and tracked systems), the majority of flying over an open stage will require a much more flexible method of suspension. Suspensions will vary to suit the scenography and therefore a 'sky hook' philosophy – the ability to rig a suspension point anywhere over the stage – is the required approach, to facilitate the suspension of an infinite variety of objects from trees to single light bulbs and everything in between.

A 'point hoist' winch system should be considered a base requirement. Point hoists come in several forms with the following characteristics:

- An electrically powered winch unit which may have one or two ropes
- A method of enabling the rope to be paid out and dropped at the correct position over the stage
- An electronic drive and control system to enable individual winches to be synchronised so that several hoists may safely suspend a single item of scenery
- Wire rope as the means of suspension.

There are five basic spatial variants available which fulfil the above criteria:

- Offstage mounted winch (mounted to the wall or in a frame with others – sometimes known as a 'winch farm') with rope paid out overhead or at grid level to the drop position via a series of modular diversion components which must be rigged for each specific use.
- Offstage mounted winch with double purchase arrangement and crane jib–style track mounted trolley to allow variable

positioning (along a linear path) of the suspension point over the stage without any requirement for re-rigging of diversion pulleys, etc.
- Winch unit suspended on an overhead travelling beam system to enable direct pay-out from the winch at the drop point. This works reasonably for a few hoists; however, larger systems quickly lead to a congested grid and there can be manual handling problems in moving units about (i.e. transferring a winch from one position to another).
- Wheeled or trolley-mounted winch unit which can be transported across a grid to the point at which the rope drop is required. This is much more flexible than the overhead travelling beam-mounted system but requires greater grid floor load capacity.
- Multi-line winch where several rope drops can be realised by individually diverting multiple ropes from the same winch drum to different points, either via the grid surface or overhead. All drops are mechanically coupled and therefore place less reliance on the control system to ensure synchronisation.

Point hoist systems require high-end control systems to ensure synchronisation of suspensions.

With linear powered flying the flying-bar is suspended by a single multi-line winch which has the benefit of mechanical synchronisation – all the ropes go to the same drum.

With a point hoist system a single item of scenery or, indeed, a performer may be suspended on two or more ropes each emanating from a different winch. Synchronisation is ensured by the electronics driving each winch and overall supervision and safety monitoring by the control system – as well as correct programming by the operator. It is therefore vital that point hoist systems are:

- Engineered to the highest level of safety as defined by EU and ISO standards applicable to the overall design of life-critical systems; for example, BS 65108 – often referred to as 'SIL 3' where SIL 3 equates to a Safety Integrity Level of 3 – applicable to life-critical systems.
- Have clear and intuitive operator interfaces – i.e. software that is easily learnt and operated.
- Have an infrastructure which permits

operators to achieve high levels of vigilance
– portable control desks, wireless systems,
etc.

- Have features to allow complex
  programming – for example, the automatic
  recording of a series of manually developed
  moves for cue playback – often referred to
  as 'teach and learn'.

Setting out the understage areas

The key requirements for the open stage's understage
areas are common to those for the proscenium house
stage. That is the need for a truly modular stage – a
stage surface made up of a regular array of removable
panels and modular riser panels to allow the insertion
of runways, staircases, etc. Ideally, the panelised floor
should be supported on a demountable structure such
as a 'drop-in bar' system where secondary horizontal
members slot into a primary horizontal spanning
structure to enable the formation of different sizes of
void. These might vary from, for example, a small ladder
trap, to a large elevator, to a swimming pool.

As deep a void as possible should be achieved to
provide the stage basement, carefully coordinated with
the audience sightlines into the pit.

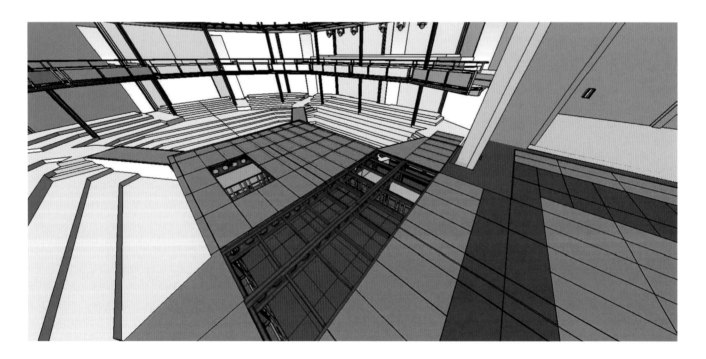

5.6.3 A modular stage floor
Image: Charcoalblue – Mark Priestley and Gregory Allan

Understage machinery

Even assuming a modular stage floor, it is unrealistic to conceive of a permanently installed simple elevator system which could meet all the reasonably foreseeable needs of an open stage show design. While large fixed elevators undoubtedly add an extra dimension, this type of system is more suited to a position upstage of a proscenium.

There are examples where the entire auditorium floor is made up of a series of 2m x 2m elevating platforms which can provide a wide variety of different riser formats and seating tiers. However, this is an extremely costly approach and likely only to be considered as part of a prestigious new-build project. While appearing to be ultra-flexible, such a system does constrain design by the imposition of a regular array.

Another approach is the 'scenery-changing machine' which has multiple elevating components and may also have a rotating configuration. Although significant constraints are placed on the production design by the machine itself, spectacular effects can be achieved by the combination of rotation and elevation. Such machines are capable of a surprisingly wide variety of uses and do ensure an original and innovative contribution to widely differing production designs. However, this is also a costly approach requiring a deep basement and is unlikely to be a realistic prospect for most theatres. The closest permanent example to this machine in the UK is the drum revolve at the National Theatre in London.

The most flexible and cost-effective approach is to combine a modular stage with stage machinery brought in for the particular show. The modular stage allows the creation of voids (of varying width, length and depth) to enable the incorporation of transportable elevator systems with or without automated doors and lids.

As with overstage systems, there is a requirement for comprehensive safety monitoring and control systems designed to meet the highest standards, applicable to life-critical systems.

SECTION EDITOR

Andy Hayles	Managing Director of Charcoalblue

CONTRIBUTORS

Peter Ruthven Hall	Sets and scenery
Peter Angier	Setting out the stage house
Richard Brett	Overstage machinery
George Ellerington	Understage machinery
Mark Priestley	Stage machinery for the open stage

Section 6
Lighting, sound and video

Contents

6.1 Introduction

This section follows a similar format to the previous one and continues the examination of the technical aspects of theatre design, focusing on lighting and sound. It also looks at video, which is becoming more widely used in productions and is likely to become increasingly important in the future.

Each technical discipline is addressed in a common format. First, an introduction to the equipment and what it is controlled by. The spatial and positional requirements for the equipment and control position requirements within the theatre are then discussed and illustrated.

As in Section 5, each subsection starts with a provocation from a leading designer or practitioner in the industry.

The level and scale of provision discussed in sections 5 and 6 is squarely aimed at the professional theatre facility. Performance facilities within higher and further education establishments may consider

a professional level of provision suitable if they are a drama school or training facility for theatre skills. Other places of education, schools and community spaces may consider a less ambitious level of provision to be more appropriate.

Regardless of the size and status of the theatre in question, in general it is considered sensible to invest in an infrastructure of the best quality that can be afforded as this will normally outlast the equipment threefold. For example, a rewire might be expected every 25 to 30 years while a lighting console is likely to have a useful lifespan of 7 to 10 years.

A theatre's technical equipment will typically cost between 10 per cent and 15 per cent of the construction cost, including stage engineering.

For producing theatres and opera houses this percentage may be considerably higher; for schools and community spaces it is likely to be lower.

6.2 Lighting equipment and infrastructure

In designing and planning your theatre and its lighting infrastructure think carefully about what you can't predict. Don't assume that every director will want to put the actors where you have put the stage.

Mark Jonathan, Lighting Director

Stage lighting electrical system

Where does the infrastructure begin and end?

Assuming a traditional installation comprising dimmer rooms and distributed power outlets, it starts with the incoming power supply, usually in the basement, or for larger venues, at the electrical sub-station. The power then needs to be distributed from the electrical intake area to the dimmer room.

Once the electricity is in the dimmer room it needs to be distributed to the dimmer racks, ideally using switch disconnect MCCB protection for each rack rather than switch-fuses. This then provides individual dimmer rack isolation for service and maintenance.

The dimmer rack is a device that allows the lighting designer to adjust the intensity of light emanating from a fixture.

Now that the dimmers are connected to the main incoming power, the electricity is distributed to the load circuits out in the theatre. Conventionally this is done using single insulated cables in trunking. Low smoke and fume cable may be required in the UK.

Once in the theatre, the cables are terminated within a facilities panel often referred to as a plug box, PLB (production lighting box) or LFP (lighting facilities position/point/post). The plug box will be a local point concentrating some or all of the following facilities: dimmer outlets, non-dim outlets, technical power, general power, worklight outlets, house light outlets, lighting network tie lines, DMX outlets or patch points.

Sometimes the plug box may be combined with a sound or video plug-in panel; though due care needs to be taken to ensure appropriate segregation is maintained.

Dimming systems

The most common system is a centralised system with a single dimmer room at the heart of the installation. The optimum position for a single dimmer room is where the load cables to the various plug boxes are of a similar length.

The second choice is a distributed dimmer room system with more than one dimmer room reducing the final circuit cable length, perhaps one dimmer room in the basement, one FOH and one in the flytower grid, depending on the size of the system.

A further option is the distributed dimmer system where the dimmers are mounted adjacent to the lanterns; this is more commonly found in television studios but can be used very successfully in other types of venue provided that the heat and noise they create is unimportant or can be controlled.

The final option is a hybrid system where distributed and centralised dimming are mixed.

Dimmer room

The dimmer room should be in a position that best suits the lighting system. It should be big enough to house all the dimmers and associated switch gear and network/data distribution. The room should be well ventilated with the ability to maintain an ambient temperature within the guidelines of the dimmer manufacturer. This often requires conditioned air.

The room may benefit from a modular 'computer' floor to allow cable access to the base of the dimmers. The layout of the room is very reliant on the type of dimming system selected – but a useful base assumption is a room that has a minimum floor area of 10m^2.

Stage lighting control systems

A stage lighting console will control the dimmers and other devices via a control network which is likely to be based on a computer network typology. The lighting console stores information and cues for a production.

A console operator runs the show from the control room. As well as controlling the lighting for a production, the operator will also need to control the working lights.

Working lights

These are permanently installed, low energy light fittings that provide light to the stage areas when a performance is not taking place.

Good working lighting of the stage area is important. Lights mounted at high level over the wings and under fly galleries will give good coverage of offstage areas. The central area of the stage can to some extent be lit from high-level side galleries but with large stages worklights rigged on flying bars may be needed. Some side gallery fittings should be mounted to illuminate the underside of the grid.

During performances there should be good dim (often blue-filtered) lighting of all galleries and work areas, arranged so as not to spill onto the acting area or be visible from the auditorium.

Ideally the fittings used will have a diffuse output (e.g. fluorescent tubes) as they cast fewer harsh shadows, it is less noticeable if a number of fittings are not working and less glare is created, making looking upwards from stage more comfortable.

Worklight control systems

The working light control system can range from a simple bank of light switches above the prompt desk to a multi-processor system capable of recording and replaying states from the lighting console.

The system should be integrated on a control level with other systems such as house lights and stage lighting but it should have no physical links with another system. If at all possible the working light system's power should come from a totally separate source to that of the stage lighting system.

Most systems will consist of a central processor, some contactors and/or dimmers to control the lights, and some form of human interface. This can be a geographic mimic of the theatre in the prompt corner; programmable touch screens; or remote push buttons around the theatre for local control of lighting circuits.

The part of the system that the staff have to use should be simple and intuitive. It is no good having an amazing system that can predict the working light setup for any given day if the cleaners have to press every button on the panel to get the auditorium lights on just to do the vacuuming.

Luminaires

The selection of the luminaires (variously called 'lights, 'lanterns', 'lighting equipment') is unique to the style and location of the theatre being built. It should not be assumed that the lighting equipment that works in a theatre in the UK will work for a theatre in Europe or the USA.

It is very important to involve the users of the venue, if they already exist, or lighting designers of similar venues. Their input is vital in conceiving a versatile lighting rig that will work for a particular venue.

Lighting equipment can fall into three main categories:

1   Generic (or 'conventional') fixed equipment that can have automated accessories added to it such as scrollers to change the colour of the light and gate accessories to rotate gobos and change the size of the iris, etc.
2   Motorised (or 'automated') fixtures that move, change colour and beam shape, etc., under the control of the lighting console.
3   Follow spots – a generic lantern that is controlled by a human being in most cases.

As soon as the lantern itself starts to move it is an automated fixture and is usually a very complex but versatile piece of equipment. The majority are fitted with discharge light sources (i.e. are not dimmed electrically) of varying intensity and colour temperatures, with a few fitted with tungsten light sources.

Automated fixtures are more expensive than generic equipment but can perform many more tasks. They can also contribute to safety when working at height as they can be focused remotely. It is important to note that while automated lighting fixtures allow for focusing to be carried out remotely, the rigging and 'plugging-up' is still a manual task that requires safe access.

Early automated fixtures have been criticised for contributing to background noise in an auditorium, though with newer equipment this issue is less of a problem. However, there are more maintenance issues with automated fixtures, due to the increased number of moving parts in the unit.

Sustainability in stage lighting

The industry's approach to controlling power consumption and emissions is improving and luminaires are now available that use 575W lamps that can equal the light output of older 1000W fixtures.

Automated lighting would appear to be more energy efficient in that fewer lamps are needed to achieve the same results. But it should be noted that a tungsten generic lantern is burning electricity only when the designer wants light on the stage while a discharge automated fixture is burning electricity from the moment the rig is turned on to when it is turned off at the end of the night. A best practice should be adopted to turn off the discharge sources when they are not needed.

In the future it is likely that LED and dimmable discharge lighting will play a much greater role in production lighting.

6.3   Lighting rigging positions

I want as many options to see the stage from as many angles as possible, and a space where the stage is the focus, not the auditorium.

Rick Fisher, Lighting Designer

The most restrictive spaces are ones where the lights are supposed to be out of sight. Hiding lanterns, especially in the auditorium, often prevents them actually seeing the stage in the way a lighting designer requires. It is much better to give the designer a large choice of positions, some of which will not be used all the time, and could be removable, than to limit the angles available.

Paule Constable, Lighting Designer

Every production has a unique lighting design. Lighting designers specify, usually on a scale drawing, where they would like each lantern to be rigged.

Once rigged, each luminaire or 'lantern' needs to be focused. 'Focusing' is pointing a lantern at the right place on stage, and adjusting parts of the lantern to adjust the beam's size, shape and 'sharpness' (i.e. the appearance of the beam edge). Each one is turned on individually.

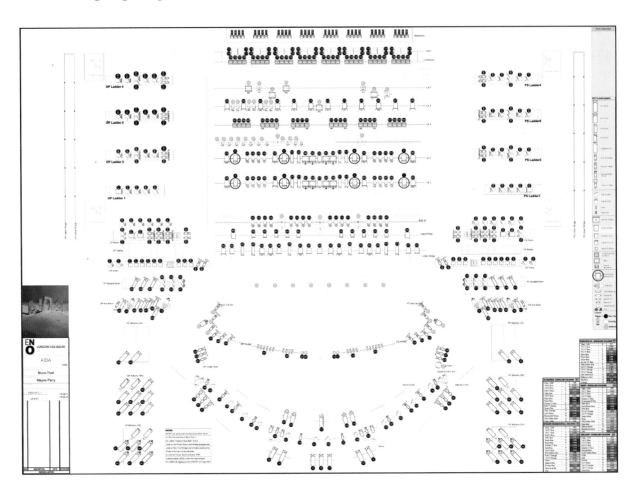

6.3.1 Typical lighting rig plan – Bruno Poet for Aida at English National Opera
Diagram: Bruno Poet

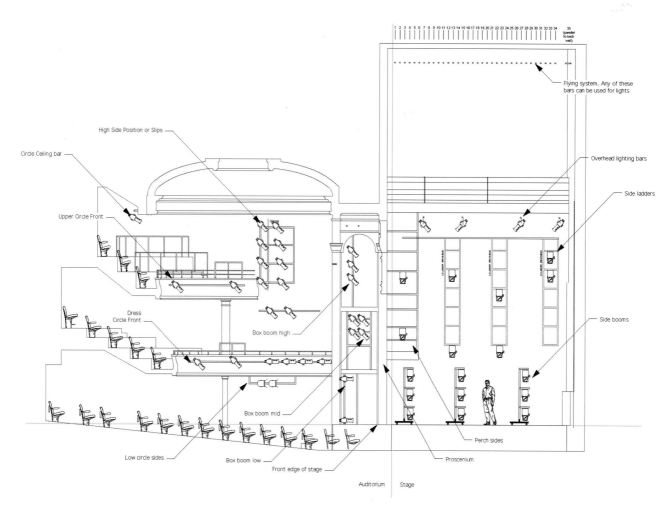

6.3.2 Section showing exemplar lighting positions, Royal Court Theatre, London, UK
Diagram: Royal Theatre Court, LX Department

Lighting rigs can use from 50 to over 500 lanterns depending on the size of the theatre and the type of show. Lanterns are awkward and heavy, so moving them around is hard work, dangerous and time-consuming, especially when working at height. A successful lighting position will make this process as safe and comfortable as possible.

Safe access is imperative and thorough risk assessment of all lighting rigging and focusing activities is required in both the design and the operation of the building. ABTT Codes of Practice provide useful guidance. Structural loading of lighting bars and access systems should be considered at the earliest stage. (The ABTT's 'Technical Standards for Places of Entertainment' provides useful advice.) The increased weight of moving

lights requires ever greater loading capacity from rigging positions.

Figure 6.3.2 of the Royal Court Theatre auditorium shows essential lighting positions, which are discussed below.

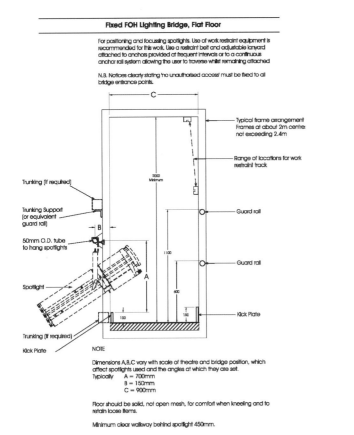

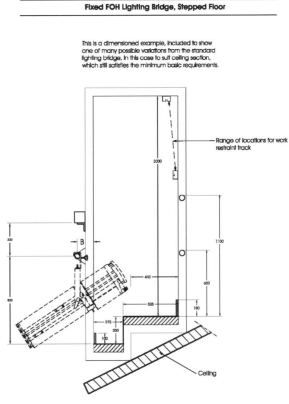

6.3.3 ABTT code of practice drawings for lighting bridges illustrating flat and stepped systems
Diagram: David Adams

Overstage

All proscenium theatres have a series of overhead bars, normally part of a flying system, on which it is possible to hang lanterns. (See subsection 5.4 – Overstage machinery.)

Lanterns are rigged at stage level and then flown up to the correct height (usually between 5m and 15m). Access to focus them is more of a problem and needs to be considered in any new theatre design. One solution is to have a series of flown 'lighting bridges' on which the lanterns are hung either side of catwalks that technicians can use to give them access to the rig.

Bridges must allow all common types of theatre lanterns and moving lights to be hung at several different heights without their movement being restricted:

- They should be safe places to work with rails and kick boards to prevent falling
- It should be possible to rig flown bridges in different positions up and down stage.

Bridges have the advantage of easy access, but they are wider than a conventional bar and will limit the space available for scenery. They are harder to move around for different productions and difficult to mask from the audience's view. They may not, therefore, be suitable for all theatres.

Sides of the stage

Ladders
Most lighting designs require side lights rigged at various heights on ladders hung at the sides of the stage. Their movable rungs start just above head height and the top rung should be just below the fly floor. They can be tracked or flown to varied positions to suit different productions.

6.3.4 Lighting ladders
Photograph: Peter Angier

Ideally there would be two ladder positions provided, one just offstage of the ends of the flying bars and another further offstage.

Booms
Booms are vertical poles with lights attached, usually supported from the floor. These allow lighting designers to use low angles of side light.

6.3.5 A ballet boom -
Royal Opera House
Photograph: Mark White

Dip traps
These are panels in the stage floor that can be lifted up to allow temporary cable to be laid safely. They often accommodate dimmer and data outlets as well. There should also be a way to run cable from the stage to the auditorium out of sight and without interfering with the safety curtain (See subsection 5.5).

The troughs revealed when the traps are lifted should be deep and wide enough to accommodate the more commonly found connectors in theatre, e.g. 16A BS 4343 ceeform connectors, socapex and Harting-type muticore connectors, etc.

Fly floor rail
Fly floors and bridges round the sides of the flytower should have one or more rails on which lights can be rigged.

Perches
Another crucial lighting position is a vertical tower or 'perch' just upstage of the proscenium. These allow the rigging of lanterns at any height from floor level to just above the height of the proscenium. They should be accessed by a series of stairs/ladders and platforms.

If the theatre has an adjustable proscenium opening these perch positions should track on- and offstage with it (See subsection 5.3).

6.3.6 A perch
Photograph: Peter Angier

Footlight positions
Footlights are sometimes used along the downstage edge of the stage. A channel with a removable lid along the very front edge of the stage should be installed to hide any cables and transformers that run to the footlights. If the theatre has an orchestra pit it will also be helpful to provide a rigging position on the inside face of the orchestra pit wall. (See Section 4.9 – Orchestra pit.)

Lighting in the auditorium

Box booms

Box booms are located at the sides of the auditorium inside what may sometimes be audience boxes. They are by far the most important lighting position in an auditorium, but can sometimes be overlooked.

It must be possible to rig lights at different heights from stage floor level to the top of the auditorium. Safe and easy access must be designed for these positions and they should be able to accommodate the rigging of large automated lanterns.

Slots

Many theatres have been designed with lighting 'slots' instead of boxes at the sides of the auditorium. These rigging positions are angled so the lights themselves are hidden from the audience. They must be wide enough to allow a lantern to see both sides of the stage.

Advance bar

If the stage extends through the proscenium creating a forestage, it is usually necessary to hang a bar or a bridge, so that it can be lit from above. A bridge is preferable because access is possible for focusing and maintenance (See subsection 5.4).

High front light

An even general cover requires high front light positions, at an angle of about 45° from head height on stage. Theatres provide these positions either with a series of bridges above the auditorium or with rigging positions at the sides and back of the auditorium.

Lighting bridges

The spacing of the bridges will vary according to the size of the stage and the auditorium, but all the bridges should be the full width of the auditorium to give the widest possible angles of view onto the stage. Where there is a series of bridges they must not restrict each other's view of the stage.

Slips or 'high sides'

An alternative to bridges is a high side or 'slip' position as seen on the Royal Court drawing in Figure 6.3.2. These have the advantage of a better side angle than bridges.

Circle fronts

Where the theatre has tiers or circles, lighting positions should be built into their fronts. These positions should follow all around the curve of the circle front, and allow a lantern to be rigged anywhere along it. Particular consideration needs to be given to how this area is to be accessed as rigging and focusing in this position can be both hazardous and ergonomically uncomfortable.

Bars in circle ceiling

This is another useful angle, but a safe system of access must be considered.

Additional auditorium positions and temporary cable routes

The most flexible auditoria will have a system built into the walls allowing lanterns to be hung in additional unusual places. There will also need to be a system for getting cable to them discretely via carefully planned temporary cable routes. These comprise a coordinated set of holes through walls and hooks over doorways and public thoroughfares that provide safe, fire-proofed and acoustically acceptable openings for cable, when put in the theatre for a particular performance.

Followspot positions

In many theatres followspots can only be placed in a central cabin at the back of the auditorium. As followspot operators usually communicate through the show to coordinate with the stage manager and their fellow operatives, it is useful to place them in an acoustically protected booth away from the audience.

Followspot positions with a side view of the stage should be provided, though it is common practice for these to be 'open' positions.

Lighting for the open stage

Vince Herbert, Head of Lighting at the RSC, suggests that as a rule of thumb, a lighting position at a line drawn 45° from the stage will be very important in providing facial illumination for the actor. (See subsection 4.7 – Lighting and sound in the auditorium.)

But in the open stage environment particular care should be taken to provide adequate lighting rigging points to cover both an actor's 'looking-out' position (where the actor is standing at the edge of the stage facing the audience) and the 'looking-in' position (where the actor is standing at the edge of the stage facing inwards). Lighting the 'looking-in' position is generally very difficult to achieve. There is a critical balance between providing enough illumination to the performer's face and ensuring that the audience in the front row is not blinded by that same light.

Top light, high side light and 'looking-in' lighting can only be provided from a position above the stage and such provision needs to be carefully integrated into the overall aesthetic of the space.

and finally...

If suitable positions are not provided, theatre designers and technicians tend to just create their own. These will usually be more intrusive than the properly designed permanent position the building's design team had avoided for fear of it being unattractive!

6.3.7 A moving light rigged on a flightcase
Photograph: Rob Halliday

6.4   Lighting control

Any lighting console, no matter how brilliant, can be rendered useless in the wrong hands. A calm, quick and knowledgeable operator is the essential addition to make a system invisible to the designer and allow us to get on with the real job, lighting the show.

Neil Austin, Lighting Designer

Evolution

Lighting control has changed dramatically through the years of electric light, from a crew directly manipulating dimmers side-stage to a single operator in a control room running a console remote from the dimmers.

The general availability of computerised 'memory' systems from the 1970s onwards fundamentally changed the process of lighting design. Without the delay required to manually 'plot' (write down) lighting levels, designers could create lighting with the actors during rehearsals rather than in special lighting sessions.

More recently, the arrival of automated lighting equipment and other new technology has increased the complexity of lighting control exponentially. Lighting operators originally dealt with one parameter per light – intensity; everything else (position, colour, size, shape) was set manually at the light. With automated lighting, the operator – now often titled the programmer – must deal with those other parameters at the console.

It is vital therefore that the lighting programmer has a good view of the stage.

Lighting control positions

Control room

For a conventional proscenium arch theatre, a lighting control room should ideally be at the centre-rear of the auditorium with an observation window giving a clear view of the stage, uninterrupted by pillars or by the heads of audience members and undistorted (by tilting, tinting or reflections). The room should be acoustically isolated from the auditorium but with an electronic relay of the show audio. It should be possible to open the window for direct contact with the auditorium if required.

The control room will require both white 'worklight' lighting and localised performance lighting, adjustable for intensity and position and masked so as not to spill through the window. Many modern lighting consoles have built-in touch screens: direct toplight often renders these illegible. If LED task lights are to be specified, it should be checked that these do not flicker when run at low levels.

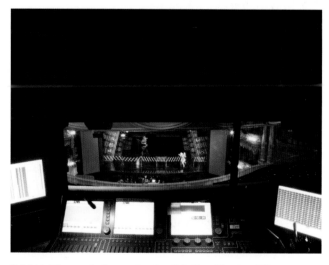

6.4.1 Lighting control room, London Paladium Theatre, UK
Photograph: Mark White

The control room will need flat working space for the console itself and any external monitors it requires, and for a laptop or notepad. Ergonomic, adjustable seating should be provided for the operator and at least one other person. Provision should be made for accommodating ancillary equipment in a rack beneath the main desk area. Multiple mains outlets should be available both above and below the desk surface, and an uninterruptable power supply (UPS) should be provided for the lighting console and related show-critical equipment (some consoles have this built in). It can be helpful to provide worklight below the desk surface.

A concealed but accessible cable route from control room to stage may be desirable to enable visiting shows to use their own cabling or to deal with future cable types.

Access to the control room should be from outside the auditorium, the route preferably separate from public areas. The route should allow equipment to be carried or flightcases to be rolled easily in and out of the control room. (Flightcases are portable road boxes used by hire companies and touring productions and can be as large as 2500mm x 800mm.)

The control room should be fully accessible for wheelchair users wherever such provision is reasonable. Where this is not possible, for example, in historic buildings, alternative operating positions should be provided.

Rear auditorium control position
Particularly in theatres that receive touring shows, there may be a need for a control position inside and at the rear of the auditorium, often shared with a touring sound desk. The position should provide a flat floor with clear access for flight cases, and offer a cable route to the stage and control room and duplicates of the lighting control, power and communication system connection points (comms) and worklight and house light controls found in the control room. Removable seats should be provided in this location, with storage for removed seats nearby.

Technical rehearsal control position: 'production desks'
Lighting programmers now usually position the control desk next to the lighting designer in a mid-auditorium location during technical rehearsals, allowing direct communication with the designer and other collaborators and giving themselves the clearest view of the stage while focusing moving lights.

Temporary desks and seating are often created from wooden boards laid over auditorium seating, but such ad-hoc arrangements are unsatisfactory ergonomically

and cause damage to the theatre's seats. A more considered solution should be provided, perhaps incorporating the ability to remove theatre seats and replace them with ergonomic office chairs. Connectivity (electrical, lighting control, comms) should be provided adjacent to this position to reduce set-up time and trip hazard risks.

6.4.2 Lighting designer and programmer at the temporary auditorium control position for On The Town, English National Opera at the Coliseum, London, UK
Photograph: Rob Halliday

Other control positions
Particularly in flexible venues, other control positions may be required. The lighting control infrastructure should reflect this by making connection points available as widely as possible.

6.5 Sound system infrastructure design

Whatever the sound designer asks for, the first tool needed for creating rewarding, memorable theatre sound is a well-designed infrastructure.

Jeremy Dunn, Head of Sound,
Royal Shakespeare Company

A well-designed sound system infrastructure is a key component in the success of any performing arts building. The basic approach to the design process is to establish the central location for sound system equipment and patching, the types of facilities needed throughout the building, and the positions where these facilities are likely to be required.

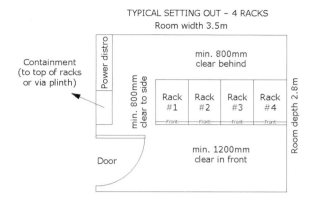

6.5.1 Drawing setting out small and large amp rack rooms
Diagram: Charcoalblue, Jon Stevens

The sound system equipment room

The equipment room is the heart of any sound system installation. It is not normally part of the main control area but may be sited next to it. The room houses the equipment racks which accommodate all of the patchbays and equipment for the various systems, with sufficient space to allow for future additions – a good rule of thumb is to allow 25 to 30 per cent of unused space in any rack.

Each equipment rack requires a dedicated power supply (generally rated at 32A SPN) with internal power distribution provided in the rear of the rack. Dedicated cooling for the room is also normally required.

Racks should be as deep as possible – 800mm will accommodate most typical theatre AV equipment – and must have at least 1200mm clear space in front and at least 800mm behind. Racks should also be as high as reasonably practicable: 41U is a common height, though taller racks are available. Allowance must be made for containment to be routed above the racks, or alternatively in a plinth in the floor. Where racks cannot be mounted to provide for rear access, they will need to be installed in pairs with clear access to one side of each rack – but this is not an ideal solution.

- A typical small theatre – a studio space up to say 250 seats – is likely to need 3 or 4 full-height equipment racks, which implies an equipment room of at least 3m x 4m.

- A medium theatre up to 750 seats would need 7 or 8 racks, requiring a space of 5m x 4.5m.
- A large theatre of 1,200 seats or more is likely to need 10 or more racks and a room of at least 5m x 6m. A theatre of this size may also need another equipment room close to the loudspeaker clusters to accommodate the amplifiers for these.

Sound system facilities in the theatre

Mic/line analogue audio
Mic/line audio points provide a connection point for use with microphones or line-level audio source equipment. They are wired in screened twisted-pair cabling and are terminated with 3-pin XLR sockets, which may be parallel-terminated with 3-pin XLR plugs. Multiple ways may also be provided.

Digital audio
Multiple channels of digital audio may be transmitted over industry-standard Cat5/Cat6 IT network cable, although care must be taken to prevent problems from arising from the latency (delay) produced by the conversion of the audio signal from analogue to digital and back again.

Increasingly, digital audio and other AV signals may also be transmitted over fibreoptic cable. Some mixing console manufacturers have custom protocols for this, while other non-console-specific systems are also available. Tielines for other digital audio protocols such as MADI (Multichannel Audio Digital Interface) or AES/EBU digital audio may also be provided where required.

Cuelights

Cuelight points provide a connection point for use with cuelight outstations fitted with red and green indicators, which are used to cue performers or effects.

Cuelights are controlled from the stage manager's desk and in large installations should be patchable.

Backstage communications

Technical intercom points are for use with dedicated beltpacks and headsets with boom-arm microphones.

The technical intercom system may also be interfaced with handheld radios/radio headsets to allow operators to move freely around the stage.

A building-wide paging/show relay system distributes voice calls and show relay (the sound of the performance) throughout the building. Front of house calls are made to the audience. Backstage calls are made to the performers and backstage staff. Paging/show relay speakers are generally wired using multipair cabling carrying 100v-line amplified audio. Paging microphone points allow the connection of paging microphones in key locations such as the stage door and the stage manager's desk.

Video

Video tielines carry composite or component video images throughout the theatre.

Video signals are often routed to the foyers to provide an image of the show for late-arriving audience members.

Video signals are also routed backstage to provide a picture of the stage to assist technicians and performers running the performance. This might include video monitors at the stage manager's desk and on circle front carrying pictures from the conductor in the orchestra pit.

Loudspeakers

Loudspeaker tielines carry amplified audio signals from amplifiers in the AV equipment room.

Assisted listening

Assisted listening points carry custom data for infrared radiator panels, which when used with an appropriate infrared receiver provide amplified audio for the hard-of-hearing and, potentially, spoken text description for the partially sighted. An induction loop may also be installed in the auditorium for audience members with hearing aids. This comprises a thin copper tape that

can be installed under carpets. Care should be taken in multiple venue complexes to avoid cross-talk between induction loops.

AV system power

AV power is wired with standard electrical cabling and is generally terminated with unswitched 13A socket outlets. Some AV power outlets may be UPS-maintained, and AV power outlets may also be contactor-controlled to provide a method for switching off groups of AV equipment when not required.

Single-phase outlets terminated with International Electrotechnical Commission (IEC) – EN60309-2 sockets may also be provided in key locations for use with large sound mixing consoles or large amplified loudspeaker systems.

To minimise the risk of interference from mains-borne noise and voltage variation, AV power is distributed via a dedicated power distribution system which is used solely to supply AV equipment and is designed and installed to minimise the possibility of electromagnetic interference being induced in the AV signal cabling.

Sound system wired infrastructure

Facilities panels

Selecting the positions and quantities of each of the facilities described above is the final element of designing an AV infrastructure.

The planning process requires the position, size and height of each facilities panel, supported by a schedule detailing each panel's facilities. Each panel is provided with facilities appropriate to its position.

Further drawings describe the system schematically, and show the setting out of the connectors on the facilities panels, and of the equipment in the audio-visual equipment racks.

Containment

Routing the wiring from each facilities panel back to the audio-visual equipment room requires careful coordination with the design team to find acceptable routes through the building, and to coordinate these routes with other wired services. Some services (e.g. Ethernet data) also have wiring length limitations which must be taken into consideration when defining the routes.

It is usual to require a number of dedicated containment groups for the audio-visual wiring, using fully enclosed metal trunking to provide protection from induced noise, and maintaining a minimum physical separation between sensitive signal wiring and mains power wiring to prevent electromagnetic interference.

6.6   Sound rigging positions

The best efforts of the system designer are all-too-often compromised through the lack of suitable and accessible rigging points in performance venues, leading to unsightly and acoustically unsuitable positioning. It's a rare venue that has sufficiently well-thought-out rigging points and cable access to make the installation of such systems simple and safe.

John Leonard, Sound Designer

6.6.1 Proscenium boom for 'Oliver!' at Theatre Royal Drury Lane, London, UK
Photograph: John Owens

Imaging of the source of sound in theatre is of paramount importance. The listening audience should feel that the sound is coming from the performer and not from a large black box hanging from the proscenium arch.

The ideal position either side of the proscenium is a fixed upright ladder beam or 'proscenium boom' from which the speaker systems (and some lighting units) can be hung.

The advantages of a ladder beam over a single pipe for a boom are rigidity and the fact that it can be used for access to the rigging locations provided that sufficient provision for PPE (personal protection equipment) is given – which includes lanyard fixing points and fall arrest systems.

A great deal of negotiation is required between lighting and sound design teams to share what is usually a very congested area of the theatre. The conflicting issues are that the sound design team will usually want the speakers to go as close to the stage as possible while still allowing the speaker fronts to be 'seen' by as many members of the audience as possible. However, they must also be far enough to one side so as not to impede the audience's view of the stage. This is always the best location for the lights as well!

The sound designer's loudspeaker palette is growing every day. Different manufacturers offer varying styles and sizes of speaker systems, designed for a huge array of uses. However a fundamental design choice these days is whether to use a 'line array' style loudspeaker, or a more conventional single cabinet design. Both types of basic loudspeaker have a place in the design process and both types and styles may be used in the same design.

Just as positions either side of the performing area are important, so are the areas above and below; if it is possible to rig in these areas, they will assist in providing an even and balanced 'picture' of sound emanating from the stage area.

Above the stage is the place to rig a central cluster. This gives an overall picture of sound from a central location. This is especially useful for the amplified 'voice' to come from.

The choice and size of speaker system will dictate how these are rigged. A standard method is to hang a truss from points in the roof from which a loudspeaker arrangement can be attached. If a single line-array hang is required then it is cleaner to hang the array from dedicated rigging points and therefore remove the need for a truss. If the sound reproduced by this system is part of the proscenium picture then these points should be as close to the proscenium opening as possible. This will ensure the sound from these boxes will seem part of the overall picture.

Any speakers that can be rigged below the acting area on the stage riser (front fills), which have a good shot at 'seeing' the audience, should be considered to be a useful addition to the sound 'picture' as they will help to pull the image to the stage rather than keep it high in the cluster, or wide on the proscenium booms.

Modern loudspeaker systems try to achieve a balanced level throughout the listening space. If this were to be attempted using only the speakers at the stage opening, there would be a considerable loss of volume the further away from the source the listener is situated. This dilemma is often overcome by the addition of rows of loudspeakers rigged further into the auditorium under the balcony overhangs or off circle front bars. The audio content that passes through these

6.6.2 Stalls delays: 'Oliver!' at Theatre Royal Drury Lane, London, UK
Photograph: John Owens

loudspeakers is delayed so that the sound picture stays on the stage. Hence the generic term for these positions as 'delays', referred to in the USA as 'under-balconies'.

The size and positions for these delay speakers will depend very much on the production design and the area that they are required to cover.

As can be seen in Figure 6.6.3, the amount of equipment required for a modern-day musical is growing every day and rigging positions that are complementary to the theatre architecture, if not thought about in the original design, can be difficult to achieve later in an aesthetically pleasing manner.

6.6.3 Circle front sound rigging: 'Billy Elliot' Imperial Theater New York, USA
Photograph: John Owens

Steve Brown of the Manchester Royal Exchange suggests that the open stage requires a particularly flexible sound system so that all sound effects sit properly in the overall sound picture being created and any music can be evenly distributed around the auditorium. The necessity to be able to place loudspeakers in many positions both in the auditorium and on the stage is important as localisation of the sound on an open stage production often explains and gives reason to certain aspects of a production.

6.7   Sound control positions

There are very few shows that would not benefit from an auditorium sound control position, and very many for which such a position is essential. My criterion is that if there are any live microphones, a sound control position which puts the sound operator in the same acoustic environment as the audience, is required. I have not yet found a sound control room, however big the window, from which it was possible to mix even the simplest musical.

Paul Arditti, Sound Designer

The role of the sound operator

Sound for theatre comprises playback of music, effects, soundscapes and atmospheric backgrounds that set mood or establish location. Cueing, fading and routing is plotted and programmed during technical rehearsal by the operator so that sequences can be accurately reproduced for every show.

The role of the sound operator is to balance microphone sources and to initiate playback of sound effects with precise timing, cued by the stage manager or taken visually from actions on stage.

A high degree of artistic interpretation and sensitivity is required from the sound operator who will respond and adjust to the subtle variations of each night's performance.

The success of an amplified musical performance therefore relies heavily on placing the operator at a prime location in the auditorium where they can hear and experience the show as if part of the audience. This is the reason why sound designers go to great lengths to get mixing consoles installed at visually prominent locations, sometimes with the loss of many high revenue earning seats. Fortunately digital mixing systems have reduced the footprint required by this position.

As a general rule the sound control room at the back of the auditorium does not provide an effective operating space for most events, and provision for an operating area within the auditorium, either temporary or permanent, is necessary.

Sound control spaces for theatre

Rear of auditorium shared control room

This is a control space shared by several personnel (lighting, stage management, automation, etc.) with a clear view to the stage.

- The window should be angled by a few degrees to prevent operators from seeing their own reflection in the glass.
- An opening window improves communications during set-up and rehearsal.
- Computer flooring is often used to manage cabling to installed patching and equipment racks.

Rear of auditorium separate control rooms

A better arrangement is to split control rooms according to function with separate rooms for lighting, sound and video projection equipment. Effectiveness of the control room for sound mixing will depend on the area of the opening window and the depth of any balcony overhang in front.

Rear auditorium mix position

The effectiveness of a rear of auditorium mixing location depends on the depth of the balcony overhang and whether there is line of sight to the loudspeaker system. The permanent sound position for the Olivier Theatre in London is an example. The operator is not centrally located but hears auditorium sound well with a clear view and easy access to the stage.

6.7.1 Sound mix position: Olivier Theatre, London, UK
Photograph: Richard Borkum

6.7.2 Centre stalls mix position (and production desk position): Cesars Palace, Las Vegas, USA
Photograph: Richard Borkum

6.7.3 Live mix area next to the main control room
Hull Truck Studio Theatre, Hull, UK
Photograph: Richard Borkum

Centre auditorium mix position

A centre auditorium mix location gives the best listening position. Access for temporary equipment and communications to the stage are good, but audience sightlines directly to the sides and rear of the position may be compromised.

A centre auditorium position works particularly well in a parterre-style stalls layout with the mixing console in a sunken pit in front of the parterre wall which minimises any impact on sightlines. A motorised elevator lift will reduce the time required to replace the mixing console wagon with a seating wagon.

Open mix balcony

An open sound mix balcony located at the back of the auditorium provides a very effective and discrete mixing position. This is often employed in the Las Vegas-style casino showroom where the venue is built around the show. It can work well in a courtyard or open stage theatre, though this may occasionally be at the expense of centreline seats at balcony level.

Making provision for sound control equipment

Sound control equipment consists of a mixing console, audio processing and playback units. There is a considerable amount of cable and connections so clear access to the rear of equipment for set-up and troubleshooting should be made wherever possible.

Digital mixing consoles have enabled space and wiring requirements for sound control to be significantly reduced. They are more compact then an analogue counterpart with equivalent channel count and signal processing is accomplished within the console reducing the requirement for outboard equipment.

Theatre playback software has replaced samplers, compact disc and mini disc players. A computer with sound card can be remotely located and triggered by the mixing console or from a remote pushbutton unit. Keyboard, monitor and mouse can be extended to the sound operator or to the designer's desk in the auditorium.

Show control systems have enabled complex sound designs to be automated and there are now many shows

6.7.4 Auditorium mixing consoles and number of seats taken
Photograph: Richard Borkum

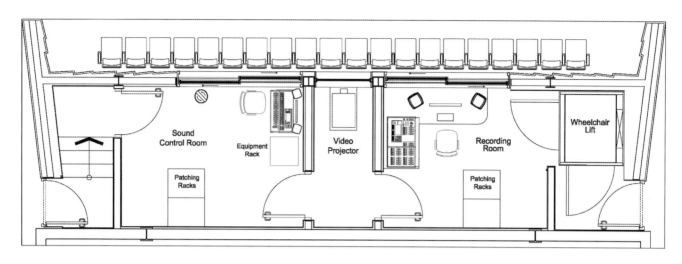

6.7.5 Concert hall control suite:
Guildhall School, Barbican, London, UK

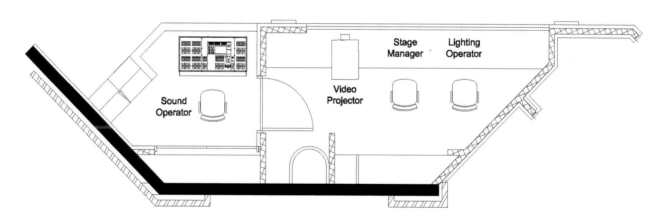

6.7.6 Main auditorium control room:
Hull Truck Theatre, Hull, UK
Drawing: Wright & Wright Architects

that can be operated by the stage manager from the prompt desk without the need for a sound operator.

Typical current mixing consoles are shown in Figure 6.7.4 to give an indication of how many seats may be lost when placed in an auditorium. Most manufacturers have ceased production of large format analogue consoles. However provision should still be made in touring and concert venues as they are likely to continue to appear on technical riders (technical specification issued to venues by touring companies) for some time.

Making provision for the stage manager

The stage manager is responsible for the technical coordination of performances and rehearsal and sits at a custom-built control desk. The stage manager's desk or prompt desk has intercom, paging, cue light controls and video monitors. In a proscenium arch theatre the stage manager's desk is traditionally located in the downstage left corner of the stagehouse. In flexible or open stage venues the stage manager usually moves to the control room or to a side auditorium box. Alternative supplementary positions downstage right and at the production desk position in the auditorium should also be provided.

Figures 6.7.5 and 6.7.6 show two control rooms, setting out examples for different types of venue:

Example 1 Concert hall control suite (Figure 6.7.5)
- The live sound room to auditorium left has a mixing console installed perpendicular to the opening window enabling the operator to lean into the auditorium.
- A recording control room is situated auditorium right.
- Installed patching and processing racks face away from the window so that equipment displays do not distract on stage. Access to rear of the racks is required for installation and maintenance.
- The lighting control room has been located at high level since both live sound operator and recording engineer require quick access to the stage for set-up and sound check.
- A video projector is housed in a separate room on the centreline and wheel-chair access is provided by a lift into the recording room.
- A cable pass in the floor provides a route for temporary cables from the stage and into the back of the auditorium for a temporary mixing console.

Example 2 Repertory theatre control suite (Figure 6.7.6)
- The control room for stage manager, lighting operator and video projector is situated auditorium right with a fixed window.
- A cat ladder provides quick access up to the amplifier and dimmer racks rooms above.
- The open live mix position is situated to the left with a locking roller shutter for security when the auditorium is not in use.
- Outboard equipment racks are housed underneath the mixing console.

6.8 Video technology in the theatre

I grew up in Manchester in the 60s. If I had been able to see Olivier's National Theatre at my local cinema, I would have gone all of the time.

Nicholas Hytner,
Director of the National Theatre

For many years now, William Dudley has been mixing live stage action with film effects ... It doesn't always work ... In Peter Pan, however ... the effect is often spectacular ... It feels, thrillingly, as if we are flying with them.

Charles Spencer, *Daily Telegraph*, June 2009

Introduction

Video within the context of a live theatre production is becoming ever more common as the moving image becomes part of everyday life, on the Internet, in our living rooms, in our telephones.

Video rarely works as a pure scenic device solely to drive the narrative of the story; a less literal treatment is often the most successful. Bill Dudley's *Peter Pan* production in 2009 set a new benchmark for computer-generated imagery (CGI) video integration with live actors to produce stunning flying sequences in-the-round.

Broadcasting and archival video is also becoming a way of improving theatre's accessibility. For example, show in recent years the New York Met, and London's Royal Opera House and National Theatre have all carried out simultaneous live broadcasts distributed nationally and internationally to local cinemas.

In many ways artistic teams are still searching for the perfect format to exploit this developing technology and the guidance given below responds to these developing techniques.

Video techniques in theatre can be considered under the following headings:

Capture	Recording/'grabbing' images for transmission live or at a later date.
Media production	Creating/manipulating/editing video images in a studio to create film or scenic video.
Presentation	Playback of images/scenic video to support productions.

NB: 35mm film projection techniques and requirements are not discussed here as this format is only rarely used to support theatrical production.

Capture

Camera positions for broadcast
Traditionally in the film world the director of photography is looking for a shot where the lens height is fractionally above the eyeline of the performer. Extreme angles such as beneath the eyeline and steep angles from a balcony can look 'alien' and difficult to integrate into the mix of a multi-camera shoot.

If a theatre anticipates that it will regularly broadcast performances, camera platforms or allocated spaces should be designed into the layout of the auditorium.

Wiring vs temporary cable routes
Wiring for visiting cameras is often particular to different camera manfacturers and formats and therefore a network of temporary cable routes should be considered rather than a dedicated infrastructure installation.

These should, as a minimum, permit visiting TV companies to install temporary cabling from the Outside Broadcast Truck parking bay (often the get-in), through any fire breaks to the rear of the auditorium and into the theatre's control rooms.

Media production

Video and digital still cameras are used for media capture but images are also created from graphics and all of these can be animated and finally composited to create media files which may then be replayed on a media server.

The following spaces are required in order to carry out these media production tasks. It should be noted that in a smaller venue or a receiving house it is likely that this production would take place at a remote facility or by a third party, and the spaces outlined below are therefore unlikely to be required.

Video recording studio
It is not anticipated that a dedicated recording studio would be required by many theatre companies – but rehearsal rooms should be suitably prepared to provide the function for occasional use. There should be wired links to a video edit suite and the theatre's control rooms.

Video edit suite
The room should be 12m^2 to 15m^2 with access to daylight. There should be a rack room enclosure adjacent (or within the space) for hard disks, media servers and other noisy heat-generating equipment. The plant space should be cooled. Access to both the front and rear of the 19-inch (483mm) equipment racking is required and in a large theatre two racks wide would be appropriate. The edit suite need not be close to the auditoria.

Video stores
10m^2 for a small company, 25m^2 for a large theatre company. No daylight needed. Step-free access to the stages, get-in and rehearsal rooms essential.

Presentation

Principally two types of video presentation need addressing:
- The presentation of films to an audience in the traditional sense
- The use of video within the set design of a show or as a graphic, illustrative element.

Film presentation
Currently, 35mm film remains the main distribution format for film exhibition. Any venue with film programming should consider installation of a 35mm projector with the usual specification of a long play system such as a tower or cake stand.

Digital film presentation is becoming widespread and high-quality digital video projection will have taken over from 35mm projection in the years to come.

Scenic projection

A multipurpose venue requiring a projector for onstage presentations should consider a high specification digital projector. The current benchmark for digital projection is the 1080P High Definition format. It is important that any projector specified for a venue should at least satisfy this picture resolution.

A digital projector is best located within a projection or control room with a glass projection window containing the associated noise. It is possible to rig a projector from the ceiling of the auditorium but this has the disadvantage of being inaccessible should there be a problem, and potentially noisy.

Ideally a dedicated, acoustically isolated projection room would be provided on the centre line. Most modern projectors allow for keystone correction so the room can be relatively high up as long as the projector has a good shot to the stage, clear of the usual lighting equipment that is also often positioned on the centre line.

The room does not have to be a dedicated space and could share with follow spot positions but not a control room. Key stoning from the side is possible but should be avoided as this forces costly and complex systems to be employed.

Small projectors can be located on the balcony front. A special pocket should be used for larger units although this is rarely achieved without the loss of some prime seating locations.

Rear projection is ideal and requires two architectural considerations – tie lines at the rear of the theatre and a sufficient stage depth to allow an image the width of the proscenium – the maximum wide lens ratio usually available is 1:0.8 where 1 = width and 0.8 = throw. So a proscenium opening of 10m requires 8m projection depth (most good theatres would allow a deeper stage depth for scenery). This then allows action to take place in front of the back projection screen but behind the proscenium or stage edge.

Projectors have also been integrated into moving light yokes with onboard cameras and media servers. They can be treated as a moving light that has digital gobos or as a conventional video source. Noise and low brightness have limited their use in theatre but this area is rapidly developing. Their obvious use is to point video into hard to reach places or move video imagery around a stage.

Where the projector carries footage that is central to the plot of a production then stacking of multiple projectors should be allowed for. Sometimes two projectors will sit one above the other providing extra brightness and back-up. Double or triple stacking is also required for some more complex scenic effects.

On the open stage, projector location can be even more problematic – especially if there is a requirement for 360° projection. Often it will be the set that needs to accommodate the projectors – and the video and temporary cable route infrastructures should support and enable this.

Screens and surfaces

Projection screens follow the principles of light and optics. Front projection screens are often white and will reflect projected light back into the audience whereas rear projection screens are pale through to dark grey and transmit light through a screen to the audience.

Professional screen materials have known characteristics for reflectivity, transmission and viewing angles. They can be welded to make any size and edges can be fastened in many ways.

For theatre stages the projectors are often required to be positioned beyond the recommended angle for optimum performance. This means the screen performance may be unpredictable and therefore screen testing is recommended.

The angle from projector to screen is the axis of the light. 'On axis' refers to the projector being perpendicular to the centre of the screen. It is possible to have a projection angle of 50°, but if this is from an advance fly bar over the stalls, the reflected light will primarily hit the downstage, making the brightness level for the circle relatively low.

Many interesting materials such as gauzes, scrims, filled cloths, plastics, foils and painted surfaces are all currently used for effects.

Video control room

An optimal film projection room for cinema was given in Roderick Ham's *Theatre Planning*. However, a modern dedicated theatre video control room is likely to be for one operator and a smaller space than a conventional projection booth.

In some productions with very few video effects it is possible to have either the sound operator or the lighting (LX) operator take on these cues – but usually only after the show has been technically put on stage by a video operator from a production desk position. The video control position requires a good view of the stage and in a proscenium house a reasonable vertical sightline to the rear of the stage.

Within the control room there should be a desk surface for a vision mixer or digital playback from a video server along with a series of video monitors. This facility can be located in the same control room as the LX operator or stage manager.

As with the video edit suite, the control room should have an adjacent rack room enclosure.

SECTION EDITOR

Andy Hayles	Managing Director of Charcoalblue

CONTRIBUTORS

Mike Atkinson	Lighting equipment and infrastructure
Bruno Poet	Lighting rigging positions
Rob Halliday	Lighting control positions
Jon Stevens	Sound system design
John Owens	Sound rigging positions
Richard Borkum	Sound control positions
Flip Tanner	Video technology in the Theatre

6.8.1 William Dudley's production of 'Peter Pan' illustrating the use of video in live theatre
Photograph: Simon Annand

Section 7
Backstage provision

Contents

7.1 Introduction

Backstage areas are there to provide accommodation and support services for those whose work is focused on the stage. But who those people are, what their work involves, and what accommodation they require, varies not just with the setting and cast numbers of individual productions but also with the changing requirements of the production process. The kind of work undertaken can include strenuous manual handling; rigging sophisticated electronic equipment; carpentry and welding. Some of those involved will need to prepare documents such as running lists or cue-sheets, others may be working with potentially dangerous chemicals or with expensive musical instruments; singers and dancers will need to warm up vocally or physically. At one moment there may be no more than a couple of painters alone in the theatre putting the finishing touches to the scenery while a few hours later there could be two hundred people – technicians, stage management, musicians and performers – all contributing to the performance.

The following is a chronological outline of the production process.

- Whether in a producing theatre or in a receiving house, scenery needs to be brought onto the stage.
- Large, awkward and heavy items including flight cases and costume rails require easy access to all backstage areas.
- Lighting equipment and suspended scenic elements are flown or rigged.
- Production floor is laid.
- Major scenic pieces are assembled, placed on stage or put ready for scene changes.
- Lanterns are focused.
- Sound equipment is installed and checked.
- Painters complete or touch up floor and scenic elements.
- Basic lighting states are established and recorded on the lighting control.
- Stage management prepare props tables and set dressing.
- Wardrobe prepare performers with final costumes and wigs.
- Technical rehearsal, including performers and all technical staff, takes place (sometimes over several days).
- Dress rehearsal as above.
- Performances.

7.1.1 Stage and auditorium during fit-up
Photograph: David Evans

What follows is a guide to the accommodation and facilities required by the largest companies and in the largest theatres. Buildings designed for a smaller scale of presentation or those limited by considerations of space or finance may not be able, or need, to meet this specification. However, even the most modest production will differ only in scale and not in nature from the process outlined above. Each of these activities will still have to take place and those undertaking them will need to be accommodated.

The on-site provision required includes:

- Get-in
- Production workshops, offices and related storage
- Dressing rooms
- Staff facilities.

Additional facilities which may be either on-site or provided elsewhere:

- Construction workshops
- Rehearsal spaces.

7.2 Circulation

Circulation is one of the most important aspects of backstage design and planning. Most people will want to be as close to the stage as possible but it is unlikely that all will be able to be so accommodated. Whatever solutions are found it is important that vertical circulation should be close to the stage entrance. The provision of alternative routes is often helpful.

A dedicated crossover corridor should be available (behind the back wall of the stage and at stage level) with easy access to both stage left and stage right. This is in addition to any understage routes linking one side of the stage with the other.

All parts of the building need to be accessible for skips, flight cases and other heavy equipment, which may need to be taken to areas such as the pit or the grid. Wardrobe, laundry and wigs need close access to all dressing rooms. All doors and corridors, particularly where there are corners to be turned, should be wide enough for costume rails or skips to pass along and, if they have to travel between floors, a suitably sized lift should be provided.

Bumper rails should be fitted to the corridor walls along all main (flight case) routes from the delivery dock throughout backstage. These should be of a durable material (hardwood timber is best) and protrude about 25mm from the wall making sure they are deeper than any skirting. Two rails should be fitted parallel to each other at about 500mm and 800mm from the floor. Doors should be protected with kick plates to a minimum height of 900mm.

A performer may have to go quickly from dressing room to stage wearing an elaborate costume. The doors through which they pass should not be less than 850mm wide and the corridors not less than 1500mm wide to avoid contact with other performers, similarly attired, going in the opposite direction. Corridor height should be not less than 2.4m to allow for headdresses. Ironmongery should be chosen to avoid door handles or similar hazards, such as unprotected ends to handrails, which might catch clothing. Fire blankets, fire extinguishers or other equipment should be recessed or situated where they do not encroach on the clear width of the corridors. Equally, wall surfaces should be such that they will not damage delicate costume fabric.

Easy access between backstage and front of house (FOH) is essential at stage level but it is also desirable to have such access by an easy route to FOH technical facilities such as the control room, lighting bridges and follow-spot positions.

Zoning of services

It is rare that all parts of the building will need to be accessed at the same time. Even during performances, when the building is at its most busy, some storage areas or repair workshops will not be in use.

During the initial get-in and fit-up period it may be that only the stage, workshops and crew facilities are needed. At other times actors may need access to dressing rooms or wardrobe when the stage is not occupied. Almost any combination of areas can be required in various circumstances.

Where there are no full-time security personnel it is important that working-light controls are such that an easy well-lit exit can be made from any part of the building. Indeed, even if there is full-time security, sections should be able to be easily closed down as it can take an individual a very long time to patrol the entire theatre, locking up and extinguishing lights.

For energy conservation reasons as much as anything else, thought should be given to systems which allow the cutting off of power to individual areas when they are not in use.

Security

Secure access is required between FOH and backstage, taking into account any local requirements for fire separation of these areas.

Most rooms will need to be secured. Some, however, may need to be accessed by more than one group of people at different times. Dressing rooms, for example, may need to be entered by dressers while the actors are on stage or before they arrive at the theatre. The personnel using the rooms will change quite frequently, particularly in touring or repertoire theatres, which means that careful thought should be given to the practicalities of keypad or card-operated systems as well as access to and security of keys.

7.3 Get-in

The get-in is one of the most important considerations in the setting out and design of a theatre. It is the access point for whatever spectacle is to be mounted, and often requires a large amount of space. The get-ins could require access for 12m long rolled cloths or lighting bars, for 7.5m x 2.3m framed flats or heavy rolling road boxes, and for larger musical instruments.

7.3.1 Get-in, Palace Theatre London, UK
Photograph: David Evans

The location of the get-in is very much dictated by the orientation of the venue. It may influence the shape and location of the stage and the auditorium and, if inadequate, could even affect the viability of a project. The impact on the architectural design is also a challenge as the access size required often takes up a large area of an outside wall.

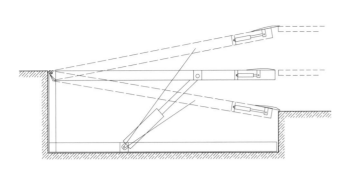

7.3.2 Diagram of a dock leveller
Diagram: Jeff Phillips

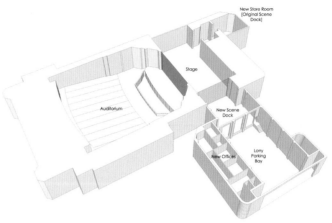

7.3.3 State-of-the-art get-in which is being constructed at the Mayflower in Southampton

Get-ins vary from direct street-level access through major lift access to high-level doors requiring a hoist or lifts to get scenery and equipment in and out. The proximity of housing also needs to be taken into account. The final get-out invariably happens during the night, directly after the last performance. However careful the operatives are, this is a noisy activity. Good lighting is essential both inside and out.

A get-in at ground level

The best possible arrangement (of all) is to have the delivery lorry's tailboard at stage level. The loading bay can then be equipped with a 'dock leveller' to allow adjustment to match varying tailboard heights. The loads can then be rolled on and off the lorry directly at stage level. This can be achieved easily if the stage is about 1m above the street.

Where the stage is at ground level, consideration needs to be given to getting the equipment off the trailer. Various ways are available such as powered ramps to allow equipment to be wheeled off and on. Forklift trucks can lift heavier loads but require increased floor loading and a place to park when not in use. Lighter equipment can be taken from the trailer and carried inside.

- Manually positioned ramps should be avoided as they are likely to be heavy to put in place.
- The loading bay should be completely flat to prevent scenery from falling over inside the delivery lorry during the get-in.
- In all cases a canopy should be provided to keep rain out and adequate lighting should be provided for night-working.
- Health and safety guidelines should be followed when setting out the loading bay.

Get-ins where stage is above or below the street

For a stage higher or lower than the street it will be necessary to provide an elevator for either the trailer or the scenery to get to stage level. The elevator can be located inside the building or outside.

A trailer lift is preferable as this allows the contents to be unloaded directly to stage level, removing 'double-handling'. Such a lift can also be programmed to stop with the tailboard at floor level.

Warehouse-type rolling crane hoists above high-level doors have been used in the past but these are an extremely slow method of operation and access may be dangerous. They should not be used as the main means of get-in for a theatre. Other items such as costumes, large orchestral instruments, nightly programmes, catering deliveries and so on need to be considered as do waste collections.

Dock doors

Dock doors should be at least 3m wide and 4m high to allow for anything in a trailer to be brought in easily. Doors can be hinged, sliding or indeed roller shutters, depending on acoustic requirements. An important consideration is good sound separation to keep street noises such as sirens from disrupting the performance. Double acoustic doors may be required to achieve this.

7.3.4 A vehicle lift at the Grand Theatre and Opera House, Leeds, UK
Photograph: Ric Green courtesy of Opera North

The scene dock

As well as outside influences, the layout inside needs to be sympathetic to the work flow required. A get-in opening directly onto the stage can disrupt stage operations, but a get-in opening onto a storage dock can get obstructed if there is much scenery to be stored.

A clear route is required through the dock with storage space at the sides and a height to match the expected built items of scenery.

High-level storage bars are an important asset, especially in a repertory house. They allow items to be laid off until required by another show in the repertory.

The frequency of use will vary depending on the current policy of the theatre. A long-running show will have a great deal of activity while mounting the production, but the get-in door may not then be needed for scenery for years. On the other hand a theatre operating a repertory system or a series of one-night stands may need to get in and out daily.

Safety considerations

Scenery can be awkwardly shaped, sometimes heavy and often delicate. It requires great care to be taken in its manoeuvring and handling. The theatre planner/architect can make a major contribution to the health and safety of the crews by careful design of the get-in.

Mechanical handling aids such as trolleys, dollies, overhead tracked hoists, pallet trucks, stacker trucks and forklift trucks should be expected. Forklift trucks require increased floor loading. A level floor throughout is essential.

Vehicle types and parking

Most scenery arrives on articulated trailers and sometimes in sea containers; small vans are used for lighter deliveries. The get-in must be able to accept all of these vehicles. In a city centre where access may be restricted, the turning circle required for vehicles will be very important. While articulated vehicles are very manoeuvrable, their overall length needs to be carefully plotted when setting out the building. Specialist traffic consultants may be required.

In a busy theatre, it may be preferable to be able to have several trailers backed up to the get-in at the same time so that different loads can be handled by different groups (stage, electrics, costumes, etc.).

The OB truck visit

With modern outside broadcast (OB) equipment, it has become preferable to make television relays direct from the theatre rather than bring productions into the TV studio. A typical relay requires at least a scanner and sound vehicle as well as equipment transport, so there may be a requirement for several vehicles to be positioned near the theatre. Easily accessed cable routes from this area to the stage, orchestra pit and auditorium should be built in to the building. It is useful to have cable trenches across pavement or pedestrian routes.

Future development

There is likely to be an increasing move towards mechanical handling of scenery, lighting and costumes. More equipment such as lighting bars will arrive pre-assembled to reduce fit-up time.

The number of venues embracing palletising of scenery is likely to increase, especially major repertoire theatres such as opera houses. This system typically consists of large pallets – commonly 9.5m x 2.3m – onto which the outgoing production is loaded. Handling equipment is then used to transfer the entire pallet and its load to the trailer, which transports them complete to the store. These systems can already be found in use in Vienna, Berlin, Munich, Gothenburg and London.

7.4 Production spaces

Workshop, wardrobe and laundry facilities are required for minor alterations and maintenance during the run of the show and have a different function to construction workshops which are used for the creation of scenery, props and costumes (construction workshops are discussed in subsection 7.6). Repair and maintenance workshops must be linked to the performance areas whereas construction workshops may be located elsewhere.

Repair and maintenance workshops

Scenery
Minor repairs to the set during the run of the show can be carried out in a small workshop opening off the stage or the scene dock. In a receiving theatre, typically in London's West End or other cases where the scenery is not built on the premises, this workshop has an even greater importance. It will require:
- a bench and vice
- a place for small hot works or spot welding
- compressed air handling for nail guns, etc.
- storage space for tools, nails, screws and ironmongery
- a cupboard to comply with Control of Substances Hazardous to Health (COSHH) Regulations
- sink
- ventilation including air extraction for solvents or sawdust
- flat floor
- lighting to workshop standards, power sockets for power tools (110 volt)
- first aid station including eyewash facilities.

7.4.1 A small repair workshop.

Properties
Properties may be found, hired or made. Where they are to be made this is best done in a properly equipped workshop which need not be near the stage area. However, there are many properties which may need to be repaired on a regular basis, or the action of the performance may demand that they are reassembled or redecorated daily. The scenic repair workshop should provide a dedicated area for this with appropriate ventilation and air extraction.

Technical maintenance workshop
Electrics, sound and audio-visual technicians will require a workshop for the repair and maintenance of stage lighting equipment, sound and AV equipment. This should be situated where there is easy access to the stage or lighting galleries and be within easy reach of the lantern store. It needs:
- at least one workbench
- another high desk/bench with vice, soldering iron
- a desk with PC and broadband/intranet for accessing on-line software updates
- storage for repair materials and racking for lanterns and cables
- first aid kit.

Stage
Cleaning cupboard including:
- low-level sink for cleaning mop and filling bucket
- cupboards for cleaning materials, mop, bucket, vacuum cleaner, brooms, etc.

Painters' facilities

It is almost inevitable that some painting will need to take place on the stage. This could be anything from a major painting of the set to a simple touching up of floor or joins in the scenery. It will always be a messy process and may involve several processes with drying periods in between. Because of the need to store paint and chemical cleaning agents and because of the inevitable mess which will be created, a room for painters near the stage should be dedicated to this purpose. It will require:

- light-coloured seamless vinyl flooring
- shelves for the storage of paint, thinners and so on
- COSHH cupboard for oil-based materials, solvents, etc.
- two large sinks (one at low level) with hot and cold water and paint trap
- a brush drying rack above the higher level sink
- a bench for preparing colours and cleaning tools
- good ventilation.

It should be noted that some of the paint will be applied with spray guns and provision should be made for easy access to a compressed air system or space provided for the use and storage of small compressors. A permanent system requires a minimum 200 litre tank fed by remote located 200 litres/min displacement compressor.

Running wardrobe

Apart from the main manufacturing wardrobe, which is discussed below, there should be separate provision for running repairs and minor alterations to be made to costumes in the current production. Even where the main wardrobe is on the same site, the differences in the working patterns of making staff and show staff and the need for maintenance facilities to be located close to the laundry and dressing rooms make this space essential in all types of theatre. It will require:

- a sewing table
- hanging space for costumes
- racks for footwear, hats and accessories
- an ironing board
- storage drawers/boxes for haberdashery.

In a theatre which takes in touring productions, plenty of space for unpacking and holding empty skips or mobile wardrobes is required.

Laundry

The laundry should be alongside the running wardrobe and should include:

- industrial standard equipment
- dryer ventilation outlets
- deep double sink and drainer
- electrical points – 2 washers, 2 dryers, 2 hot boxes, twin tub, iron and steamer – which might all be used simultaneously
- fixed costume rail
- good ventilation.

Wig room

While only the largest organisations will make their own, wigs require daily maintenance. The use of hairspray and acetone and heat from wig ovens mean that this room needs careful thought. It will require:

- good lighting, from at least two sources, overhead and wall-mounted
- air extraction close to work benches
- shelving (for wigs and wig blocks)
- a fixed work table (long but not deep – like a dressing room counter) with 35mm thick overhang for attaching wig clamps and a mirror behind on the wall
- sink and drainer
- electrical points for wig oven, heated rollers, tongs and dryers.

Running properties

A store for properties used by the actors in the current production/s should either open directly off the stage or be close to the actors' main entrance to it. The stage manager and his/her team will lay out properties from this store on tables at the side of the stage for collection by actors before their entrances.

Many plays require the use of food as part of the action. There should be a dedicated area for its preparation. This area should be independent of the similar facilities for painters or cleaners and include:

- a large sink and drainer
- separate hand-wash sink plus soap dispenser and towel supply
- clean kitchen surfaces for food preparation
- fridge, microwave and cooking rings
- lockable storage cupboards for food and for cleaning materials.

Storage

Lighting

Theatres can collect a great many luminaires, not all of which will always be in use. The best way of storing them is by hanging them on 48mm pipes each taking 6 to 8 lanterns. These should be stacked vertically approx 750mm apart, either fixed 500mm off the wall or, commonly, to a trolley with luminaires each side of a steel frame. In addition, adjustable shelves are required for the storage of a stock of lamps or bulbs for stage lighting equipment and other light fittings which will be of various sizes and may include fluorescent tubes.

The electrician also needs hooks on which to hang the coils of flexible extension cable and space for stands, clamps and other accessories. It may be useful to have small local stores close to areas where there is a high concentration of lighting equipment in use.

Stock sheets of colour filters should be found a place where they can be stored flat. They need an area of 1300mm x 650mm on a shelf or in a drawer and bench space where they can be cut to size.

If the electricians are responsible for pyrotechnics and other stage effects they will need a dedicated storage space which should comply with local regulations.

Sound

A similar storage space will be needed to keep and maintain speakers, speaker stands, microphones, cables and so on. Increasingly, space will also be needed for video equipment used in productions.

This equipment is often packed in flight cases and these, too, need storage space.

7.4.2 Lighting/sound store

Props

Apart from those laid out for immediate use in the performance, requirements for the storage of properties fall into a number of categories.

- An area near the stage for replacement props, larger quantities of running props, etc. This should ideally be lockable or should have lockable cupboards, one of which should be for the storage of firearms.
- In a producing theatre, a storage area for props being accumulated during the rehearsal period, often best located in or near the rehearsal room.
- A permanent company will require storage for stock items and rehearsal props. It should be dry and well ventilated (but need not be on-site).

Musical instruments

Large opera, dance or musical theatres may require climate-controlled storage for pianos and other large musical instruments such as harps and percussion, with easy access to the get-in and to the orchestra pit.

7.5 Personnel accommodation

General requirements

Separate accommodation should be provided for male and female staff.

Backstage areas should have an environmentally friendly supply of drinking water, easily available to all performers and staff.

Smoke detectors may be set off by fumes from hair lacquer and spirit gum. Ensure that they are connected to alarm and sprinkler systems via a buffer allowing time to verify that fire or smoke is present.

Either wireless or direct connectivity to broadband is required in all dressing rooms, green rooms, workshops and offices.

All backstage rooms require loudspeakers with volume control to receive paging calls and show relay.

Production staff facilities

All backstage staff will require changing rooms, lockers, lavatories and access to showers. During production periods and performances these rooms will be used for changing from street clothes into protective clothing or performance dress (e.g. black trousers and shirts).

During performances and technical rehearsals, staff may have to be available for long periods and need somewhere to wait until they are required. Adequate numbers of comfortable seats should be provided.

Accommodation/technical offices

Stage
The chief stage technician should have a small office near the stage. If there is easy access to the repair workshop during performances this office may be located there but should, as far as possible, be protected from dust. Space for a drawing board and telephone and Internet access are required.

Lighting
The chief lighting technician should have a similar office with space for a drawing board, computer, A0 printer, and with telephone and Internet access. This could be near the technical maintenance workshop or the control room rather than the stage.

Stage management
A typical drama stage management (SM) team consists of three people, although for larger shows it may be as many as six or seven. In theatres with more than one performance space, a repertoire system or occasional incoming tours then a number of teams may need to be accommodated at the same time.

During the rehearsal period their focus will be on the rehearsal room whereas during the performance their focus will be on the stage. However in both cases they will have a considerable amount of work which requires good telephone and internet access and office facilities. Where the stage management office cannot be near both the rehearsal room and the stage it may be necessary to duplicate some of the facilities.

A dedicated stage management office should be secure as it may contain sensitive personal information. It should either have built-in desk space or enough room to accommodate the entire SM team or teams (see above), notice board, shelves, filing cabinet and other storage. In addition to usual office work, this room will also be used for changing into show clothes, the making of paper and other small props and the storage of items as they are collected through the rehearsal period. The allocation of space should take these needs into account.

It also requires:
- windows that open with blinds for privacy where necessary
- telephone and Internet points
- a safe for petty cash and valuables
- lockers for personal items and hanging space for street clothes and performance clothing
- full-length mirror
- washbasin.

Company management
In touring theatres there may also be a need for a dedicated office for the company manager. The requirements are similar to those for stage management but the CM is less concerned with the running of the show. However, they need to be able to concentrate on paperwork, have confidential telephone conversations, and be able to see company members and other staff in private.

Rest and treatment
It is extremely useful to have a small 'quiet' room for someone who is temporarily unwell or has a minor injury. It should include a lockable cupboard for first aid supplies, a small washbasin and a bed.

Many musicals and dance shows now tour a dedicated physiotherapist and they will require a treatment room. It needs to be big enough for a physiotherapy bed with space around it, a desk and two chairs, large sink, cupboards (for towels, etc.), fridge (for ice packs), first aid kit, and a small area for a gym mat and Swiss ball.

Visiting/freelance staff
Increasingly designers of sets, costumes, lighting and sound, together with choreographers, fight directors, voice coaches and others, are engaged on a freelance basis. During production periods, they require space where they can leave their coats, have access to the Internet and work between rehearsals. Tables, chairs and a drawing board would be useful.

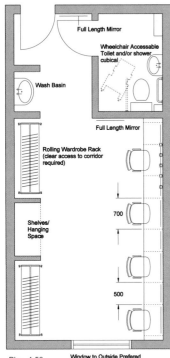

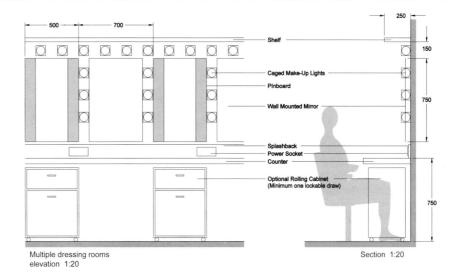

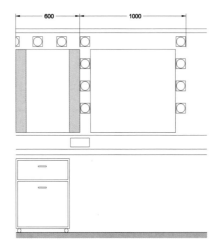

Full Length Mirror

Wheelchair Accessible Toilet and/or shower cubical

Wash Basin

Full Length Mirror

Rolling Wardrobe Rack (clear access to corridor required)

Shelves/ Hanging Space

Plan 1:50   Window to Outside Prefered

Shelf

Caged Make-Up Lights

Pinboard

Wall Mounted Mirror

Splashback
Power Socket
Counter

Optional Rolling Cabinet
(Minimum one lockable draw)

Multiple dressing rooms
elevation 1:20

Section 1:20

Typical chorus dressing room

Single dressing station
elevation 1:20

7.5.1 Dressing room layouts
Diagram: Theatre Projects Consultants

Dressing rooms

Actors often have to spend long hours in their dressing rooms during and between performances and rehearsals. Although the putting on of stage make-up has to be done in artificial light of similar quality to that used on stage it does not follow that all daylight must be excluded. Indeed it is of great benefit for performers to have not only natural light but also contact with the outside world through a window. Blinds will provide privacy or cut out daylight as and when required; those that pull up from the bottom may be particularly suitable.

Each performer must be able to see head, shoulders and headdress in the dressing room mirror while in a sitting position. The table top should have a hard-wearing, easily cleaned surface and should not project further than 500mm from the face of the mirror or the actor will be pushed too far away from it to see properly.

Doors should have a facility for displaying actors' name cards. A small pin board adjacent to the door is also useful.

Lighting
Traditional dressing room lighting is bare tungsten bulbs ranged around the mirror. The quality of the light used to make up the face should be the same as used on stage. It should be clear, uncoloured, not fluorescent, and come evenly from left, right and above so that hair and wigs can be adjusted. In chorus rooms or where space is very limited a continuous run of mirrors with bulbs above may be used but this is less effective than lighting from all sides.

These dressing-table lights should not be the sole illumination and each position should be individually switched. When actors wish to relax it is a great advantage to be able to switch off the more dazzling lights.

Each dressing room should be provided with one long mirror so that performers can check their costumes before leaving to go on stage. Lighting should be arranged so that they are illuminated when standing in front of the mirror.

Power

Shaving sockets should be provided between each pair of dressing room positions. The authorities have often frowned upon ordinary power sockets in dressing rooms, largely because of a fear that they will be used for heating or cooking equipment which might be a fire hazard. However, where dressing rooms are properly heated and where there is a green room for the preparation of hot drinks, these abuses are less likely.

Power sockets are useful for equipment such as hair dryers and styling equipment and are essential for vacuum cleaners. They should be on residual current device (RCD) protected circuits.

Storage in dressing rooms

A small cupboard with a drawer underneath the make-up top between each position is useful for personal possessions. These should be lockable, perhaps with padlock hasps, and be big enough to take a laptop computer. Mini-safes allow each person to set their own combination without the need for keys or key-codes.

There should be dedicated hanging space for day clothes and costumes, of which each performer may have more than one. Costumes will often be stored temporarily on wheeled hanging rails and it should be possible to move these to and from the wardrobe and straight into the hanging spaces. The fixed rail should, therefore, be high enough to clear the portable one. A minimum length of 600mm per performer should be provided but double that is not unreasonable for ladies' period dresses or numerous changes of costume.

Hats and wigs need a shelf, which can be over the dressing-table mirror or over the hanging rails. Boots and shoes should have a rack, probably under the hanging space, and should keep footwear off the floor to aid cleaning. Hooks at 1m height are useful for hanging swords and similar costume accessories. Hooks are also useful for dressing gowns. They could be on the back of the door if this is not being used for the full-length mirror.

Pin boards are an essential provision in dressing rooms for greetings telegrams and notices.

It is extremely useful to have a hook or hooks outside the dressing room doors so that costumes can be delivered when the performer does not want to be disturbed or to save a busy dresser having to lock and relock the door.

Furniture

Most dressing room furniture is built-in but the most useful chair is armless, upholstered, swivelling and adjustable. It is desirable to make room for a day bed in at least some of the dressing rooms.

Washing facilities

A washbasin with hot and cold water should be provided in every dressing room holding up to four performers. In larger rooms there should be at least one for every four positions. Basins should be large enough for a hair-wash and have a splashback and mirror over and a towel rail within reach. They should not be set into the make-up top.

Showers should be provided on a similar scale to washbasins. These may open off the dressing rooms but it may be preferred to group the showers together, especially for the larger dressing rooms. In this case access from the dressing rooms must be easy.

7.5.2 A two-person dressing room at MTC Theatre, Melbourne, Australia. All the dressing rooms have humidifiers; dimmable lights around the mirror and in the ceiling; openable windows; and separate toilet and shower accessed from within the room.
Photograph: Marshall Day Architects

Toilets

A 'star' single-occupancy dressing room can become something like a hotel room with its own small bathroom containing shower, washbasin and WC. However, in general, toilets should not open off dressing rooms. Local regulations may lay down the required provision of lavatories for performers, but these are unlikely to prove adequate. Performers are often under stress and dancers and singers are likely to consume larger than average quantities of water.

There should be toilets close to the entrances to the stage on either side and for each sex on each dressing room level.

Finishes

It might be assumed that bare feet and the need for quiet would suggest a carpeted floor. In general this is not popular as it is hard to clean and is unsuitable for areas near washbasins or showers. A soft, warm, vinyl may be preferable.

As with the wardrobe and corridors, wall finishes should be such that they will not damage delicate costume fabric if it should come in contact or be rubbed against them.

Children's dressing rooms

When there are children in the cast there are strict regulations about how they are to be treated. In the dressing rooms they have to be accommodated in separate rooms from adult members of the cast and supervised by chaperones, who may also require facilities for administrative activities. They must have toilets for their exclusive use.

Summary of provision

- Principals' dressing room: normally 1 person but large enough for 2, en suite toilet and shower
- Group dressing rooms: able to accommodate between 4 and 6 persons, en suite double showers, toilets accessed off corridor
- Chorus dressing rooms: able to accommodate up to 15 persons, en suite triple showers, toilets accessed off corridor

The number of each type will vary as to type of theatre/company. Typically a No.1 touring house requires up to 100 people (See Figure 7.5.3).

Notes:

Two of the group dressing rooms should be designed to be accessible for disabled performers, i.e. adjustable counter height, wide door, en suite level shower, toilet, close to lift and or stage.

Two others could double up as children's dressing rooms (but then need dedicated toilets).

Other artists' rooms

Conductor

Many of the above recommendations may equally apply to changing rooms for conductors or concert performers. Single rooms for conductors should be able to accommodate a piano. If it is upright the minimum area required is 14m² although it is often useful to have a room big enough to hold auditions or a small ensemble practice.

Single rooms should have a hanging cupboard for street clothes, a cupboard and drawer for personal possessions, a washbasin with mirror over, a wide shelf (600mm) with a resilient covering for resting musical instruments, a table and armless chair, a sofa and/or an easy chair. There should be a long mirror. It is preferable for single rooms to have their own toilets and showers.

In an opera house the conductor's room will be grouped with the dressing rooms of the principal singers rather than with the musicians and it should be placed near to the stage.

Number and type	To accommodate	Size	Equipment
6 principals' rooms	1 or 2 persons each	15m²–20m²	WC, shower, 1.5m mirror, counter
6 group rooms	4–6 persons each	15m²–20m²	showers 0.75m to 0.9m centres
4 chorus rooms	Up to 15 persons each	35m² minimum preferable 45m²	continuous mirror and lighting along top edge

7.5.3

Band room

Even theatres which are predominantly used for drama will often require facilities for musicians. Whether or not they are appearing on stage they will be required to wear evening dress or, at the very least, black clothing. A reasonable provision might be for 15 musicians with the facility to provide separate accommodation for unequal numbers of men and women. Musicians are less likely to spend time in the band room other than to get changed but they will require full-length mirrors, lockers for personal belongings and enough space for musical instrument cases. Broad shelves with resilient surfaces on which musical instruments can be placed are also required.

This room should be located near the entrance to the orchestra pit. Since it is likely to be used for occasional individual practice or tuning it should, where possible, have a level of sound insulation both from the auditorium and the dressing room area.

For large musical theatres or opera and ballet companies the room(s) may need to accommodate up to 70 or 80 musicians.

Green room

The green room is a common room for communal relaxation where snacks and drinks can be served. The scale of the green room facilities depends on the nature of the company. Current thinking is that generally a single facility should be available for all performers, technicians, workshop staff, front of house and administration. As it is for use during rehearsals and performances the green room should be near the dressing rooms and the stage. It must have daylight and, wherever possible, a pleasant outlook. It should be furnished with easy chairs, coffee tables, sofas and perhaps writing tables and chairs and a television.

In smaller venues a kitchen with sink, cooker or microwave, refrigerator, and crockery and cutlery storage, will serve for food preparation by individuals. In larger theatres or opera houses a separate dining room with a canteen kitchen and self-service facilities will be required.

Stage door

Traditionally there is a separate entrance for artists and technicians, supervised by a stage door keeper. The main functions are to control access, keep a record of who is in the building by means of a signing-in book, and to receive mail and other small deliveries. The stage door keeper will also be responsible for keys or other security measures for dressing rooms.

The usual planning arrangement is to have a doorkeeper's office with a counter open to a lobby just inside the stage door. The lobby acts as a sound lock between the outside and the corridor leading to the dressing rooms and the stage. It also acts as a reception area with seats where visitors can wait. There should be a notice board in a prominent position in the lobby.

For reasons of economy, space or ideology some companies prefer to combine backstage access and deliveries with the main reception desk located in the public foyer. This decision should be taken with care and in consideration of the implications for signing-in facilities, security and the management of performers' visitors.

7.6 Construction spaces

Production spaces for the construction and painting of scenery and props and the making and dyeing of costumes are only needed in theatres where productions are originated. Even then there is an increasing trend to out-source some or all of these activities to independent contractors with their own facilities. In any event these spaces do not have to be on the same site as the performance spaces although there are obvious advantages when they are. They should be planned to make the process of manufacture as simple and efficient as possible. This is best achieved where there is plenty of space, rather than on a congested site in the centre of town. However, the advantages of moving out may be outweighed by the cost of transport and the labour of loading and unloading as well as the time taken by these activities.

Production spaces are, essentially, workshops manufacturing a range of specialised products. Their industrial nature should be understood.

- No serious theatrical enterprise can get along without its own scenery being specially made for each production.
- Stage sets are often bulky and expensive to move about and store.
- The materials used can include timber, metal, fibreglass, gauzes, canvas and projection materials, among others.
- The making of larger properties often has materials, techniques and equipment common to scenery building.
- Costumes are easier to store and it is also easier to divide the making up between a number of freelance costumiers. Often it

will be more economical to hire costumes (such as uniforms or men's period suits) than to make them.
- Only the largest companies are likely to make their own wigs.

Scenic workshop

The process of manufacture of a set begins when the designs and outline construction methods have been agreed with the production manager and others. Sketches, working drawings and set models are provided by the designer. Further draughting work will almost certainly be required and the workshop should include a separate space for a drawing board and computer-aided draughting, including a printer capable of producing plans and elevations at 1:25 scale. This room should be large enough to house the set model and accommodate a meeting of up to six people.

There should be changing and shower facilities with secure storage for personal items and tools. In all but the smallest facilities, metal shops and timber workshops should be separated.

As they are built, the various components of the set will pass to an area where a trial assembly can be made. The space required for this will vary but height will always be important and there should be enough to clear the tallest piece of scenery.

It is useful to have suspension points and a flexible system of hoists in the roof structure so that parts of the set which will be suspended can be dealt with in a similar manner for the trial assembly, and to aid the movement and building of heavy pieces. This has implications for the load-bearing capacity of the roof.

The floor should be level and smooth to facilitate the alignment of parts of the set which must fit accurately together. Other requirements are:
- Carpenters' benches against the wall to provide easy access to power sockets for hand tools and wall racks, and for handling larger assemblies a bench with space all round it is more useful. Power sockets should be placed on the front of the bench not on the wall behind. Alternative or additional power sockets on suspended blocks also assist in ensuring that trailing cables do not pass across working surfaces.
- Some of the larger woodworking machines must have a clear area in which to manoeuvre the pieces of timber which are being shaped.
- Likely equipment will include: circular saw, planer, band saw mortiser, grindstone, cross-cut saw and tenoner.
- Metal is as common as timber in modern scenery construction and provision for angle-grinding, cutting and welding is required.
- Power outlets for machines should have local switching which may take the form of a 'panic button'.
- Compressed air system and air lines for tools such as nailers and staplers.
- Separate power supply of the same voltage as stock stage machinery such as revolves or lifts.

Dust extraction
Sawdust and shavings have to be cleared away. A dust extraction plant should be installed with extract points located close to the cutting blades of machines from which sawdust will be carried away in ducts to a discharge point for collection.

In addition, provision should be made for portable dust extraction at various locations.

Heating
Probably the most comfortable environment for working is provided by radiant panels overhead. With a high ceiling the source will be far enough away to avoid the unpleasant feeling of heat at head level which is sometimes associated with this form of heating.

In hot countries the problems and their solutions will be quite different and air conditioning may be required.

Lighting
Daylight should come from roof-lights or windows high up in the walls as the walls of the workshop will often be used to stack timber or pieces of scenery. Most light should ideally be from the north to avoid overheating problems in summer.

Artificial light should be bright and be from several directions as tall assemblies will often block a single source. In many circumstances some element of scenic art will be applied before the set is moved to the paintshop. It is important that the lighting here takes that into consideration and is full-spectrum.

Finishes

Finishes in the workshop should be appropriate for industrial use: robust, easily cleaned and cheap.

Particular attention should be paid to the floor. Accurate levelling is extremely important. A double, staggered, layer of good-quality plywood, net 36mm thickness, is a good standard. That thickness allows adequate fixings for machinery without the need for piercing the substrate and is more than enough for temporary fixing of scenery. The upper layer is replaced as necessary. Painted concrete floors are to be avoided.

This workshop may include a dedicated area for the making of properties with appropriate ventilation and air extraction.

Storage

- The maximum length of timber or metal is not likely to exceed 7m and a convenient method of storage is along a wall of this length on 50mm galvanised tube cantilevered 900mm from a wall at about 400mm centres. Alternatively a similar mobile rack system mounted on heavy duty castors enables flexibility in the use of the workshop.
- Rolls of canvas and other materials need shelves about 1m deep.
- Although sheet materials keep their shape better if they are laid flat, they are easier to select if they are stacked upright and this method should be used if the turnover of material is fairly rapid.
- Nails, screws, ironmongery and other odds and ends can go on shelves or in cupboards and drawers. Some adhesives, fillers and sealants are volatile and require separate safe storage.
- Workshops require a three-phase power supply. The supply for portable equipment should be 110 volt for light equipment. There should be no provision of 240 volt outlets in the workshop.

7.6.1 A scenic workshop within TR2, the Theatre Royal's award-winning Production and Education Centre in Plymouth, UK
Photograph: Ian Ritchie Architects

Paintshop

The paintshop will be required to paint and/or texture built scenic pieces from the workshop and also backcloths and gauzes which will be brought directly from the makers or from a store. Backcloths are still common in many productions, particularly in opera and ballet. They may be painted laid out on the floor or suspended vertically on a paintframe. Provision for both methods is ideal. General requirements are:

- Dimensions that allow built pieces of scenery to be easily reached and that can accommodate the largest likely backcloth.
- A rolled backcloth can be up to 15m long so it is important that it can be easily moved out of the paintshop either directly onto the stage or out of the building.
- Two large sinks with hot and cold water and paint trap. Taps should be high enough to accommodate the filling of buckets.
- Gas rings or a small cooker hotplate.
- Much work is done by spray gun so a permanent system is worthwhile. Minimum requirement is a high pressure (HP) system: vane or rotary compressor (ideally remotely located to avoid distress from noise), producing 800 litres/min displacement at 12 bar to 300 minimum litre buffer tank. Piped at 20mm bore to connection points at 10m intervals at 1200mm above floor around whole paintshop perimeter. Connection points each to have pressure reducer, water and oil purge.

7.6.2 A paintframe: TR2 Production and Education Centre, Theatre Royal, Plymouth, UK
Photograph: Ian Ritchie Architects

- Low pressure system: in addition and to reflect changing preferences a high volume low pressure (HVLP) system should be available. This can take the form of small self-contained units requiring local electric power, or adaptors to reduce and clean HP air for use, or central turbine units with dedicated 50mm bore pipe distribution. In the case of adaptors attached to HP systems, considerable additional air usage should be anticipated and the buffer tank should be increased in size to compensate.
- Air supplies to paintshops should never be shared with other users.

Armoury

Theatres housing large classical companies and opera houses will need a workshop for the manufacture and maintenance of swords, guns and other weapons. It should be equipped with welding, brazing, grinding and polishing machinery. Storage in the armoury should be particularly secure and should be in line with local legislation.

Recording studio

Sound is becoming an increasingly important aspect of theatrical production. A room equipped for creating and editing digital sound effects and music is a requirement for many theatre companies.

It is often worth combining this with a facility for recording music and effects. The size will depend entirely on expected use but, in any event, it should have:
- extremely good sound insulation and the approach to it should be through sound lobbies with acoustic seals around doors and sound-absorbent material on the walls;
- ventilation should be as near silent as possible;
- recording equipment should be in a control room separated from the studio by a double-glazed sound-insulating window.

Wardrobe

The main manufacturing wardrobe is distinct from the costume maintenance facilities which are described earlier in this section (under 7.4). Although, like the scenery workshop, it is not essential that this activity takes place in the main building it is much better if it does. It will usually take up less space than that needed for scenery construction and there is a requirement for closer liaison with rehearsals and with performers.

Costume making is a manufacturing process which must be carried out in a proper sequence if it is to be efficient. In addition to cutting, sewing and fitting costumes, facilities should be provided for dyeing and painting cloth, for millinery, for making accessories and, in the larger companies, for making boots and shoes.

The designer's sketches are discussed in the supervisor's office and a programme of work is decided. The actors' measurements are taken or checked and paper patterns are cut out on a draughting table. The next stage is cutting the cloth which is done at cutting tables. The rest of the process will involve the use of tailors' dummies, sewing tables and ironing facilities. The following equipment needs to be accommodated:

- *Draughting table*: about 900mm x 1800mm x 850mm high with space all around.
- *Cutting table*: 1200mm x 1800–2400mm x 1000mm high with all-round access and shelves under for fabric storage. An allowance of 12m^2–14m^2 per table should be made.
- *Tailors' dummies*: both male and female in a range of sizes, mobile but requiring 3m^2–4m^2 floor space.
- *Sewing machines*: each on its own table with a chair and a space around it; about 1100mm x 1100mm with 13 amp socket outlets in a convenient position for each machine.
- *Sewing tables*: 750mm x 1200mm with a chair, requiring 5m^2 or 6m^2 of floor space.
- *Ironing boards*: portable with a bench nearby for standing irons and equipment. Each board needs 6m^2–7m^2 and adequate accessible power points.
- *Portable storage*: a wheeled cabinet or trolley with shallow drawers for boxes of pins, needles, cotton reels, etc.
- *Hanging rails*: room for hanging rails for completed costumes.
- *Lighting*: good overall illumination from both daylight and artificial lighting with adjustable lamps near each sewing machine.
- *Access*: skips of costumes, hanging rails and heavy bolts of fabric will regularly need to be brought into the wardrobe. Where it is on the ground floor access should be level and where it is on upper floors nearby suitable lift access is essential.
- There should be a sink and draining board with hot and cold water supply.

Storage

Ideally raw materials should be stored in a separate room. Rolls of dress fabric are usually about 1m wide but curtain fabrics are more likely to be 1.3m wide. A system of deep pigeon holes or shelves can be used for bolts of cloth and drawers or boxes on adjustable shelves for small supplies and haberdashery.

7.6.3 A theatre wardrobe: TR2 Production and Education Centre, Theatre Royal, Plymouth, UK
Photograph: Ian Ritchie Architects

Fitting rooms

Although it is likely that men's and women's costumes will be made in the same area it may be necessary to have separate fitting rooms of about 10m^2 with a wall mirror in which a full-length view can be obtained.

Dye shop

A separate area is needed for dyeing and painting cloth for costumes. This will require:

- a heated dyeing vat alongside a large sink with hot and cold water
- shelves and cupboards for dyestuffs and acids
- surface for weighing dyes – traditionally marble-topped
- bench for mixing colours – faced with laminated plastic
- plastic-topped bench with space all-round
- good ventilation/extraction as sprays will be used.

Drying room

A drying room should adjoin the dye shop. The wet cloth will be draped over a drying rack which can be made of steel tube, galvanised or plastic-covered. The tubes of the rack should be fitted at about head height at about 0.5m intervals and each tube should be about 1.5m long. Moisture will drip onto the floor which should be laid to fall to a floor gulley. A suitable floor finish should be chosen. The speed of drying will depend on a good circulation of warm, dry air.

Millinery and accessories

Although related to the work in the costume shop, this work should have its own separate area. Making hats and accessories involves sewing by hand and machine but also employs other techniques related to prop-making. The work will usually be done seated at worktops about 750mm wide and with about a 1m run for each person.

Each position should have a drawer for tools, shelves for materials, hat-blocks and wig-blocks, an adjustable lamp, and access to a 13 amp socket outlet.

The room should have a sink with hot and cold water and a bench with gas rings or a small cooker hotplate. There should be good overall illumination from both daylight and artificial lighting and good ventilation/extraction.

Wig room

Even where wigs are not made on the premises they will require maintenance and dressing on a regular basis. This will require a well-ventilated room with 300mm deep shelves for storing wigs in boxes or on wig-blocks, a fixed table 35mm thickness for attaching wig clamps, and electrical points for wig oven, heated rollers, tongs and dryers.

A wig-making workshop will have similar requirements.

Shoes

Boots and shoes are an important element in stage costumes and some production organisations may include a separate shoemakers' workshop. Like other workrooms it requires a bench, a sink with hot and cold water, good light, both natural and artificial, power sockets, storage drawers and cupboards for tools and materials, and racks for the products.

Jewellery

Where jewellery is made by the company it will probably be in a corner of the property workshop. A proper jewellers' bench is fixed at a height of about 1050mm and has a semi-circular cut-out of about

45mm diameter at each work position. Gas is needed for soldering and there should be a sink and a drainer with resistance to the acid which is used.

Storage

Within the building, costumes are best hung on rails, either fixed or mobile. When they are taken out of the building (to go on tour, for example) they may be packed in skips of average dimensions 900mm x 650mm x 650mm.

7.7 Rehearsal facilities

Rehearsal rooms

In a busy theatre or opera house there will be great demands on the stage area and it will not be available long enough or at the right times for a continuous programme of rehearsal. Very often companies have to find space away from the theatre, a situation which can be expensive and inconvenient.

Whether for drama, opera or dance, the dimensions of the rehearsal room must be related to the size of the stage upon which the production will eventually appear.

For opera and drama the rehearsal rooms should have the same dimensions as the acting area of the stage, plus a minimum margin of about 1m at the back and sides. There should also be a space of about 3m at the front for the director and stage management and (for opera rehearsals) a piano, repetiteur and conductor. The height of the room should be related to the height above the stage floor. Where large choruses are required the space around the acting areas should be much larger.

For dance and ballet productions the maximum space is required with a minimum clear height of about 4.5m. A sprung floor is essential. The walls should have large areas of mirror up to a height of 2.4m which can be curtained off. There should be a practice barre 300mm from the wall at a height of 1.2m.

If the rehearsal room is to be accommodated in the same building as the main theatre it should be close to the dressing rooms and the stage management office. It is also an advantage if it is close to the stage and workshop since it is very useful for rostra or other scenic elements to be easily moved into the rehearsal room. If none of this is possible or if the rehearsal room is to be located at some distance from the theatre then facilities for costume fittings, props storage, stage management administration work, personal lockers and green room facilities will need to be replicated.

In all cases care should be taken to ensure that the acoustic properties of the rehearsal room are fit for purpose or able to be adjusted to various requirements.

7.7.1 Rehearsal room: Tricycle Theatre, London, UK
Sliding shutters allow lower windows to be closed off for privacy, when required, while still retaining the high-level daylight.
Photograph: Courtesy of the Wales Millennium Centre

Sound insulation is also important to avoid disturbance both of and by rehearsals. The floor finish should be similar to that of the stage. Daylight should not be excluded but wall space and a background that does not distract are essential, so windows should be at a high level. Artificial lighting must give a high, evenly distributed illumination.

The rehearsal room should have hooks for performers to leave their personal belongings and a rail for rehearsal costumes.

Temperature and humidity control and other environmental conditions are also important, particularly for dancers and singers.

Practice rooms

Particularly in opera or in musical productions, individuals or small groups will need to practise. A series of practice rooms should be provided, sized according to the number likely to use them.

SECTION EDITOR

A K Bennett-Hunter

The following have advised on or contributed to this section:

Petrus Bertschinger
Dennis Charles
Marilyn Cutts
Terance Dickson
Barbara Eifler
Mark Jones
Jeff Phillips

Section 8
Additional spaces

Contents

8.1 Introduction

This section looks at all the ancillary space required
for the smooth operation of a theatre. It begins with
information on management structures. While this
may seem a little odd, it is important to know how the
organisation is to be structured, what departments there
will be, and how many staff are to be accommodated,
in order to evaluate the number, type and size of offices
and other facilities which need to be provided. The
information needs to be assessed at the planning stage
and incorporated into the design brief. This also applies
to education and community activities which are now
fundamental parts of most theatre organisations. Each
has its own individual space requirements.

It is important to think about flexibility so that certain areas of the building can accommodate a range of uses. For example:

- Foyers
- Bars and catering
- Rehearsal rooms
- Meeting rooms.

Flexibility is also an important consideration for other spaces if they are to be utilised in the most cost-effective way, notably offices and storage. If these spaces are poorly planned at the outset, with provision that is inadequate or where no allowance is made for growth or change, the results can prove costly in the longer term.

As explained in Section 1, theatres can be broadly classified into two main categories:

1 Producing theatres
2 Receiving theatres.

The extent and nature of the office space required will, to a large extent, be determined by the type and nature of the operation. A producing theatre will need to take into account space for production staff (those concerned with initiating and mounting productions) whereas a receiving theatre will focus more on the administrative aspect of running the venue.

Regardless of whether it is a producing or receiving venue, every organisation's staffing structure will vary, reflecting the vision and values of the venue, its purpose and its objectives. Some organisations, for example, may focus on developing and presenting new work; some on outreach and creative learning; for others commercial activities and fundraising may be a priority. The office space and related accommodation needs to reflect the requirements of the individual organisation.

While the overall size of the venue and its operation will obviously affect office size and layout, a similar range and level of tasks need to be undertaken in all theatres. They will, however, vary in levels of complexity and this must be factored in when allocating spaces.

8.2 Management structures

Board and chief executive

Theatres are normally run by a board of management which has ultimate responsibility for the organisation. The board is likely to be one of the following:

- Charitable trust comprising trustees and management representatives

- Local authority comprising councillors and local authority officers
- Commercial company comprising shareholders and executive management.

A producing house is generally headed by an artistic director who is responsible for the overall artistic policy and for the productions. A receiving house, which primarily hosts touring productions, is generally headed up by a chief executive whose prime responsibility is programming each season.

Areas of responsibility

Thereafter, structures will vary to reflect the size, priorities and operational style of the individual theatres. For example, in smaller organisations several areas of responsibility might be undertaken by one person while, in larger organisations, the same responsibilities are split into separate departments.

As a general guide, the operational areas that will need to be covered are as follows:

- programming
- marketing
- ticket sales
- financial control
- front of house management and sales
- customer care
- security
- development (fundraising and sponsorship)
- health and safety management
- human resources management
- technical management
- building management
- legal compliance
- external relations (e.g. with local community, supporters and funding organisations)
- room bookings and possible hires
- education and related activities
- ancillary events.

A producing theatre will need to include additional functions such as:

- Commissioning – writers, designers, directors, etc.
- Casting
- Production management
- Workshop management.

Each organisation will need to make its own list.

Examples

The following examples of management structures are taken from both producing and receiving theatres of varying sizes. They emonstrate that each organisation is different. There is no right or wrong way to structure an organisation, provided that the areas of responsibility are clear and that all aspects are adequately covered.

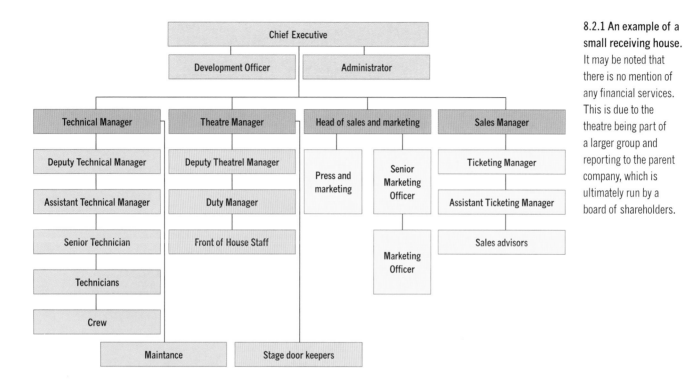

8.2.1 An example of a small receiving house. It may be noted that there is no mention of any financial services. This is due to the theatre being part of a larger group and reporting to the parent company, which is ultimately run by a board of shareholders.

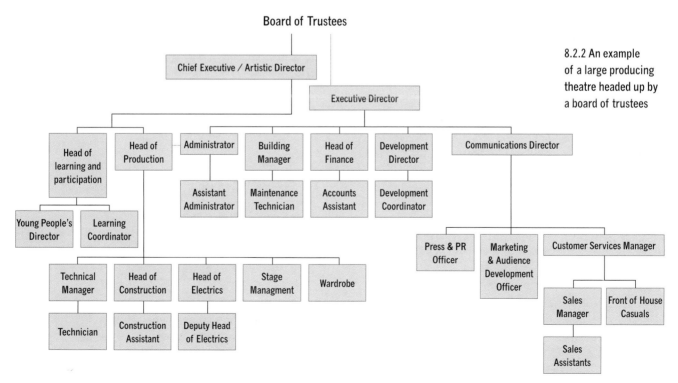

8.2.2 An example of a large producing theatre headed up by a board of trustees

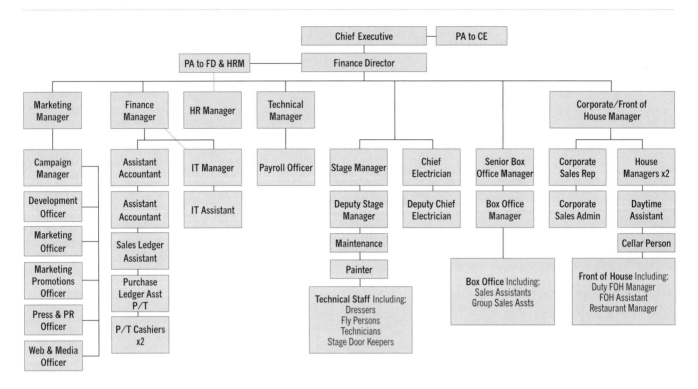

8.2.3 Structure of a large receiving theatre which is headed up by a board of trustees (though they are not shown here)

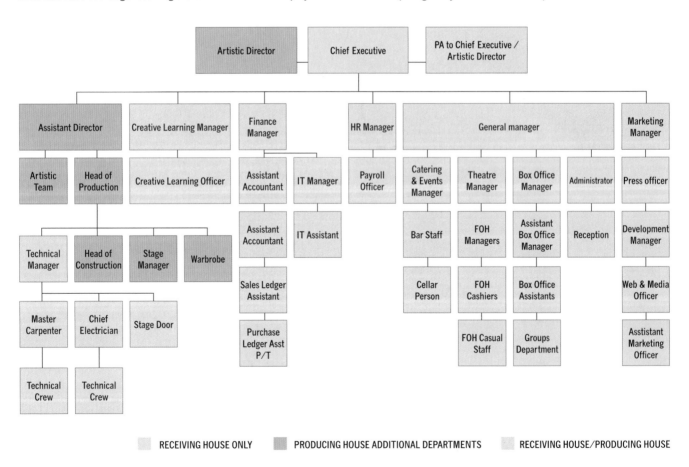

RECEIVING HOUSE ONLY   PRODUCING HOUSE ADDITIONAL DEPARTMENTS   RECEIVING HOUSE/PRODUCING HOUSE

8.2.4 Generic organisational chart indicating the additional departments a producing house typically needs to accommodate.

8.3   Functions and requirements

The table aims to provide a checklist of departments and responsibilities within a theatre organisation. The extent of the office accommodation is determined by the administrative structure of the company that is to occupy the building and needs will vary widely according to the size and kind of operation anticipated.

Function	Accommodation
Board Meetings will probably take place quarterly but smaller committee meetings may happen more frequently.	A meeting room big enough for the whole board (12 to 20 people with staff) to meet in comfort. This room should be designed to accommodate comparable uses such as production conferences, interviews and staff meetings.
Producing theatre	
Artistic Director Responsible for overall policy, choice of productions and commissions.	An office large enough to hold meetings and conferences of heads of departments.
Assistant Director Assists Artistic Director.	Office space close to the Artistic Director.
Associate Directors A company may have directors who have responsibility for particular productions either on a permanent basis or for a specific task.	Where the establishment is known, office space should be included in the schedule of accommodation. Alternatively, space needs to be provided that can be allocated to visiting directors.
Playwright, Musical Director, Composer A company may have creative teams working on current and forthcoming productions.	Where these posts exist, they will need an office space/s close to the department most associated to their work. Provision may also be needed for a piano (both in use and stored).
Creative Team Costume, lighting and set designers will be needed for each production.	If these posts require office space it should be in the same area as the Associate Directors.
General Manager Where the organisation is headed by an Artistic Director a General Manager is often appointed to run the building and the non-production staff.	The office should be located near that of the Chief Executive or Artistic Director, depending on how the organisation is structured.

Company/stage management teams (See Section 7)

Receiving theatre	
Chief Executive Leads the management team, chooses the shows and negotiates with the producers.	An office large enough to hold meetings with heads of departments.

All theatres

Management Team	
Finance Director	An office space preferably near the rest of the management team and the Accounts Department.
HR Manager	An office space with a meeting area (that can be private for confidential meetings) and space for secure cabinets for staff files.
Marketing Manager	An office space preferably near the rest of the management team and the Accounts Department.

Backstage Department (See Section 7)

Marketing Department	
Development Manager Marketing Officer Press and PR Officer Web and Media Officer	These people and their teams need to be located near one another as they all work closely together. Regular access will be needed to storage for all materials relating to their roles. Access to photocopiers/scanners/fax machines will be needed daily so should be incorporated into their working area.

Box Office Department (See Section 3)

Administration Department	
Accountant Sales Ledger Purchase Ledger Payroll	The size of this department will depend on the size of the organisation, but the most important factor to note is that a significant amount of filing space will be needed.
Receptionist	Situated at the entrance to the main administration offices.
Office Administrator Personal Assistants Administration Assistant	All these roles will depend on the size of the organisation and in some small theatres could be carried out by the same person.
IT Manager	An office and in some cases a workshop for repairs and storage of IT equipment.
Education Officer	In most organisations this role is now seen as part of the senior management team and so should be located in the same area.
Health and Safety Manager	Depending on the size of the organisation, this role may be contracted out. Most large theatre organisations have a full-time person in this role.

8.3.1

8.4 Office accommodation – specifications

Working environment

Office space is strictly covered by legislation, which tends to be specific to a particular country or region and changes quite frequently. UK legislation (*The Workplace – Health, Safety and Welfare Regulations 1992*) specifies a minimum workspace of 11m³ for each person permanently occupying that space. This is based on a maximum ceiling height of 3m.

In practice, the amount of workspace needed for each person may well be higher. Employers must ensure that work areas and work stations are laid out so that people can carry out their tasks safely and comfortably. Workers must have enough free space to move about the work area with ease.

The amount of space required needs to be assessed taking account of:
- the needs of each worker based on the nature of the work and space taken up by personal equipment and storage
- access and disability requirements
- the dimensions and shape of the overall work area
- the number of people working in the area
- space taken up by columns, alcoves, traffic routes, shared equipment and shared storage.

On a very practical note, essential elements of an office can take more space than anticipated, including:
- Photocopier
- Franking machine
- Stationery
- Filing systems
- Pigeon holes
- IT servers
- Telecommunications equipment.

Functionality and flexibility

Offices need to be seen as an integral part of a theatre building. To work effectively, administrative and support staff should feel that they are part of the production and presentation process and this will not be the case if their offices are isolated in a separate wing or cut off from the main activities. Ideally, office space should be situated centrally within the building, offering accessibility for everyone including staff, suppliers and visitors. This can rarely be fully achieved even within a new building so, essentially, staff need to be close to their areas of operation in order to be 'close to the action'. For example:

Front of house
- Theatre Manager
- Box office Manager
- Catering Manager.

Backstage
- Technical Manager
- Chief Electrician
- Master carpenter.

Over time, organisations may change their objectives and this could have a significant affect on staffing requirements and structures. Departmental collaborations and working practices may also alter, so the challenge for any office space is to maintain functionality while offering maximum flexibility.

Open-plan offices

There are many advantages to open-plan offices. They engender a sense of identity, simplify the informal flow of information between individuals and departments, and offer flexibility for the number and position of work stations to be adapted to the current needs of the organisation. At the same time, they need to give every member of staff a sense of permanence so that they feel they have ownership of the space where they work. Features such as space between desks and the use of carefully placed plants and low partitions can provide a level of privacy without impeding social interaction.

'Hot desk' facilities should be provided to accommodate temporary workers needed during busy periods of operation as well as staff normally located elsewhere (either within or away from the building).

Meeting rooms/areas must be available and, again, some flexibility could prove extremely beneficial enabling them to accommodate different sized groups and adapt to future needs.

The following equipment may need to be accommodated:
- Wipe boards
- Overhead projector
- Retractable screen
- Appropriate variable lighting
- DVD/laptop facilities.

Safety, security and confidentiality

While open-plan offices may be the preferred accommodation for many of the staff, it is likely that some individual offices will be needed both for confidential discussions and for the handling and storage of sensitive information. There are also times when people need private and personal space; for example, the Chief Executive, Artistic Director and Financial Controller may require greater privacy.

Cash handling features heavily in most venue operations and consideration needs to be given to providing adequate security both for the money and for those handling it. Cashiers' offices need to be located close to the front of house operation and have appropriate safe facilities. Cash should not be walked through the public areas. If the cash is to be banked by a security firm consideration needs to be given to its safe collection.

Provision needs to be made for the storage of personal possessions. Lockers will need to be installed, especially for staff that are peripatetic or working in places where there is no provision for personal belongings. Digital or coin-operated lockers are preferable to those with keys so as to avoid the cost of replacing lost keys and to deal with people coming and going on a regular basis (visiting companies and staff turnover).

Staff welfare

Many theatre staff will be working outside normal office hours and this means that some form of refreshment facilities may well be required. The type and scale of provision will depend on the size of the organisation, its style of operation and its geographical location. It could range from a fully functioning canteen through to a room with kitchen facilities for staff to make their own refreshments.

Adequate toilet facilities and changing rooms for both sexes should be identified. Showers may also need to be provided.

(See Section 7 for backstage staff provision.)

Physical factors

Temperature control and air circulation also need to be considered if staff are to work effectively. Emphasis should be placed on enabling staff to control their own environment with natural ventilation being preferable to mechanical ventilation.

Natural lighting is also the preferred option but, where this is not possible, diffused lighting with similar characteristics to daylight may be considered.

Communication

Good communication is vital to the success of any organisation, whatever its size. Within a theatre, shift patterns and the different areas of work can pose barriers to effective communication.

Keeping the office space as central as possible, as well as within the locality of each department's area of responsibility, will prove beneficial.

A welcoming and functional staff kitchen area can also hugely boost morale, aid communication, break down departmental barriers and generate a feeling of organisational unison. This could be combined with the company green room to break down the potential barriers between front and backstage staff.

8.5 Education and community activities

Introduction

The place of education in theatres – or Creative Learning, Creative Development, Participation, Learning or Engagement to give just some of its many names – has grown significantly since the earlier ABTT theatre design guides were published. In the UK, this work is often a condition of funding for publicly funded venues, and its status, breadth and diversity will reflect this necessary relationship. However, even commercial theatre operators have begun to appreciate the value of such work in relation to audience development, community relationships and public relations, and may be just as likely to include education activities in their programme.

It is also worth noting that the term 'Education' does not just mean hosting school groups. In fact, this association is why so many organisations have moved away from using it as a name for their work, although it is used in this section as the generic term for a wider area of activity.

The work of an education department reaches many different people, from the very young to the retired, across a wide range of ability. It aims to offer opportunities for all these people to become creatively engaged in the work of the venue. It can take the form of traditional learning-based sessions, clearly led by an educationalist, or more open-ended participatory activities where the learning outcomes are less prescribed. It also usually encompasses outreach work, which may bring groups into the venue as well as taking activities directly to them.

Theatre education is increasingly embedded in the daily working life of venues. Theatres must, therefore, have the resources not only to support it on a basic operational level, but to enable all patrons to have the best experience possible, regardless of whether they are seeing a show or participating in a workshop.

In order to make sense of a complex area, this subsection is divided as follows:

- Theatres with additional educational spaces (which will be the majority)
- Practicalities – the detail you will need to consider in this format
- Finding the best fit – the relationship between programme, space and audience.

The design of education-based performance spaces attached to independent organisations, such as schools and colleges, is discussed in subsection 2.3.

Creating space for education activities

If a theatre is to deliver a wide range of educational activity, then the best scenario is to have the dedicated use of one or more studio spaces in which to work. This will provide flexibility and ease of use and offer the best environment for the widest range of participants.

Where space is more limited, the studios may have to be multi-purpose and shared between education, rehearsals, corporate entertaining and even commercial hires. In such cases, it is important that the different uses are detailed and planned for at the briefing stage. Plans need to look at timing and frequency of use as well as space and equipment requirements.

The day-to-day sharing of spaces can create friction. Where provision is being made for an existing organisation, all potential users need to be properly consulted from the outset.

The work of an education team is not always workshop based and it is worth considering whether space can be made available to extend what is on offer within the theatre programme, for example by creating somewhere for small-scale professional work to be presented to children. This would require space for a temporary stage/backstage area to be created, as well as appropriate seating.

Anyone planning such a space should obviously consult the theatre's education team (where one exists) to ensure their particular needs are met. It would also make sense,
for those designing a new facility, to visit other theatres to see how such spaces operate in practice. Talking to

8.5.1 Informal event in the foyer of Wales Millennium Centre, Cardiff, UK
Photograph: Courtesy of Wales Millennium Centre

education managers and practitioners will also highlight the problems which can arise and identify those that could be avoided in newly built premises if they are well designed and fit for purpose.

Finding the best fit (matching space to audience to programme)

It may appear self-evident but thinking about what will take place in the space as well as who will be using it is an important consideration at the planning stage. Not every education programme is the same, and not every educational space will have the same requirements. If the theatre's programme is focused on outreach activities or work with adult learners, the spatial requirements will be very different from those required for a programme which concentrates on delivering regular workshops to schools.

To give an example, where the main house offers little of interest to young children and their families, then programming work for these groups in a smaller space may be a priority. In this case, the education space needs to be geared to this particular audience, who may need a place to keep buggies and easy access to toilets throughout the performances. Similarly, if a large part of the theatre's education activity is with older people, they will want to sit down on chairs, even when participating in what is mainly a physical workshop. While teenagers and young children are happy to sit on the floor, most adults are not.

Elements of the programme which impact on the design

The following is a checklist of points which need to be considered at the planning stage for new or improved education provision.

- Likely range of ages of participants and associated needs.
- Anticipated frequency of use and likely numbers per activity: during one week, one month, one year.
- Turnaround: will the typical day be densely packed with workshops?
- How many spaces are needed on a regular basis?
- Timings of the activities – will they be mostly daytime, or after school/work? Will there be simultaneous use?

- Needs of disabled users (including those with learning difficulties and those who experience difficulties with socialising).
- Nature of activity – physical dance/drama workshops, or more sedentary such as a playwriting group or story-telling.
- Will the space be used for any form of public performance?
- Will there be the need for catering on any regular basis (for example, for children's birthday parties)?

Practicalities

The practicalities which need to be considered when creating an educational space for a theatre are many. The list which follows is by no means exclusive.

Size and accessibility of space

Visiting school groups will often comprise one or more classes of up to 30 children, plus the requisite number of adult supervisors. Space will be needed to accommodate this number, plus the theatre practitioners, and provide sufficient room for everybody to move around or divide into small groups. The minimum space which is appropriate for this sort of work is in the region of $70m^2 – 90m^2$, even before storage is considered.

A practical problem faced by all schools when organising trips is where to take the children for lunch, for example, when attending a workshop followed by a matinee performance. Ideally, this will be an additional, smaller space (or means of dividing one larger space) which can be simply furnished with tables, benches and bins and used for coat and bag storage when necessary. Such a space will also benefit from being readily adaptable to other uses. It is essential that drinking water is available, especially when physical activity is involved. It is more cost-effective and environmentally sustainable if this is provided for in the design of the building rather than leaving people to bring in bottles.

The space should be accessible to disabled visitors with consideration being given to aspects other than simple access and egress. For example, there may be visits by groups of children with special educational needs, where several are wheelchair users with complex disabilities. Good practice requires that they be able to enjoy a workshop experience comparable to that of non-disabled children.

Toilets

Ideally, a purpose-designed educational space would be served by toilets located close by with a sufficient number to ensure workshop time is not lost in queuing. The toilets should be safe and easy to use by children without the need for adult supervision and, in the interests of children's safety, preferably not open to the general public at the same time. For pre-school children and their parents, there should be adequate baby-changing facilities. All of the above also applies to accessible toilets.

Storage space

Most theatre education departments will have a treasure trove of materials, props, costumes, worksheets, etc. all of which need to be easily accessible by whoever is delivering the workshop (often a freelance practitioner). It is therefore important to have sufficient storage for these items either within the educational space itself or close by. It is also worth bearing in mind that, in the UK, many activities require emergency or medical information on children to be provided by parents which is confidential yet needs to be stored safely near to the activity in case it is needed. A small, lockable store or safe would therefore prove useful.

Furniture and fittings

Another challenge for education space in theatres is that needs may change each time the space is used. For example, sometimes lots of furniture will be required while at other times the space will be cleared for physical drama or dance activities. This tension can be exacerbated when the space is dual-use, for example, with the educational usage sitting alongside corporate entertaining. Expectations of the type and condition of furniture are very different. Lightweight, stackable furniture which can be easily moved and stored may help provide a solution. Where damage is likely to be a problem, providing robust coverings that can be laid out when needed will serve to protect the tables and other fittings and furnishings.

Workshop activities may include 'making' or design-based work, which requires paint and other 'wet' materials. It is therefore useful to have a separate sink of a height which allows children to use it and to help keep the space clean and tidy.

Where workshops involve technical theatre activity, good provision of power sockets will facilitate the introduction of specialist equipment into the space, such as sound desks, lighting desks and computers.

Selecting suitable flooring is complex. Some work is better conducted on carpet (for example with very young children who will tend to sit on the floor and roll about) while other work is much better on wooden or laminate floors. Dance work needs to be conducted only on specific types of floors (either sprung or with sufficient 'give' to soften the impact). Where a wooden floor is specified, for example, a piece of carpeting will make it more comfortable for the very young and a removable dance floor, which can be rolled out when needed and then stored elsewhere, will extend the use of the space further.

Lighting

A balance of artificial and natural light is desirable. However, it is also worth considering whether some basic theatrical lighting will be beneficial, perhaps enabling an ordinary room to double as a very basic studio theatre. Blackout facilities may also be installed. Facilities of this type could be used by a youth theatre or hired by local groups (generating additional income and bringing in new audiences). The equipment should be easy to use so that it does not need specialised theatre staff to operate it.

Offices

Wherever possible, the educational space(s) should be located close to the offices which the education department uses. There is invariably a good deal of running to and fro when workshops are in progress and it is advisable to have the permanent staff on hand should an emergency arise.

8.6 Rentals and hires

Opportunities and motivation

Many theatres hire out spaces within their buildings and, increasingly, new theatres are designed to facilitate this. An example of such hires could be:

- Play readings
- Photo shoots
- Film shoots
- Corporate training sessions
- Student showcases
- Award ceremonies
- Charity fundraising events
- Seminars, meetings and discussion groups
- Book and product launches.

Although the need to generate additional income is a key motivation, there are other good reasons for opening the building to more general use. These come under the broad heading of 'public relations' and include:

- Audience development by bringing different groups of people into the theatre.
- Strengthening support within the local community by providing space for local events and activities.
- Attracting sponsorship through 'packages' which include occasional use of the theatre's space.

A successful policy for 'lets and hires' needs to recognise that these are secondary to the theatre use. Spaces must be designed to suit the requirements of their primary function and any adaptations made to cater for other uses should not detract from this. As with all theatre activities, these additional uses are accommodated most effectively when planned for at the outset. This means that the potential for lets and hires and the related policy issues need to form part of the initial business plan and then be incorporated into the design brief. (See Section 1.)

The main space

In some places, the theatre may be one of the few spaces available where large numbers of people can be accommodated. Many theatre auditoria work well for conferences and larger meetings, especially middle scale venues with a flexible auditorium layout and the potential for a thrust stage.

The opportunities for letting the main spaces depend on how the theatre is operated. Theatres may consider hiring out the main auditorium:

- During the day (pre-performance and avoiding matinees)
- On 'closed' days (some theatres are dark for one or two days a week – e.g. Sundays and Mondays)
- Between productions (though this time is often used for setting up the stage and for rehearsals)
- Out of season (some theatres still work to a season of plays with the period of closure varying according to local circumstances).

There are, however, many theatre-related activities which take place in the auditorium throughout the day. Even during a long run, there will be adjustments to be made to the equipment and aspects of the production which require additional rehearsal. Most theatres will also want to maintain the 'integrity' of the set and not allow members of the public access to the main stage. Closed days and 'between season' periods may also be earmarked for maintenance, cleaning and refurbishment.

Ancillary spaces

There are a number of other areas within a theatre which have the potential to be hired out either commercially or for community activities. They include:

- *Meeting rooms* Well-designed and located rooms can be used both during the day and while a performance is taking place in the main auditorium.
- *Rehearsal rooms* Space for rehearsal is generally in short supply and may well be hired by other companies as well as by community groups.
- *Studios* A producing theatre might use studio space to broaden its programme by hiring it out to small professional touring companies, local theatre groups, school performances, youth theatre companies, or music, film, and other arts-related events.
- *Foyer* Depending on the size, design, location and amenities, foyers can be used for receptions, presentations, displays, parties, exhibitions, informal performances, etc. both for commercial organisations and community events. Design requirements for such uses are discussed in Section 3.7.

8.6.1 Set up for a banquet, Wales Millennium Centre, Cardiff, UK
Photograph: Courtesy of Wales Millennium Centre

Planning for rentals and hires

Location and access

The performance space lies at the heart of the theatre, and is quite rightly the primary focus within the building. The theatre will be designed to ensure that the audience can enter the building and make their way to the auditorium quickly and easily and bars, toilets, etc. will be located so that they are easily accessible to the theatre audience. The challenge is to cater for the additional uses and to make them part of the visit, without compromising the principal function of the building.

Where possible, these spaces should be designed so that they can be independently accessed and be self-contained. The main performance space should be able to be used without any of the activities in these secondary spaces affecting either the performance or the audience's enjoyment of the bars and restaurants and access to toilet and cloakroom facilities.

Issues to be considered include:

- *Noise* Audiences entering and leaving the main auditorium (before and after the show and during intervals) could cause a distraction for events taking place elsewhere in the building.
- *Provision of toilets, etc.* These need to be accessible for general use or additional facilities will be required.
- *Safety* Events and activities which coincide with the main performance will increase the number of people within the building at any given time. This could impact on the safety requirements.
- *Economy* It should be possible to light and heat/ventilate individual areas so that small meetings do not incur large energy costs.
- *Security* Ancillary lettable spaces need to be designed so that those using them do not wander round other parts of the building where equipment is stored or where fit-up or other work may be taking place.

Furniture, equipment and storage

If a space is to be used for a wide range of activities, it will need to be flexible in both furnishings and equipment. When these are not required they have to be stored, preferably where they can be easily moved out again to serve a different function.

A list of items to be considered includes:

- *Furniture* Chairs and tables capable of being used in a variety of meeting formats or cleared away and stored when an open space is required.
- *Communications* Wireless, computer points, etc.
- *Display* Projector, screens, blackout facilities.

Additional costs/overheads

Staffing overheads are a major consideration in deciding whether or not an outside event can be accommodated. The add-on costs need to be set against potential income when the business plan is being drawn up, before the decision is made to incur additional capital expenses to cater for lets and hires. These operational costs could include:

- Opening and closing the building
- Servicing the meeting or event
- Heat and lighting
- Cleaning
- General wear and tear
- Sound provisions.

Careful planning can help to keep overheads to a minimum.

Catering

The style and scope of catering within a venue will vary. It may have facilities designed to cope with a range of uses at different times in the day (more usual in a venue with an 'open foyer' policy) or may be geared to bar sales before and during performances.

Each additional use will have its own requirements. Where these cannot be met by the theatre's main catering facility, additional provision will be required. For example, if caterers are to be brought in for specific functions they will need space to store and prepare food as well as wash-up facilities and staff changing areas.

Meeting rooms which are used when the bar is closed will benefit from having a small area where tea and coffee can be prepared (plus related storage).

Where the theatre's catering spaces are used, numbers can be an issue. Theatregoers and other regular patrons (if the café or restaurant is a public facility) will not appreciate it if their visit is disrupted because an outside let has taken over all the available space.

More detailed information on theatre catering is given in Section 3.6.

Conference use

Hiring the theatre out for conference use can prove lucrative but it is also demanding in terms of the amount of space required and the equipment needed. In all but the largest venues, a conference is likely to take over the whole of the front of house and the auditorium. In addition to the main space, conference use will require:

- *A reception area* Greeting and signing in delegates takes longer than checking theatre tickets.
- *Rooms for break-out sessions* The delegates may need to divide into a series of working groups.
- *Catering* As many as five breaks may need to be catered for:- pre-conference refreshments, mid-morning coffee, lunch, mid-afternoon tea and a closing drinks party/reception.
- *Technical support* Particularly in the auditorium when video, projection and sound equipment may well be used.
- *Staff areas* An office with computer, telephone, printer, etc.
- *Display space* For promoting the organisation or 'branding' the venue.

8.6.2 Conference breakout session in the foyer of the Unicorn Theatre, London, UK
Photograph: Ed Webb. Courtesy of The Theatres Trust

Technical requirements

If a venue is to cater successfully for a range of non-theatre events, the additional technical requirements need to be reviewed at the planning and design stage.

The events industry has developed considerably in recent years and to attract lucrative high-end commercial opportunities the following services must be available:

Adjustable lighting facilities

These should preferably be low energy in consumption and in heat output, so as not to affect the temperature of the space. Users should have full control over the lighting, specifically the intensity and the ability to focus lights in individual areas. Ideally there will also be the opportunities to provide a colour wash, for example by using red, green and yellow LEDs.

AV capabilities

The majority of events today rely heavily on audio-visual equipment. The ability to supply this service must be taken into consideration; whether for a small-scale presentation that requires projection facilities or for a high-end corporate function that requires a small sound desk with microphone output points and LCD (liquid crystal display) screens to showcase a company. The equipment does not necessarily all need to be fitted as it can be hired from event suppliers. However, if it is available 'in-house', the theatre may be able to increase the hire fee.

Wireless access

Even the smallest of companies can be dependent on their ability to connect to the internet in order to retrieve important files and documents for their presentations. Multinational companies often want to conduct live link-ups via the Onternet during their events.

Decor

The majority of event companies want to be able to dress the space to reflect the theme or style of the event being held. Many theatres (such as historic buildings and those with sensitive acoustic finishes) will place strict limitations on what can be done within the auditorium itself but consideration can be given to enable the introduction of free-standing equipment, fabrics and marketing materials, so that the company's image can be projected without causing any damage to fixtures and fittings. Lighting and video can also be used effectively if good provision is made at the outset.

Where a rehearsal room is designed to accommodate dance (rehearsals or classes) it will probably need a mirror and a barre fitted along one side of the room. If the room is to be used for other purposes it may be necessary to provide some form of covering, for example, curtains that can either be run on tab tracks or alternatively be hung off one of the lighting bars.

When planning a new building, it might be worth considering including spaces which could be used to host exhibitions and art installations. As well as offering scope for the theatre to extend general activities, this would have the added advantage of providing corporate clients with an area to use for 'branding' their events.

Staging

A small stage or podium may be required even for the most basic of events. If this can be designed as an option in an adaptable auditorium it will improve the marketability of the space to the corporate sector. Where permanent fixtures are restricted, it may be worth considering some form of temporary fitting (such as low-rise steel decking) which can be set up as and when needed. See also 'Rostra' below.

Technical facilities in a rehearsal space

A rehearsal room is a valuable asset as far as potential hire income is concerned and it is worth giving consideration to the technical facilities which could extend the use of the space.

Lighting

For the principles of open rehearsals, play readings and other such small performances a minimum of four LX bars would provide adequate back, front and overhead lighting. They need to be linked to a small desk with simple sliding dimmer controls.

Sound

A small sound system with inputs for iPods/MP3 players, etc. should be available and located in a position which allows the operator to see the stage/performance area.

Rostra

Rostra may be required in order to create a tiered seating system to accommodate the audience for a public performance. These rostra could also double as staging units to create alternative formats or for events held in other areas of the building.

8.7 Storage

Introduction

Effective storage provision should allow for a specific allocation of appropriate storage space both front of house and backstage, taking into account operational and production requirements (as distinct from just blocking off a spare area and marking it 'storage'). The location of such space needs to be carefully planned, with careful consideration being given to what will be stored and how often it will be needed.

Failure to provide for adequate and suitable storage areas could lead to additional spaces being sourced externally (with significant cost implications both in hire charges and operational efficiency) or to other spaces being used (also reducing operational efficiency).

Information on the storage requirements of specific areas such as backstage workshops and front of house catering is given in the relevant earlier sections.

Conditions

Some items will have very specific storage requirements. A detailed assessment needs to be carried out and good provision made at design stage. Aspects to be considered include:

Heating, cooling and ventilation

A suitable level of ventilation (natural) will help regulate storage conditions in terms of airflow. The storage of certain items, for example, kegged (draught) beer and ambient food, may require more specific temperature control measures.

Fire protection

The inclusion of sprinklers, fire extinguishers and fire blankets within the store may be appropriate and break glass points within a reasonable proximity are essential.

Where hazardous chemicals, gases or combustibles may be stored, specific guidance should be obtained from the relevant regulatory bodies.

Flooding

Careful consideration needs to be given to storage areas that house drainage access points and mains water isolation valves that could potentially, in the event of flooding, damage or destroy stored goods.

Confidential information

There will be a need to keep confidential information such as personnel files, accounts and credit card details in both long-term storage and in an accessible short-term storage area. The restriction of access to such stores should be factored in.

Location of storage areas

The location of storage areas can have a major impact on the smooth running of the venue. Poorly sited spaces can lead to operational problems including loss of man hours, a reduction in sales and related income, and a risk of health and safety violations. Storage needs to be positioned so that goods can be easily transported from the delivery areas as well as taken to where they are eventually needed.

The examples shown below are not exclusive but serve to provide a broad range of variable options that can be applied to most areas where storage is required. When designing a building for an existing organisation, proper consultation with all relevant departments will ensure that spaces are fully optimised.

Cellar

Cellars will be required to store stock for the bars and kiosks. Risk assessments and extensive planning will need to be conducted before deciding on the location of these areas, ensuring that manual handling issues are explored.

Given the potential volume and weight of wet stocks, i.e. kegs, cases of wine, spirits, etc., it is imperative that the point of delivery to the cellar is as short and obstruction-free as possible.

Some stock will be stored at the point of sale, but consideration should be given to an appropriate centralised store/cellar that can fully facilitate the venue running at capacity.

Events equipment

Events, meetings and conferences all require a wide range of equipment; tables, chairs, IT equipment and so on. Suitable provision needs to be designated for such items. These items will be used regularly so need to be accessed easily and stored close to where they will be most used.

Merchandise

Needs will vary according to the types of performances held. If there is a long-running show the same merchandise will be sold over a prolonged period and merchandise points are likely to be static. If the venue follows a rolling programme the merchandise will change on a regular basis, as will the size and location of the sales points. Sales points and associated storage need to be flexible to accommodate a wide variety of lines.

There should be enough display and storage at each sales point to carry sufficient stock to last an entire show – if stock runs out pre-show or during an interval the impact on revenue can be significant.

Print and display boards

Where a venue houses its own marketing department, it will need a large centralised store that can be accessed daily. It may be worth involving marketing specialists with the planning of such areas, as the amount of stock housed could be sizeable.

Display boards can vary in shape, size and weight. It is very likely that each will have an allocated position when in use and should have a specified storage place close at hand.

Safes and lockers

In the interests of security, adequate storage space should be considered within dressing rooms, green rooms, staff rooms and band rooms, etc. for safe and secure storage of valuables and personal effects.

Uniforms/stationery/disposables/glassware, etc.

Storage space for items such as uniform stock, stationery, disposables and so on will be needed and is likely to require frequent access.

Cleaning

All areas within the building need to be cleaned on a regular basis. Some will require specialised equipment.

Consideration needs to be given to both the front of house and backstage areas and provision made which takes into account the various levels and corridors and the likely number of cleaning staff in operation at any one time. More centrally located areas may be needed for larger items such as floor scrubbers, strippers, pressure washers and vacuums.

To operate efficiently, cleaners need power services with an adequate number of well-located power points, good working lighting (which does not require the whole theatre to be illuminated), and sinks and water supplies.

Allowing for growth

Taking into consideration the size and scale of the operation it should be possible to estimate a year-on-year growth projection, which will identify the amount of space to be provided for areas that have an obvious growth potential such as ticket stubs, personnel files, accounting history, etc. If no allowance is made for long-term storage and expansion, after a while, additional space will either have to be created or hired.

Labour
Consider the time that is taken from delivery, to storage, to distribution and replenishment. Taking more time to execute these tasks effectively will impact on productivity and output.

External storage
Hiring outside space to house the extra conference seats or the spare crates of accounts and personnel files could impact on the operational costs and could undermine the initial business planning on which they are based. This needs to be offset against any savings incurred by using cheaper 'out-of-town' provision.

SECTION EDITOR
David Blyth   Operations and Building Development Director, Ambassador Theatre Group

CONTRIBUTORS
Julien Boast   Theatre Royal Brighton, UK
Sue Morley   The Ambassadors, Woking, Surrey, UK
Julia Potts   Ambassador Theatre Group
Colin Chester   Ambassador Theatre Group
Russell Miller   Ambassador Theatre Group
Ruth Close   Ambassador Theatre Group

Section 9

Restoration, conversion and improvement of existing buildings

Contents

9.1   Introduction

This book focuses on new buildings but many theatre projects relate to the modernisation, refurbishment and improvement of existing facilities. Some will be major redevelopments while others will be relatively minor additions or modifications. Theatre buildings have always been subject to change – to keep abreast of fashion; to meet the current needs and expectations of audiences, operators and performers; to introduce new technology; and to increase the operator's profit. Almost invariably what is seen today reflects a gradual evolution over time.

In the days when theatres were lit by candle or gas they were not expected to last. Fire was the great enemy and the average life of a theatre building was less than 20 years. During the second half of the twentieth century, the increasing appreciation of theatre heritage, combined with the escalation in building costs and the scarcity of good city and town centre sites led people to consider how existing theatres could be adapted to meet modern needs. Since then a considerable body of experience has been accumulated.

This section looks at the merits of the existing stock of older buildings and the arguments for and against upgrading them. It outlines the planning and procedural issues and the particular problems that may be encountered when applying the principles described in previous sections. It also considers how these lessons can be applied to adapting other types of buildings for theatre use.

9.2 Existing stock of theatre buildings

Pre-1945 theatres

The traditional image of a theatre is one with an audience seated on a number of different levels, on plush seats or wooden benches, in an ornately decorated auditorium with a proscenium arch framing the stage. This represents a style that had gradually evolved since the mid-eighteenth-century and culminated in the boom years of theatre building during the late nineteenth century. The architects who designed these theatres had plenty of experience, learning from one commission to the next, and their buildings worked in a practical way.

What they produced was a highly functional and successful machine. But it was labour-intensive and predominantly commercially run; it inevitably demanded maximum audience numbers and minimum financial outlay in order to balance the books. A theatre that was closed was not generating income, so few improvements were carried out and any alterations were done in whatever way was simplest, cheapest and quickest.

The years between the First and Second World Wars were really the era of the cinema. Few new theatres were built and theatre attendance was in decline. Money, even for basic maintenance, was in short supply.

As a result, any early theatre that has survived substantially unmodernised will probably need a structural overhaul as well as work to unpick some previous alterations. The services will need to be completely replaced and the building is unlikely to comply with current access standards or meet audience expectations in terms of convenience and comfort. Nor will it be readily capable of providing acceptable working conditions. While such a theatre can command great affection among some sectors of the audience, others will regard it as an anachronism.

Theatres from the second half of the twentieth century onwards

Since 1945, there has been a revolution in the design of theatre buildings with a wealth of new ones being created. Many of these bear little resemblance to their predecessors. During the immediate post-war period, particularly in Europe, there was an emphasis on 'civic theatres'. Their style of architecture has tended to make them unloved, as has the fact that many of them tried unsuccessfully to cater for a range of uses and had flat-floored auditoria.

There was also a growth of college and campus theatres, particularly in the USA, which experimented with different types of formats and performer/audience relationships. The great chimera was the quest for a format that could be readily adapted to provide everything – from an intimate studio theatre in-the-round, to a concert hall for a symphony orchestra.

9.2.1 The auditorium of the Savoy Theatre, London, UK
Showing the 'traditional' three level format of a late Victorian building, but clad in geometrical art deco style in 1929 and meticulously restored after being gutted by fire in 1990.
Photograph: Ted Bottle

Towards the end of the last century, the greatest growth was in small-scale and community ventures, often created by adapting redundant existing buildings or 'found space'.

As a result of these developments, theatre practitioners and audiences have become accustomed to different styles and types of auditoria, including flexible layouts and less formal surroundings. They expect to find the building open throughout the day for refreshments, events and other activities. A new theatre today is also likely to have a second separate smaller studio space and to be able to offer facilities for hiring out in order to generate additional income. It may form part of a larger cultural or social facility. There is now no longer even common agreement as to what a theatre or performance space should look like, from outside or within.

Particular problems with post-1945 theatre buildings

Some of these buildings are undoubtedly distinguished, both architecturally and technically, and some also work well theatrically. But these three essential qualities are too rarely found together. Quite a few of the post-1945 theatre buildings are considered to be worthy but dull, while others are best regarded as interesting experiments, if not fundamentally flawed in their design. Some of these 'modern' theatres were built cheaply, some experimented in structure and materials. Many have not worn particularly well or have been poorly maintained and are now just as much in need of major surgery (or replacement) as their predecessors.

Even the best and most successful buildings need regular attention and require some upgrading and renewals after a period of 30 years. Some theatres have been allowed to just tick over for much longer than this.

As a result, it is almost impossible to generalise on how best to improve buildings of this period or even whether it is worth keeping them. Each building has to be examined on its own merits and in relation to the brief that the client has set.

Briefing

The process of briefing is discussed in Section 1, but it is worth drawing attention here to the added complexities of working within the constraints of an existing theatre building. The client is often the resident company with great experience of their own theatre and its virtues and shortcomings, but with little knowledge of how to commission a major project. This inexperience can lead to a short-sighted brief and the company (and its successors) will then have to live with the consequences. There is a vital role here for the services of historic building specialists as well as theatre consultants and others who have previous practical experience of what may or may not be feasible in any given set of circumstances.

While the revolution in the design of new theatre spaces has been producing mixed results, many of the older theatre buildings have been restored or brought back to life. Some have even been rescued from other uses. The most successful have been modernised in ways that enhance their best features, retaining their historic interest alongside improved facilities, modern services and new technical equipment. The same treatment has been given to some later buildings that started their lives as cinemas and, more recently, to some of the first generation of 'modern' theatre buildings created since 1945. The process of adapting and improving existing theatre buildings is in effect a continuous one, just as it has always been.

9.3 Opportunities and constraints

Existing buildings – a known commodity

An existing building will usually have some following within the community, even when it has been closed or in other uses for many years. Committed theatregoers have surprisingly long memories and can usually be relied upon to help support a campaign for opening or reuse. If the building is already in theatre use it should have the advantage of being a known quantity with a loyal audience. It will quite likely occupy a site that has a long tradition of established theatre use and that has been zoned accordingly by the planning authorities. The building may also be prominent in the townscape and centrally located. It is likely to be close to associated businesses such as bars and restaurants and convenient for public transport. The cost of acquiring a similar town centre site is likely to be prohibitive today, even were the space to be available.

Even the most down-at-heel building could well have some redeeming features that are worth retaining and it is not unusual to discover, after an exhaustive search, that in terms of location and existing ownership there is simply nowhere else available that is better than the existing site.

Remodelling is good for us – and kinder to the ghosts

As a general rule, it is less expensive to remodel and restore than to rebuild from scratch. It may also prove more sustainable to reuse an existing building, in terms of the energy embodied in it compared to the energy required for a new construction. It is generally agreed that we all need to become better at recycling existing buildings. Although old ones often need sympathetic help and, sometimes, radical surgery to achieve worthwhile reductions in their CO_2 emissions, it is often feasible to do so.

There is another, less tangible, reason why many theatre practitioners prefer to adapt an existing building rather than create a new one. Spaces like Wilton's Music Hall in London's East End, the Majestic in New York's Brooklyn and the Bouffes du Nord in Paris possess an indefinable, almost haunted quality, as if the ghosts of past performers and audiences somehow live on and contribute to the atmosphere that makes theatregoing there such a very special experience.

In purely practical terms however, it is usually necessary to make some fairly radical decisions. Most typical theatre buildings can be analysed on fairly predictable lines. One overriding issue that has to be considered right at the outset is whether there is likely to be sufficient scope to increase the floor area, should it prove necessary.

Typical analysis of an existing building

The auditorium is often the most prominent and well-regarded feature of an existing theatre and it may be feasible to adapt this, provided that the client is happy to maintain a version of what is likely to be a proscenium arch format. However, the front of house and circulation areas are more likely to need to be extensively remodelled and enlarged so that the whole audience can use the same entrance and have sufficient circulation space and proper facilities. This will normally necessitate the acquisition of some additional land adjacent to the front of the theatre. Additional space may also be needed to increase backstage accommodation. Often this will have to include a new stage house with a larger and higher flytower. Provision for vehicle loading access for modern container loads and a new and larger get-in are also likely to be needed. The remodelling of the old Empire Theatre in Edinburgh from its former use as a bingo hall to create the Festival Theatre presents a well-known example of this process (Reference project: p.224).

Obtaining official consent

The other main factor to be considered at the outset is whether the planning authorities are likely to impose constraints on what can be done, for example, by requiring the external appearance to be maintained as existing (or reinstating the original) or by placing limits on the scale of the building in the context of its surroundings. If a building has been officially listed or designated as having a heritage interest, it will be necessary to take careful account of this. There are only a few dozen theatres in the world from before 1800 that remain substantially complete and these are all likely to be heavily protected. In the UK anything prior to 1880 is considered a rarity, and a good example of a theatre building of any period up to 30 years ago is quite likely to fall into the 'heritage' category. The UK planning system also recognises and seeks to protect theatre use, so that existing buildings and their sites are not needlessly lost to other, more commercially lucrative, purposes. Over the past 35 years this has done much to encourage the reuse of existing theatre buildings, as well as their replacement where appropriate.

Finally, it is worth remembering that a planning or licensing authority may decide that the alterations proposed trigger a requirement for 'consequential improvements' in other parts of the building fabric or systems. For example, a proposal to rebuild the stage house could lead to a requirement to improve disabled access throughout the backstage areas. This might be required to correct perceived shortcomings in the original design or in an attempt to try to bring it into line with more modern practice. Early consultation with the appropriate bodies to agree what can reasonably be achieved is essential.

Get to know your building and agree what is worth keeping

The key to a successful scheme is to start with a thorough understanding of the building, its history and how it has developed over the years. This is a field where it really is worth engaging expert advice.

The best way to achieve this is to commission an independent expert with knowledge of historic theatres to prepare a Conservation Plan. This will outline the construction history of the building, highlighting those features that are of special architectural or historic interest. It should also indicate those aspects that are of lesser importance and where the removal of fabric may be justified. A good Conservation Plan should also recognise those aspects of a building that do not work well and need to be changed to enable it to continue to operate as a theatre. It should never be assumed that just because a theatre is old, or was designed by a well-known architect, it will necessarily be free from significant defects. Unfortunately, this stricture applies equally to some modern theatres.

Even if the building appears to have no particular merit, it is worth finding out as much as possible about its construction history, including researching the original plans and contemporary descriptions and illustrations. Unravelling the history of a theatre building is usually quite a complex business, but the process can yield valuable clues on how best to modernise it, especially when space is at a premium. It is always worth talking to people who have worked in the building for many years and who know its quirks, and the reason why some things are as they are. This will help reduce the risk of the unknown causing surprises during refurbishment.

Heritage issues

If the building has been listed or landmarked or otherwise designated by heritage authorities it will be necessary to obtain formal consent for any alterations that may affect its special interest. Fortunately, national conservation policies relating to historic buildings generally assume that the best use for a building is the one for which it was originally designed. This means that heritage authorities are often willing to agree to quite radical changes provided that these are demonstrated to be necessary. In making the case for change it is important to be armed with the Conservation Plan and to be supported by recognised experts who can point to precedents elsewhere and put the proposals and the theatre building itself into the broader regional or national context. It also helps if the client has appointed architects who are experienced in working on historic buildings. If some heritage fabric has to be lost, it is often possible to demonstrate how this may be offset by recovering and restoring other aspects of the building that are currently unseen or dilapidated.

Consent is more likely to be granted if the proposals work with the grain of the building. Radical changes of scale, trying to turn a proscenium arch format into an end stage, or stripping out elaborate period decor in order to change the ethos of an interior, are among those things best avoided.

Is there room to expand?

Once the brief is established and it has been agreed which aspects of the existing building are worth retaining and what adaptations can be made, attention may then need to turn to securing additional space for expansion.

The best solution will often entail the acquisition of an adjacent property or properties. Some theatre owners have to wait many years for such an opportunity to arise. When the chance comes along it is essential to take it, even if this then means sitting on a vacant site until the time is right to build, or subletting the space on a short-term basis.

Exploiting underused space

Building above an existing theatre may be an option but this is likely to prove expensive. There is an added difficulty in introducing the structural supports that will be required and valuable space is also likely to be lost when the necessary lifts and staircases are installed. A further consideration is whether the extra accommodation provided will be at the level where it is most needed, namely for public or backstage use. However, a lightweight construction on an existing flat roof could be an option and help to release other space below. There could also be usable space within a roof void, though this may well have already been filled with ducts for ventilation and other services.

Excavating below an existing building is also likely to be expensive. There are precedents, however, and this option is certainly worth investigating, particularly if there are existing basement areas which have not been previously exploited.

Careful thought should always be given to whether some activities could be rehoused in less expensive accommodation off-site. Likely candidates include scenery construction workshops and storage, including the main wardrobe.

Where expansion onto an adjacent site is not readily feasible, the first line of investigation is to see whether any underused space can be reclaimed within the existing theatre building. The initial researches into its history should offer some clues. Likely options include:

- bringing back former front of house space previously colonised for office use, relocating the offices elsewhere;
- utilising space at basement level or below the auditorium, never previously in use or fully fitted out;

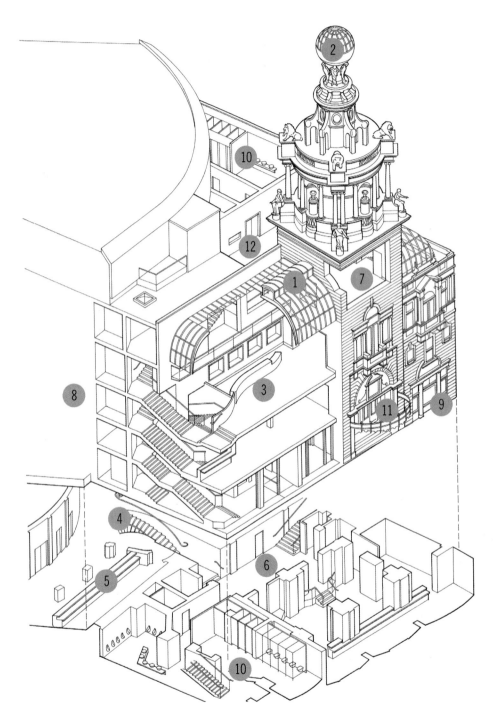

New features

1   Glass roofs
2   Fully restored globe
3   Terrace bar
4   Promenade staircase
5   New stalls bar
6   Lower ground level expansion
7   Tower room
8   Refurbished auditorium
9   Relocated box office
10 Increased number of toilets
11 Main entrance to all levels
12 Balcony bar

9.3.1 London Coliseum

Diagram showing how space in the original architect's design was recreated above the façade following war damage, and at lower ground level to create additional FOH space, and staircases re-designated so that everyone could come in via the one main entrance.

Drawing: RHWL Architects

- the area at the rear of the stalls under the circle with its poor sightlines may be better used to give additional foyer/bar or toilet space;
- the rear part of the uppermost seating tier may be floored over to create bar or office space at that level;
- the cellar and basement that originally contained machinery under the stage of an old theatre will often have become disused or used as a storage dump, but may be readily adapted to provide a band room, technical stores and crew rooms.

There are some examples of worthwhile schemes being achieved totally within the confines of the existing theatre, utilising areas such as those listed, but there are often limitations on what can be achieved. For example, the Prince of Wales Theatre, like the London Coliseum as illustrated, occupies a land-locked site in London's West End with no scope to expand the site or improve backstage facilities. But the original (rather unattractive) auditorium was sensitively remodelled and clad in a way that did no harm to the original historic fabric beneath. Bar and circulation space was radically improved by taking over rooms previously used for offices and by reducing the depth of the auditorium stalls. Capacity has been increased and comfort improved by reinstating seats of authentic design and the whole experience of going to this theatre has become a more enjoyable one.

9.3.2 Auditorium of London's Prince of Wales Theatre, before and after recladding and subtle modifications to improve lighting and make the audience feel closer to the stage.
Photographs: Ian Grundy

Is it better to rebuild?

Whenever a major refurbishment is being considered, the fundamental question needs to be addressed as to whether a complete rebuild on the existing site would be a better solution than working within the constraints of the existing building. Obviously heritage considerations may rule this out in some cases. However, in others, this could prove to be the best course of action, possibly less expensive overall, and making better use of the site than trying to restore a fundamentally unsatisfactory building. The new Wexford Opera House is a good example of what can be achieved (Reference project: p. 272).

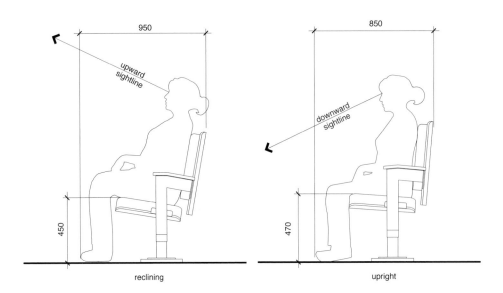

9.4.1 Diagram showing low and more upright seating positions

9.4 Some quick hits

There are often some relatively simple things that can be done to enhance an old theatre building, even if there is no opportunity to rebuild or insufficient money to undertake a major refurbishment.

As every building is different, not all of the options below will be available, but it is worth considering them alongside the list of potential spaces for expansion set out above.

- Many theatres have been subjected to ill-advised modifications over the years, and much may be achieved simply by correcting previous mistakes; for example, replacing an unsuitable decorative scheme, or removing unsightly false ceilings and partitions and light fittings.
- There may well also be scope for some subtle remodelling of an unattractive auditorium.
- One very common mistake earlier in the twentieth century was the replacement of the original seating with seats that were designed for use in cinemas. In a cinema one sits in a low seat, leaning back to look ahead or up to the screen, whereas in a theatre most positions require one to sit upright and to look down to the stage. The difference in terms of leg room and sight-lines is all too evident in the diagram.

- Almost invariably there will be a lack of adequate toilet facilities, particularly for women. It is worth going back to the original plans for clues, as the number could have been reduced over the years. Traditionally men were always given more space, whereas they actually need significantly less than women both because of the shorter time spent and the male/female ratio of audiences. So a simple expedient could be to swap some of the available spaces between the sexes. (See Section 3 for guidance on current recommendations.)
- It is always worth looking again at staircases and the original escape routes, as theatres are no longer designed to segregate different classes of society with separate and distinct circulation routes. It may be possible, with modern fire-engineering advice, to create additional space by removing or rerouting one or more staircases, particularly if seating improvements have led to a significant reduction in audience numbers.

Where it proves impossible to find the space to make a historic theatre workable by current standards, the only alternative could be a complete change in the nature and scale of the operation. The transformation of the former Whitehall Theatre to create the new Trafalgar Studios in central London is a good example of this approach (Reference project: p. 268). Like the Prince of Wales, it would probably have closed down completely had the planning and heritage authorities not been prepared to grant consent for a radical remodelling.

The following text looks at some of the significant issues that are regularly encountered when undertaking a full refurbishment of an existing theatre building.

9.5 Public areas

Access, circulation and increased front of house space

Providing level access for all sections of the audience through one common entrance is likely to prove a significant challenge. The problem is often best solved by creating a new main entrance and foyer areas in an extension, complete with a lift and service core from which the main levels of the existing structure can all be readily accessed. However, no two buildings are alike and it is well worth looking to see what has been done elsewhere. At London's Hackney Empire, for example, audiences still have the option to use the original doorways and staircases but a substantial element of new build incorporates a new staircase and a lift that connects all levels (Reference project: p. 236).

Where the seating is tiered, simply creating a new entrance and service core will obviously not ensure level access to all parts of the auditorium, and wheelchair access will have to be restricted accordingly. Converting more than single steps inside a building to a ramp is most unlikely to be a solution, as a ramp takes up far too much space.

Entrance (and egress) points to an auditorium circle or balcony are normally situated at the original lower and mid-sides and upper levels of each tier, and these are likely to be the only positions where wheelchair positions can be located. In practice, the best (and safest) positions are usually at stalls level and the least satisfactory (in all respects) at the uppermost levels. Rather than attempting to offer wheelchair users and their companions a full range of seat prices and positions, it may be acceptable to provide spaces at stalls level and discount the price accordingly. (See subsection 2.6 – Access for people with disabilities.)

One of the key factors which influences the amount of front of house space required is the range of ancillary activities that the theatre wants to house. Even though the seating capacity in a 100-year-old theatre that has been refurbished to modern standards is likely to be only a third of that claimed when it was originally opened, the space for toilets could well need to be trebled, and the bar and foyer space at least doubled. (See Section 3 – Front of House).

9.6 Within the auditorium

Seating capacity

When preparing the business plan, it is important to calculate what the potential seating capacity is likely to be. Increasing the volume of an existing auditorium is rarely a realistic option, either technically or aesthetically. In many theatres it will prove impossible to create a significant number of worthwhile seating positions at the uppermost levels and the need to provide leg room and seat widths to modern standards at other levels will inevitably reduce capacity still further. Once this is accepted by the management, unsatisfactory space can be released for other purposes. Even with fewer seats on sale, the ticket income could well increase, as the quality and comfort of those seats that remain will have improved sufficiently to allow higher prices to be charged. (Information on modern seat and seatway dimensions is given in subsection 4.4.)

Removing pillars

In older theatres, built before the introduction of cantilevered balcony construction in the late nineteenth century, the view from many parts of the house may well be obscured by pillars. It is tempting to consider removing these but, unfortunately, the cost and disruption involved usually rules this out. However, with careful planning of individual seating positions it is often possible to mitigate the worst effects.

Seat spacing and tiers

At stalls level, reseating should present few problems. It may be feasible to increase the stalls floor rake slightly, particularly if the rear wall is brought forward. Sightlines will be further improved by staggering the seat spacing. If possible, centre gangways should be avoided

9.6.1 Ironmongery at upper levels
Contrast the view of a forest of ironmongery on the left with the more sensitive treatment of the upper levels of a traditional theatre.
Photographs: Ian Grundy

as they create an unnecessary gap in the audience from the performers' viewpoint. Continental seating can provide a more unified audience and allow greater space between the rows without any loss in the overall seat count (see subsection 4.4).

The old dress circle will probably need reseating, but it should be possible to work within the constraints of the original tiering, provided a suitable type of seat is used. It may be worth researching and adapting the original seat designs, as these will have had a higher seat base and this will both maximise the amount of leg room available and improve sightlines.

A more radical solution is likely to be needed in those upper parts of the theatre originally designed for bench seating. Subsequent attempts to improve conditions tended to make matters worse so it could well be worth stripping back to the original structure. There are then likely to be two main options.

1   The most popular solution was to build onto the original structure to provide two new tiers for every three original ones, thus creating fewer rows but with more modern seats. But the steepness of the rake is likely to lead to demands from licensing bodies for a higher railing on the balcony front and sometimes even new railings inserted

between each row of seats. This is likely to prove detrimental to the sightlines and to be unpleasing aesthetically. More than one old theatre that has been carefully restored in other respects has been spoilt by the enforced insertion of a forest of ironmongery at its uppermost level.

2   In recent years a number of theatres have been successfully restored by creating more comfortable versions of the original benched seating system at the top level, retaining the original tiering but adding upholstery. The rationale for this is that it provides a quantity of seating at low prices for those who want this option. The sightlines and acoustic, at least from the front few rows, are often very good and in some instances the front couple of rows have been seated while the rear section remains benched, echoing what often happened when these theatres were first built.

9.6.2 Hackney Empire, London, UK
The refurbished auditorium
Photograph: Hélène Binet. Courtesy of Tim Ronalds Architects

However, it is not always possible for the whole of the uppermost tier to remain in use. Sometimes it will be completely closed to the public, or have only the central portion retained in use. If closed, the space is likely to be set aside for lighting positions and to create a lighting control box.

Spaces at the sides (or slips) of an auditorium vary greatly in their comfort and sightlines, particularly at their upper levels. As a general rule, it should not be assumed that the slips can be made saleable simply by reinstating a modern version of what was there originally. But having seating positions at the sides of a traditional auditorium does have a vital function, i.e. that of 'papering the walls with people', and it is important to try to retain this feature, even if these seats have to be sold at a lower price. The same may be said of boxes, although those closest to the stage are likely to have been long colonised for lighting and control positions. (See Section 6.)

Decor

Adapting an existing theatre building for modern use does not automatically involve a full restoration of the original decor. While many decisions will be influenced by the heritage merit of the building and the requirements of planning authorities, there are also practical and artistic considerations.

A hundred years ago the decorative scheme varied from expensive wallpaper, gold leaf and carpet in the front stalls and dress circle, to plain ceramic tiles, painted brickwork and bare boards in the cheaper parts of the building. Current practice is less discriminatory.

An ornate auditorium with gold leaf and rich upholstery is not to everybody's taste. Some may consider that it runs counter to the artistic ethos of the programme that is planned or that it may not appeal to the expectations of a young audience. A slavish return to the original colour scheme can result in an auditorium that appears 'bleached out' under modern house and stage lighting, which is very significantly brighter than the gas (or candlelight) for which the original was designed. The pale colour will reflect light and may make it impossible for an effective 'blackout' to be achieved.

Although there have been notable examples of a full and authentic decorative scheme being reinstated with minimal compromises, such as the Theatre Royal at Bury St Edmunds (Reference project p. 266), the Gaiety on the Isle of Man, and the London Coliseum, most restorations have opted for an overall scheme throughout the public areas that respects the historic

nature of the building while being practical and reflecting contemporary tastes. Hackney Empire provides an example of the latter approach (Reference project: p. 236, illustrated on page 189)

In some places the whole auditorium has been painted out in a dark colour to give a neutral effect, although fortunately this fashion now seems to be on the wane. An alternative solution (where plush finishes are not considered to be appropriate) is for the original to be retained in its 'unrestored' state, as at the Majestic in New York or the Bouffes du Nord in Paris (Reference project: p.198).

Lighting and sound

Similar decisions and compromises are necessary when deciding how to incorporate positions for modern stage lighting and loudspeakers. As these were not available when the historic theatres were built, no provision was made. Over the years, lighting positions will have been created in stage boxes, on the front of circles, and suspended above the auditorium. Speakers will have been fastened to the side of the proscenium arch. One of the objectives of any scheme should be to remove unnecessary clutter and to design in appropriate positions for modern lighting, sound and video equipment in a way that is as unobtrusive as possible. Nevertheless, modern production lighting and sound systems and other services do need substantial space for installation in areas such as balcony fronts (see Section 6). Integrating these services while preserving the fabric and character of an old building requires a respectful approach.

The natural acoustic of most traditional theatre auditoria was very good and it will be important not to jeopardise this by removing drapes or ornamental plasterwork. What will have changed over the years is the amount of extraneous noise from transport and, of course, the greatly increased noise generated from inside the building with amplified sound systems. It is as important to prevent complaints from neighbours as well as from audience members and this may not be easy in an old building. Providing the necessary acoustic isolation may well entail cladding the stage house and its roof with appropriate materials and installing and soundproofing lobbies on external doors from the auditorium.

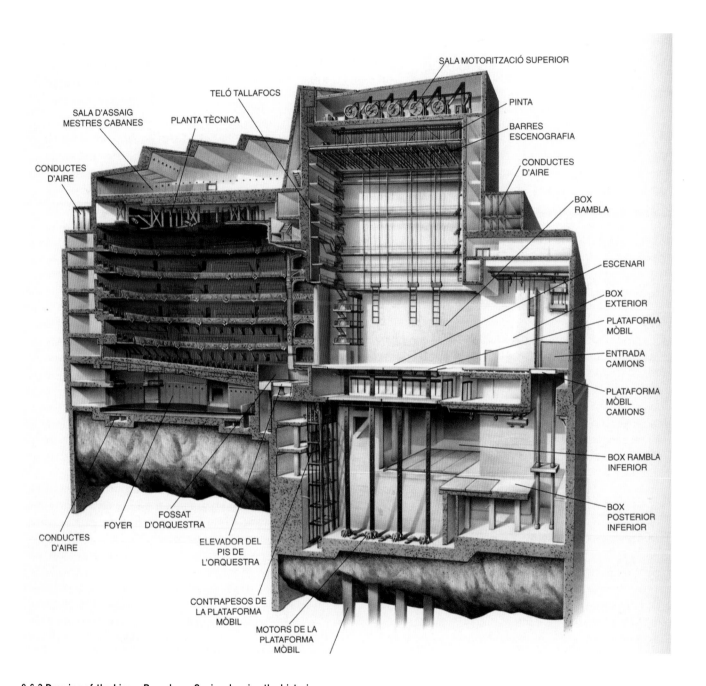

SALA MOTORITZACIÓ SUPERIOR

TELÓ TALLAFOCS

PINTA

SALA D'ASSAIG
MESTRES CABANES

PLANTA TÈCNICA

BARRES
ESCENOGRAFIA

CONDUCTES
D'AIRE

CONDUCTES
D'AIRE

BOX
RAMBLA

ESCENARI

BOX
EXTERIOR

PLATAFORMA
MÒBIL

ENTRADA
CAMIONS

PLATAFORMA
MÒBIL
CAMIONS

BOX RAMBLA
INFERIOR

BOX
POSTERIOR
INFERIOR

FOYER

FOSSAT
D'ORQUESTRA

CONDUCTES
D'AIRE

ELEVADOR DEL
PIS DE
L'ORQUESTRA

CONTRAPESOS DE
LA PLATAFORMA
MÒBIL

MOTORS DE LA
PLATAFORMA
MÒBIL

**9.6.3 Drawing of the Liceu, Barcelona, Spain, showing the historic
theatre and its new additions**
Drawing: Courtesy of the Liceu, Barcelona

Heating and ventilation

Ensuring that there is adequate heating and ventilation is likely to have been a continuing source of frustration over many years. A refurbishment programme could well provide the opportunity to return to first principles and start again. Most older theatre buildings were originally constructed on the principle that air, heated by the audience and the lighting, rises naturally. Theatres were designed to allow heat to escape at ceiling level and equipment such as 'sunburners' were installed to promote this process. Attempts have been made to reverse this process (feeding hot air in from the top, partly in order to prevent draughts) but these have rarely proved successful.

The main difficulty in introducing a displacement system (i.e. one that works with the natural buoyancy of hot air rather than against it) is finding space to install the necessary input ducting at lower levels, though there is usually space to fit extract vents in the roof voids above the auditorium's decorative plaster ceiling. With both under-seat and overhead ventilation, the rear of the stalls and balconies need to be considered very carefully as these are often areas where air stagnates and overheating occurs. It is also important to understand how air and moisture moves when a building is modernised so that damage to delicate historic material may be avoided. (Section 4 provides more detailed information on auditorium ventilation.)

9.7 Backstage

The stage house

A new stage house is normally an essential component of any full refurbishment project (although there is still a tendency for theatre owners to concentrate on those parts of the building that the public sees and then for the money to run out before the backstage areas are tackled). While a complete demolition and rebuild of the stage house will not necessarily be either feasible or appropriate, it is likely that the grid will need to be raised and mechanised flying installed. Wing space, get-in and storage will also need to be improved and dressing room, crew room, wardrobe and stage management accommodation will probably need better provision. The case study on the Edinburgh Festival Theatre demonstrates the full treatment (Reference project: p. 224). At the Hackney Empire the existing stage tower was simply extended upwards using a lightweight construction while the historic Theatre Royal at Newcastle had its stage tower extended upwards and refitted using glass reinforced plastic (rather than steel) to reduce the weight on the original structure.

Levelling an old stage

Until around 1900 all theatre stages were raked (i.e. there was a built-in slope upwards away from the audience) but from the early years of the twentieth century onwards, flat stages became the norm. Some of the older ones were levelled but as this necessitated altering all the supporting structure into the wings and scene docks many stages still retain their original rakes. However, it was not only cost which stopped many managements from altering the stage format. Stage rakes were introduced to improve sightlines from the stalls level and to give an enhanced perspective effect. Removing a rake can seriously damage the view of the stage for those sitting in the stalls and, unless the slope on the stalls floor can be increased to compensate, it may still be best to leave things as they are.

Historic technology

It is tempting to assume that the historic interest in a theatre building will be confined to its front of house areas with everything beyond the proscenium arch being regarded as expendable. However, an unmodernised theatre building will often contain significant elements of historically important stage machinery or other equipment that is of technological interest. It is worth bringing in expert advice before any building work starts so that appropriate steps may be taken, with the agreement of the heritage authorities, to record any technical installations before removal or, if appropriate, to safeguard them *in situ*.

9.8 Incorporating elements of new build

The initial researches into the building's history should have identified the parts of the existing structure that have special significance and the elements that may be replaced. Where additions are planned, the relevant authorities need to be consulted at the outset in order to reach an agreement as to how such new work is to be treated. Current opinion is that pastiche is best avoided, and it seems now to be generally accepted that the 'joins' between old and new work should be clearly delineated.

At the London Coliseum, designed by Frank Matcham, an agreement was reached that all work within the surviving 1904 structure and any reinstatements of elements originally designed by him should be as historically authentic as was feasible, whereas any new work could be in a contemporary style. At the Hackney Empire a similar division between old and new was agreed (Reference project p. 236).

Others, however, have taken a different approach. For example, in 1988 the foyers of Newcastle's Theatre Royal were extended and a new main staircase installed which was designed to be indistinguishable from the original. In Spain, at the Liceu Theatre in Barcelona, the front of house areas of this historic opera house were rebuilt in a modern style after being destroyed by fire, but the traditional auditorium was meticulously restored to its original state (Reference project: p. 240).

Replacing signage

One element that is often overlooked at the outset is the need for signage and advertising material on the outside of the building. An authentically restored façade is likely to show only the name of the theatre with possibly a couple of poster spaces. Neon lights and illuminated display boards may have been added later, probably in a piecemeal fashion, and could well be regarded by the planning authorities as inappropriate. It is important to include display facilities as part of an overall scheme and to obtain official consent at the outset. Westminster City Council, for example, whose area includes a high proportion of London's historic theatres, has prepared policy guidance in conjunction with theatre owners, setting out realistic guidelines on what may be permitted.

9.9 Other approaches – and some more radical solutions

This section has tended to concentrate on nineteenth- and early twentieth-century theatre buildings because that is where the greatest problems are likely to be encountered. In more recent auditoria-based structures, such as cinemas from the 1930s, leg room and row tiering at the upper level should be less restricted, there will have been one large main entrance rather than four or five, and there will be far more foyer, bar and circulation space. On the other hand, few cinemas were equipped with proper stages, and those stages that do exist are likely to have been built with limited depth, flying capacity and wing space. Dressing rooms are also likely to be in short supply. But defects such as these are relatively easy to overcome, and there are many examples of former 'super cinemas' being successfully adapted for theatre use.

Remodelling

Sometimes a cinema auditorium will be too big, even to create a large theatre. At the former Regent Cinema in Stoke-on-Trent, one of the two sets of (false) boxes on either side of the auditorium was removed to allow a new proscenium to be installed; thereby extending the depth of what would otherwise have been a shallow stage and reducing the overall auditorium length. Since then a drape/curtain has also been introduced to reduce further the apparent volume of the auditorium space on those occasions when a smaller audience is expected.

Buildings may also be remodelled in more radical ways. The exterior and foyers of the former Odeon Cinema at Scarborough were restored while the auditorium was divided up to create a 400-seat theatre in-the-round (the Stephen Joseph) and smaller studio space, with offices and dressing rooms looking onto a day-lit atrium inserted between the two new auditoria.

Precedents for this type of remodelling had already been established at the Majestic in New York. The disused old theatre was given a new life and a totally new look, with the former proscenium format replaced by an open stage that projects out into the audience at first-floor level to be encompassed by the original circle. The former stalls area below has thus been released to create other facilities.

Conversions from other building types

There is in theory no limit to the ways in which existing spaces can be converted to create a theatre. The Stephen Joseph at Scarborough started its life in a temporary conversion of a room above a library, and later moved into a redundant school building, before creating its more permanent home in the former Odeon Cinema. The Royal Exchange Theatre in Manchester is a free-standing module sitting inside a nineteenth-century trading hall: (Reference project p. 264). London's famous Mermaid Theatre was originally a dock warehouse; and the Roundhouse started its life as a shed for railway engines (Reference project p. 258).

When an existing building is being considered for conversion, attention tends to be focused on the part of it that might house the auditorium. But a theatre building requires more than a large core space – perhaps twice as much area again – and it is important not to prejudice future success by failing to find a building that can also provide adequate backstage and front of house accommodation or one with sufficient land for these facilities to be added.

In previous centuries the early theatre companies would often travel from place to place, setting up their makeshift stages in whatever space was available. Permanent theatre buildings, often only to be used for a few weeks each year, were created later. Elements of that tradition whereby theatrical performance can take place anywhere, and where the ad hoc nature of the surroundings add to the magic of the event, still survive. Unfortunately though, it is now far more difficult to create a theatre, let alone a temporary one, in a found space as all today's increasingly stringent fire, health and safety, and disabled access requirements will need to be met before a license can be obtained. Anyone considering such a space should seek expert advice and be aware that obtaining the necessary consents will take time and that the costs of meeting these requirements could prove prohibitive. Reference projects, the King's Cross Almeida (p. 238) and the Royal Shakespeare Company's Courtyard Theatre (p. 212) illustrate temporary use; The Young Vic (p. 278) shows how a temporary theatre became a permanent one.

9.9.1 Scarborough's Stephen Joseph Theatre with its two auditoria, created inside the former Odeon cinema.
Drawing: Concept by Harry Osborne of Osborne Christmas Architects
The former Whitehall Theatre in London's West End (now Trafalgar Studios) demonstrates a similar approach (see Reference project p. 268).

Final words

Those who decide to adapt an existing building will have to be prepared to accept some compromises, but if they do their researches properly at the outset and employ people who have relevant experience of this type of project, they will probably be surprised at how much can be achieved. Not only will they have made good use of an existing space, but they will discover that its spirit somehow lives on and contributes to the 'magic' quality that they in turn hope to create.

SECTION EDITOR

Peter Longman

The section takes account of advice and comments received from theatre historian, John Earl.

Reference projects

REFERENCE PROJECTS

Note:

Plans and sections are 1:500 scale

Théâtre des Bouffes du Nord
Paris, France

Peter Brook's internationally renowned theatre, the Bouffes du Nord, demonstrates how the retention of an original interior, rich in theatrical history, can create an atmosphere rarely found in new buildings or conventional renovations. It is a theatre, tailored by practitioners rather than by architects, designed to respond to Peter Brook's personal dramatic vision (as set out in his book *The Empty Space*). It captures the essence of 'found space' and has served as an inspiration for several generations of theatre directors and designers.

Located behind the Gare du Nord in Paris, the theatre building dates from 1876. For the next hundred-odd years, it had what has been described as an 'interesting' history with a succession of artistic directors trying and almost invariably proving unable to make enough money to keep it open. Its use became increasingly episodic until it was shut down completely in 1952 for failing to meet safety standards.

Peter Brook discovered Bouffes du Nord in a state of terminal decline in 1974 and recognising theatrical value in its decay, literally stopped the rot at that specific point.

We made our way through a dusty tunnel until we found the Bouffes du Nord, dilapidated, charred, ruined by rain, its walls pitted by age, but at the same time noble, humane, light, breathtaking, the quality of sound extraordinary. We took two decisions; one, to leave the theatre as it was and not to erase the marks that a century of use had left, the other to bring it back into use as quickly as possible.

Peter Brook in his book *The Shifting Point*

Within six months the theatre opened. The structure was cleaned and made safe. The wooden bench seats in the gallery were retained and covered in fabric and the basic technical equipment installed. The only other work which was done at that time was adding doors as a fire safety modification, flattening the floor of the stalls and adding benches. A more serious refurbishment was undertaken in 2005, with structural work, acoustic doors and new ventilation equipment being installed.

The acting area is brought forward into the centre of the space with the stage reaching out into the audience, wrapped around on the remaining three sides by stalls and balcony seating. The stage is at stalls level, flattened out from the back of the former stalls. The two lower balconies each have only a few rows of seating and the upper level is reserved for lighting and technical equipment.

While the 'feel' of the original decorative finishes has been retained, the colours have evolved over the years: grey to begin with, brown/ochre for *The Mahabharata*, white and green for *The Tempest*; and red for the *Impression de Pelleas*.

Summary

Theatre type and operational format
Mostly receiving and co-productions with the occasional work by Peter Brook. High proportion of music (chamber, jazz, some rock).

Location and web reference Paris, France. www.bouffesdunord.com

Building dates Original theatre built in 1876. Renovated in 1904. Reopened 1974 – after being made structurally sound and fulfilling safety requirements. Further extensive renovation for code compliance in 2005.

Auditorium Traditional proscenium and galleries space, adapted to be used with central stage/performance area in former stalls section.

Stage 'Double depth' apron stage with former proscenium at approximately the mid-point in the stage's depth; the proscenium walls are used scenically with doors at stage level.
Very limited technical provision from stage ceiling (suspension points for a grid or a few bars), no flying space as office floors were built in the stage tower by the owner prior to Brook's arrival).

Dimensions 17m deep from front row to back wall; 13m wide in front of proscenium (widest part of curve of front row), proscenium 8m opening, stage 14m to 15m wide behind proscenium.

Architect Louis-Marie Emile Lemenil.

Theatre (design and technical) consultants In-house staff and designers.

Building cost £10,000 for first renovations in 1974.

Auditorium showing the galleries
Photograph: Jean-Guy Lecat

Dome and original stage
Photograph: Jean-Guy Lecat

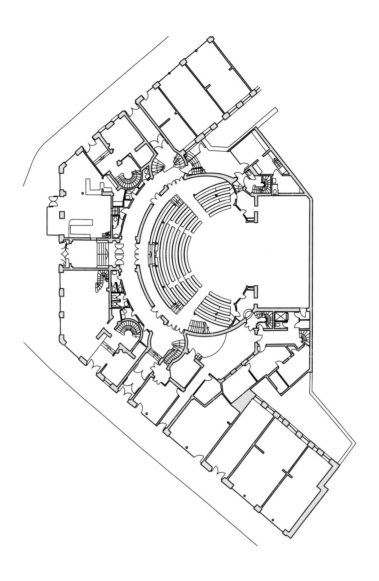

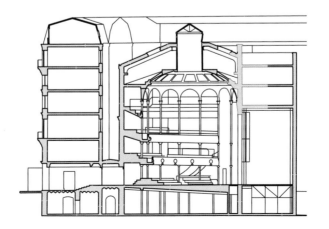

Cerritos Center for the Performing Arts
Cerritos, California, USA

Cerritos Center for the Performing Arts (CCPA) opened in 1993 but it is still regarded as one of the most flexible theatres in the world. This is achieved through the intensive use of mechanisation, pioneered in the UK and USA, to create a venue capable of housing many different arts and social activities. The Center is owned and operated by the City of Cerritos and functions both as a performing arts and a conference facility. The performance season runs from August through to May and consists of an eclectic mix of music, dance and drama with events ranging from pop concerts to chamber music to Broadway shows.

Part of the initial phase of the Cerritos Town Center, CCPA established an identity for the surrounding capital development by creating a building composed of pavilions that contrast with the adjacent high-rise office buildings and hotel. The Center is clad in glass, polished red granite and horizontal bands of limestone with the roof, overlooked by commercial development, being treated as the fifth façade. A transparent lobby links the Center to the hotel plaza and establishes an open and inviting entrance.

The shape of the auditorium is based on that of the classic concert hall such as the Musikvereinssaal in Vienna or the Boston Symphony Hall. While the balcony seating remains fixed, a system of hydraulic lifts and air castors is used to raise, lower or remove seats and floors, ceilings and stage areas. This enables the space to be configured in five basic formats: arena, concert, lyric, drama and banquet (flat floor) and change from a relatively intimate space seating an audience of 900 to a large open area accommodating up to 1,950 people. The towers, which hold the Center's distinctive three-level box seating, are also equipped with air castors and can be angled to face the stage in any one of a number of positions. The team is able to change from one format to another in less than eight hours.

Similar systems allow the second performance space, the Sierra Room, to be changed from performance to banquet to conference use. This flexibility enabled CCPA, within two years of opening, to become the highest grossing theatre of less than 3,000-seat capacity in California and the third highest in this category in the whole of the USA.

Summary

Theatre type and operational format
Major civic venue running a ten-month mixed programme of performances as well as conference and related use throughout the year.

Location and web reference Cerritos, California. www.cerritoscenter.com

Building dates Opened 1993 as part of a larger development.

Auditorium Rectilinear concert hall dimensions equipped with high-level technology to enable space to be reconfigured to five basic formats. Seating capacity ranges from 900 (drama configuration) to 1,950 (concert hall configuration).

Stage Varies with format in width and depth from 9m to 18m width and 10m to 15m depth.

Architect Barton Myers Associates, Inc., Los Angeles, California, USA.

Theatre (design and technical) consultants Theatre Projects Consultants, South Norwalk, Connecticut, USA.

Acoustic consultants Kirkegaard Associates, Boston, Massachusetts, USA.

Building cost $50 million (1994).

The auditorium in concert format
Photograph: Tim Street Porter

A mobile tower
Photograph: Barton Myers Associates

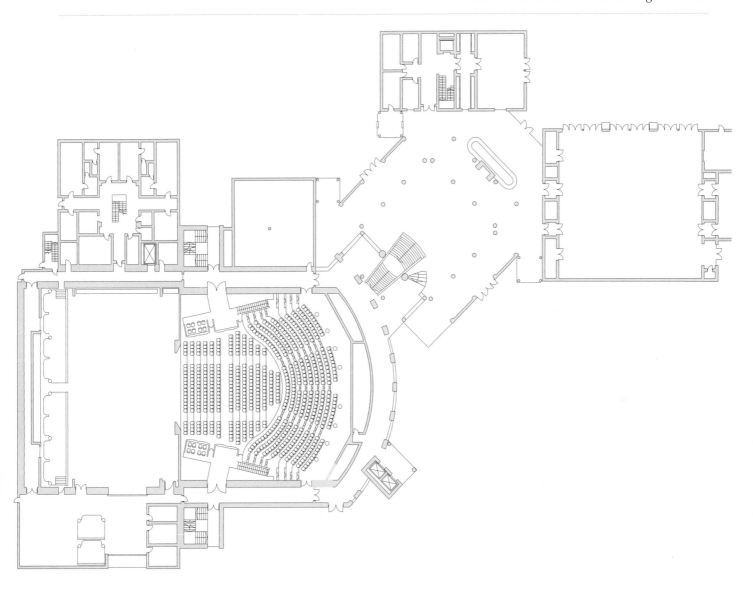

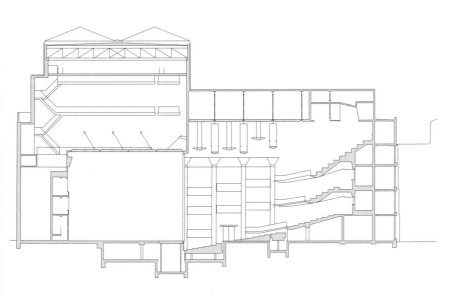

Copenhagen Opera House
Denmark

Copenhagen's new Opera House, which opened in 2004, was a private project financed by the A.P. Møller and Chastine Mc-Kinney Møller Foundation, donated to the Danish State to be operated by the Royal Danish Theatre.

The building occupies a prominent, artificially created, island position at the shore of the harbour of Dokøen, on an axis with the Royal Palace. Designed by Danish architect Henning Larsen, it is one of the best equipped opera houses in the world, as well as being one of the largest. The building totals 41,000m² spread over 14 floors, five of which are below ground level.

The building has two main parts – the stone-clad façades of the main section housing the stage and backstage accommodation, and the steel and glass of the front of house areas. The structure is unified by a vast metal roof which floats over the whole complex and extends out over the granite podium along the front façade, providing the strong identity that the Opera House's civic status requires.

The main auditorium has a classical form with four horseshoe-shaped galleries wrapping around the stalls (three for the audience and a technical gallery above). The balconies are clad in maple, modelled to enhance the natural acoustic of the room. The auditorium seats an audience of about 1,500 (with the orchestra pit in use). The pit is capable of accommodating just over 100 musicians).

The stage is supported by five additional spaces, designed to accommodate a demanding repertoire of opera and ballet, as well as scenery preparation and rehearsals with full settings. Four double-deck main stage elevators raise and lower 5m from stage level while a series of wagons move without guide tracks over all five stage spaces and into the main rehearsal room. There is also a 15m diameter revolve and a ballet floor wagon stored under the rear stage.

A second auditorium (the Takkelloftet, meaning rigging loft) is a totally flexible black box studio. Its 200 seats are partly on retractable tiers and partly on 13 mobile towers, which move on air-bearings to enable the space to be configured in a variety of performance formats.

The maple-clad drum of the exterior of the main auditorium takes on a sculptural form within the extensive glazed foyer space where a series of radial bridges connect to the foyer balconies and provide views across the water to Renaissance Copenhagen. The work of Danish and Icelandic artists features strongly both in the foyers and in the auditorium.

Summary

Theatre type and operational format Opera House, base for the national opera and ballet companies and receiving venue for opera, dance and other major works.

Location and web reference Ekvipagemestervej, Copenhagen, Denmark. www.operaen.dk

Building dates Construction November 2001 to October 2004. Opened for performances in January 2005.

Auditorium Maximum capacity (no pit): 1,647. Regular pit: seating reduces to 1,468 (removing 179 seats in five rows removable as two and three rows on two seating wagons on two elevators). Very large pit: seating reduces to 1,434 (removing an additional 32 seats in one row). Takkelloftet is a highly adaptable 'black box' studio theatre seating around 200 people.

Stage The main stage is 30.2m x 22.7m in plan, with the grid at +30 m. The flying hoists are in a room above with some dimmers and through which the air ducts for the main auditorium pass from the plant room behind the flytower. The portal is adjustable from 16m x 11m down to 12m x 7.5m.

The Studio Theatre is 22.7m x 16.6m with a tension-wire grid at 6.9m above.

Architect Henning Larsen Architects, Copenhagen, Denmark.

Theatre (design and technical) consultants Theatreplan LLP, London, UK.

Acoustic consultants Arup, London, UK.

Building cost Not published but estimated to be around $450 million (2004).

The Opera House frontage
Photograph: Adam Moerk. Courtesy of
Henning Larsen Architects

Main auditorium
Photograph: Adam Moerk. Courtesy of
Henning Larsen Architects

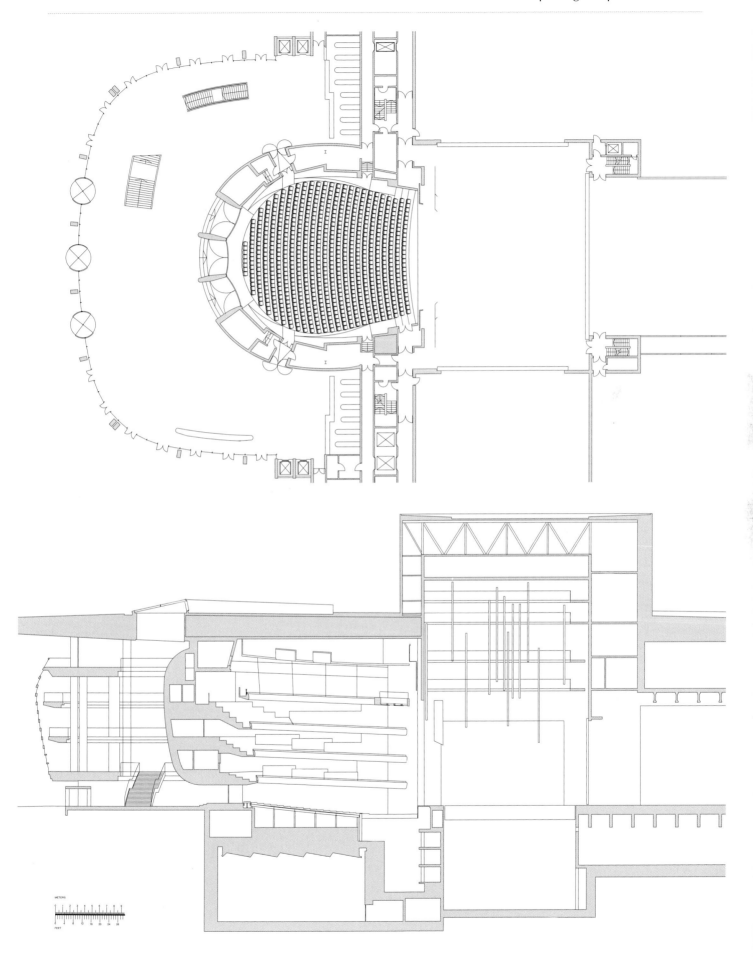

METERS

FEET

The Cottesloe, National Theatre
London, UK

After decades of planning, a prestigious Board set up by the UK government and the Greater London Council finally delivered the National Theatre, which opened in 1976 on the South Bank of the Thames. With such high-level input, it is interesting that the smallest of its three auditoria is almost universally regarded by theatre practitioners as being the most successful and possibly the only one to offer a prototype for the future.

The courtyard-style Cottesloe was not part of the original brief. It was designed as a space for experimental and developing work at the instigation of Peter Hall, when appointed as Director after building work on the complex had already started. The Cottesloe was set out in a void under the much larger Olivier theatre and is entered via its own street-level foyer, giving access to the middle of three seated levels.

The theatre successfully combines flexibility with simplicity. It is a dark-walled rectangular room with a central area defined by two tiers of pillared galleries around three of the walls. There are two fixed features: the two gallery slabs, with removable hand rails, and the fixed end stage platform. The space can be configured in a number of different end stage, in-the-round, traverse and flat floor arrangements by means of a mid-auditorium elevator and a retractable seating tier – retracting manually under the rear auditorium first-level gallery, or manually set steel-framed rostra and stacking chairs. The seating capacity depends on how the space is formatted with the maximum audience being around 400.

The first- and second-level galleries extend halfway up the end stage and these positions are available to actor, audience or technician, depending on layout.

Five technical bridges extend halfway up the end stage, giving way to a flying grid with a small number of motorised flying bars shared between lighting and scenery. Lighting positions are provided between bridges on all four sides of three bays across the theatre. The flying grid is supplemented by chain hoists for scenic assembly.

The auditorium in its courtyard format
Photograph: Courtesy of Theatre Projects Consultants

Alternative layout set for the production 'Vincent in Brixton'
Photograph: Philip Carter

Summary

Theatre type and operational format
Experimental and medium-scale work within a larger performing arts venue – The National Theatre.

Location and web reference Lambeth, London, UK. www.nationaltheatre.org.uk

Building dates The National Theatre opened in 1976 with the first performance in the Cottesloe being given in March 1977.

Auditorium Adaptable courtyard format seating an audience of between 200 and 400 depending on the format.

Stage Flexible rectangular stage. Fixed platform 9.144m deep and 9.9m wide between side galleries. Flying height 7.38m above end stage.

Architect National Theatre architect Denys Lasdun and Partners, London, UK.

Theatre (design and technical) consultants Theatre Projects Consultants, London, UK.

Building cost £16.6m for the whole of the three-theatre complex (1976).

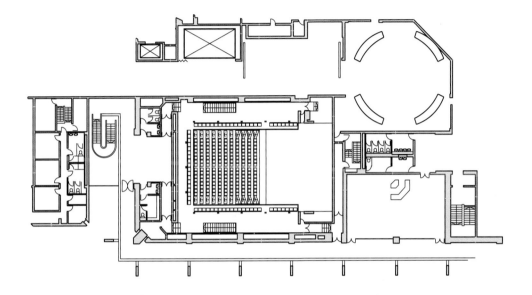

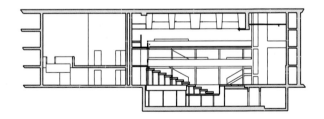

The Courtyard Theatre, Royal Shakespeare Company
Stratford-upon-Avon, UK

The Royal Shakespeare Company (RSC) has had a purpose-built theatre in Stratford-upon-Avon since 1932. It was a competition-winning building, designed by Elisabeth Scott in art deco style, and has listed status. Unfortunately, the auditorium had long been considered to have shortcomings as a performance venue and, by the 1990s, was becoming increasingly at odds with the ambitions of the RSC and the way it wanted its work to be presented.

The RSC took the radical decision to demolish the 1932 auditorium and remodel it as a thrust stage space for the twenty-first century. While this was taking place, they needed somewhere in Stratford to perform their work, which, at the same time, would also serve as a prototype for the new auditorium. Thus the idea of the Courtyard Theatre was born. The resulting space was industrial and edgy, with its 'rusty' corten steel finish contrasting with the traditional red brick of the rest of the RSC complex.

The new auditorium layout was developed in response to the RSC's ambition of bringing the audience much closer to the action than other thrust forms at this seating capacity. The length of the auditorium was limited by the overall depth of the existing theatre between the listed foyer and the proscenium wall, and the width was determined by what was needed to contain 1,000 people able to see the stage. These two constraints resulted in a U-shaped auditorium wrapping around a deep thrust stage. All dimensions were tested in three dimensions in a scaffolding mock-up.

The structural solution was to use a series of shallow-pitch portal frames, braced in a longitudinal direction, and clad with 5mm thick corten steel. This virtually free-standing auditorium frame was then built within the box. The interior finishes picked up the industrial aesthetic with steel balustrades and plywood-clad walls. The overall dimensions of the steel box were 40.8m x 26.6m with a height of nearly 14m. This approach enabled the foundations to be independent of the adjoining building 'The Other Place', the company's studio theatre, which was converted to provide the foyer and front of house for the temporary theatre.

Although temporary, the Courtyard features all the attributes of a permanent facility: – fully air-conditioned using an innovative displacement system through recyclable fabric ducts, thermally and acoustically insulated, with powered flying and with international standards of lighting and sound equipment.

When the transformation of the Elisabeth Scott theatre is complete, the Courtyard is to be dismantled. Planning permission for the steel structure was only granted on a temporary basis. However, the lessons which were learnt and the *joie de vivre* which the temporary space elicited should live on in the new theatre, due for completion in 2010.

Summary

Theatre type and operational format
Temporary structure to house the Royal Shakespeare Company (which produces and tours it work) while the permanent theatre is redeveloped.

Location and web reference Stratford-upon-Avon, London, UK. www.rsc.org.uk

Building dates Construction started on the Courtyard in January 2005 with a contract duration of 58 weeks. The theatre was in use from 2006-2010.

Auditorium Modelled on Elizabethan theatre formats with the audience wrapped around a thrust stage. Seating capacity is 1,050.

Stage End stage and modular thrust stage with limited height flying facilities, 7.4m wide and 9.6m deep to the upstage setting line. Crawl space substage.
Architect Ian Ritchie Architects, London, UK.

Theatre (design and technical) consultants
Charcoalblue Theatre Consultants, London, UK.

Acoustic consultants: Paul Gillieron Acoustic Design, London, UK.

Building cost Construction cost £5.68 million. (2005).

The auditorium with the audience wrapped around the thrust stage
Photograph: Stewart Hemley. Courtesy of the Royal Shakespeare Compnay

Entrance through 'The Other Place' leading to the corten steel-clad auditorium (on the right)
Photograph: Stewart Hemley. Courtesy of the Royal Shakespeare Compnay

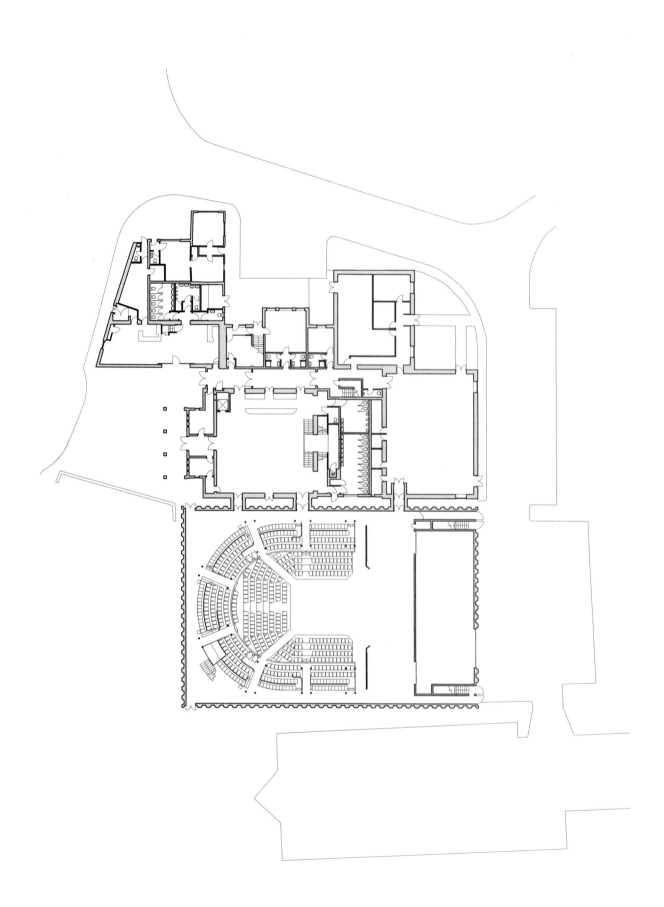

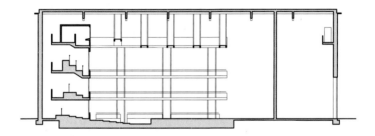

The Crucible Theatre
Sheffield, UK

The Crucible Theatre opened in 1971 and is now the main producing venue in Sheffield. It is generally regarded as the best example of a Guthrie thrust stage theatre in the UK and in 2008 was listed by English Heritage as a building of architectural and historic importance.

The architects worked closely with Tanya Moiseiwitsch, Tyrone Guthrie's designer, to create a space accommodating an audience of 980 with no seat more than 16m from the stage. This is achieved by wrapping the audience around three sides of a narrow promontory stage which extends out into the auditorium. The stage is encircled by steps and a moat allowing performers to get onto the stage from the auditorium as well as from diagonal vomitory entrances. The format focuses attention directly on the performers with scenery being kept to the minimum so as not to block sightlines. It also enables the theatre to host the annual World Snooker Championship which both raises its profile and provides additional income.

The complex contains a studio-style theatre, its flexible design allowing the seating to be adjusted to play on one, two or three sides or in-the-round. It hosts a mix of small-scale in-house and touring productions as well as a music in-the-round festival.

After 35 years of theatrical activities, a major redevelopment was undertaken, with the first phase being completed in 2009. The refurbishment programme included fitting a new roof, reinforcing foundations and installing new outside cladding and glazing. It also added a new entrance, box office and bar. The original stage was replaced, the seating made more comfortable, and access improved. A second phase focused on the refurbishment of the backstage spaces and also further improvements to the Studio Theatre, installing new seating and finishes and new ventilation and electrical services. The work was part of a European Regional Development Fund programme.

Summary

Theatre type and operational format
Producing theatre run by the consortium 'Sheffield Theatres' in conjunction with the adjacent Lyceum Theatre (designed by WGR Sprague in 1897).

Location and web reference Sheffield, South Yorkshire, UK. www.sheffieldtheatres.co.uk

Building dates Opened in 1971. Studio Theatre refurbished in 1994. Major improvement/refurbishment project completed 2009.

Auditorium Main auditorium seats 980 in single rake of 14 rows on three sides of the stage (an encirclement of over 180°). Studio seats a maximum of 400 in a space which can be adapted to various formats including in-the-round.

Stage Main auditorium has a thrust stage 10.2m x 10.2m with encircling steps and moat (often filled in to provide a larger performance area).

Architect Original theatre and studio refurbishment RHWL, London. Improvements and refurbishment Burrell, Foley, Fischer Architects, London (2009 onwards).

Theatre (design and technical) consultants (original theatre) Theatre services: Theatre Projects consultants. Stage consultant: Tanya Moiseiwitsch.

Acoustic consultants (original theatre) Hugh Creighton.

Building cost £0.88 million in 1971. Studio refurbishment £266,000 in 1994. Redevelopment (estimated) £15.3m in 2009.

The entrance to the Crucible with the historic Lyric Theatre (to the right)
Photograph: RHWL Architects

Main auditorium showing the stage encircled by steps and moat
Photograph: RHWL Architects

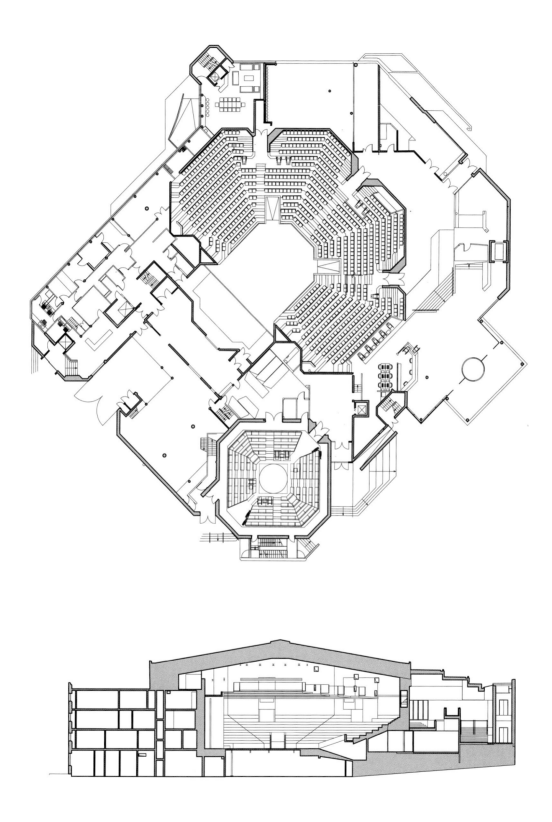

The Donmar Warehouse
London, UK

The Donmar Warehouse has established a reputation within the theatre industry which belies both its small size and low-key street presence. Despite what many would regard as constraints and disadvantages (such as limited space and an irregular seating and stage format), the theatre continues to attract international 'names' both to direct and to perform.

The theatre also merits its place as a Reference project in this publication both as an example of a 'found space' and as one of the very few theatres in the UK to have been successfully redeveloped as part of a larger commercial initiative. The Donmar site falls within half an acre of central London, just north of Covent Garden Market, that was acquired in the 1980s to house residential units, shops and offices.

The building itself dates back to the 1870s, a hop warehouse for a local brewery which became a film studio before reverting back to a depot for ripening bananas. Its first connection with famous names was in 1961 when it was bought by Donald Albery (of the London theatre family) and the ballerina Margot Fonteyn (Don and Mar), who formed DonMar productions and converted the warehouse to provide a private rehearsal space for the London Festival Ballet. The Royal Shakespeare Company used it as their London base from 1977 to 1981. It then hosted cutting-edge touring productions with Sam Mendes taking over the management in 1990 and overseeing the redesign of the space. Donmar Warehouse now houses a resident company which produces work for its London base as well as for other theatres both in the UK and worldwide.

The Donmar is essentially a thrust stage space. At stalls level, four rows of seats wrap around its relatively wide acting area with a two-row gallery above. A further row of vertiginous slips seats are set at high level to each side. At stalls level, the first two rows of seats are set into the stage floor itself, with a third row sharing the stage surface. This subtle design feature philosophically gives the floor of the room to the performers.

There are two lighting bridges that traverse the space, and an open high-level lighting and sound position located above the audience on the rear wall. The audience side galleries link to the stage wall, creating small band or production platforms.

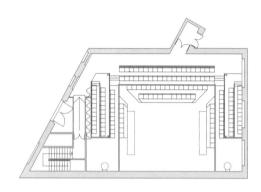

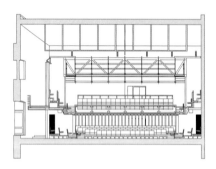

Summary

Theatre type and operational format
Small producing theatre. Operated by the Ambassadors Theatre Group with all shows being produced by Donmar Warehouse Projects Ltd, a registered charity.

Location and web reference Covent Garden, London, UK. www.donarwarehouse.com

Building dates Opened 1992 as Donmar Warehouse Theatre. Previous incarnation of the space as The Donmar originally opened in 1961.

Auditorium Thrust/open stage, with total seating capacity of 251 (plus 20 standing) arranged on three sides of a shallow raked stalls, with a three-sides gallery above.

Stage Thrust stage, 8.4m wide and 7.2m deep. Clear working height of 6.2m.
Architect Arts Team, RHWL, London, UK.

Theatre (design and technical) consultants
Technical Planning International, London, UK.

Acoustic consultants Arup, London, UK.

Building cost £1.35 million in 1992 (plus £250,000 theatre equipment installation).

The auditorium
Photographs: RHWL Architects

Lighting signals the entrance to the theatre

The Egg, Theatre Royal
Bath, UK

The Egg is a theatre created for children, young people and their families. It is housed within a former parish hall which was used as a cinema before being bought by the neighbouring Theatre Royal. Both the hall and the theatre (a traditional proscenium arch theatre originally dating from 1805) are listed buildings.

The architects dropped a free-standing, steel structure into the cleared interior space of the hall to support an elliptical (i.e. egg-shaped) 125-seat auditorium. The mellowed Bath-stone walls of the original building were retained and now contrast with the bright red structure and leather bench seating, in a space designed in response to the young advisers' request for a simple but exciting style of theatre. The aim was to create a space with the 'glamour of the main nineteenth century auditorium without the pomposity'. The auditorium is clad with translucent red corrugated plastic sheeting which glows with reflected light, providing a further playful reference to the interior of the adjacent Theatre Royal.

The large windows of the original building have also been retained and now form a backdrop to the stage, enabling either a full blackout or day-lit use of the auditorium which can be configured in end-on, in-the-round, as a flat-floored workshop space, or traverse formats. A rehearsal space has been slotted in at rooftop level while the basement has been used to accommodate the technical workshop.

A key feature of the scheme is the street-level café which was designed to draw young people in by offering them a place to meet, hang out, and take part in events and activities, as well as get something to eat before or after a performance.

The auditorium created within the original stone hall
Photographs: Philip Vile. Courtesy of Haworth Tompkins Architects

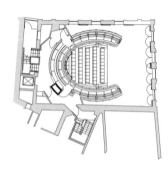

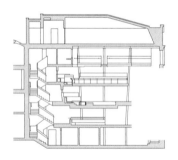

Summary

Theatre type and operational format
Purpose-built theatre for children and young people. Owned and managed by the adjacent Theatre Royal, Bath.

Location and web reference Bath, UK.
www.theatreroyal.org.uk/the-egg

Building dates Built within a listed nineteenth-century building. Opened 2005.

Auditorium Elliptical auditorium seating a total audience of 125 on bench seats. Variable formats.

Stage Flexible end-on-end format. 7.5m high, 6m to 10m deep and 6m to 11m wide, depending on configuration.

Architect Haworth Tompkins Architects, London, UK.

Theatre (design and technical) consultants Anne Minors Performance Consultants, London, UK.

Building cost £2,264,000 in 2005.

The mirrored ceiling
gives a feeling of
height to the café area

Festival Theatre
Edinburgh, Scotland

The Edinburgh Festival Theatre demonstrates how a historic theatre can be successfully restored to create a venue capable of receiving national and international companies.

For more than four decades, the city of Edinburgh searched for a site on which to build a new opera house before deciding to convert the existing, but redundant, Empire Theatre. The 1928 theatre was well positioned and was regarded as having one of the finest lyric theatre auditoria in the country but its stage was small and it lacked many of the facilities which a contemporary theatre/opera house requires. The solution involved rebuilding everything behind the proscenium arch and the whole of the front of house (wrapped around the 1928 auditorium), purchasing additional properties to provide the space required. The theatre now combines the best of the old with the up-to-date technology and good front of house and backstage provision of a modern lyric theatre.

The most evident change was the street frontage with a striking three-storey glazed façade replacing the original discreet entrance, tucked between two shops. The front of house cafés and bars now open directly to the street, drawing people into the theatre during the day and providing an illuminated centre of activity during the evening. A grand staircase links the different levels, easing access and adding vibrancy to the foyers.

The Festival Theatre hosts a programme of musicals, large-scale drama, popular entertainment and concerts as well as providing Scottish Opera and Scottish Ballet with an Edinburgh home. It has one of the largest stages in the UK, full flying facilities, generous backstage provision and a seating capacity of up to 1,913. An adaptable orchestra pit is able to accommodate the largest orchestras while providing additional seating when the full version is not needed.

The whole transformation was achieved at a significantly lower cost than for an equivalent new-build theatre with the added advantage of having an auditorium which was known to work well for a wide range of art forms and types of production.

Summary

Theatre type and operational format
Large-scale receiving theatre for national tours of dance, drama and opera as well as a wide-ranging programme of entertainment. Major venue for the annual Edinburgh Festival.

Location and web reference Edinburgh, UK. www.eft.co.uk

Building dates Auditorium building from 1928. Redevelopment completed in 1994.

Auditorium Traditional proscenium style originally designed for use as both a lyric theatre and a cinema. Substantially upgraded to meet modern technical, safety and comfort requirements.

Stage Completely rebuilt with large wing space, adaptable orchestra pit and full flying facilities.

Proscenium width 13.6m, height 9.62m.
Stage to grid 23.8m.
Stage width 20m. Wing width: Stage left 11m. Stage right 2.8m.
Depth 17.3m (front stage to last flybar), 29.9m front of stage to rear of scene dock.

Architect Original: W and T R Milburn. Redevelopment: Law & Dunbar-Nasmith (LDN Architects), Edinburgh, UK.

Theatre (design and technical) consultants, Theatre Projects Consultants., London, UK.

Acoustic consultants Sandy Brown Associates, London, UK.

Building cost £14 million (excluding the site acquisition costs) in 1994.

The glazed street frontage of the Festival Theatre
Photograph: Paul Bock

View from the stage through to the original 1928 auditorium
Photograph: Paul Bock

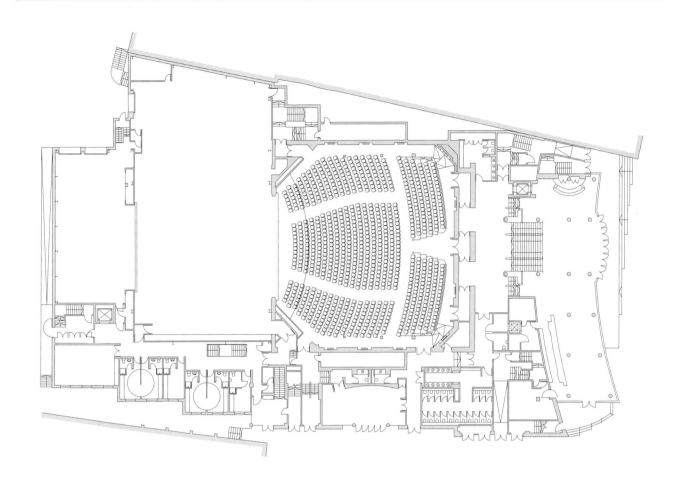

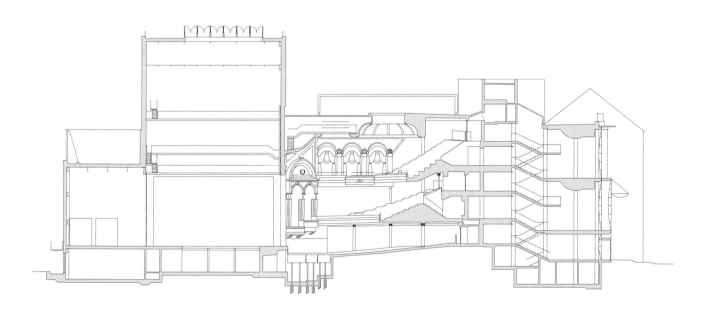

Glyndebourne Festival Opera
East Sussex, UK

The original Glyndebourne theatre had just 300 seats. It was built in 1934 as an extension to a large country house in the Sussex Downs, owned by opera lover John Christie. Though the theatre had been extended over the years to provide 800 seats, it had become increasingly obvious that more radical changes were needed if the Opera Festival, which it housed, was to survive.

The brief established the criteria for the new building: the theatre was to blend into its surroundings but be 'of its time'; the auditorium needed to be enlarged to provide 1,150 good seats while the intimacy of the original was to be retained; the acoustic had to be excellent. Facilities for staff, singers, orchestra and audience also needed to be radically improved.

The architects responded with a building which occupies the same site but is turned through 180° to improve the links between the auditorium and the gardens, which provide one of the attractions of the Summer Festival. This reorientation also enables some of the bulk of the new building to be disguised by digging 10m into the slope of the site. The auditorium, with its flytower and extensive side and backstage areas (needed for the changing repertoire of productions during the Festival), forms the core of the building. Foyers and the back-up spaces for production, performers and administration are wrapped around the circular drum of the auditorium at three levels. This is a seasonal theatre, only used during the warmer months, so foyers take the form of open galleries, overlooking the landscape. They reflect the galleries of the auditorium within and also serve to break up the exterior massing.

The auditorium is based on circular geometry with a lyre-shaped parterre enclosing the stalls and every seat close to the stage enabling performers to be heard clearly, whether singing or speaking. The building

uses a limited palette of natural materials both internally and externally. The interior of the auditorium is clad in century-old pitch pine. The load-bearing walls are built of imperial size bricks, selected to match those of the adjacent house, while the roof and rectangular mass of the flytower are clad with lead panels. The other main structural material is concrete, washed in acid to create a finish which blends more naturally with its surroundings.

The new Glyndebourne opened in 1994 to celebrate the sixtieth anniversary of the company's founding. Seven years later, the second rehearsal room was added adjoining the main stage, completing the master plan of the new opera house.

Summary

Theatre type and operational format Opera house producing and touring own work. Performances for Festival season from late May to late August followed by short pre-tour season in October/November.

Location and web reference Near Lewes, East Sussex, UK. www.glyndebourne.com

Building dates Original opera house opened in 1934. Current building completed in 1994 with second rehearsal room added in 2001.

Auditorium Semi-circular horseshoe format with stalls and three tiers of seating. Total capacity 1,342 (including private boxes and standing room). Public seating 1,182.

Stage Proscenium (11.6m wide) with orchestra pit (one elevator) and flytower. Stage dimensions: width 37.2m, depth 17.4m, flying height 20.6m.

Architect Michael Hopkins and Partners, London, UK.

Theatre (design and technical) consultants Theatre Projects Consultants, London, UK.

Acoustic consultants Arup, London, UK.

Building cost Construction costs £23 million in 1994. Project costs £33 million.

Auditorium
Photographs: Richard Davies

View of the Opera House from
the gardens

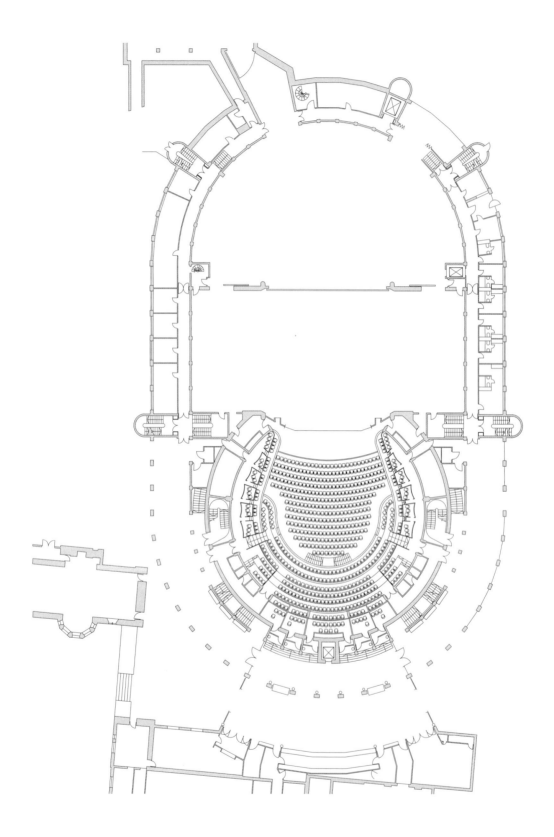

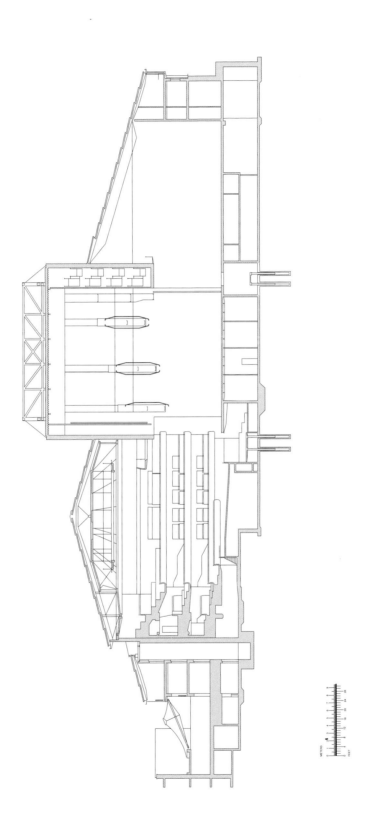

Guthrie Theater
Minneapolis, Minnesota, USA

The Guthrie Theater in Minneapolis, first established in 1963, was among the earliest regional theatres in the USA. Its extraordinary thrust theatre, designed by architect Ralph Rapson, was a unique and idiosyncratic response to the flaws Rapson perceived in earlier thrust theatres, where long circular rows followed the model of classical amphitheatres and seemed to exaggerate the width of the room and make the stage seem small by comparison. Rapson instead chose to create an asymmetrical thrust stage surrounded by an irregular arrangement of rows.

After nearly 40 years the Guthrie had outgrown the original building. When studies concluded expansion in-place was not possible, a site was secured on the Mississippi River, and planning began for a new consolidated and expanded facility. The new building contains three performance spaces: the Wurtele Thrust Stage, the McGuire Proscenium Stage and the Dowling Studio Theater, plus production and support spaces. The three stages accommodate a season of up to 13 productions in a mixture of classics and new plays.

Architect Jean Nouvel chose to organise the project vertically. The ground floor is given over to an open public concourse, the box office, bookshop and restaurant. From here escalators rise nearly 50 feet to the first level of lobby space serving the thrust and proscenium theatres, where an enormous 175ft-long cantilevered viewing platform provides sweeping views of the river. The Dowling Studio is on the eighth floor. Large freight elevators on both sides of the street provide access for materials and goods to all three stages.

The design objective for the Wurtele Thrust Stage was to replicate the original Rapson design as closely as possible while making improvements to comfort, safety, disabled access, acoustics and a couple of sightline problems. Originally seating 1,300, the capacity was reduced to 1,100 in order to prevent the room from expanding beyond its original dimensions. The flytower itself was enlarged but the original thrust's unique shape and size were maintained, as were the asymmetrical vomitory entrances to the stage; one ramped and the other stepped.

Jean Nouvel and Artistic Director Joe Dowling felt that the new proscenium theatre should provide a clear contrast to the thrust stage, and Nouvel's notion of 'radical frontality' became the organising principal for the proscenium theatre. The McGuire has a wide 'panoramic' proscenium opening and straight rows that climb to the rear of the room where there are two balconies of two and one rows respectively.

The Dowling Studio Theater is a flexible space that can be used in a variety of configurations. One long wall can be raised, expanding the space to encompass its lobby, which has extraordinary panoramic views of the river and the city beyond.

Summary

Theatre type and operational format
Purpose-built theatre complex with three performance spaces designed to house the Guthrie Theater company, and its educational programmes.

Location and web reference Minneapolis, Minnesota, USA. www.guthrietheater.org

Building programme Design started in June 2001 and the building opened in June 2006.

Auditoria Three spaces of differing scale and format: the Wurtele Thrust Stage (1,100 seats), the McGuire Proscenium Stage (700 seats) and the Dowling Studio Theater (flexible, up to 250 seats).

Stages The Wurtele Thrust Stage: irregular, asymmetrical thrust nominally 38' by 38' forward of a 100'w, 24'd, 60' grid, 50'w, 24'h proscenium.

The McGuire Proscenium Stage: 39'd, 78'w, 67' grid. 40'w, 24'h proscenium.

The Dowling Studio Theater: flat-floored rectangular space 48' by 58', 32' tall including a wire-rope grid.

Architect Design by Architecture Jean Nouvel, Paris, France. Executive architect: Architectural Alliance, Minneapolis, USA.

Theatre (planning, design and technical) consultants Fisher Dachs Associates, New York, USA.

Acoustic consultants Talaske Group Chicago, Illinois, USA.

Building cost US$96m building cost; US$125m project cost in 2006.

The Wurtele, designed to recreate Guthrie's original thrust stage auditorium
Photographs: Courtesy of Fisher Dachs Associates

View across the Mississippi River showing the Guthrie Theater (left) and one of the area's historic flour mills (right)

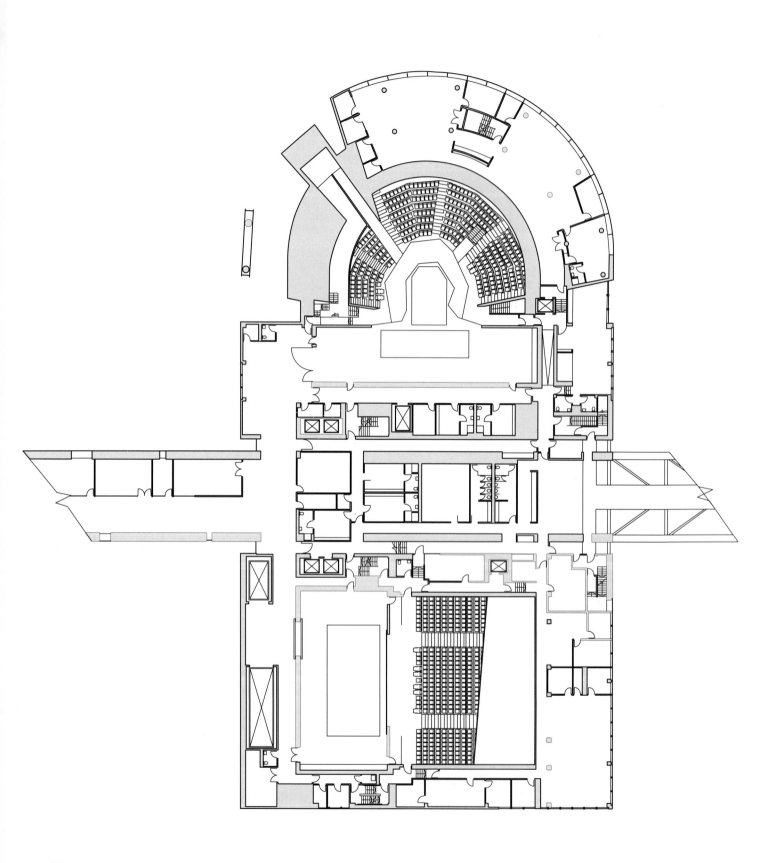

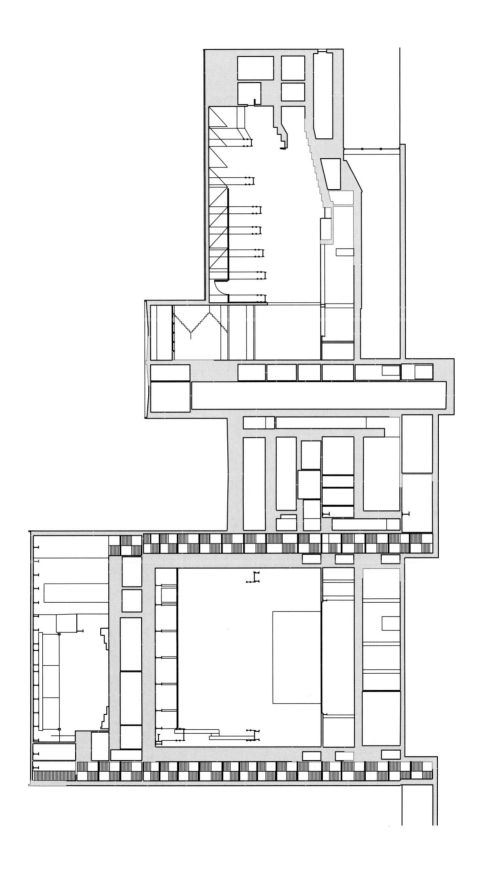

Hackney Empire
London, UK

There are only 25 theatres remaining from the 150 or so which were either designed or remodelled by the prolific theatre architect Frank Matcham (1854–1920). One of the finest of these is Hackney Empire in London's East End. For many years, the magnificent interior with its grand vestibule and double staircase, marble finishes and ornamental ceilings served as a backdrop to bingo. It was rescued by a group of enthusiasts, brought back to life and improved on a shoestring until the money was found for a major refurbishment.

The work that was undertaken enabled Hackney Empire to reclaim its role as a leading variety theatre offering an eclectic mix of entertainment, 'something for everyone', to Hackney's increasingly multicultural audience. The theatre creates and tours its own product; hosts international dance, drama and opera companies; and mounts a varied season of comedy, music and family entertainment.

The refurbishment and redevelopment involved two major additions to Matcham's theatre. At the rear, cramped backstage areas were replaced with a new extension providing dressing rooms, wardrobe, green room, kitchen and technical offices and workshops. The small stage was extended, an orchestra pit created, the flytower was increased in height, and a modern counterweight flying system installed. These new facilities made the Empire a viable touring theatre.

The historic theatre was refurbished and equipped with new bars, performance systems, a modern ventilation system and lift access to all levels. Much care was taken not to lose the atmosphere of this dilapidated Palace of Varieties. The auditorium was repainted in a more subtle version of its bingo red and gold, rather than reverting to the original white interior, which worked with gaslight but was too pale for contemporary theatre lighting.

At front of house, on the site of a former public house on the corner of the theatre block, a new building, the Marie Lloyd, houses a theatre bar, a studio theatre, hospitality spaces, and all the plant and equipment needed to modernise the theatre. On its exterior giant terracotta letters spell out the name 'Hackney Empire', identifying the theatre not only from street level but also for airline passengers as they fly into the nearby City Airport.

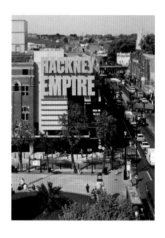

Bold signage identifies the theatre within Hackney's busy high street

The refurbished auditorium
(Note: Larger image available on p.189)
Photographs: Hélène Binet.
Courtesy of Tim Ronalds Architects

Summary

Theatre type and operational format
Producing and receiving theatre with additional spaces for smaller scale, education and community activities.

Location and web reference Hackney, London, UK. www.hackneyempire.co.uk

Building dates Opened in 1901. Major restoration and development programme started in 1997 with the theatre reopening in 2004.

Auditorium Lavishly decorated auditorium with three balconies – dress circle with boxes at the back. Marble proscenium flanked by buttresses topped by Moorish domes. Square, deeply coved ceiling with sliding centre. Equipped from outset with cine-projection box. Seating capacity 1,311.

Stage Small variety act stage now extended with full flying facilities and orchestra pit. 18m wide, 12m deep, 20m high to underside of grid.

Architect Original theatre designed by Frank Matcham. Renovation and development by Tim Ronalds Architects, London, UK.

Theatre consultants Carr and Angier, Bath, UK.

Acoustic consultants Arup, London, UK.

Building cost No record of original cost. 1997 to 2004 programme of work cost £15 million.

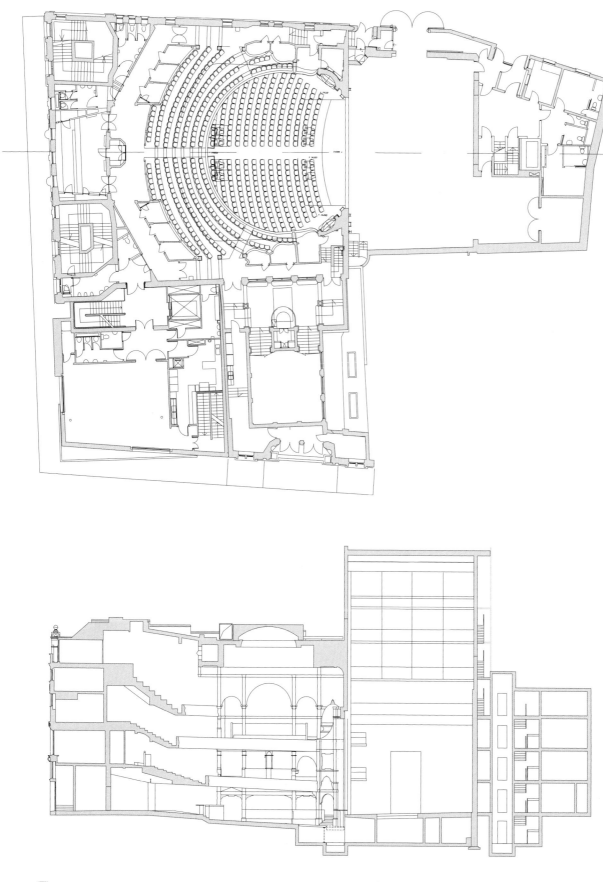

King's Cross Almeida (temporary theatre)
London, UK

This is an example of a low-cost reclamation of a 'found space'. In 2001, London's Almeida Theatre Company needed to find temporary premises while their own building was closed for refurbishment. Their search identified an old bus depot, in an area near London's King's Cross Station long scheduled for redevelopment. The bus station itself was semi-derelict and due for demolition but the spaces within the decaying structure suggested that it could house the theatre that Almeida needed. 'Remarkably, some of the spaces have nearly perfect classical proportions; it may be made of tin, but it has a secret grandeur' (Steve Tompkins, architect).

Just 17 weeks after its being discovered, the building opened as a theatre with two auditoria and full front of house and backstage facilities. The main auditorium exploited a wide, low space to create an unusual proscenium stage while the other housed more flexible facilities. Both had simple padded bench seating offering good views from all positions.

The industrial interiors were left in their raw state, with a series of 'architectural installations' (stairs, bar, toilets, etc.) positioned to adjust the proportions and divide the space. Materials were selected to convey a sense of the provisional nature of the building and its surroundings while the lighting and mirrors were specifically designed to add sparkle to the entrance foyer and to create intimacy within the bar area.

The old corrugated steel cladding on the exterior of the building was covered in sedum matting. Originally specified as being the cheapest form of sound and thermal insulation available at short notice, the planted roof not only worked effectively but the interest it generated proved to be a valuable asset in publicising the temporary location. The dingy surroundings were also brightened by the installation of a long panel of back-lit yellow plastic sheets reaching out into the street and guiding audiences down the narrow alley which led to the entrance to the theatre.

For the next two years the King's Cross Almeida became both a theatrical and architectural destination.

Main auditorium
Photographs: Philip Vile. Courtesy of Haworth Tompkins Architects

Summary

Theatre type and operational format
Temporary space housing a small producing theatre.

Location and web reference The temporary building was demolished in 2002. The company has since returned to its refurbished premises in Islington, London, UK. www.almeida.co.uk

Building dates Opened in 2001. Closed in 2002.

Auditorium Main auditorium: horseshoe format with adapted proscenium seating 550. Second more flexible space seating 400. Both theatres with bench seating in a single rake.

Stage Main stage zone 25m wide and 14m deep. Flexible stage in second space.
Architect Haworth Tompkins Architects, London, UK.

Theatre (design and technical) consultants Haworth Tompkins Architects, London, UK.

Building cost £850,000 in 2001.

The bright yellow sheeting marks the route into the theatre.

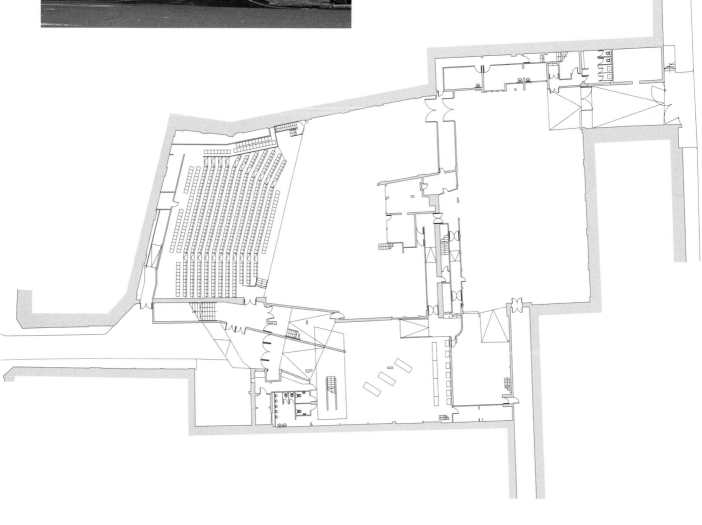

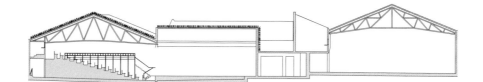

The Liceu
Barcelona, Spain

The Gran Teatre del Liceu, in Barcelona's famous Paseo de las Ramblas, may look as if it was built in the mid-nineteenth century but it has been twice destroyed and recreated since it first opened in 1847. The most recent catastrophe to hit the theatre was in 1994 when the whole of the auditorium and stage area was destroyed by fire. Five years later, the theatre was reopened and restored to its former state but with considerably improved facilities.

Even before the fire, there had been discussions about renovating the Liceu. The auditorium was one of the largest in Europe, originally seating nearly 3,000 people, but the public areas and the backstage provision were constricted and the site offered little scope for expansion. The fire served to rally support, with contributions coming from both public and private sources. This enabled the Liceu to buy about 90 adjacent apartments, taking over a whole block in the tightly packed Ramblas district.

The horseshoe-shaped auditorium with its five tiers of balconies has been reinstated, retaining the acoustic quality which had been praised by generations of singers and audiences. The lavish red, gold and brown neo-classical decoration has also been restored. Some sections of the original building, such as the finely decorated entrance foyer and Mirror Room, were not destroyed and these have been renovated.

The new Liceu has a vastly enlarged backstage area, cleverly designed to make best use of the limited site. In order to overcome the restrictions and to keep some backstage accommodation at ground level, only one side-stage was provided, with two others positioned 16m below served by a pair of major stage elevators. The flytower is comprehensively equipped with a power flying installation consisting of 63 across-stage bars, two panorama bars each side, 11 across-stage tracks each with six point hoists and 30 free point hoists.

In addition, there is proper stage delivery access from Las Ramblas, some new rehearsal rooms, a gift shop and large underground foyer that is also used for small concerts and receptions. The rebuilding also provided the opportunity to upgrade the technical provision in the auditorium as well as in the backstage and production areas. The international status of the Liceu and the quality of the auditorium is now matched by its support facilities.

A drawing showing the extent of the new work can be seen in Figure 9.6.3 (p.191).

Summary

Theatre type and operational format International opera house.

Location and web reference Barcelona, Spain. www.liceubarcelona.com

Building dates Opened 1847. Destroyed by fire and rebuilt in 1861. Destroyed by fire again in 1994. Reopened 7 October 1999.

Auditorium Horseshoe format with five tiers of balconies. Currently seats 2,292. Permanent orchestra pit.

Stage Proscenium arch 14m wide with opera portal reducing this to 11.5m. Height between 7m and 10.5m.

Stage 29.1m wide by 26.1m deep (iron to rear shutter). Side stage at this level 15.9m wide by 19.9m deep; tapering rear stage space. Two further side stages 16m below stage.

Stage to underside of grid is 29m and the scenery clearance height is 9.5m at stage level but 10.5m for scenery brought up from the lower side stages.

Architects Francese d'Assis Soler (1844); Josep Oriol Mestres (1861). After the 1994 fire the theatre was rebuilt to the designs of Ignasi de Solà-Morales working with Xavier Fabré and Lluís Dilmé.

Theatre (design and technical) consultants Theatreplan LLP London, UK.

Building cost Total cost estimated to be around $80 million in 1999.

The Mirror Room
Photographs: Antoni Bofill. Courtesy of the Liceu Theatre.

The historic auditorium, fully restored after being virtually destroyed in the 1994 fire

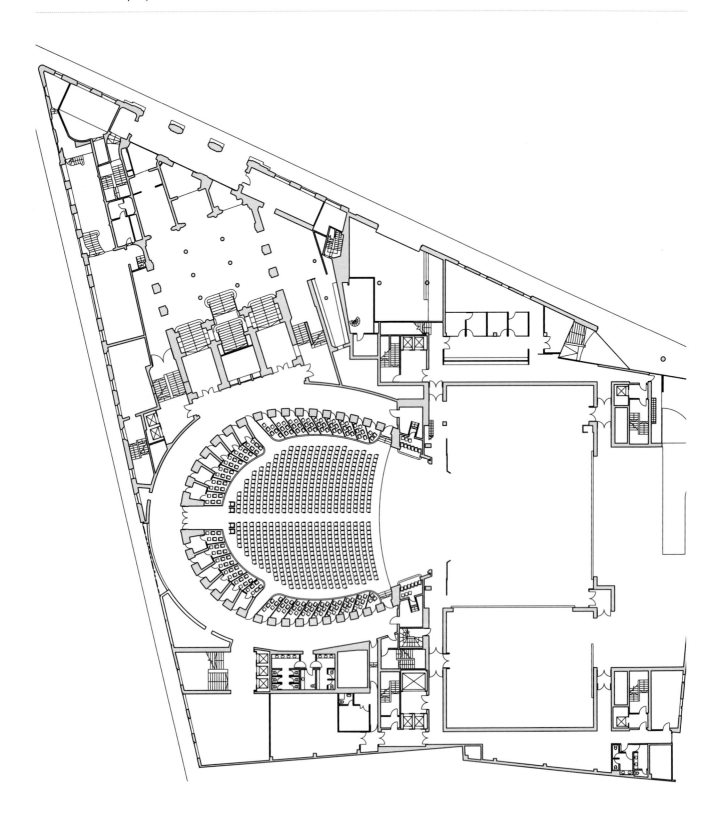

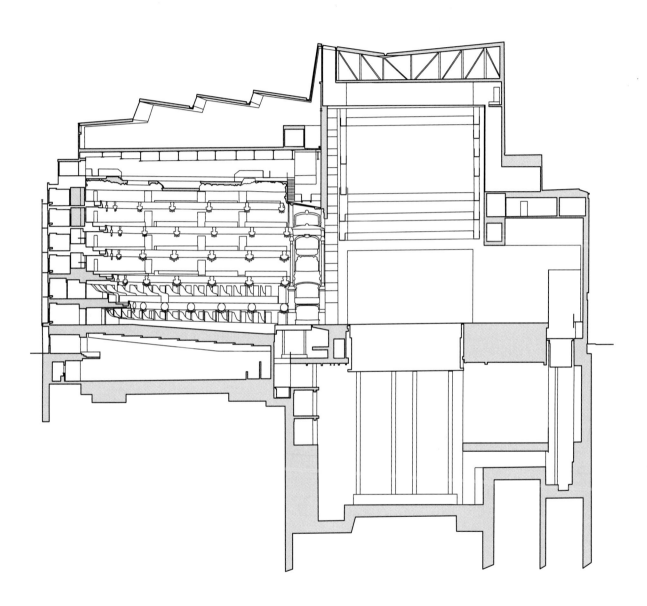

The Lowry
Salford Quays, Greater Manchester, UK

The Lowry provides a platform for both the visual and the performing arts; including a large lyric theatre; a smaller, more adaptable, flexible performance space; a studio theatre; the UK's first 'hands-on' gallery for children; and a gallery displaying over 350 paintings by the Salford artist L S Lowry. It is the final project by the architectural partnership of Michael Wilford and Sir James Stirling (completed after Stirling's death in 1992).

The Lowry is one of 12 major urban projects which were funded by the UK's National Lottery programme to mark the new millennium. It is an example of the arts being used as the focus for economic and physical regeneration, in this case aimed at bringing more businesses and tourism to the once thriving but subsequently derelict Salford docks on the Manchester Ship Canal.

The building is designed to make an impact. It is striking in its form, use of materials and location. The complex is made up of a sequence of geometric shapes – hexagon, circle, triangle and rectangle – forming a single unit which evokes the image of a ship moored at the end point of the quay. The glass and stainless steel used to clad the structure serve to enhance this image, reflecting both the sky and the water.

The form of the Lowry aims to draw people in and encourage them to explore what is on offer. A promenade runs all around the building providing easy access to the different spaces – the large open foyer areas as well as the theatres and galleries. A restaurant, cafés and bars are sited along the south side of the building and open onto waterside terraces.

Bright colours, orange and purple and blue, are used throughout the interior spaces.

The two main theatres are contrasting in their ambience, colour and production values. They provide facilities for a wide range of events and productions (drama, opera, ballet, dance, musicals, children's shows, popular music, jazz, folk and comedy). The main theatre is a successful modern interpretation of the late nineteenth- and early twentieth-century lyric theatre, designed on three levels to bring the whole audience as close to the stage as possible. The Quays theatre is a flexible 400-seat horseshoe auditorium owing much to both the late eighteenth and late twentieth-century courtyard theatres, with considerable mechanisation to facilitate changes of layout.

Summary

Theatre type and operational format Three performance spaces house a mixed programme of arts and entertainment.

Location and web reference Salford Quays, Greater Manchester, UK. www.thelowry.com

Building dates Master planners appointed 1991. Planning approval 1996. Start on site 1997. Opened in April 2000.

Auditorium Main theatre: Lyric style with proscenium and flytower, seating 1,730. Flexible courtyard theatre seats up to 466. Flexible studio theatre seats up to 218.

Stages Lyric: 29m wide x 17.5m deep. Height to grid 23m.

Courtyard: 20m wide x 10.2m deep. Height to grid 9m.

Studio: 10m wide x 11m deep.

Architect Michael Wilford and Partners. (Original master plan developed with Sir James Stirling.)

Theatre (design and technical) consultants Theatre Projects Consultants, London, UK.

Acoustic consultants Sandy Brown Associates, London, UK.

Building cost £106 million in 2000.

The Lowry with its canal side terraces and
the Lifting Footbridge leading to Trafford
Wharfside and Imperial War Museum North
Photograph: Len Grant

The studio theatre
Photograph: Courtesy of Theatre Projects
Consultants

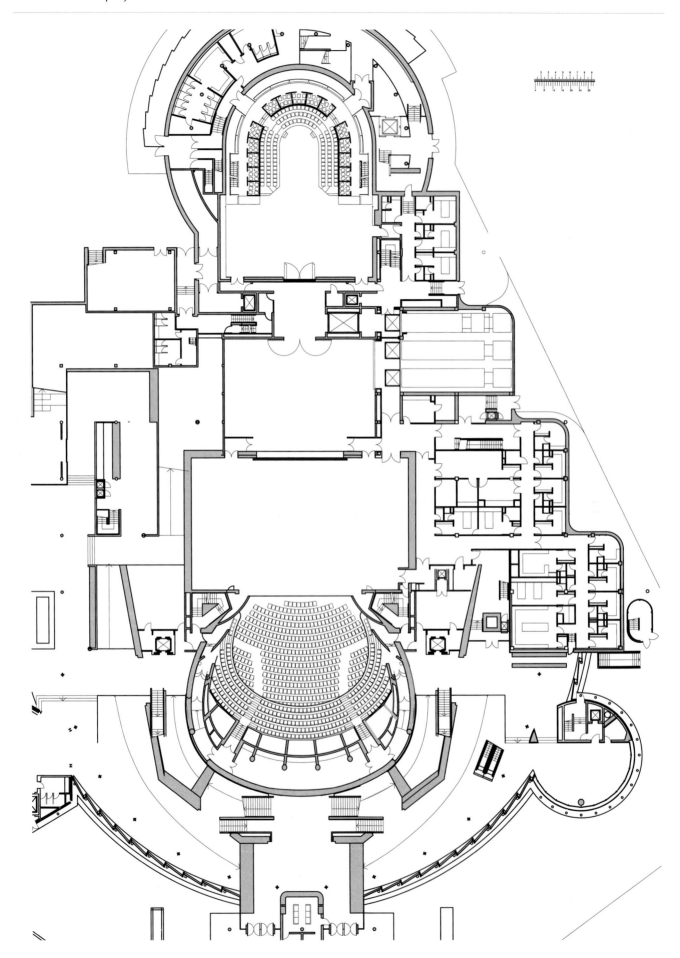

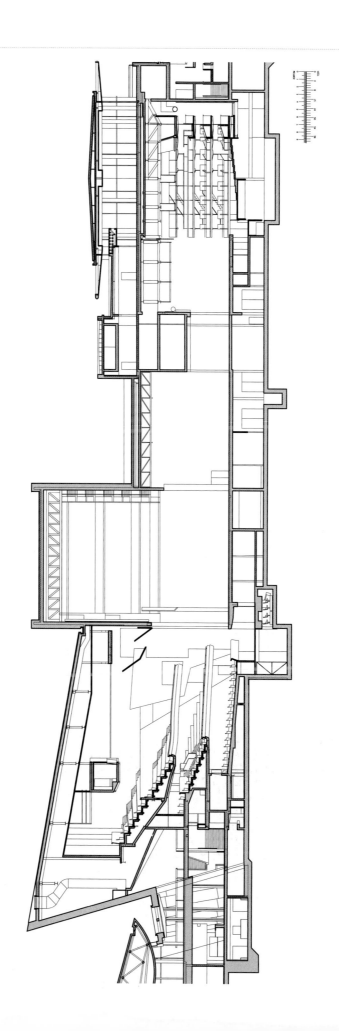

Mahaffey Theater
St Petersburg, Florida, USA

The Progress Energy Center for the Arts Mahaffey Theater is an example of a 1960s theatre which has been remodelled and extended to create a successful venue for the twenty-first century. It is now a 2,030-seat multi-purpose theatre, home to the Florida Orchestra and hosting dance, popular music and family entertainment including Broadway touring productions. The Mahaffey Theater also mounts 'Class Acts', a programme enabling school children to experience the performing arts.

The original Bayfront Center auditorium was built in 1962, and consisted of an auditorium and an 8,000-seat arena. In 1988, the auditorium was completely redesigned and renovated to form a new venue for the City of St Petersburg and renamed the Mahaffey Theater after the family that helped fund the project. The original fan-shaped auditorium was reduced in width, while sidewall boxes were added to improve ambience and acoustics. An orchestra pit and side stage were also created during the renovation.

After a 2004 market analysis and demand study, the arena was demolished and a $22 million expansion/renovation planned for the theatre front of house area. The renovation and expansion more than doubled the theatre's lobby size and added audience facilities that had been impossible to accommodate previously. The spacious foyer now offers spectacular waterfront views and is used for a range of events including weddings and other social gatherings.

In 2006, Progress Energy and the City of St Petersburg entered a 20-year partnership to support the theatre programme, adding the name of Progress Energy Center for the Arts to the Mahaffey Theater.

The theatre interior retains the art deco references of the 1962 building, now enhanced by the red, blue, cream and gold colour scheme which carries through from the lobby to the rich red seating in the auditorium.

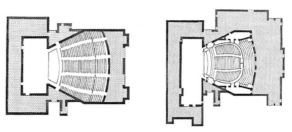

The auditorium, remodelled in 1988

Photographs: Courtesy of the St. Petersburg City Council

Summary

Theatre type and operational format
Large-scale multi-purpose receiving theatre and home to the Florida Orchestra..

Location and web reference St Petersburg, Florida, USA. www.mahaffeytheater.com

Building dates Originally constructed in 1962. Renovated and refurbished in 1988 (concentrating on the auditorium) and in 2005 (improving the foyer and audience facilities).

Auditorium Original wide fan adapted to provide a more proscenium-style format with end stage, sidewall boxes and optional orchestra pit. Seating in stalls, raised back-stalls and gallery. Capacity 2,030.

Stage Proscenium width adjustable from 44' to 60'. Standard performance size is 44' wide and 40' 6" deep (pits chaired) and out trim for borders of 22'.

Architects ARCOP Toronto and Montreal, Canada (1988); Robert Aude Associates, Clearwater, Florida, USA (2004 onwards).

Theatre (design and technical) consultants Theatre Projects Consultants, London, UK (auditorium 1988); Schuler Shook Associates, Minneapolis, Minnesota, USA (2004 onwards).

Acoustic consultants Kirkegaard Associates, Chicago, Illinois, USA (1988 and 2004).

Building cost Unavailable (1962); $19 million (1988); $20 million (2005).

The extensive
new foyers
reflect the style
of the original

Melbourne Theatre Company Theatre
Melbourne, Victoria, Australia

Melbourne Theatre Company (MTC) is Australia's oldest theatre company. Since its foundation in 1954, it has occupied various different homes while remaining a Department of Melbourne University (which it still is).

The MTC finally moved into its own building early in 2009 – a striking complex comprising the Sumner Theatre (seating 500–550) and the Lawler Studio (seating 180). Immediately adjacent is the Melbourne Recital Centre, designed by the same architects and built at the same time.

The brief for the theatre called for an egalitarian, dynamic working space, emphasising the importance of flexibility in use and ease of operation. MTC also wanted a sense of theatricality and of destination. The specialist design team was selected by competition.

The exterior of the theatre comprises an exoskeleton of highlighted white piping that is brought forward off the satin-finished black aluminium cladding of the actual mass of the structure. This animates the building both during the day, when the piping appears to shift and change as you pass by, and by night, when it is illuminated. The two auditoria share generous foyers, with a café and bars, offering views across the city. Striking forms and bright colours serve to animate the spaces.

The main auditorium picks up on the requirement for theatricality with its dark timber walls illuminated by quotes from past plays, dimmed or colour changed as productions require. The proscenium for the Sumner is fully adjustable, allowing the room to be varied to fit the scale of the productions on stage. There are full power flying facilities, a modular stage floor, ample dressing room space, centralised offices for staff and significant installations of technical infrastructure – including power, data and rigging points across the entire venue. Likewise the Lawler Studio space is fully reconfigurable with a flown truss grid, modular seating system, and its own dressing rooms and high-quality equipment.

Access around the entire building has been designed to facilitate cast, crew and audience movement. There is flat-floor travel from the entry of the building to all dressing rooms, stage areas and offices and lift access to all levels of the building. Various hidden doors enable cast and crew to move through the building without being caught in audience crushes and allow directors increased flexibility for actors' entry or exit points around the entire auditorium.

The exterior of the theatre with its white piping exoskeleton

Summary

Theatre type and operational format Purpose-built theatre with two auditoria designed to house Melbourne Theatre Company productions.

Location and web reference Melbourne, Victoria, Australia. www.mtc.au

Building programme Construction stage ran from June 2006 to December 2008. Building opened early 2009.

Auditorium Main auditorium (seating 500 – 550) – designed primarily for drama with deep stage, full flying facilities and orchestra pit. Smaller auditorium (seating 180) – adaptable space.

Stage Flat, traditional proscenium (variable up to 9m high x 16m wide) with an optional forestage or orchestra pit. Stage width is 26m (with wing space) and 21m between fly galleries. The stage depth is 19m including 6m of rear stage. The height is 20m to grid and 9m to fly galleries. Fully modular stage floor.

Architect Ian McDougall and Peter Bickle of Ashton Raggart McDougal, Melbourne, Australia. Project managed by: Major Projects Victoria for Victorian State Government.

Theatre (design and technical) consultants Melbourne Theatre Company with Entertech Theatre Consultants.

Acoustic consultants Arup.

Building cost AUS$55 million in 2009 (AUS$40 million contributed by University of Melbourne of which MTC is a Department).

The main auditorium and its 'wall of quotes'
Photographs: James Grant. Courtesy of Melbourne Theatre Company

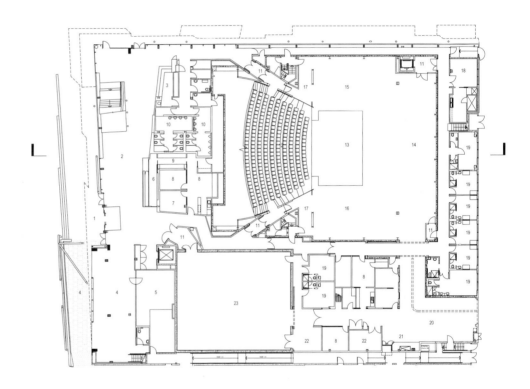

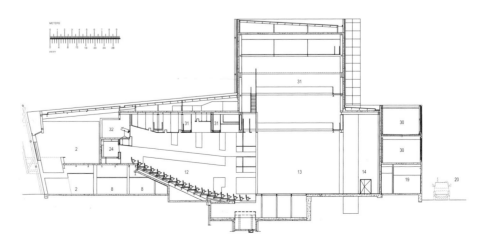

Milton Keynes Theatre
Milton Keynes, UK

Though planned for from the outset, the UK's new city of Milton Keynes lacked major cultural facilities for the first 25 years of its existence. This long recognised gap in cultural and leisure provision was filled by a complex of buildings which includes the theatre, a gallery, a restaurant, the tourist information office and, this being the city of the car, a multi-storey car park.

The complex occupies a key site between the open green space of Campbell Park and the iconic 1970s shopping centre. The theatre, gallery and restaurant all open onto a new central square which provides a link between the buildings as well as an area onto which activities can spill out in good weather.

The largest structure in the complex is the new theatre, instantly recognisable by its undulating roof with the mass of the auditorium projecting through. The foyers and staircases are partly suspended from the waveform roof and enclose the concrete drum of the auditorium, providing open vistas and generous areas for gathering and circulation.

The materials for the theatre building mainly comprise concrete, steelwork and glass all finished to a high quality. This low-key palette contrasts with the deep blue, red and gold decorative finishes and auditorium seating, which give a sense of luxury and of intimacy to the main spaces.

As the only large receiving house between London and Birmingham, the theatre was designed to accommodate a broad range of productions from intimate drama through to musicals, opera and full orchestral concerts. Each of these different uses requires a different acoustic. The key feature of the main auditorium is a 30-tonne mobile acoustic ceiling designed so that it can be raised or lowered by up to 10m. The lowest position reduces the volume and seating capacity to suit plays and the spoken word; the intermediate position accommodates musical theatre and opera; while the highest position extends the volume of the space to create a concert hall acoustic. This method of achieving physical and acoustic adaptability builds on the experience the architects first gained while working with Peter Moro on the Theatre Royal in Plymouth, UK.

Main auditorium in 'concert' format
(Note: drawing of theatre complex available on p. 89)
Photograph: Courtesy of Andrzej Blonski Architects

Summary

Theatre type and operational format
Receiving house for national productions of drama, dance, music and opera operated by the Ambassador Theatre Group.

Location and web reference
Milton Keynes, Buckinghamshire, UK.
www.miltonkeynestheatre.com

Building dates Competition winning scheme selected 1994. Theatre opened 1999.

Auditorium Arranged over three tiers with a movable ceiling reducing the capacity to 1,040/800, and acoustic volume which can also be increased for orchestral concerts.

Stage Flat stage with three stage front positions achieved with forestage lifts. Proscenium width can be varied from 11m to 14m with a maximum height of 8.5m. Depth of stage varies from 15m to 18.5m. Orchestra pit is formed in three independent lifts. All lifts are double decker and the pit can be formatted to accommodate from 20 to 100 players.

Architect Andrzej Blonski and Michael Heard, London, UK.

Acoustic consultants Arup, London, UK.

Theatre (design and technical) consultants Carr and Angier, Bath, UK.

Building cost £25 million (for the total complex including the art gallery, etc.) in 1999.

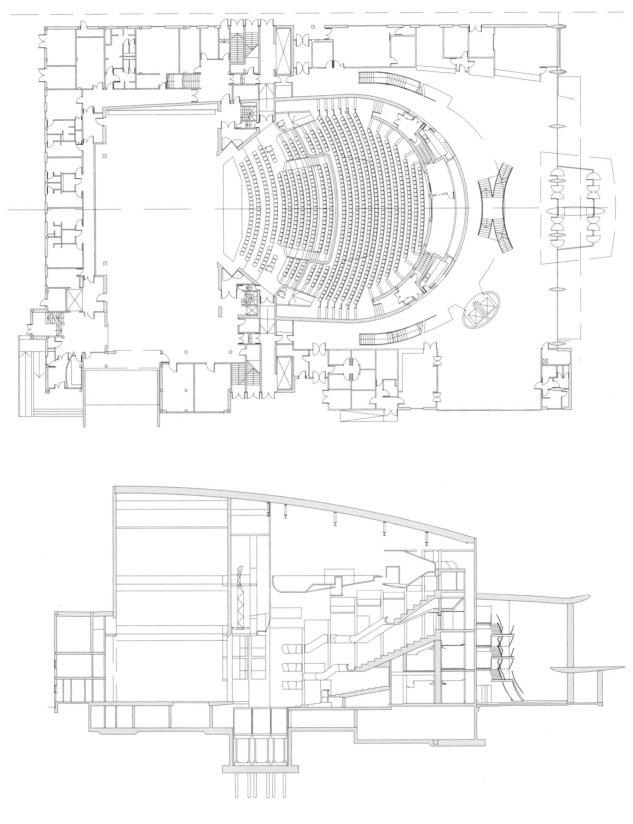

The Opera House
Oslo, Norway

The Operaen opened in 2008, designed to provide a home for the Norwegian National Opera (Den Norske) and the national ballet company and described by the architects as 'the largest single culture-political initiative in contemporary Norway'.

It is a striking building, sited on the waterfront with the joint aims of providing a venue for Norway's leading opera and dance companies and of rejuvenating the harbour area in the centre of the city. The main structure slopes down into the water like a ski-slope – an image which is strengthened by the building being clad in white marble – with the horizontal and sloping planes creating a series of terraces, open to everybody, and offering views across the Oslo Fjord. The overall height of the building is, however, deceiving as just under half of the accommodation lies below sea level.

The main space – Hovedscenen – is designed for opera with a horseshoe-type plan and a high ceiling, providing good natural acoustics. The auditorium seats around 1,350, in the stalls and in three balconies, stacked almost vertically in order to ensure that the furthest seat is no more than 33m from the stage. Each seat back has its own individual screen enabling subtitles to be made available in eight languages. The interior is simple in treatment using Baltic oak to provide a wall between the public areas and the performance spaces and also for the balcony fronts where it has been hand-carved by Norwegian boat builders to celebrate their craftsmanship.

The smaller theatre (Space 2) is designed mainly for use by the resident ballet company so the brief required a large orchestra pit and deep stage to be provided as well as flexible seating layouts and a flat-floor option. This was achieved through the installation of pneumatic lifts (to raise and lower the floor) and a series of wagons to move blocks of seating.

The backstage areas contain all the facilities needed to produce an opera or ballet to an international standard. They are housed over five levels and designed to offer sufficient flexibility to enable the theatre to respond to different requirements in the future.

Hovedscenen. The main auditorium with its carved oak balcony fronts
Photograph: Jaro Hollan Statsbygg

Summary

Theatre type and operational format
Opera house, base for the national opera and ballet companies and receiving venue for opera and dance.

Location and web reference Oslo Fjord, Oslo, Norway. www.operaen.no

Building dates Opened 2008.

Auditorium Three auditoria. The main space seats 1,369 in classical horseshoe format. Space 2 is an adaptable 'box' designed mainly for dance (end stage, flat floor and in-the-round) and seats about 400. The third space seats 200 and doubles as a rehearsal room.

Stage The Hovedscenen has a main stage area of 16m x 16m, which comprises 16 individual elements that can be elevated, angled, or rotated so that landscapes/settings can be constructed on stage. Flytower above main stage is 35m in height, equipped to enable complicated theatre-technical solutions. The more simple second space – Space 2 – has the option of a large orchestra pit and a 52' deep stage for dance.

Architect Snøhetta, Oslo, Norway.

Theatre (design and technical) consultants
Theatre Projects Consultants, London, UK.

Acoustic consultants Arup.

Building cost €500 million in 2008.

Open Day – the public were invited to explore the building while it
was still under construction
Photograph: Courtesy of Theatre Projects Consultants

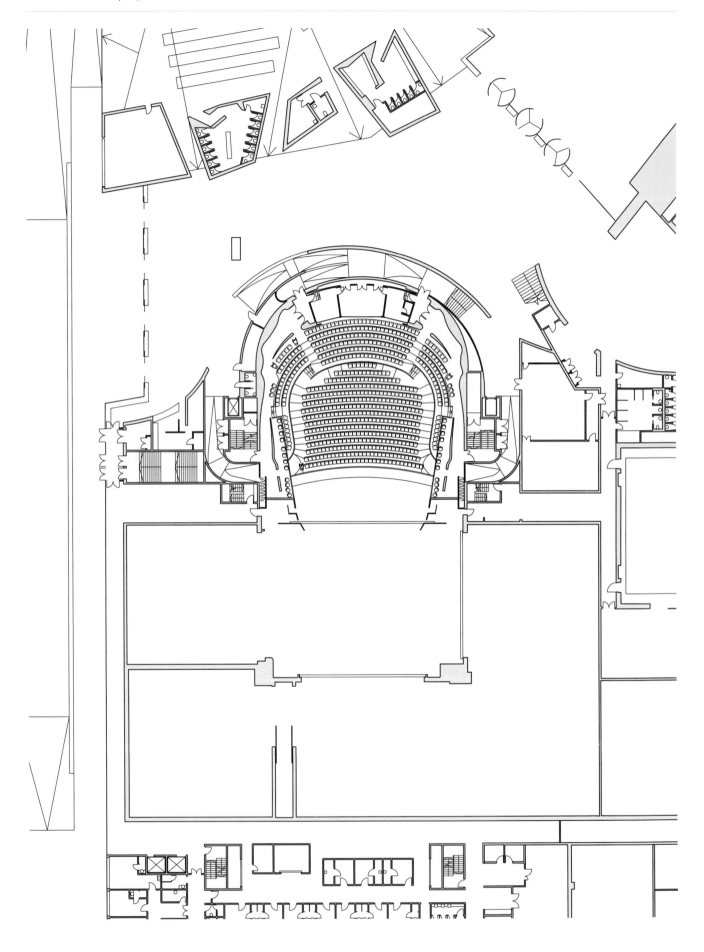

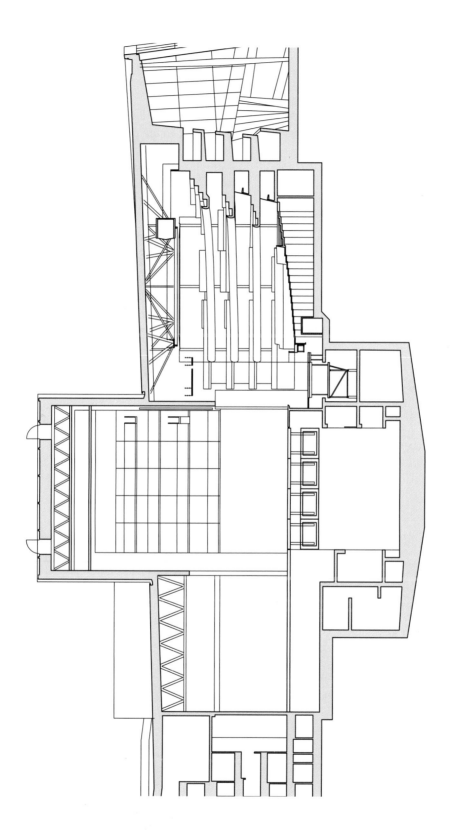

The Roundhouse
London, UK

A mid-nineteenth-century shed built to turn around steam engines at the end of the Birmingham London run would seem an unlikely candidate for iconic status and a programme of refurbishment and improvements costing some £27 million. The Roundhouse, in north London, first grabbed people's imagination in the 1960s, a 'found space' which continued to attract support through decades of decline and a variety of attempted rescue projects. Its future was secured when sufficient money was raised to redevelop rather than just make do.

What makes the Roundhouse special is the scale and structure of the interior space, its brick drum forming a natural auditorium capable of housing a range of events – from experimental drama to popular music gigs. A major challenge was to devise a roof with sufficient acoustic mass to contain loud music but without imposing additional loads on the slender cast-iron roof structure. The problem was solved by a new conical steel-framed over-roof, resting on rubber mounts on top of the heavy outer brick walls, adding the necessary acoustic mass and supporting the 20-tonne load from the new technical grid.

In the spectacular Main Space, adaptable seating in end-on, thrust and in-the-round configurations can be removed for standing events. A new circle at second level adds a different perspective and brings the total capacity to 1,800 seated (or 3,300 standing). The central glass lantern has been restored and the original roof lights triple glazed.

In general, structural interventions were minimised in order to retain both the Victorian sense of grandeur and the early industrial aesthetic. New additions were designed to both complement and contrast with the existing building. In order to maximise the use of the Main Space for performances and events, a three-storey curved and glazed wing was added to one side of the building. It houses a café, bars, box office and public areas, as well as backstage and office facilities and includes a studio theatre.

Provision is also made for the Roundhouse's new role of working with local young people to develop skills and explore their creative potential. The vaulted Undercroft has been converted into a series of studio spaces: rehearsal rooms, sound and recording studios, video editing and production areas.

Summary

Theatre type and operational format
Arts venue promoting an eclectic mix of live music, theatre, dance and circus as well as developing related activities with young people. Owned and run by The Norman Trust with high-profile donors and celebrity support.

Location and web reference
Camden, London, UK. www.roundhouse.org.uk

Building dates Original engine shed dates from 1846 (designed by Robert Dockray and railway pioneer Robert Stephenson). First converted for performance in 1964 (led by playwright Arnold Wesker). Closed in 1983.

Bought by Norman Trust in 1996. Reopened in 2006.

Auditorium Arena capable of accommodating 1,800 seats (including the balcony level) or up to 3,300 standing.

Stage In-the-round, thrust and end stage formats can be achieved.

Architect John McAslan + Partners, London, UK.

Theatre (design and technical) consultants Theatre Projects Consultants; Charcoalblue; and Anne Minors Performance Consultants Ltd, all of London, UK.

Acoustic consultants Paul Gillieron Acoustic Design, London, UK.

Building cost Original – not known. Redevelopment £29.7 million (completed 2006) plus £3 million purchase price (1996).

The Roundhouse within its street context
Photograph: Hufton and Crow

**The structure within the refurbished
engine shed**
Photograph: Hufton and Crow

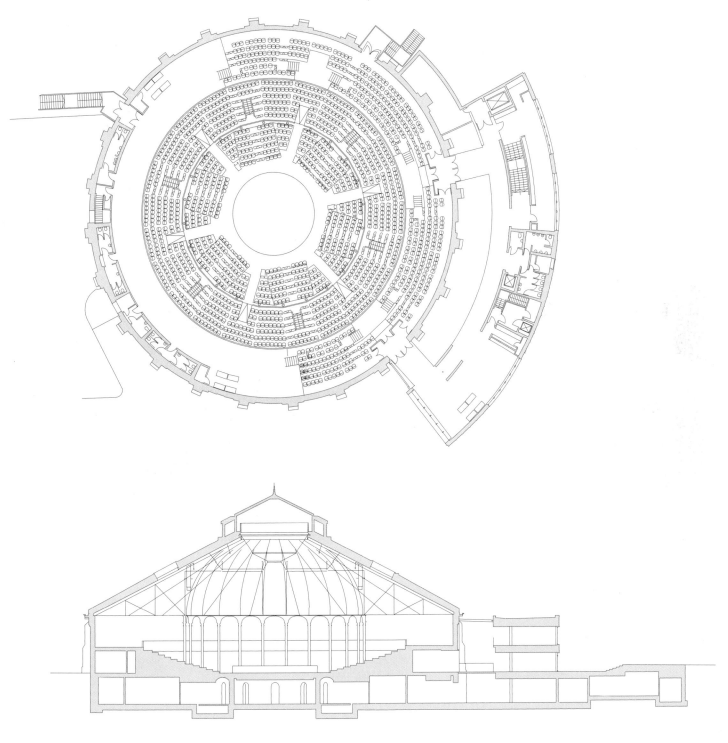

Royal Academy of Dramatic Arts (RADA)
London, UK

In 2000, the UK's best-known drama school celebrated both its centenary and the completion of its new building. Funding from the National Lottery enabled RADA to redevelop its existing site and properties to provide three theatres as well as workshops, rehearsal rooms, teaching areas, a public café/foyer bar and support facilities. All is contained on a tight urban site 15m wide and 60m deep, running between two parallel streets (Malet Street and Gower Street). The Gower Street building, RADA's original home, was retained and converted to provide the main administrative and teaching spaces while the rest of the site was cleared.

The new building is 10 storeys at its highest point with three of these below ground level, housing production spaces. Though densely packed, the whole development is designed to provide a relaxed environment for students and uses two full-height atria to bring light into the heart of the building.

The horseshoe-shaped main space (the Jerwood Vanbrugh Theatre) is designed as a training ground to enable students to experience a wide range of scale and format – with a full flytower, orchestra pit and variable proscenium arch. It feels much larger than it actually is with the open stretched wire balcony fronts giving a greater sense of space than conventional solid fronts. In the proscenium format, the theatre accommodates an audience of 204 spread over three levels – a circle and two balconies, the upper one being largely technical. The theatre is very flexible. The proscenium arch folds away and the electro-mechanical raking allows a flat floor to be created for a variety of formats, including in-the-round. A tension wire grid (one of only three in the UK when it was installed) enables students to gain experience of lighting a range of theatre styles and layout formats.

The two other theatres are smaller both in capacity and scale; the new black box John Gielgud Studio seats 80 and the historic (now refurbished) George Bernard Shaw (GBS) Theatre seats 60.

Workshop space
Photograph: Courtesy of Theatre Projects Consultants

The Jerwood Vanbrugh Theatre – RADA's main auditorium
Photograph: Courtesy of Avery Associates

Summary

Theatre type and operational format
Drama school with three theatre spaces used both for teaching and for public performances.

Location and web reference
Camden, London, UK. www.rada.org

Building dates Redevelopment started on site in July 1997 and was completed in December 2000. (Gower Street building was built in 1927.)

Auditorium Main auditorium: seating 204 in proscenium format in circle and balconies. Capable of being adapted for other formats.

Stage 10m wide x 6.8m deep. Flytower height (stage to grid floor) 13.8m.

Architect Bryan Avery of Avery Associates, London, UK.

Theatre (design and technical) consultants
Theatre Projects Consultants, London, UK.

Acoustic consultants Paul Gillieron Acoustic Design, London, UK.

Building cost Total cost £17 million in 2000. (Building costs £14.6 million.)

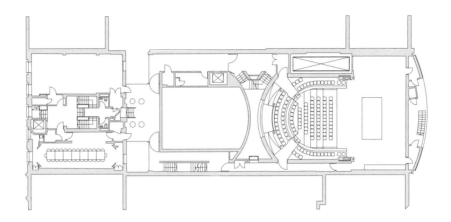

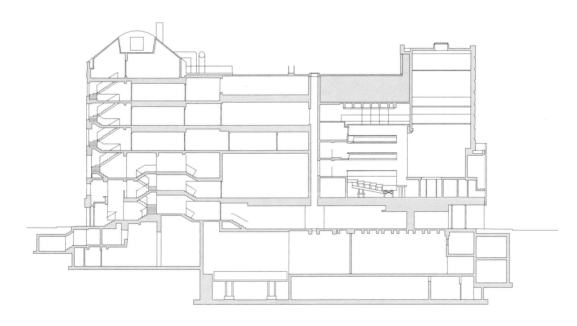

METERS

FEET

The Royal Exchange Theatre
Manchester, UK

For two centuries the Royal (Cotton) Exchange was central to the commercial life of Manchester. When the current building opened in 1874 it was described as the biggest commercial room in the world. It then doubled in size before gradually becoming redundant as the cotton trade moved elsewhere. Since 1976, the Royal Exchange has housed the theatre of the same name. This multi-level theatre in-the-round is highly influential for its intimacy and intensity and could well claim to be the most innovative theatre space created within the UK in the last century.

The auditorium was developed by the theatre company, under the direction of Michael Elliot, who had a very clear vision of how their work was to be presented. A prototype, conceived by designer Richard Negri, was first built in scaffolding before architects were invited to develop a permanent structure.

The auditorium is designed to sit within the massive stone hall, independent of the historic structure. The architects devised a seven-sided 'theatre module', with a diameter of 21.3m and a height of 13.7m, constructed of steel and glass. The seating rises all around a central acting area. The module was conceived as a free-standing unit with a transparent supporting framework within which the audience, performers and stage crew all share the same intimate space. The foyer makes use of the surrounding areas of the Great Hall while the support facilities are housed in other parts of the building.

In 1996, the centre of Manchester was devastated by an IRA bomb. It severely damaged the Royal Exchange building, though the auditorium structure itself remained unscathed. While the necessary work was undertaken to restore the historic hall, the theatre took the opportunity to make radical changes to the front and back of house, including the introduction of

an adaptable 100-seat studio theatre. At the same time the auditorium's technical installations were improved, and restaurant, bars and front of house facilities renewed. The street entrances were also redesigned. A new glazed lift and bridges were installed, linking all public levels for the first time and bringing an iconic 1970s theatre into the twenty-first century.

Open day – the theatre module seen within the historic Great Hall
Photographs: Courtesy of Theatre Projects Consultants

Audience seated within the theatre 'module'

Summary

Theatre type and operational format
Medium size producing theatre for drama.

Location and web reference Manchester, UK.
www.royalexchange.org.uk

Building dates Royal Exchange 1874, extended 1921. Theatre opened in 1976 (intended to last for 25 years). Damaged by bomb attack in 1996, reopened 1998.

Auditorium In-the-round format within a seven-sided structure. Seating on three levels. Capacity 740.

Stage Round, floor-level stage. Variable but set at 8m diameter. Flying height 7.6m.

Architect Levitt Bernstein Associates for 1976 theatre installation and for the restoration and improvement work undertaken 1996–1998.

Theatre (design and technical) consultants
Richard Negri (theatre design); Theatre Projects Consultants (equipment); Ove Arup and Partners (structure), all London, UK.

Acoustic consultants Arup, London, UK.

Building cost £1.2 million in 1976. £18.5 million in 1998.

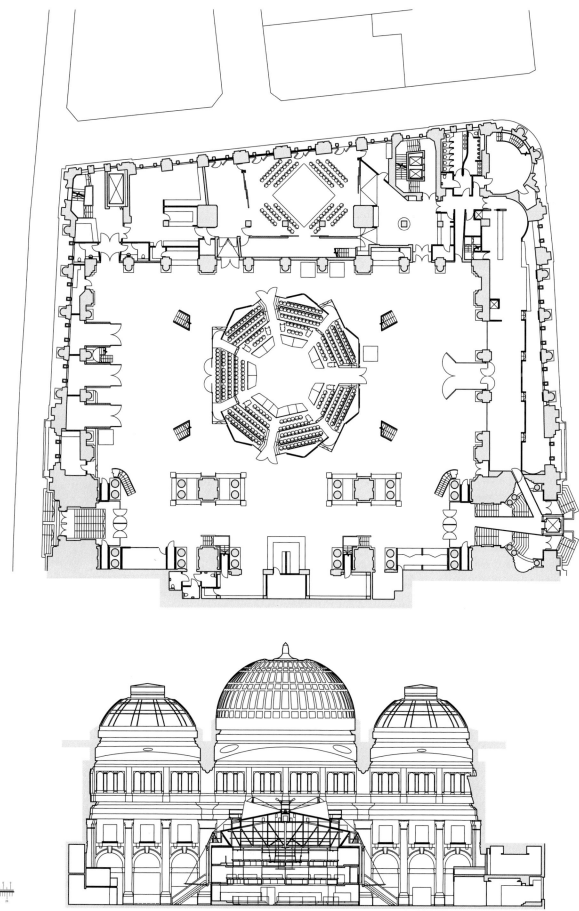

The Theatre Royal
Bury St Edmunds, Suffolk, UK

The significance of the Theatre Royal lies, in part, in that it is the last remaining example in the UK of a type of theatre which could once have been found in towns across the UK and in Europe. Built in 1819, the building was designed to house a theatre genre which has also virtually disappeared. The project launched with the support of heritage interests in 2005 had two aims, first to restore the historic theatre building and second to facilitate the revival and study of early nineteenth-century writing, acting and theatrical presentation.

Over the years the building suffered a series of inappropriate changes and a long period of neglect, including being used as a barrel store for a nearby brewery (it still owns the theatre freehold which is leased to the National Trust). The theatre was partially restored in 1965 and since then has been fully operational, housing medium-scale professional touring product and local amateur productions. The problem which faced the design team responsible for the major, heritage-funded, restoration project was that of maintaining a working theatre rather than creating a museum, meeting the needs of current audiences and of modern productions while restoring the historic building as close to the original as possible.

The work was preceded by an intensive period of research. The seating and decor have been restored to the original design which featured a double row of boxes and two levels in the stalls. The stage, modernised in 1965, remained unchanged. It was already a large one and now has a forestage which draws the performer towards the audience, creating a level of intimacy not found in later nineteenth-century theatres. Within this framework, production facilities have been upgraded and all services have been removed and completely redesigned.

The most significant visible change is the addition of a new foyer, adjacent to the existing site and providing more circulation space and extra bar and catering facilities. As well as making theatre visits more enjoyable, the new facilities enable the theatre to accommodate corporate events and generate increased earned income.

Exterior of the 1819 theatre
Photographs: Dennis Gilbert. Courtesy of the National Trust

Summary

Theatre type and operational format
Historic theatre running a varied programme of medium-scale tours and local productions as well as mounting plays of heritage interest appropriate to its style and period.

Location and web reference
Bury St Edmunds, Suffolk, UK.
www.theatreroyal.org

Building dates First opened 1819. Initial restoration 1965. Full restoration 2005-2007.

Auditorium Horseshoe-shaped theatre with double tiers, each with 15 boxes. Reported to have originally seated 780. Current capacity 360.

Stage Proscenium arch 7.3m wide and 5.5m high. (24ft wide by 18ft high).

Stage width 13m wall to wall. Depth behind proscenium approx. 10.5m.

Forestage 2.4m deep; 10.3m wide; height over 8.1m.

Architect Original theatre designed by William Wilkins (the architect responsible for the National Gallery in London's Trafalgar Square). 1965 renovation by Ernest Scott. 2005 to 2007 restoration by Levitt Bernstein Architects, London, UK.

Theatre (design and technical) consultants Arup Venue Consulting, London, UK.

Acoustic consultants Arup, London, UK.

Building cost £3.67 million (2007). Earlier expenditure not recorded.

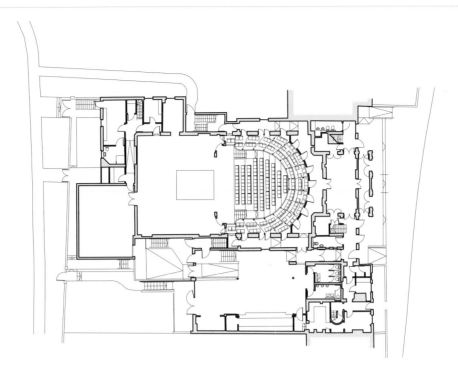

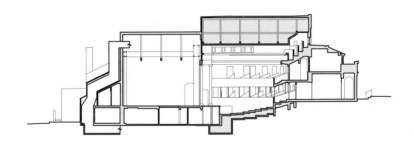

View towards the stage

Trafalgar Studios
London, UK

Two studio theatres have been created at low cost within the former 1930s Whitehall Theatre (listed Grade II), providing a new lease of life for a historic theatre building and new style of venue for central London. Though recognised for the quality of its art deco interior, the original theatre was hampered both by its size (seating just 650 with restricted stage depth) and by its position on the 'wrong side' of London's Trafalgar Square. It finally closed in 2003 having proved unable to compete successfully within the West End commercial theatre market.

The building reopened early the following year. Renamed 'Trafalgar Studios', the theatre now houses two studio spaces: a larger space seating 380 and a small space seating 100. The larger space was designed to create an open stage transfer theatre providing a much-needed central London showcase for visiting work created in similar open stage venues by organisations such as the Royal Shakespeare Company and the Young Vic. Such work does not transfer successfully to conventional West End proscenium theatres.

To create the larger studio, the original circle front was removed and the steeply raked dress circle tier extended forward by four rows to meet a new raised stage, projecting in front of the original proscenium. A single downstage vomitory entrance is shared by audience and actors and the front row of seats is at the same level as the stage. The seating is mainly fixed but with some flexibility around the new apron stage. The original rear stalls, below the circle, has become Studio 2, a small-scale studio with seating on three sides.

Planning consent was given on the basis that any alterations which were made to the listed building were reversible, so a lightweight method of construction was used which had the added advantage of being quick to build. All original decoration within the auditorium was retained but covered over to enhance the studio atmosphere.

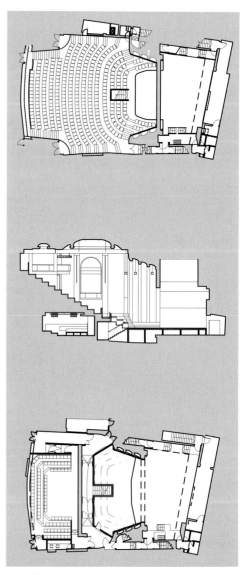

Summary

Theatre type and operational format
Receiving theatre, owned and operated by the Ambassadors Theatre Group.

Location and web reference: Westminster, London, UK. www.trafalgar-studios.co.uk

Building dates Original theatre built in 1930. Converted to provide two studio spaces in 2004 to 2005.

Auditorium Two auditoria, the larger seating 380 and the smaller seating 100.

Stage Studio 1: Original stage: 10m x 5m. Apron stage forward of proscenium: 3.5m x 7m. Studio 2: 4m x 6m.

Architects Edward A. Stone (1930). Tim Foster Architects, London, UK, and Jaques Muir and Partners, London, UK (2004 to 2005).

Theatre (design and technical) consultants Tim Foster Architects (design); Howard Eaton Lighting Ltd (Studio 1 – electrical); White Light Ltd (Studio 2 – electrical).

Acoustic consultants Paul Gillieron Acoustic Design, London, UK.

Building cost 2004 to 2005 conversion £0.8 million.

The former Whitehall Theatre
now Trafalgar Studios
Photographs: Courtesy of Tim
Foster Architects

The larger auditorium

The Tricycle Theatre
London, UK

The first Tricycle Theatre opened in 1980, housed in the Forester's Hall, in Kilburn, north London. Working within a limited budget and timescale, the auditorium was constructed inside the old Hall with a brightly coloured scaffolding system, timber floor decks and canvas gallery fronts being used to create one of London's first contemporary courtyard-style theatres.

In 1987, the auditorium was almost totally destroyed by a fire (started in a neighbouring timber yard). The theatre reopened two years later with the original theatre structure rebuilt within a new outer shell, with improved front of house, rehearsal and production facilities. In 1998, funding from the National Lottery enabled further improvements to be made and a cinema and rehearsal room to be added on adjoining land. The Tricycle now comprises a 230-seat theatre; a 300-seat cinema; a large rehearsal studio; a visual arts studio for educational use and a smaller theatre/workshop space; as well as a café/bar, art gallery and the 'Creative Space' for community/participatory activities (added in 2001).

The design of the auditorium with its easy audience/performer contact and the relaxed, informal style of the building as a whole serve the theatre company well. The dimensions and form of the auditorium are closely modelled on the Georgian Theatre in Richmond, Yorkshire (built in 1788), demonstrating that traditional formats can be successfully adapted to use modern construction techniques and to meet current theatrical needs.

The entrance. The main theatre is hidden from the street
Photograph: Tony Quill. Courtesy of Theatre Projects Consultants

Summary

Theatre type and operational format
Small producing theatre with additional arts facilities.

Location and web reference Kilburn, London, UK. www.tricycle.co.uk

Building dates Opened 1980, rebuilt after fire and reopened in 1989. Further improvements and new-build additions 1998 and 2001.

Auditorium Courtyard format seating a total audience of 230 housed in raked central 'stalls' and the surrounding lower and upper gallery spaces.

Stage Simple proscenium-style end stage (7.2m x 6.1m from edge proscenium and pillar to pillar) with removable forestage (1.4m x 6.1m lip and pillar to pillar).

Architect Tim Foster Architects, London, UK (1980, 1989, 1998).

Theatre (design and technical) consultants Theatre Projects Consultants, London, UK (1980, 1989).

Acoustic consultants Paul Gillieron Acoustic Design, London, UK.

Building cost £1.5 million in 1980.

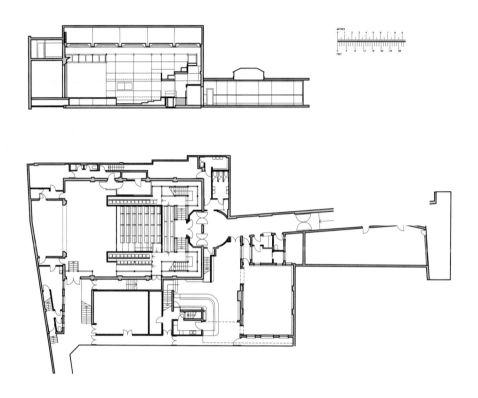

The courtyard-style auditorium
Photograph: Courtesy of Tim
Foster Architects

Wexford Opera House
Wexford, Ireland

Wexford's Annual Opera Festival, first established in 1951, is now seen as an integral part of the cultural life of Ireland and attracts visitors from around the world. Its original home was the former Theatre Royal, a traditional nineteenth-century theatre which, despite a series of refurbishments, had become increasingly difficult to maintain and operate. In 2000, the decision was taken to build a replacement on the same site, extending onto adjacent land which had become available.

The result is a new building designed for the Opera Festival which also provides a year-round arts venue housing other Wexford Festival productions and work by visiting companies. Like the original theatre, this larger building has been successfully integrated into the historic fabric of Wexford's medieval centre.

The main entrance is deliberately understated – a simple doorway in a row of reinstated terraced buildings hiding the main building from the street. The scale of the theatre, with its copper-clad flytower, is only apparent from the far bank of the River Slaney which runs through the old town.

On entering, theatregoers are led through a discrete box office area into a top-lit atrium from where a wide stairway leads up through four storeys to the top of the building, revealing views of the old town and estuary. The main auditorium follows the traditional horseshoe operatic format. The stage can be adapted through a series of lifts to accommodate an orchestra pit of varying dimensions or an optional forestage for drama and dance. Full flying facilities are provided. The back stage area includes provision for directors, conductors,

designers and singers; as well as dressing rooms, chorus rehearsal rooms and prop making.

Fitting this range of accommodation into the tight town centre site involved designing and constructing a series of component parts which were then assembled on site, starting with the most landlocked corner and working through to the more accessible areas.

The theatre seen from across the River Slaney
Photographs: Courtesy of Keith Williams Architects

The main auditorium
(Note: Larger image available on p. 93)

Summary

Theatre type and operational format Purpose-built theatre with two auditoria designed to house Wexford Festival Opera productions as well as a varied programme of smaller scale dance and drama touring.

Location and web reference Wexford, County Wexford, Republic of Ireland. www.wexfordopera.com

Building programme Design started in July 2003 and the construction stage ran from June 2006 to August 2008, completing on schedule for the autumn 2008 Wexford Opera Festival.

Auditorium Two spaces of differing scale and format: the larger (780–850 capacity), purpose-designed to house opera with deep stage, full flying facilities and orchestra pit. Smaller adaptable auditorium (seating 175) provides for performance in a variety of formats.

Stage Flat, traditional proscenium (9m wide by 7.5m) with an optional forestage or orchestra pit. Stage width is 21m (with wing space) and 16.8m between fly galleries. The stage depth is 10.5m, 13m or 16m depending on positioning of stage lifts. The height is 20m to grid and 8m to fly galleries.

Architect OPW (Office of Public Works) Architectural Services, Republic of Ireland; with Keith Williams Architects, London, UK.

Procurement Specialist design team selected by competition.

Theatre (design and technical) consultants Carr and Angier, Theatre Consultants, Bath, UK.

Acoustic consultants Arup, London, UK.

Building cost €33 million in 2008.

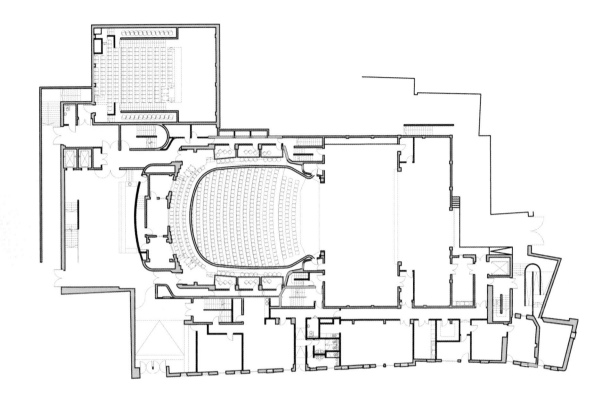

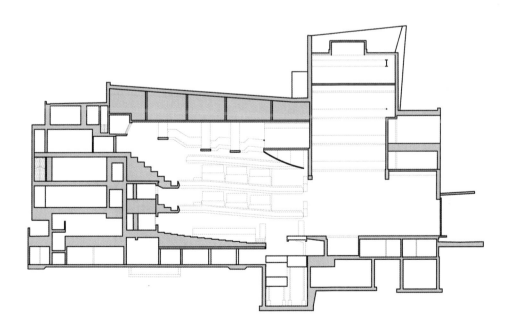

The Winspear Opera House
Dallas, Texas, USA

The Dallas Center for the Performing Arts, which opened towards the end of 2009, comprises four new venues within a 10-acre public park. It is the result of a 25-year plan to create a world-class arts district in the centre of the city.

One of the key buildings is the Margot and Bill Winspear Opera House, designed as a base for the Dallas Opera and the Texas Ballet Theater as well as a venue for visiting opera, ballet, music-theatre and other large-scale productions. The 2,200-seat main auditorium (the performance hall) has been described as a twenty-first-century reinterpretation of the traditional horseshoe opera house. The audience is stacked on a series of vertical tiers to ensure that each seat is as near to the stage as possible. Variable acoustics are achieved by using retractable screens and interior finishes have been specified to improve the resonance for the human voice so that the hall can be adapted for both music and drama. The pattern to the balcony fronts acts as a sound-dispersing surface, distributing it more evenly to create a better overall acoustic.

The auditorium floor plays an important part in the energy strategy of the building with cool air outlets positioned to provide a cool comfort zone where the audience is seated. The Winspear complex also has a second space, an Education and Recital Hall that can house performances seating up to 200 people as well as classes, rehearsals and meetings.

There are 'destination' facilities for the general visitor, which include a restaurant and café, open throughout the day. This sense of being 'open to all' is evident in the design of the building. The glass walls give a sense of transparency, revealing views of the public concourse, foyers and grand staircase as well as the outer drum of the performance hall, which is clad in vibrant red glass panels. The colour was chosen to define the outer shell of the auditorium – an inversion of the traditional use of red for seating.

Part of the glass façade is retractable, opening the public areas to one of the adjacent outdoor performance spaces, while an expansive canopy extends on all sides of the building. The canopy not only reduces the solar gain by stopping the direct solar radiation, but also creates a micro climate beneath.

Summary

Theatre type and operational format
Large-scale performance venue, designed to function as a high-quality opera house as well as accommodate tours and act as a civic space within an arts quarter.

Location and web reference Dallas, Texas, USA. www.dallasperformingarts.org

Building dates Start on site 2006. Opened late 2009.

Auditorium Oval shaped auditorium with contemporary-style proscenium. Audience of 2,200 seated in stalls and vertically stacked tiers.

Stage Dimensions 132' x 64'.

Architect: Foster and Partners, London, UK.

Theatre (design and technical) consultants Theatre Projects Consultants, London, UK.

Acoustic consultants Sound Space Design Ltd, London, UK.

Building cost not published.

The main auditorium
Photographs: Courtesy of Foster
and Partners Architects

**The approach to the Winspear
Theatre**

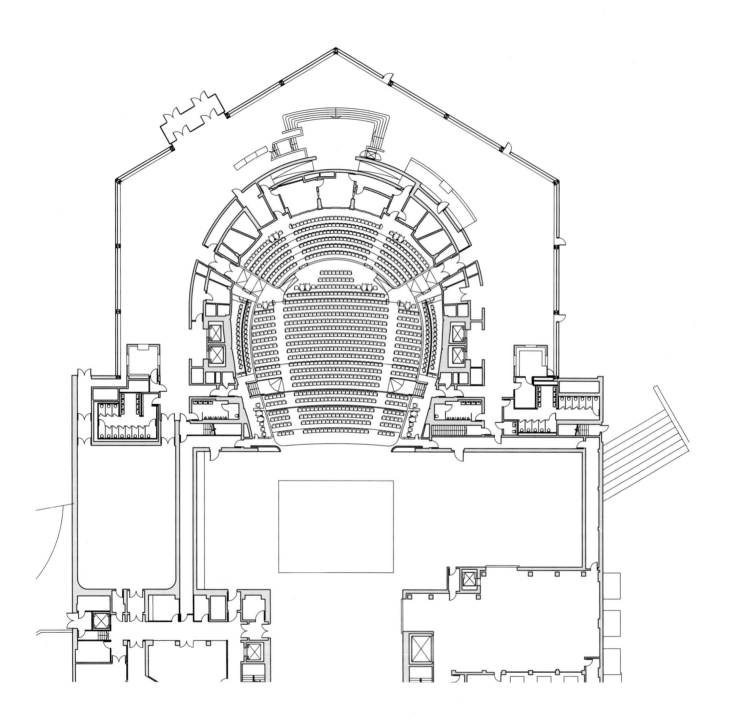

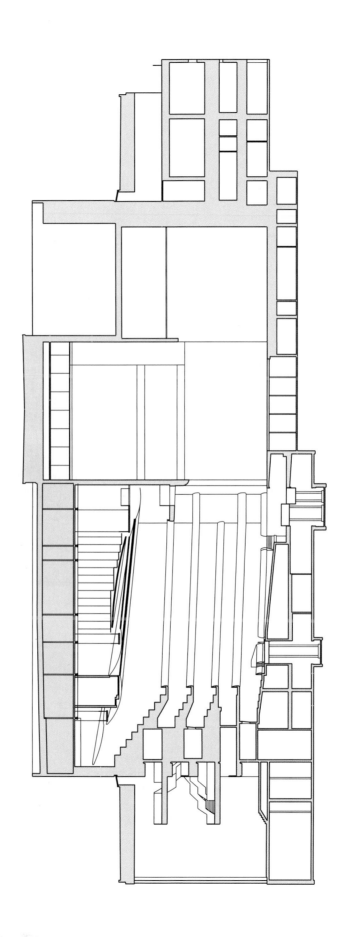

The Young Vic Theatre
London, UK

The Young Vic is one of the UK's leading venues where young theatre professionals and established 'names' come together to create and present work predominantly for a young audience. It was built as a second temporary space for the National Theatre, just down the road from the Old Vic Theatre, where the company was then housed. It was designed as a new theatre for a new generation – one that was experimental, open, circus-like and cheap.

The challenge which faced the theatre nearly 40 years later was to improve radically what had been deliberately designed as a low-cost, low-key, temporary structure and to do so without losing the ambience which had drawn in successive generations of young people. The theatre also wanted to keep the best aspects of the original design, in particular the idiosyncratic but very effective auditorium – an early example in the UK of a Guthrie thrust stage combined with the vertical element of galleries. Bench seating and demountable stage units provided a degree of flexibility.

The new building retains much of the original fabric (including the former butcher's shop which formed the entrance to the 1960s theatre) while providing vastly improved facilities for the company and for its audience. The auditorium has been upgraded to increase the technical provision with the height raised to accommodate a new lighting grid. A new layer of get-round and more entrances have been added and a movable wall with demountable gallery now leads into the large new workshop so that an extended thrust stage can break the boundary of the square auditorium format. The seating capacity has been increased by some 25 per cent within the same footprint.

Two further studio spaces have been added and both backstage and front of house provision has been rebuilt and extended.

The materials used in the new theatre reflect the ad-hoc and semi-industrial style of the original: with plywood and steelwork being widely used in the interior spaces and aluminium mesh and customised concrete blocks cladding the exterior.

The success of the new space owes much to the quality of the 1969 theatre – to the original concept of a young, egalitarian space and to the design of the building that gave it expression.

The auditorium is clad in aluminium mesh while the original 'butcher's shop' entrance has been retained

The auditorium

Photographs: Philip Vile. Courtesy of Haworth Tompkins Architects.

Summary

Theatre type and operational format
Producing theatre specialising in work for younger people and providing opportunities for new writers and directors. Significant education and community programme, touring and co-productions.

Location and web reference Lambeth, London, UK www.youngvic.org

Building dates Original theatre opened 1969. Major refurbishment 2004 to 2006.

Auditorium Flexible octagonal space with gallery on all sides. Seating capacity 420 but capable of accommodating a maximum audience of 550. Two further flexible spaces: Maria Theatre seating 140–180 and Clare Theatre seating 65–80.

Stage Variable formats with in-the-round and thrust stage option. Flexible stage size, in-the-round, the smallest, is 6m x 6m.

Architect Original, Bill Howell, HKPA Architects, London, UK. Remodelling: Haworth Tompkins Architects, London, UK.

Theatre (design and technical) consultants Studio Todd Lecatt and Theatre Projects Consultants with Charcoalblue, both London, UK.

Acoustic consultants Paul Gillieron Acoustic Design, London, UK.

Building cost Original theatre cost £60,000 (1969). Total cost of major remodelling work £12.5 million (construction costs £7 million).

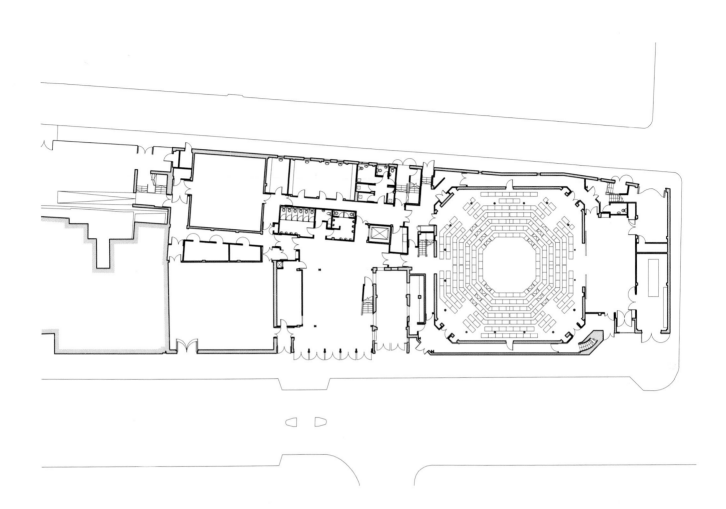

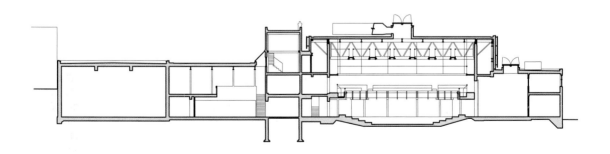

Glossary

Stage directions
These are taken from the viewpoint of an actor facing the audience.

Downstage
Towards the audience.

Upstage
Away from the audience. Historically stages were usually *raked* or gently sloped towards the audience. Hence the part of the stage away from the audience was at a slightly higher level than that closest to it.

Stage left
To the actor's left (the audience right). Usually where *Prompt Corner* is located.

Stage right
To the actor's right.

Off stage
That part of the stage house invisible to the audience, blocked by scenery, drapes or sightlines.

On stage
In view of at least some members of the audience.

A
Acting area
Those portions of the stage in which any action of a performance takes place.

Amphitheatre
Stepped banks of seating surrounding an arena. Also describes the curved uppermost level of seating in a large theatre.

Apron
The extension of a stage projecting outwards into the auditorium. May be permanent or demountable.

Automation
Precise control of scenic elements by means of computer-controlled winches and motors.

B
Backstage
That part of the theatre to which the public do not normally have access. Sometimes referred to as *back of house*. See *front of house* and *pass door*.

Band room
Musicians' changing room. May also be a temporary structure located behind the scenery on the stage for a large musical production.

Band shell
Movable sound reflector placed behind a group of musicians on the stage or in the open air to improve the acoustics.

Bar/barrel/pipe
Length of metal pipe (usually 48mm o/d) suspended on a set of lines to which scenery or lighting may be attached. See *Truss*.

Barre
Horizontal rail usually of wood used by ballet dancers when practicing.

Bastard prompt
See *prompt corner*.

Batten   Length of (usually) wood used in scenery construction or used for hanging scenery cloths and the like.

Border   Abbreviated cloth hanging or semi-solid pelmet used to mask the line of sight to hide the staging technical equipment.

Brail line
Generally a length of rope used to pull a piece of hanging scenery away from its normal vertical position in order to make room for a moving scenic piece.

Bridge
1. A gallery bridging across the stage or auditorium used for lighting and sound equipment.
2. A lift in the stage floor extending across the stage floor to usually the proscenium width.

Bridle
A short length of certified lifting cable or sling used to distribute the load of a hoisted pipe or truss.

C
Call
Warning to be ready for part of a performance. Usually given via a backstage-only public address system.

Carpet cut
Series of flaps in the stage floor, generally on the proscenium line, by which a stage cloth can be held in position.

Cleat   Wooden or metal fitment round which a line may be turned and/or made fast. See *pin rail*.

Cloths   A hanging painted cloth. May be *cut* to reveal part of another cloth behind, or a *stage cloth* used to cover the stage floor, usually painted to represent paving, etc.

Control room
Room(s) housing lighting and sound desks with a good view of the stage as a whole. Require soundproofing but with openable windows into the auditorium. Can also house audio describers, surtitle operators and the like.

Counterweight system
A mechanical system for flying scenery in which the weight of the pieces of scenery are counter-balanced by the addition of metal weights in the counterweight cradle. The cradles move in guides via a loop of rope known as the *hauling line*.

Crossover
A passageway behind or under the stage for actors or technicians to cross from one side of the stage to the other.

Cue
A signal for action during the performance by an actor or technician. Cues may be given verbally via headsets or via a cue light invisible to the audience.

Curtain line
Imaginary line drawn just upstage of the proscenium (if fitted) marking the position of the house tabs when closed. Also known as the *setting line*.

Cut
Any long opening in the stage, generally across. See *dip traps*.

Cyclorama
Plain, curved, stretched cloth or rigid structure used as a background to a setting to give an illusion of great depth.

D

Dead
A predetermined position to which a scenic piece is raised or lowered or brought on or off stage.

Dip Traps
Hinged covered shallow troughs generally running up and down stage at the edges containing outlets for lighting and sound equipment plus providing spaces for cables to prevent tripping hazards at stage level.

Dock
A storage area next to the stage. Scenery is unloaded and taken through the 'dock door' to the stage.

Double purchase
A system of pulley blocks and suspension ropes which gears the movement of the counterweights to half of that of the associated scenery load. See *counterweight system*.

Drapes
Any unspecified fireproofed fabric hanging in folds as a scene or part of a scene, especially curtaining fabrics such as wool, velvet, etc.

Drencher
A perforated sparge pipe that will, in the event of a fire, spray water on the upstage face of the safety curtain to stop deformation.

F

False proscenium
Also known as a show portal or opera bridge. A permanent or removable structure immediately upstage of the proscenium opening. May be structural in order to place lights and sound equipment or purely scenic.

Fire Curtain
See *safety curtain*.

Fireproofed
Treatment of scenic elements with flame-retardant chemicals in order to slow the spread of fire. Fireproofing does not necessarily render the item treated non-combustible.

Flight cases
Rugged, rigid, wheeled enclosures usually specially constructed required for the transport of delicate equipment such as speakers, luminaires and the like. Have disadvantage of taking up as much space when empty as when full.

Floats (footlights)
A trough at the very front of the stage for placing of lights and other equipment so as not to obscure the audience's view of actors' feet, etc.

Flown
Suspended on lines as distinct from standing on the stage floor or hanging from fixed rails, etc.

Fly
Lift above the level of the stage floor by means of sets of lines run from the stage grid. The term *flys* or *flies* is also used as an abbreviation for fly gallery.

Fly gallery
A gallery extending along the sidewall of the stage, some distance above the stage floor, from which the machinery used in flying scenery is operated. This machinery may be manually operated or automated. Also known as the fly floor.

Fly rail
Heavy rail along the on-stage side of the *fly gallery* fitted with cleats to which scenery suspensions may be made fast.

Flyman
A technician with skilled ability in the suspension, rigging and operation of flying scenic elements.

Flytower
An elevated section above the stage into which scenic pieces can be hoisted out of view and stored by means of the flying system. Generally at least twice the height of the proscenium opening, with often three times the height required for repertory theatres. Contains galleries such as the *fly gallery*.

Follow spot
A manually operated high-intensity spotlight used to follow lead performers during a production. Formally known as 'Limes' from Limelight.

Forestage
Portion of the stage floor in front of the curtain line. Generally forms the upstage edge of the *orchestra pit*.

Front of house (FOH)
The areas of the theatre to which the public has access.
In auditoria: the parts in front of the curtain line.

G

Get-in/out
The process of placing a production in the theatre and removing it when finished to leave a bare stage. Also refers to the related access doors, parking area, lifts, etc.

Grave trap
An oblong trap, usually downstage centre (DSC) used for making actors appear and disappear during the course of the performance.

Green room
A communal room, generally close to the stage, where performers and others involved in the performance may prepare and wait before being required on stage. A relaxation area after the performance or rehearsals.

Grid
Framework of steel or timber beams at high level over the stage used to support sets of lines used for flying scenery.

Ground plan
Plan of the stage (usually 1:25 scale) on which is marked the position of scenery and technical equipment such as lighting, sound, projection, etc.

H

Hauling line
Used by the *flyman* in a counterweighted system to move the counterweight cradle to position a piece of flown scenery.

Head Block
Device comprising three or more sheaves set together in a line or parallel on a common shaft and attached to the grid or flytower soffit directly above the fly gallery. The suspension lines of rope or steel are passed over to the fly gallery.

Hemps
The term usually employed to signify lines used for flying scenery made from vegetable fibre or even synthetic materials as distinct from steel wire ropes used in a counterweight flying system. A *hemp house* is a theatre equipped only with a direct lift flying system as opposed to a counterweighted or automated system.

House border
Adjustable height decorative pelmet suspended immediately in front of the *house tabs*.

House tabs
The main curtains in a theatre, usually decorative and heavy. May be *drawn* (opened horizontally), *swagged* (opened so as to form bunches at the high-level corners of the proscenium) or *guillotined* (opened vertically). Derived from *tableau curtain*.

I

Iron
See *safety curtain*.

L

Lantern
1. Stage lantern or haystack lantern is the term for the automatic smoke ventilation opening located in the roof of the flytower. May also be manually operated.
2. Term for a stage lighting instrument. See *luminaire*.

Legs
Vertical length of fabric used in place of a *wing*.

Lift
Section of the stage that can be raised and lowered, sometimes also tilted to enable changes of setting to be made and provide a changeable acting area. See *bridge*.

Lines
Ropes used for suspension or repositioning of scenic elements. May be fibre, steel or synthetic composites. See *set of lines*.

Loading gallery
Narrow gallery above the *fly gallery* used for storing and loading the weights used in counterweight flying systems.

Locking rail
Rail on *fly gallery* or floor used to attach *rope locks* that hold the hauling lines stationary and so keep the flown scenic piece in position.

Loft block or grid pulley
Sheave in a metal frame bolted to the grid or flytower soffit and used to pass a suspension line, one block for each line in a set.

Luminaire
A stage lighting instrument. Also known as a lantern or a fixture.

M

Masking
A piece of scenery used to cut off the view of parts of the stage.

O

Opposite prompt
Stage (actors') right. The left off the stage as seen by the audience. Known as OP.

Orchestra pit
Lowered area to accommodate musicians between the audience and the stage. The floor is usually adjustable in height to suit different forms of performance. May become the *apron*.

P

Packing rail
A 'stacking rail', usually a horizontal steel tube projecting from the stage wall used for tying to or stacking against large (flat) pieces of scenery.

Paint frame
A frame to which backcloths, flats, etc. may be vertically attached for scenic painting. Vertical access often provided by a paint bridge suspended from the ceiling.

Pass door
Fireproof door linking the flytower and the auditorium. Usually contains a lobby. Generally locked during performances.

Pin or cleat rail
Used in direct-hauled flying systems. The flying scenery suspension lines are taken over loft blocks and head blocks and brought straight down to the pin or fly rail for paying out and tying off. There are no counterweight or other means of sustaining the load of the scenery when the lines are free of the cleats.

Point hoist
A single line powered winch for flying scenic elements. Generally used in groups. The suspension point on the grid is via a relocatable spot block (pulley).

Portal
A unit of permanent masking comprising legs and a border set between the show portal and the backdrop or cyclorama.

Powered flying
System of scenery flying utilising motors only. Manual operation is usually only possible in an emergency.

Prompt box
The traditional position for the prompter in opera is a box let into the front of the stage extending into the *orchestra pit*.

Prompt corner
Usually located downstage left. the stage manager's control point. See *bastard prompt*.

Prompt side
Traditionally stage (actors') left, regardless of the actual position of the prompter. Known as PS.

Properties or props
Objects such as furniture, pictures, carpets, ornaments, weapons, etc. used in a production.

Proscenium or pros.
The theoretical fourth wall of a stage comprising the proscenium opening and its surrounding treatments. See *false proscenium*.

Proscenium opening
The opening through which the audience views the stage.

R

Rake
Sloped floor of an auditorium or stage. A rake of less than 1 in 24 is regarded as flat.

Rig
To set up scenery on stage. 'Rigging' is a collective term for the suspension equipment.

Riser
1. Vertical front of a raised stage where it faces the audience.
2. Vertical enclosed compartment stretching over many floors containing building services such as plumbing, electrical mains, air handling ducts, etc.

Roller
Where there is no flying space over the stage, a backdrop can be rolled known as a roller or a roll drop. Also known as 'Tumbling'.

Rope lock
See *locking rail*.

S

Safety curtain
Fireproof screen or shutter comprising a framework of steel or iron faced with sheet steel and fireproof heat absorbing fabric. Mounted immediately behind the proscenium in guides, the shutter quickly creates a fire barrier between the auditorium and the *stage house* by means of an automatic closing system. See *drencher*.

Set
Arrangement of scenery units that together represent a single location. The term is also used as a verb to mean to put up or assemble scenery for use (e.g. to set a stage).

Set of lines
Unit group of suspension lines hanging from the grid or the flytower soffit for the attachment and flying of scenery; there are usually three or four lines in a set. See *counterweight system* and *pin or cleat rail*.

Setting line
The imaginary line across the stage, in front of which scenery cannot be hidden by the *house tabs*. See *curtain line*.

Sheave
Grooved wheel or pulley over which a suspension line may be passed.

Single purchase
A suspension system where there is no gearing of pulleys. The counterweight and its travel will be the same as that of the object that is being suspended.

Stage house
That part of a theatre housing the technical areas such as the stage, the flytower, dressing rooms, wardrobe, workshops, rehearsal rooms, etc.

Swag
Looped up curtain, border or leg.

T

Tormentor
Substantial wing, placed immediately behind the proscenium opening to mask the off-stage edges of the setting.

Trap
An opening in the stage floor generally with a mechanism to raise and lower actors. The trap cover slides over to form a continuous floor when not in use.

Truck
Low trolley, either running in tracks or free-moving, on which scenery, etc. may be mounted for horizontal linear movements of settings.

Truss
A latticed girder of steel or aluminium welded construction of square or triangular section used for supporting temporary lighting or scenic elements. Stronger and more rigid than a *bar/barrel/pipe*.

V

Vomitory
An entrance through a block of seating as distinct from through the surrounding wall.

W

Wagon
1. A large *truck,* usually guided, on which sets are assembled and moved on and off stage when required.
2. Vehicle in which scenery is transported between venues.

Winch
A rope-winding mechanism for moving scenic or other elements such as curtains, acoustic panels, etc. May be powered or manually operated.

Wings
Off-stage spaces to left and right of the acting area.

Contributors

SECTION EDITORS AND STEERING GROUP MEMBERS

A K Bennett-Hunter has over 35 years' experience of theatre as a stage manager, production manager and general manager. He has worked in both the West End and in the funded sector including the National Theatre, English National Opera and Opera North. For six years he was Administrative Director of the Theatre Royal Stratford East.

He has been executive producer for productions at Strindberg's Intima Teater and the Royal Dramaten Elverket Theatre in Stockholm and has contributed to management training courses in Finland and South Korea.

As a consultant, his clients have included the Abbey Theatre in Dublin, the Royal Court and London's South Bank Centre. He is a commissioning editor for *The Stage* newspaper and editor of the Association of British Theatre Technicians' journal *Sightline*.

David Blyth is Operations & Building Development Director with the Ambassador Theatre Group, a role which encompasses responsibility for overseeing all Building Services, Maintenance, Health and Safety, Retail, and General Management departments for ATG's portfolio of over 23 buildings. Prior to joining Ambassador Theatre Group in 1992, David was involved in theatre and arts entertainment management in both the commercial and the subsidised sectors. Between 1983 and 1987, he worked in a managerial capacity with two major West End theatre owners – Maybox Group and Stoll Moss Theatres. He then became Head of Operations for the local authority-run Fairfield Hall Arts Complex in Croydon before moving to ATG as Chief Executive of the Ambassadors Theatre in Woking, UK.

Tim Foster is the senior partner in Foster Wilson Architects (formerly Tim Foster Architects). He trained at Cambridge University School of Architecture, where he also worked as a stage designer. Before establishing the practice in 1979, he worked for Roderick Ham and Partners and as consultant architect to Theatre Projects Consultants.

Tim has been responsible for all major arts projects carried out by the practice including the Tricycle Theatre and Cinema, The Cliffs Pavilion, Southend-on Sea, the Salisbury Playhouse Redevelopment, The Broadway, Peterborough, Trafalgar Studios, London, The Broadway Theatre, Barking, the redevelopment of Theatre Royal Norwich and a number of school theatres, including those at Dulwich College, St Paul's Boys School, The American School (all in London) and Cheltenham Ladies College. Current projects include a Carnival Arts Centre in West London and work to the Polka Children's Theatre in Wimbledon.

Tim is chairman of the ABTT Theatre Planning Committee and represents the UK on the OISTAT Architecture Commission. He is a board member of the Tricycle Theatre Company and in 2009 he was appointed a Trustee of The Theatres Trust.

Andy Hayles is Managing Director of Charcoalblue, a multidisciplinary theatre design consultancy whose clients include the National Theatre, the Royal Shakespeare Company, Glyndebourne and English National Opera. Prior to co-founding Charcoalblue in 2004, Andy sat on the board of Theatre Projects Consultants where his work included the Royal Court Theatre, RADA, Regent's Park Open Air Theatre (all in London) and the Lowry in Salford.

His recent projects include the Young Vic, the Roundhouse, the RSC's Courtyard Theatre, and the redevelopment of the Cottesloe at the National Theatre.

Andy is a visiting lecturer to Cambridge University, Kent University, Royal Welsh College of Music and Drama, LIPA and RADA. He is a full member of the Society for Theatre Consultants, a member of the Society for the Preservation of Ancient Buildings, a Director of the ABTT and a PLASA Innovation Award Judge.

Peter Longman has been involved with theatre buildings for most of his career. He was a Trustee and then Director of The Theatres Trust, advising on theatre buildings throughout the UK, for a total of 16 years to 2006 and continued as a Consultant until 2008. He is currently a non-executive director of theatre consultants Charcoalblue, on the boards of two theatre companies, and an active member of the ABTT Historical Research Committee.

He ran the Arts Council's grant scheme for arts buildings from 1969 to 1978, and was the Government's chief adviser on museums from 1984 to 1995. He has lectured and written extensively on theatre buildings and was the author of 'Act Now', the report on the need to upgrade London's West End theatres published in 2003.

Julian Middleton is a Director of RHWL Architects. He leads the design of auditoria for Arts Team, the practice's specialist group. Alongside his specialism in auditoria design, he also works on the early stages of project development including: brief writing, feasibility and conceptual work.

His new-build projects include the Donmar Warehouse, for director Sam Mendes; Northern Stage – European centre for the performing arts; Bridgewater Hall in Manchester; and the international dance venue of Sadler's Wells in London. Restoration projects include Sir Cameron Macintosh's Prince of Wales Theatre in London's West End and the Theatre Royal in Waterford, Ireland. His work on spaces for younger performers includes the home Chicken Shed, the integrated youth theatre company; the naturally ventilated Auden Theatre in Norfolk; and the Winterflood Theatre, part of the City of London School. Brief development work has included collaboration with companies ranging in scale from the Royal Shakespeare Company to Hull Truck.

Anne Minors Dip Arch is Director of Anne Minors Performance Consultants Ltd (AMPC) founded in 1996, a multidisciplinary consultancy specialising in the design and equipping of theatres, opera houses and concert halls. Previously Anne was head of design at Theatre Projects Consultants (TPC) where she worked on the Esplanade in Singapore; Chan Centre Vancouver; Disney Concert Hall and Glyndebourne Opera House.

Among AMPC's first projects was the remodelling of London's Royal Opera House (including the new Linbury and Clore Studios) and of the Barbican, London. Other clients include the Theatre Royal Bath (main house and the Egg) and collaboration with the Royal Shakespeare Company to explore the new 1,000-seat thrust stage format. Recent openings include an opera house in Kazakhstan; the Menuhin Hall, Surrey; Hull Truck Theatre; and the Koerner Hall for the Royal Conservatory of Music in Toronto.

Anne is a regular music performer and organiser of arts for children. She has also lectured students at the Architectural Association in London and at Sheffield, Dundee and Hong Kong Universities. She is an ABTT Council member and past-Chairman of the Society of Theatre Consultants.

Barry Pritchard is a Principal Director of RHWL Architects. He leads Arts Team, the practice's specialist team that designs theatres, concert halls and arts centres. His practical theatre experience was gained as a member of the National Youth Theatre before becoming an architect and obtaining a Master's degree in architectural conservation.

Barry has been involved with the majority of Arts Team's 85 built arts projects including refurbishments of Theatre Royal Nottingham; the Old Vic Theatre, London; Theatre Royal Newcastle; the Lyceum Theatre Sheffield; and The Prince Edward Theatre in London. New buildings include Royal Concert Hall Nottingham and Bridgewater Hall in Manchester. He has also worked on restoration projects at the Brighton Dome and the London Coliseum, extensions to Royal and Derngate Theatres in Northampton and Belfast's Grand Opera House as well as a range of smaller education and community facilities.

Barry is a member of the ABTT Theatre Planning Committee and was a Council Member and Honorary Secretary of the ABTT (1992 – 1998).

David Staples is Chairman of Theatre Projects Consultants (TPC) where he specialises in feasibility and planning studies. He prepares preliminary building programmes and briefs for architects. His work includes theatre planning, project planning and organisation. Much of his more recent work is in Asia, the Middle East and Europe.

He joined TPC in 1974 and was subsequently based in the Middle East with responsibility for the company's operations, advising governments on arts development before moving on to conduct major planning and economic feasibility studies for theatres and arts centres in the USA and Canada. Recent projects include the Lowry in Salford, UK; the New Opera House in Oslo, Norway; the Royal Opera House in Muscat, Oman; and a theatre and concert hall in Kristiansand, Norway.

David is a Fellow of the Chartered Management Institute, a Fellow of the Institute of Business Consultants and a certified Management Consultant (USA). He is a member of the International Society of Performing Arts, a former Chairman of the Society of Theatre Consultants, and a member of the ABTT.

Judith Strong set up a-ap consulting (formerly Arts & Architecture Projects) in 1991, supporting and guiding clients through the initial stages of building projects. Prior to that she was Competitions Officer and Director of London Region at the Royal Institute of British Architects and then Housing the Arts Officer for the Arts Council.

Her consultancy work includes: the National Youth Centre for Performing Arts, Gloucester; the Circus Space, London: The Boilerhouse, Royal Holloway,

Surrey; the replacement of Westminster Theatre (for Talawa Theatre Company); and Normansfield Theatre, Surrey. Recent clients include the Old Vic, Leeds Grand Theatre, the Gardner Centre (University of Sussex), Hoxton Hall, CABE (Commission for Architecture and the Built Environment), The Theatres Trust and Arts Council England.

Publications include: *The Arts Council Guide to Building for the Arts*; *Winning by Design – Architectural Competitions*; and *Encore – Strategies for Theatre Renewal*.

She is currently an Enabler for CABE. Other appointments include Chair of the Arts Advisory Committee for the London Borough of Richmond upon Thames; board member of Action for Children's Arts; board and building committee member for the Orange Tree Theatre, Richmond.

Mark White is Director of Electronic Theatre Controls Ltd and has been Chairman of the ABTT from 2002 until the present.

Mark takes a keen interest in theatre technology and the way that buildings use energy for performance. This interest extends to practical measurement of the amount of electricity used by a cohort of theatres in the UK. This has led to realistic expectations of energy consumption in theatres around the world using currently available technology. These baseline consumption figures have provided yardsticks by which the outcomes of moves towards sustainability may be measured.

Having worked in various backstage and management roles within the performance industry, he is acutely aware of how design issues in the planning stage impact on the financial, artistic and safety aspects of live productions.

Mark plays a key role in the works of the legislative review and commentary process of the ABTT, a body encompassing many experts from the theatre industry. The Association provides a mechanism for commentary on proposed introduction of or reform of legislation effecting performance venues as well as practical guidance on compliance with introduced requirements such as Disability Access, Fire Regulations, Safety Legislation and a raft of other concerns.

GRAPHICS

Richard Penman studies Architecture at London Metropolitan University. His professional work includes experience in both the private and commercial sector of architecture. Collaborations have involved working with Architecture Studio, Paris, on projects ranging from hospitals to research centres. In the UK his work has varied from working with private developers to working with CZWG Architects under Piers Gough.

Under the tutorship of David Grandorge, Richard has developed a passion for working with detail and precision, while engaging in the nuances within architectural history.

Emma Savage has worked as a theatre consultant since 1989, first with Artec Consultants and then with John Wyckham Associates before joining Carr and Angier (where she has worked from 1995 to the present). Her fields of specialisation include the planning of stages and all associated backstage and technical areas; seating and sightlines; orchestral layouts and pit designs; room acoustics; and stage equipment planning and layouts.

She has an Honours degree in Music and Drama and is a professionally qualified flautist. This, together with a Diploma in Sound and Vibration Studies, gives her a particular interest in music performance and acoustics. A further area of expertise is computer science and computer draughting.

Lee Wren studied Architecture at Bath University. He is an architectural assistant with a wide range of experience in a variety of architectural types including social housing, educational buildings and performance spaces.

He has worked in the public sector for Barnsley Council and Lincoln University, where he was involved in the design of a new Drama Centre on the campus. On the completion of this project Lee embarked on an extended sabbatical of working/travelling abroad in Eurasia.

Upon his return he joined Arts Team at RHWL Architects and worked on the detailed development of new performing spaces for the Guildhall School of Music and Drama. He is currently helping to develop the design of a faculty of Islamic Studies in Education City Qatar.

Index